Wellington's Waterloo Allies

How Soldiers from Brunswick, Hanover, Nassau and the Netherlands Contributed to the Victory of 1815

Andrew W. Field

Pen & Sword
MILITARY
An imprint of
Pen & Sword Books Ltd
Yorkshire - Philadelphia

First published in Great Britain in 2022 by
PEN & SWORD CRIME
An imprint of
Pen & Sword Books Ltd
Yorkshire – Philadelphia

ISBN 9781399090377

A CIP catalogue record for this book is available from the British Library

Typeset in Chennai, India
by Lapiz Digital Services.

Printed and bound by CPI Group (UK) Ltd, Croydon, CR0 4YY

Pen & Sword Books Ltd incorporates the imprints of Pen & Sword
Archaeology, Atlas, Aviation, Battleground, Discovery, Family History, History, Maritime, Military, Naval, Politics, Social History, Transport, True Crime, Claymore Press,
Frontline Books, Praetorian Press, Seaforth Publishing and White Owl

For a complete list of Pen & Sword titles please contact

PEN & SWORD BOOKS LTD
47 Church Street, Barnsley, South Yorkshire, S70 2AS, England
E-mail: enquiries@pen-and-sword.co.uk
Website: www.pen-and-sword.co.uk

Or

PEN AND SWORD BOOKS
1950 Lawrence Rd, Havertown, PA 19083, USA
E-mail: Uspen-and-sword@casematepublishers.com
Website: www.penandswordbooks.com

Contents

List of Maps and Diagrams

Maps

Diagrams

Acknowledgements

I claim no credit for the discovery and translation of the primary source material that I have drawn on in this book. The full credit for this goes to the incredible pioneering work carried out by a relatively small number of authors and enthusiasts over the last twenty years who have striven to bring to a wider English-speaking audience the rich and fascinating original reports, and particularly the eyewitness accounts, that have been hidden away in various national archives and museums throughout Europe.

I have drawn heavily on the outstanding work of the following authors whose books appear in the references and bibliography:

Gareth Glover and John Franklin for their tracking down, translation and publication of Hanoverian, Nassau, Brunswick and Netherlands accounts that has made them available to such a wide audience.

Erwin Muilwijk for his very detailed, four-volume account of the Netherlands army and the 1815 campaign from a Netherlands perspective, drawing heavily on the Netherlands archives and Netherlands' eyewitness accounts.

André Dellevoet for his detailed study of the Netherlands cavalry during the Waterloo campaign, also drawing heavily on the Dutch archives and first-hand accounts.

Pierre de Wit for his pioneering website (www.waterloo-campaign.nl) covering the campaign in incredible detail from every nation's perspective that has informed and inspired so many enthusiasts of the campaign for many years.

I also need to thank the following people who have answered the myriad of questions I have put to them on their own specialist subjects and who have given up so much of their own time to help me; they are truly experts in their own fields who deserve more credit than they receive:

Michael-Andreas Tänzer and Dr Jens Mastnak of the *Arbeitskreis Hannoversche Militärgeschichte* in Hannover, who have helped me so much on the Hanoverian contribution, and Thomas Musahl, Hans Kolmsee and Andre Kolars of the *Herzoglich Braunschweigische Feldcorps e.V*, whose knowledge of the Brunswick contingent of 1815 must be second to none.

I would also like to thank my friend Robert Pocock, founder, owner, director and lead guide of Campaigns and Culture, for his calm advice and priceless proofreading which has no doubt made this a much better book than it would otherwise have been.

Thanks are also due to Rupert Harding of Pen & Sword Books for his lasting patience as I have bounced from one project to another and never quite made up my mind which one I want to do next.

Finally, many thanks to Mandy for her love and infinite understanding of my passion for Waterloo and spending so many hours locked away in my study. One day I really will get round to doing all those jobs...

Introduction

The English appear to want to claim for themselves all the glory of the triumph of Waterloo, as if the troops of the other nations that were there did not take a large part in this fierce struggle, where they spilt their blood, just as well as the insular British.[1]

They were the rankest cowards that ever formed part of an army[2]

The Belgians behaved vilely...[3]

For the best part of 180 years, the British perception of the battle of Waterloo was that it was a great British victory gained over the French tyrant Napoleon, and that the victory was achieved in spite of, rather than because of, the contribution of the allied contingents in Wellington's army. Indeed, the early campaign accounts by British authors, perhaps exemplified by William Siborne, based on eyewitness accounts by British soldiers and officers, and encouraged by the doubts of their military efficacy expressed in Wellington's own despatches, denigrated and vilified the courage and prowess of their allies. Indeed, so many examples are there that it serves no purpose to repeat them all here. For whatever reasons, some of the countries did not want or dare to challenge the slurs made against them, but some Belgian senior officers,[4] seeing the courage of their troops in particular called into question, tried to put the record straight; their efforts were lost in the outpouring of British triumphalism and jingoism.

It is only in the last twenty to thirty years that modern authors, with better access to the accounts and archives of the allied nations, have tried to present a more balanced view,[5] and their efforts have been rewarded with a change in attitude by many modern students of the Waterloo campaign. Indeed, in these days of political correctness and in their determination to prove that the contributions of the allied contingents were vital to the Waterloo victory, and with this particular axe to grind, there is a danger that these views are almost as distorted as those of the early British accounts. Indeed, despite their worthy efforts, some have been distinctly subjective and biased pieces of work which appear to have deliberately avoided an in-depth and objective analysis of the potential and battlefield performance of the allied contingents.

My aim, therefore, is to present an objective assessment of the contributions of the allied contingents of Wellington's army to the victory of Waterloo.

I have already thanked the many historians who have tracked down the primary sources from the archives of the foreign contingents and I do not pretend to have done much original research myself except for ruthlessly exploiting a number of enthusiasts who have been kind enough to agree to help me (these are also named in the acknowledgements). I have only collected, collated, interpreted and analysed. And while the many pages of enthralling accounts start to give us a new perspective and insight into what truly happened during this short campaign, they do so without real context. This is one of the key aspects I have also addressed in this book; I have tried not to include too many long quotes by eyewitnesses that are available in the works of others, but carefully selected those I have used to illustrate a particular aspect of the action as part of my analysis. By trying to place them in the context of what was going on around them at the same time, perhaps can we truly see their place in the narrative of the battle and how their actions and movements contributed to it, therefore giving us a better idea of their true value. Having read all these sources before, I was surprised what a different perspective my more recent study of them revealed when considering them in the context of the battle for this book; this has forced me to re-evaluate some of my understanding of the battle.

In order to look at the contribution of each of these contingents, we cannot look solely at their numbers. We must also look at their training, experience and other key factors which would affect their performance; in short, we need to try and measure their potential military effectiveness. This is what the modern military call 'military capability', but in this technological age of increasingly complex warfare the term is probably not suitable for the rather low-tech warfare of Napoleonic times. Having looked at this as the contingent's 'potential', we then need to balance it, with all the benefits of hindsight, with what they actually achieved on the battlefield.

Sources

In order to look at this whole range of factors, and especially when trying to objectively analyse battlefield performance, we must be careful which sources we use and be clear-sighted about the inevitable biases that will appear in both official reports and individual accounts. As archives and digitisation have made once-hidden information far more accessible, recent histories have increasingly relied on these individual accounts and reports to try and deliver more accurate narratives of military history. Yet such accounts, while a priceless source of fascinating information, present their own problems. Individual accounts and official reports, written by eyewitnesses, were initially considered sacrosanct and any challenge was considered blasphemous. However, as more have become available, it has become clear that they are often contradictory. There is a growing awareness that they cannot be accepted as the absolute truth just because they were written by someone present at the action they are describing. Many accounts are likely to have been influenced by personal, regimental, political and national prejudices, and/or affected by memory loss over time and/or the influence of having read other accounts or discussing them with others. More recent books which present, or are based on, individual eyewitness accounts, now start with a lengthy explanation of why these accounts must be treated with caution, my own included. I do not wish to repeat what has already been written, but refer the reader to those books if they wish to explore this subject further.

In an effort to be entirely objective, wherever possible I have used a nation's own reports and eyewitness accounts when analysing its capabilities and assessing its battlefield performance, only using accounts from other contingents to corroborate details. Accounts from other nations are only used in isolation when they have something new to add or when they counter clear national bias.

I have also tried to limit myself to using primary source material and avoiding general histories. Even with careful reading, only some of this primary source material gives the low-level detail that is not covered in general campaign histories, yet it gives us a glimpse of the lives and tactical actions that individuals experienced first-hand. Therefore, although I have consulted national histories for context, I have rarely relied on them for detail as, just like English-language histories, they have their own biases and agendas, often, though understandably, promoting the actions and successes of their own national contingents.

The fact that Waterloo was a decisive victory meant there was no need for the allies to conduct a post-mortem and no need for scapegoats; everyone could bask in the reflected glory and the veneer of victory did not need to be picked at to see what lay beneath. Everyone could write up their own claims to fame and courage and there was little chance of challenge unless it reflected poorly on others or stole their laurels. We shall see later how Wellington was prepared to turn a blind eye to unfortunate incidents which might have taken some of the shine off the victory, and for similar reasons he was unenthusiastic about the avalanche of books on the battle that inevitably followed. There was certainly no reason to challenge the view that everyone did their duty. Wellington wrote:

> You cannot write a true history of a battle without including the faults and misbehaviour of part at least of those engaged. Believe me, that every man you see in a military uniform is not a hero… it is better for the general interests to leave those parts of the story untold than to tell the whole truth.[6]

Some of the evidence presented to prove the effectiveness and courage of the allied contingents has often quoted the letters to sovereigns from contingent commanders or the army commander and official reports, but these letters and reports were influenced more by political expediency and a nationalistic pride in victory than they were an accurate reflection of the achievements of the contingents on which they reflected. They can hardly be used as an objective assessment of true battlefield performance and were never meant to be so.

Of far more utility are the reports written to a nation's military authorities, often solicited some years after the event, when a calmer, more objective approach has been used, to try and learn the lessons from a particular conflict in order to modernise and improve military forces or doctrine. This 'lessons learned' process (as it is now called) was particularly effective in the Prussian army of the time, and was later copied by the Hanoverians and Netherlanders, but ignored by the British.[7] Furthermore, the individual recollections of the participants of lower rank, whether officers or soldiers, are often rather more honest in their descriptions of what actually happened than official reports designed to feed royal or political leadership and national morale, though they inevitably offer a very localised view of battle.

The value, or lack of value, of official reports is well illustrated by the following example, even though it was written by a Polish officer writing of an experience during the Peninsular War:

> On the next morning Solnicki, the former commandant of Monzon, called me into his room and I found him rather agitated. 'I have received,' he told me, 'the order to write a full report on yesterday's battle. Would you sit down there and set the ball rolling. Here is a pen, ink and paper.' I sat down, and regurgitated a brief resume of what had happened, adding the number of dead and wounded, some fifteen men. I read all this off to the captain and he pointed out that I had missed a couple of essential details. He then dictated some additions and corrections which had the effect of turning this minor skirmish into a colourful struggle of heroic proportions and accorded full credit to its fortunate outcome to himself. 'That, my friend, is how you write a report,' he boasted and then got me to write out the report once again, scribbled his name with difficulty at the bottom of the page and rewarded me with a cup of coffee, a luxury I had been deprived of since Pamplona. Military histories are all too often written in the manner of Solnicki's report, if not all histories.[8]

Let us also look at two shorter examples from Waterloo. The first was written by Captain Jean-Baptiste of the Netherlands artillery staff who was responding to a request for information from Captain Ernst van Löben-Sels, who was collating the Netherlands' accounts of the campaign for the general staff; the letter was dated 20 July 1841:

> I had little time to compare the reports [from the batteries that were at Quatre Bras] to substantiate their validity; for as you yourself have observed, it is very difficult to identify the truth within these events, for after a battle won the contributions to the victory are invariably enlarged, and errors disregarded.[9]

The second is a good example of how poor battlefield performance was glossed over in national official reports. At Waterloo, the Hanoverian Duke of Cumberland Hussars, having suffered some casualties from long-range artillery fire, but not directly engaged with the enemy, turned bridle and left the battlefield, despite a number of staff officers being sent after them to persuade the commanding officer to return; he refused, and the regiment didn't stop until close to Brussels. In his report as the senior Hanoverian officer present at the battle, General von Alten wrote in his report to the Duke of Cambridge, 'Of our cavalry, only the Duke of Cumberland Regiment was present in the battle but did not attack. It was exposed to the cannonade for a considerable time and sustained significant losses.'[10] The commanding officer was later court marshalled and cashiered.

Scope of the study

Although the King's German Legion (KGL) was essentially an all-Hanoverian organisation, I have not included them in this study. There are several reasons for this. Firstly, strictly they were not an allied, national contingent, but a formal part of the British army. Secondly, due to their long experience in the peninsula, but also in other theatres, they were considered, even by the British themselves, as every bit as professional and effective as their British comrades, indeed more so in some areas of their performance. Finally, I am restricted by space, and while the KGL have had much exposure in the many histories and writings on the Peninsular War, I did not want to cut back on the detail I have accumulated on the other contingents in order to accommodate them.[11] Their vital contribution to Waterloo must not be underestimated.

I have also chosen not to include Wellington's steadfast allies, the Prussians. These of course warrant a book of their own and there are detailed studies of their contribution to the campaign for those interested. That is not to say there is no room for a modern, objective assessment of their contribution to the campaign, but this is not the place for it.

I have also chosen to avoid a study of uniforms and unit internal organisations and manning, as this information is now widely available in many other excellent publications.

Objectivity

I have no personal axe to grind in this study and have approached it by trying to be as objective as I possibly can. However, I accept that this is *my* interpretation; I have chosen which accounts to quote from and which parts to use as evidence. The analysis is also mine, based on the evidence of the whole accounts I have consulted rather than just the extracts I have included in this book. This analysis is based on my own military experience, my military education, logic, common sense and intellect. I am certainly not so dogmatic that I think all conclusions are absolutely the right ones. For those who do not agree with my interpretation then I welcome your feedback; healthy discussion and debate is a vital part of an interest in military history, and I long ago learnt to challenge everything I read and not take it as the absolute truth. If this encourages more people to read all the evidence available and come to their own conclusions, then that is to be welcomed.

Chapter One
Military Effectiveness

Measuring military effectiveness

If we are to objectively assess the effectiveness of each of the allied contingents within Wellington's army, we must consider two things: firstly, their potential, and secondly, their actual performance in battle, which may exceed their potential, or fall short of it.

For this study I shall call the true combat value of a force its 'military effectiveness', which can be defined as its ability to achieve a specified wartime objective, such as winning the war or a battle.

Military effectiveness is made up of different physical components and capabilities.[1] Some of these are tangible and measurable, such as manpower, structure and composition (an effective mix of staff, infantry, cavalry and artillery) and other key factors that we shall consider shortly. But other elements that need to be considered are quite abstract and intangible, which may require some subjective judgement if we are to try and evaluate them. These may include the quality of leadership, discipline and ethos. The consideration and value of all these components and capabilities establish the potential of a force, but must then be balanced against their performance on the battlefield before we can judge their true, proven military effectiveness.

However, accurately assessing battlefield performance is fraught with difficulty as it relies on complete objectivity in the analysis of that performance based on eyewitness accounts and official reports, which may be controversial and biased, especially if they come from partisan observers from a different nation to the one being assessed.

Therefore, to fully establish military effectiveness, it is necessary to examine a combination of both tangible and intangible factors. For each of the contingents, these will be examined to the extent that we have dependable evidence as to how they affected each contingent. If no evidence is available, the factors will be ignored to avoid speculation or hearsay.

All the foreign contingents of Wellington's army were forced to raise new armies after their countries had been absorbed into either France itself (the Netherlands and Belgium) or into, or as, French satellite states (Brunswick, Hanover and Nassau). This is not to say that these states lacked manpower with military experience, but only Nassau had any truly national military forces of its own after French annexation or domination, and prior to the end of 1813 when it was liberated. The new, independent armies had therefore effectively had to be raised almost from scratch.

The basic building blocks of an army are straight forward and include the following:

Manpower

Manpower is the most basic requirement for an army and can be raised by volunteers, conscription or a mixture of both. The size of a force, or army, was largely dependent on the size of the pool of military-aged males and the ability of a state to pay for what was an enormously expensive tool. Although a large army may be imposing and capable of achieving many tasks a small army may not, the value of any army cannot be based on raw numbers alone. History has many examples of small, well-equipped, well-trained and highly disciplined armies that have comprehensively defeated much larger, but less well-equipped, less well-trained and poorly disciplined armies, even though they may have been well-motivated and enthusiastic. Although a lack of numbers can be mitigated to a certain extent by strength in other factors we will consider, there is a point when a small army, however professional and effective it is, will be overwhelmed by a numerically superior, but less efficient force. Britain, which had long maintained a small but professional army in preference to a much larger conscript army, had almost inevitably relied on allies providing extra bulk in order to face much larger continental armies. In 1815, unable to field the 150,000 men it was obliged by treaty to provide, Britain subsidised its allies to make up the shortfall, making the other national contingents a vital contribution to the viability of Wellington's army.

Organisation

To form an army, manpower needed to be organised into units and formations, to have a command structure and include the basic combat arms of infantry, cavalry and artillery, as well as the supporting arms such as engineers and a transport train. Even in the Napoleonic era, it was an established principle that effective military operations required combined arms cooperation of all three arms – infantry, cavalry and artillery – to become more effective than the sum of the individual parts. A contingent without one or more of these three arms would be forced to rely on allies to provide the shortfall or fight without them, and this risked poor coordination and a drop in effectiveness.

Equipment and arms

A new force needed to be uniformed, armed and equipped to be able to operate on campaign and in battle. However, in a state which had previously not produced its own arms and equipment, mobilising new means of production could be problematic, especially if funds were low. In 1815, some of the allied contingents relied on the British to a greater or lesser extent to provide the shortfall in uniforms, arms and equipment, without which they may well only have been able to field a smaller, or less effective, force.

Logistics

A new force needed to be fed and watered and provided with ammunition to fight, with sufficient transport to move the necessary supplies. The failure to have an efficient logistic system could have a huge bearing on the performance of the frontline troops and particularly on their acceptance of a system of discipline. The army that had an effective system of obtaining and transporting vital supplies would often have an advantage over an army which did not. *In extremis*, food could generally be obtained from the local community, with or without renumeration. However, the same was not true of ammunition and a failure to efficiently replenish stocks could have serious consequences. The difficulties of resupply were increased if there were a variety of different calibres across a polyglot allied army and we shall see how the various mix of muskets and rifles had an impact on the battlefields of 1815.

Drill and training

To compensate for the poor accuracy of muskets of the Napoleonic era it was necessary for men to maintain a tight formation to ensure effective control and maximum concentration of fire. For these units to be able to move efficiently around the battlefield and change formation when conditions demanded, they were regulated by drill. Although the drill regulations inevitably differed from country to country, the basic formations and evolutions were generally similar. However, for those armies with long experience of battle, certain adaptions, and more efficient ways of applying drill, could give an army an appreciable advantage over its adversaries. It was also found that different armies preferred a particular formation that, although it gave them an advantage over one enemy, might not have an advantage over another.

Throughout the Peninsular War, although the professional British units had generally formed columns to move and manoeuvre quickly, they had almost invariably engaged in a line that was two ranks deep to maximise their firepower against the more densely packed French columns. In this formation they had consistently beaten the French in all the major battles of the war. However, the large conscript continental armies had generally formed their lines three ranks deep, believing that the extra rank gave their line more solidity and the soldiers more confidence. They believed that a two-rank line, especially if made up of young and inexperienced troops, was frail and that if taking casualties, the line was at risk of breaking up. They also adapted their own drill and tactics to reflect that which had been used by the French during their years of military success on the battlefields of Europe.

Ideally, all the formations and units of an army would use the same drill regulations to ensure consistent manoeuvre and avoid confusion on the battlefield. Unfortunately, the complications of drawing together a multi-national army such as that commanded by Wellington made this impossible.

Raised in haste, the various contingents of 1815 had either adopted the drill regulations of other countries or tried to adapt what they were already practised in with particular aspects of the regulations drawn from others. Allied to the British and influenced by senior commanders who had experience with them, the Netherlands contingent adopted the British practice of two deep lines, while the Nassauers adopted the French regulations, with lines three deep, which most of their officers were familiar with. The Hanoverians and Brunswickers used Prussian practices which were immediately available in their own language. We thus see a variety of drill regulations being used among the contingents which could potentially result in confusion, particularly when trying to manoeuvre together. This also meant that it became difficult for experienced officers and NCOs from one nation to assist with the training of other nationalities that used different regulations to their own. Furthermore, as we will see at Waterloo, what suited the troops of one nation might not be suited to those of another. There was a danger that this lack of consistency between contingents may have had significant implications on the battlefield.

Well-trained troops will inevitably have a better chance of success in combat compared to those who are not. During wartime, when reinforcements are desperately needed, it was often difficult to find the time to train recruits sufficiently as well as finding suitably experienced men to conduct that training. In Napoleonic times, the amount of time required for training was much shorter than in more recent wars and in 1813 and 1814, French conscripts were often trained on the march from the depots to the front line in just a few weeks. This may have worked well enough for individual training, but it was also vitally important for complete units to train together so they were able to manoeuvre cohesively under fire on the battlefield without becoming disordered.

In 1815 many units had had the time to conduct training before the campaign opened and had become proficient at drill. However, there were some notable exceptions who arrived with the army just as the campaign opened. As we examine each contingent, we will be able to identify those units that had the time to train and those that did not, and we will often see how the lack of training impacted on their battlefield performance.

These building blocks were generally the same in all armies of the period; manpower was a basic requirement for all armies, and organisation, weaponry and drill were similar across the continent; logistic systems were also generally the same (apart from the French, whose system of living off the land meant they were not encumbered by a large logistical chain) and if there were differences during the Waterloo campaign, they had little impact on the result of the battle itself. But these basic building blocks will provide only a soulless army; true performance on the battlefield was determined by some rather more intangible factors, and it was these, and their differences between contingents and armies, that were to have the most significant impact on battlefield performance. These include the following factors.

Leadership

It is insufficient to have a chain of command in an army. Its leaders must be professional, courageous and determined, an example for the other ranks to follow and have trust in. Good leaders add considerably to the morale and capabilities of an army and poor ones will inevitably lead them to defeat. There is an oft-repeated mantra that there is no such thing as bad soldiers, only bad officers.

The importance of good leadership in any army, from the most junior officer to the commander-in-chief, can hardly be overemphasised. It does not matter how well-motivated, experienced or professional your troops: if they are poorly led, they will almost inevitably face defeat due to the incompetence of their officers.

After Waterloo, Napoleon, while praising the morale and conduct of his troops, was quick to blame the defeat on the failures of his subordinate commanders. In Wellington's situation, where he had little or no control over the leadership of the various contingents and where those contingents were of varying experience and quality, it was vital that he employed them with much thought and consideration to ensure he could derive the maximum benefit from their attributes and not expose their identified weaknesses. In this respect, the experience he had gained from working with the Spanish and Portuguese armies during the Peninsular War was significant, and the lessons he learnt there can be seen in the way he handled and deployed his allies in 1815. It is noteworthy that in the actions where he was not present, or his hand was forced and he was obliged to give them missions for which they were unsuited, the outcome was often failure. We shall see some examples of this later.

Commandant Colin, a French officer and military theorist writing in the mid-nineteenth century, echoed many famous generals when he wrote, 'There are no troops so bad that good generals cannot fire them. Perhaps the value of the leader outvalues all others'[2] and this is not only true of generals, but also, and perhaps just as importantly, low-level, battlefield leadership. While all officers needed to know their drill and the required manoeuvres on the battlefield, for the more junior officers, doing their job among the soldiers of their company, the men looked to their officers for an example of courage, honour, determination, coolness in adversity and endurance and as long as their officers were able to 'stick it' then they were honour-bound to do the same.

Discipline

The need for people to obey orders is a vital requirement of an effective army; without discipline the officers have no control over their men with obvious implications for their performance on the battlefield. However, discipline in good units helps to develop the self-discipline which stops individuals avoiding difficult times and moments and being prepared to fight on when things are not going well. Discipline implies the use of punishment to control behaviour, but a well-disciplined unit generally has high morale and does not require the use of punishment as much as those which are less so.

Ethos

Ethos seems little considered in the attributes of an army. Yet it is the spirit of an army; what motivates it, maintains its cohesion when things are not going well, and helps to forge trust between the officers and their men and between each other. In many armies, the cause for which it fights will often have less influence on a soldier's willingness to fight than his preparedness to fight and die for his comrades and his unit, which promotes the importance of discipline. The ethos of an army helps to motivate less experienced units to emulate those that have excelled in battle and therefore pervades the whole organisation.

Support for the cause

Even given that a soldier's will to fight for, and with, his comrades was probably one of his greatest incentives, it is quite possible that he would not even be on the battlefield if he did not believe in the cause for which he was fighting. Among the contingents at Waterloo there were many officers, some very senior, as well as soldiers, that had fought for the French in some guise; either in French regiments or within contingents that were allied to France. Some senior allied officers had reached their high rank commanding French soldiers and been decorated and ennobled by Napoleon, often amassing considerable fortunes along the way. In the case of the Belgians in particular, but also the Dutch and Nassauers, there were many in the allied army that doubted their loyalty to the cause. As we shall see, Wellington wrote of his concerns about the loyalty of some of the senior officers of his army. Even Napoleon believed that many Belgian soldiers would change sides to serve him and established a depot to recruit Belgian deserters into French service.[3] There is plenty of contemporary evidence to support the view that many of Napoleon's old officers and soldiers retained some loyalty to him, and it is only natural that others should doubt their dependability on the battlefield. We shall see the extent to which this was reflected in their battlefield performance later in the book. But if there were some who harboured an affection for Napoleon, there were many others who had cause to hate him, and the memories of the French invasion and rule of their own countries had generated much motivation for revenge.

Experience

The value of having a good level of experience of campaigning and of battle in an army should almost go without saying. Campaigning hardens the soldiers, teaches them how to look after themselves in arduous conditions, develops confidence between officers and men, and establishes unit cohesion and an almost mutually agreed level of discipline. Experience in battle takes those same factors forward, conditions the men to the sounds and sensations of battle and teaches them how to deal with them, how to control their fear and to develop their trust in the men who surround them. And hopefully, experience of victory develops confidence in the individual and in the unit and starts to establish a feeling of superiority over the enemy. As long as there is a hard core of veterans, a unit can absorb batches of new recruits without a drop in effectiveness and those recruits will quickly pick up the lessons which we have just explored from the veterans around them. We have already studied the importance of having good leadership in inexperienced units as good officers will know how best to exploit the enthusiasm of new troops without letting it draw them into situations for which they are unprepared. But while campaigning experience is inevitably of value to soldiers, experience of defeat can be demoralising and lead to a lack of confidence in the chances of bettering an enemy that has beaten you on previous occasions. Experience of defeat can have a debilitating effect on battlefield performance through low morale, or, under strong leadership, can increase the determination to avenge previous humiliations.

Courage and morale

The basic building blocks of an army, but more the intangible factors we have just described, contribute to morale. Courage and morale, high or low, will be reflected in battlefield performance. High morale is vital to an army; no army with low morale is likely to win a battle and the morale of a unit is fundamental to its potential performance on the battlefield. Equally, a high level of courage does not guarantee effective battlefield performance – perhaps just the ability to stand and 'take it' when things are not going well.

High levels of courage and morale, and the resulting determination to fight hard, can be infectious, and this is why Wellington was so keen to mix his experienced units with those which were less experienced. But the same is true of low morale; it is unusual to read of single units that broke and ran in battle without dragging others back too.

As these are both abstract, variable and complex concepts, there is no room to examine them in detail in this comparatively short study. Both are almost impossible to quantify accurately in advance, can change in seconds on the battlefield, and are rather easier to assess with the benefit of hindsight. No military experience or training is required to have morale or courage, and this is why inexperienced troops are often described as having both. Certainly, the accounts by officers of all the contingents at Waterloo are full of such descriptors when speaking of their men and there is no reason, in the circumstances that prevailed, to doubt that they were telling the truth. As the aim of this study is to assess what each contingent actually achieved on the battlefield this should clearly establish whether it was their enthusiasm and courage that were lacking, or something else.

Battlefield performance

An objective examination of a force based on the factors discussed above may suggest a high level of potential, but its true military effectiveness can only be accurately established after assessing its battlefield performance. Avoiding a premature examination of the allied national contingents at Waterloo, a good example of this is the French Imperial Guard. A cursory examination of all the factors we have just discussed would anticipate exceptional battlefield performance, but any student of the battle will know that their final attack against a much-weakened allied line was an abject failure. While there are many reasons why this was so, it admirably illustrates how assessed potential, and supposedly high morale and courage, do not guarantee battlefield success.

Each of the factors we have discussed will have an impact on battlefield performance and each to a different extent, although it would be difficult to accurately quantify the relative importance of each as they could also have a variable impact at different times and in different circumstances. While a high training proficiency in a unit suggests high performance, if logistics have failed and they have no ammunition, they are unlikely to reach their full potential.

As the level of each of our factors (and there are certainly others that might have an impact as well), is likely to be different from unit to unit, let alone contingent to contingent, we cannot expect their battlefield performance to be the same. This is why it is inherently unfair and unhelpful to compare the allied contingents with the most experienced British regiments. And to go a step further, beyond the factors we have looked at, a unit's place on the battlefield, its mission, the time it is exposed to enemy fire and to close combat will all affect its ability to demonstrate, or not, its effectiveness.

Therefore, the best we can hope for is to assess the extent to which each unit, brigade or contingent fulfilled its potential: did they perform as well as could be expected in the unique circumstances that each of them faced? It is this that will help us assess their contribution to victory, rather than trying to construct a league table of achievement in combat, and importantly it is also this that will determine whether they were correctly handled and managed in order to maximise their effect.

What does the level of casualties tell us?

In many ways, the level of casualties may well reflect the intensity of the fighting that a unit has been involved in and its ability to 'stick it', but we must be wary of concluding that a unit's casualty rate reflects its battlefield performance. However, while the level of casualties is an important indicator of a unit's staying power (discipline, courage, unit cohesion etc), casualty figures must be balanced against the role the unit played in the fighting and the battlefield environment in which it was engaged.

A unit's tactics and role can affect its level of casualties. Units formed in column were likely to suffer heavier casualties under artillery fire than units in line; careful use of terrain often protected a unit from heavier casualties, while those fighting from buildings or behind any kind of cover against the rather primitive firearms of the day may have suffered far less, even though they may have been engaged for much longer. A unit may have suffered heavy casualties from being exposed to artillery fire without having fired a shot or coming into close contact with the enemy.

A unit's level of casualties therefore has to be looked at in the context of the intensity and conditions of the fighting in which it found itself before we can form a view on how far casualties reflect battlefield performance.

A low level of casualties can tell us a number of different things. The unit could have found itself on a quiet sector of the battlefield where no serious fighting took place; it could have displayed poor morale, discipline, cohesion and a lack of effective leadership and withdrawn early from, or avoided, heavy fighting; and yet equally it could have executed a brilliant tactical manoeuvre that quickly overwhelmed the enemy before they had an opportunity to fight back. At Waterloo, many eyewitnesses speak of a unit suffering heavy casualties, yet the actual casualty figures do not reflect this.

A high level of casualties may also have been for a variety of reasons; a prolonged engagement at close quarters showing discipline, courage and tenacity against an equally determined enemy; they could have stood immobile and determined in the face of heavy artillery fire without the means or opportunity to fire back; or they could have broken early and run from a mobile and determined enemy and been cut down and/or captured in large numbers without offering resolute opposition.

Each of these two scenarios – light or heavy casualties – offers the extremes of courage and resolution; from cowardice or ineffectiveness to heroism and military prowess. Many of them may also have been a reflection of good or bad leadership, training, tactics and so on; indeed, a mix of the very factors that we have discussed when measuring potential and all, or none of them, may have reflected the courage and willingness of the individual soldier or collective unit. We must take care to examine the context of a unit's role before drawing conclusions on battlefield performance from the level of casualties it suffered.

Missing

We must be equally wary, if not more so, of how we interpret the number of men reported as 'missing'. These are often assumed to have made a deliberate and cowardly effort to slip away from the fighting for either the short term, to reappear with their units after the battle had finished, or to have departed with the intention of deserting their army altogether and returning home. In an article in the *Nineteenth Century Magazine* of 1900, Sir Charles Oman, a well-known English historian of the late nineteenth and early twentieth century, used the numbers of missing of the various allied contingents at Waterloo to conclude that large numbers had run away and that they were all cowards. This of course is far from the truth, for there are many other, more legitimate reasons why men were missing from their units at the end of an engagement.

While the numbers of missing were often used as an indicator of rocky unit morale, this may not be essentially true. All units, from all nationalities, had men that went missing during battle; some had helped wounded comrades to a field hospital or been sent for more ammunition, and for equally legitimate reasons failed to return during the battle (for example, soldiers were often kept back at field hospitals to help the medical staff deal with particularly heavy casualties). Cavalry units were likely to have had relatively large numbers of men that had been dismounted and struggled to find a new mount and/or to locate and rejoin their units in the hours and days after battle. Many men had been killed or wounded and fallen unobserved (indeed, this seems to have been the major cause of those missing), while very few had deliberately absconded.

However, in units of high morale, discipline, cohesion and confidence, individuals who had a legitimate reason or excuse for becoming separated from their unit would often make every effort to rejoin their comrades before the battle was over, while those from inexperienced units, or inexperienced themselves, might wait until the battle was over before returning.

Some units honestly recorded those missing, while others attempted to cover up the numbers to protect the reputation of their unit. Creative accounting was also used; those missing were often included in the numbers of killed and wounded. Some units were very open and not only reported those missing under a separate heading, but also included the names of those who were known to have deliberately avoided combat in post-action reports. Examples of all of these will be seen in the following chapters.

Inexperienced troops

All of the allied contingents that fought in Wellington's army at Waterloo were composed of a relatively large number of young and inexperienced troops. Some, as we shall see later, had not been long in uniform, lacked training and only arrived with the army a few weeks, or less, before the campaign opened.

It is not hard to imagine what a shock their first experience of battle must have been to these young men.

All the allies who contributed forces to Wellington's army faced the same problem; they were forced to raise the majority of their troops quickly and, for some, without a substantial campaign or battle experienced cadre to build on. All the nations we will examine were raising much of their force virtually from scratch; the majority had only been raised in the previous twelve months. And even those who had been in uniform since the end of 1813, a relatively small proportion of the whole, had no campaign or battle experience and were inevitably very young.

It is therefore worth spending a little time and space looking at how the capabilities and shortcomings of such troops were discussed at the time, as this should help to more objectively assess their performance at Quatre Bras and Waterloo and ensure we do not judge them too prematurely or too harshly.

After the catastrophe of the retreat from Russia, Napoleon had miraculously raised a large, new army to face the increasingly overwhelming forces that were massing against him. This army, like the allied contingents of 1815, was largely composed of young conscripts who were poorly equipped and lacked training. The performance of these young conscripts on the battlefield, much commented on by the French commanders of the time and the historians that looked back on them, gives us a good idea of what the new levies of the allies of 1815 would be capable of and how they were likely to perform.

Reading the various accounts of the 1813 campaign and the conduct of the young French conscripts, named '*Marie-Louises*'[4], the same two words were used again and again by different authors to describe their battlefield performance: 'enthusiastic' and 'courageous'. It is unsurprising to find that these same words appear in the accounts written by the officers of the allied contingents in 1815. But enthusiasm and courage alone do not make effective soldiers. In his famous book *On War*, Clausewitz writes: 'Military virtues should not be confused with simple bravery, and still less with enthusiasm...'.

We briefly return to the importance of good leadership; Commandant Colin, whom we have already met, wrote:

> Newly raised levies generally only achieve decisive results when they have a great superiority in numbers. Especially without well trained officers, they become masses with which it is difficult to perform evolutions, cannot achieve decisive results by manoeuvre and consequently, are incapable of bringing off a decisive success. Well officered troops on the contrary, compensate for their numerical inferiority by the quickness of their manoeuvres.[5]

In 1813, Napoleon ensured that the best of the young conscripts were placed in new battalions of the greatly expanded Young Guard, as he was able to supply them with the very experienced officers (and NCOs), of which Colin speaks, from his Middle and Old Guard regiments.

The newly raised regiments of Wellington's allied contingents, particularly the Brunswick, Hanoverian and Netherlands contingents, had only limited cadres available and many of the NCOs and junior officers were as young and inexperienced as the troops they were to lead. Indeed, some contingents, particularly the Hanoverian and part of the Nassau contingents, were so desperately short of experienced officers that even relatively senior regimental officers had little or no previous campaign or battlefield experience.

Wellington was clear; firstly, that without capable officers, young recruits are almost valueless and secondly, being proficient at drill is not the same as being effective on the battlefield. He made his preference for experienced soldiers clear when he wrote to the military secretary of the Duke of York in 1813, 'I am of opinion from long experience that it is better for the service here to have one soldier or officer, whether of cavalry or infantry, who has served in two campaigns, than it is to have two or even three who have not. Not only the new soldiers can perform no service, but by filling the hospitals they are a burden to us.'[6] Inevitably, seasoned and battle-hardened troops are the best, but in the absence of fighting experience it is the cohesion, mutual confidence, the habit of shared hardships, military training and education, and above all, the quality of the officers and NCOs that impart real value to the troops.

Maximising utility

During his experiences in the Peninsula, Wellington had become adept at getting the best out of his allies; whether it was the uncooperative and unpredictable Spanish, the increasingly effective Portuguese, or the many Germans (Hanoverian Kings German Legion, Brunswickers or other Germans serving in British regiments) who served in the army. Their positioning on the battlefield, his tactics, his mixing them with British units and the use of British officers in some foreign units all contributed to maximising their effectiveness. Wellington attempted to make use of all these approaches during the Waterloo campaign with various levels of success.

Use of British officers

In order to improve the efficiency of the Portuguese army during the Peninsular War, Wellington attached British army officers to the Portuguese units and had British senior officers in the key command positions, replacing them with Portuguese officers when these had gained campaign experience, learnt their roles and proven themselves on operations. In 1815 he was unable to use this sensible policy, lacking the full command status or agreement of the nations involved who understandably, if possibly short-sightedly, wished their own officers to command their own units. His only minor success in this regard was, having failed to bring the significantly understrength KGL units up to strength with the fine raw material of the Hanoverian militia, that he reduced the KGL infantry units to six companies from ten and sent the officer and NCO cadres from the disbanded companies to the Hanoverian militia, who were short of officers and experienced NCOs. However, some of the commanding officers of these units had no military experience at all and even one of the Hanoverian brigade commanders was dubiously qualified for his command: Colonel von Vincke, commander of the 5th Hanoverian Brigade, had had no military service since leaving the Hanoverian army as a captain in 1803.

Mixing formations of one nation with another

In the Peninsula, Wellington had successfully mixed Portuguese formations with British, experience having shown that after time, this improved the performance of the Portuguese troops. Wellington would have liked to have done the same thing in 1815[7], and requested that a sizeable force of Portuguese join his army for the coming campaign. Before a decision on this request had been delivered, he accepted that he did not have the same freedom to do so with the other contingents in his army, because he did not have the support of the contingent's government or sovereign or because they had their own fully established staffs and chain of command. On 12 April he wrote to Earl Bathurst:

> There is likewise this advantage in Portuguese troops, viz., that we can mix them with ours and do what we please with them, and they become very nearly as good as our own. The others [Netherlands, Nassau and Brunswickers] must remain separate. They have their Generals and staff, and they must form separate divisions, if not separate corps.[8]

In fact, Wellington had made an effort to convince the Prince of Orange to authorise him to mix some of the Netherlands units with experienced British units, but his efforts had failed. He had raised the issue in a meeting of 11 April, but Erwin Muilwijk writes of it:

> The duke took the initiative in the discussion and proposed to amalgamate the rather inexperienced Dutch and Belgian troops with his own, to bolster the morale of the first and give them positive examples for a role model. Even though he pressed this matter, the Netherlands officers likely responded that this amalgamation was far too early, as they themselves were in the middle of such an affair themselves; each brigade was composed of both Dutch and Belgian units, who had to get to know each other better.[9]

Even on the night before Waterloo, a Dutch staff officer, Major van Gorkum, was told by Colonel de Lancy, Wellington's quartermaster-general, 'that it was the duke's will to have the younger troops covered by veteran ones and were placed with the English in the front line, the cavalry behind them and in between the intervals. That the German veterans were to occupy the wings and the forward posts and be divided over the line between the English...'.[10]

Although Wellington appeared to accept that he could not break up the Netherlands formations, and they started the campaign under the central authority of the Prince of Orange and his chain of command and fought under that authority at Quatre Bras, Wellington did not feel the same reticence on the day of Waterloo, deploying the two brigades of the 2nd Netherlands Division to different parts of the battlefield. Indeed, he even took a single battalion (the 1st/2nd Nassau) from the 2nd Brigade, which was deployed on the very left of the allied line and sent it to defend Hougoumont on the extreme right.

In contrast to the Netherlands troops, Wellington did have the freedom to mix Hanoverian brigades with British ones; he broke up the Hanoverian division and placed one of their brigades with each of his British divisions in order to surround them with capable, mainly experienced, troops. However, this did not go down well with the Hanoverian troops, even if they understood the reason for it; Captain Carl Jacobi, of the Lüneburg Field Battalion, wrote:

> Regrettably, we Hanoverians soon lost much of our willingness to serve and of our feelings of pride in our independent status, although hopefully not our courage. By the terms of a General Order from the duke [of Wellington] of 26th April, the Hanoverian brigades were assigned to various English divisions...
>
> With regard to the order of battle, discipline and provisions, the troops were completely subordinated to their English divisional commanders.
>
> There were substantial military considerations that justified this step; the Hanoverian troop complement had only recently been organised; only the field battalions formed in 1813 had proven themselves in battle; and the numerous Landwehr (15 battalions) had not any experience. This would, of course, explain the Duke's point of view of the desirability to provide these new units with an example and a firm support by their close attachment to the old and battle tested English regiments.[11]

Another officer, Captain Weiz of the very inexperienced 1st Battalion of the 1st Nassau Regiment, also recognised the value of mixing inexperienced with experienced units; he wrote:

> Also to be noted is the foresight of placing old battle tested regiments in between the less seasoned ones; as an example, the 1st Battalion of the 1st [Nassau] Regiment was posted in the first line, with an English regiment to its right, and to its left a battalion of the German Legion, etc., etc., The 2nd and 3rd Battalions of the 1st Regiment stood in second line, about 150 paces behind the 1st [Battalion], and behind those were the artillery reserve and a large corps of heavy cavalry.[12]

Tactics and positioning on the battlefield

At Waterloo, Wellington tried to deploy his allies to areas of the battlefield where the ground offered more protection, such as the broken ground around Papelotte and Smohain, or covering less likely enemy approaches such as around the right flank at Braine l'Alleud. Apart from using the reverse slope to protect all his troops, he also put many of his allied contingents into the second and third line so as not to expose them to close combat too early in the battle and to protect them from the inevitably heavy French artillery fire. While there were notable exceptions to this, such as Bijlandt's Netherlands brigade, this approach was largely followed with all the allied contingents; as part of the army's reserve, under Wellington's personal direct command and control, the whole Brunswick contingent and the 1st Nassau Regiment were initially deployed in the third and second lines respectively where they were largely protected from the heavy artillery fire and the fighting that took place in the initial stages of the battle, leaving them with relatively low casualties, still fully provisioned with ammunition and their morale generally intact for when they were needed in the front line later in the afternoon. These tactics left what he largely considered his most experienced and reliable troops in the front line throughout the battle.

It is axiomatic that recently formed, imperfectly trained and inexperienced troops are unlikely to be able to manoeuvre confidently or efficiently on the battlefield. Other than moving units from one place to another, out of contact and preferably out of the fire of the French, Wellington clearly chose static roles for his less experienced troops and was prepared to use them offensively only when the situation or the odds were clearly favourable. Where circumstances forced his hand, or if commanders at the point of contact made independent decisions, we will see that offensive manoeuvre by inexperienced units seldom ended well.

Wellington was also aware of the impact that the formation of the troops can have on their determination to hold. We have already mentioned that troops in line formation were not considered as secure as in column, and while British units had the confidence and experience to fight in line, most continental armies tended to fight in the more compact and robust column which gave them a better feeling of security. This is well illustrated by the following conversation between Wellington and the military theorist Jomini. In his well-known book *The Art of War*, Jomini wrote:

> I asked the illustrious general [Wellington] if at Waterloo he had not formed the Hanoverian, Brunswick and Belgian troops in columns by battalions. He answered, 'Yes; because I could not depend on them so well as upon the English,' I replied that this admission proved that he thought a line formed of columns by battalion was more firm than long deployed lines. He replied, 'They are certainly good also; but their use always depends upon the localities and the spirit of the troops. A general cannot act in the same manner under all circumstances.'[13]

Summary

Accurately assessing the military effectiveness of the allied contingents at Quatre Bras and Waterloo is no straightforward task. We must consider in detail the factors, both tangible and intangible, discussed above to establish their potential, and then to examine their battlefield performance to analyse to what extent this potential was realised given the individual circumstances each operated in and faced. As these will be different from contingent to contingent – indeed unit to unit – their success on the battlefield should not be compared to that of others, but to the extent to which they fulfilled their potential. Only then can we come to an objective and fair assessment to the contribution of each to the allied victory at Waterloo.

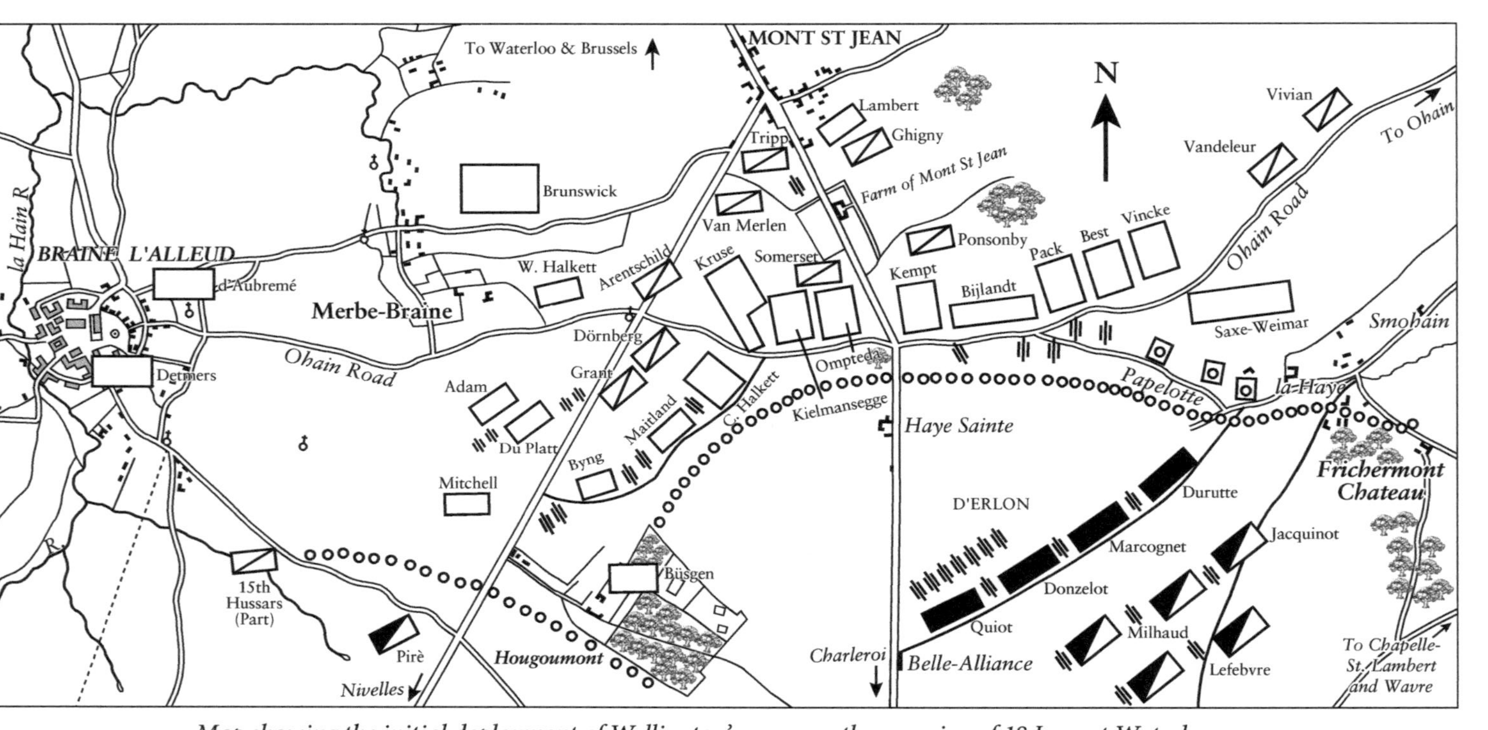

Map showing the initial deployment of Wellington's army on the morning of 18 June at Waterloo.

The Allied National Contingents in the Waterloo Campaign

It is impossible to be precise about the number of soldiers who fought at Waterloo in Wellington's army as sources inevitably vary. Although parade strengths are a good indication of a unit's overall strength, even on the day of battle, it is not true to state that all these men were deployed on the battlefield, as sickness and detachments for a wide variety of legitimate reasons inevitably reduced the number of men who actually fought. As an example, in his book *The Waterloo Companion*,[1] Mark Adkin records the strength of the 2nd/30th of Foot at Waterloo as having a total strength of 635; de Bas has the battalion as having a strength of 615 men on 12 June, yet Ensign Edward Macready, in his account of the campaign, wrote, 'From the number of sick, and on detached duties, it [the battalion] did not enter the field above 460 bayonets…' having suffered just 40 casualties at Quatre Bras. We must therefore understand that the figures given throughout this book are approximate.

The strength of Wellington's army at Waterloo was approximately 68,000. Because of the difficulty of accurately assessing the true strength of individual units, Mark Adkin uses battalions, squadrons and batteries to give a better feel for the contributions from each of the contributing nations and offers the following breakdown:[2]

British
Infantry: 25.5 battalions (30% of all infantry battalions).
Cavalry: 45 squadrons (49% of all cavalry squadrons).
Artillery: 13 batteries (a total of 77 guns which represent 49% of the army's total).

King's German Legion
Infantry: 8 battalions (9.5% of all infantry battalions).
Cavalry: 16 squadrons (17% of all cavalry squadrons).
Artillery: 3 batteries (a total of 18 guns, 11.5% of the army's total).

Nassau
Infantry: 8.5 battalions (10% of all infantry battalions).
Cavalry: Nil.
Artillery: Nil.

Brunswick
Infantry: 8 battalions (9.5% of all infantry battalions).
Cavalry: 5 squadrons (5% of all cavalry squadrons).
Artillery: 2 batteries (a total of 16 guns, 10% of the army's total).

Hanoverian
Infantry: 17 battalions (21% of all infantry battalions).
Cavalry: 4 squadrons (4% of all cavalry squadrons).
Artillery: 2 batteries (a total of 12 guns, 7.5% of the army's total).

The Netherlands
Infantry: 17 battalions (21% of all infantry battalions).
Cavalry: 23 squadrons (25% of all cavalry squadrons).
Artillery: 4.25 batteries (a total of 34 guns, 22% of the army's total).

Overall
The following figures reflect the contribution of the contingents *at* Waterloo and reflect a 'best guess' based on the variations of casualty and strength reporting of each contingent.

British: 35%
KGL: 8%
Nassau: 10%
Brunswick: 8%
Hanoverian: 18% (But this increases to 26% if the largely Hanoverian KGL is included.)
The Netherlands: 21%

Chapter Two

The Nassau Contingent

Background

The smallest contingent in Wellington's army, though not by much, was that of the minor German state of Nassau. Nassau had long been associated with the House of Orange that ruled the Netherlands. In 1815 its population was less than 300,000 people and was considerably smaller than that of Wales. In July 1806 Nassau joined Napoleon's Confederation of the Rhine and contributed two infantry regiments and a small cavalry contingent to the French army, fighting most notably in Spain, where they took part in forty-two combats, including at the battles of Medellin, Talavera, Ocana, Vitoria and on the Bidassoa. The 2nd Regiment defected to the British when Nassau was overrun by the allies in 1813; the 1st was disarmed by the French. The 2nd Regiment was evacuated by the Royal Navy and taken to Holland, where it immediately entered the Dutch service. After its liberation, Nassau only slowly began to rebuild its army and those men with experience under the French were absorbed into the units that were sent to supplement the Netherlands army as the latter struggled to meet its own targets for military manpower. In 1815 Nassau actually had more men under Netherlands' command than it did its own; while five battalions were raised for Dutch service, only the tardily re-raised 1st Regiment served under its own national commanders as part of Wellington's designated reserve.

Contingent size

Despite its small size and population Nassau contributed a considerable number of soldiers to Wellington's army; about 7,500 men in three regiments of infantry. Given the population of this time the percentage of military-aged males must have been low, and few could have escaped the conscription.

As two of the three regiments that made up the Nassau contribution to Wellington's army actually formed part of the Netherlands army, it is not strictly accurate to include them in the Nassau national contingent total, but as we are considering the contribution of individual states it seems appropriate to do so in this case. Nassau regiments were recruited by the Netherlands because of their failure to recruit enough soldiers into their own army to reach the target they had set themselves.

In early 1815, the 1st Nassau Regiment, formally titled the 1st Nassau-Usingen Light Infantry Regiment, was still being formed and did not arrive in Brussels to join the army until just two weeks before Waterloo. The 2nd Nassau-Usingen Light Regiment (these will be abbreviated to 1st or 2nd Nassau Regiment from now on), which had a much higher proportion of experienced officers, non-commissioned officers and soldiers, had formed part of the Netherlands army on its return from Spain. The remaining men formed the cadre of the new 1st Nassau Regiment. Each of these two regiments consisted of three battalions. As the Netherlands army struggled to fill its ranks, Nassau provided further troops; the Orange-Nassau Regiment of two battalions was formally incorporated into the Netherlands army and was numbered the 28th Netherlands Regiment (Orange-Nassau), and also a company of volunteer jägers, the *Freiwillige Jägers*, that was attached to this latter regiment. The Orange-Nassau Regiment also had a fair proportion of officers and men that had fought for the French. With the 2nd Nassau Regiment, the Orange-Nassau Regiment formed the 2nd Brigade of the 2nd Netherlands Division. The 1st Nassau Regiment formed an independent national contingent which was a part of the army's Reserve Corps. Nassau produced no cavalry or artillery units for the campaign. The Nassau contingent wore a French-style green uniform.

When the campaign opened, each Nassau regiment consisted of the following numbers:

1st Nassau Regiment: sixty-six officers and 2,834 men in a regimental headquarters and three battalions. Each battalion numbered over 900 men.

2nd Nassau Regiment: eighty-three officers and 2,575 other ranks in a regimental headquarters and three battalions. Each battalion numbered around 850 men.

The 28th Orange-Nassau Regiment: The regiment was made up of two battalions for a total of 1,581 all ranks.

Volunteer jägers: 177 men.

At Waterloo, the contingent represented approximately 10 percent of the allied army.

The leaders

There are two senior Nassau commanders who are worthy of a quick study. The first, August von Kruse, was born in Nassau and had much military experience leading Nassau troops under French command. The second, Prince Bernard of Saxe-Weimar, was not a Nassauer by birth, but found himself commanding over half the Nassau troops at Quatre Bras and Waterloo.

Major-General August von Kruse was born in Wiesbaden, Nassau, in 1779 and joined the Brunswick military aged seventeen before transferring into the expanding Nassau army as a major. He served under French command in the war against Prussia in 1806 and was promoted lieutenant colonel at the end of that campaign. In 1808 he deployed to Spain where he commanded a battalion of the 2nd Nassau Infantry Regiment and later the regiment itself. The regiment served in a number of key battles as well as many skirmishes. Von Kruse was wounded at the battle of Medellin, where he was also noted for his bravery. At the end of 1813 von Kruse oversaw the defection of the Nassau troops to the allied side. The Nassauers and von Kruse earned a fine reputation in Spain and Wellington was aware of von Kruse's record fighting there. Von Kruse was thus an experienced and capable veteran, proven on campaign and in combat.

Colonel Prince Bernard of Saxe-Weimar was born in Weimar in 1792. He first joined the Prussian army and fought against the French in 1806. In 1809 he joined the Saxon army and fought with the French against the Austrians at Wagram the same year, after which he was awarded the *Légion d'Honneur* by Napoleon himself. In 1810 he was in the Saxon Guard but was prevented by his parents from going to Russia. He served as a garrison commander in Saxony during the 1813 campaign. As large parts of Saxony were given over to Prussia in the peace of 1814, he looked for service elsewhere, being accepted into the Dutch army as colonel of the Orange-Nassau Regiment in February 1815. The regiment was part of the 2nd Brigade of the 2nd Netherlands Division; the other regiment in the brigade being the 2nd Nassau Regiment. The 2nd Brigade was to have been commanded by a Nassau officer, Colonel von Goedecke, but this officer having had his leg broken by a kick from a horse as the campaign opened, Saxe-Weimar confidently assumed command of the brigade as it arrived at Quatre Bras, commanding it through both that battle and Waterloo. He must be credited with directing the initial defence of Quatre Bras, having had the command thrust upon him by the absence of the nominated commander, and successfully commanding the brigade in the defence of the extreme left of Wellington's line at Waterloo. However, it is apparent from a number of comments from Nassau officers that he was not well respected by them[3] and appears to have lost considerable support from his officers by suggesting some of the Nassau troops ran away when the Prussians mistook them for the French at the end of the battle. However, Sergeant Doring, of the 1st/28th Orange-Nassau Regiment, called him 'A very brave and courageous soldier…'.[4] Saxe-Weimar was still only twenty-three years old at Waterloo, but had both campaign and combat experience, and although young, certainly did not shy away from responsibility, having almost ten years' experience in uniform. When the extra responsibility of brigade command was thrust upon him, he did not waiver and he was to command his men with a sure hand.

Even in the most recently formed regiment, the 1st, the level of campaign experience in the more senior officers was high. The regimental commander, Colonel von Steuben, started his military career in 1801 and reached the rank of lieutenant colonel in 1809 having served in Prussia in his early career and then in Spain; he was a recipient of the *Légion d'Honneur.* All the battalion commanding officers had served in Spain, and even the militia (3rd) battalion commander, Major von Preen, had served since 1801, fought in Prussia in 1806 and Spain 1810–11 (he retired as a lieutenant general in 1848).

Many of the more junior officers of the Nassau contingent also had considerable experience with the 1st and 2nd Nassau Regiments that had fought in Spain or had been serving with the Orange-Nassau Regiment since its creation, and these are often praised in accounts of the fighting. However, the officers of the recently formed 1st Nassau Regiment were generally less experienced. But even those with considerable experience were not necessarily well regarded or performed competently; in the exigencies of the moment, it is quite possible that some were promoted beyond their capabilities. Captain Weiz, who served with the 1st Regiment at Waterloo, wrote:

> The 1st Battalion was commanded by Major von Weyhers, a well-educated man and in the highest degree an energetic and brave officer; he, however, lacked the talent and competency to train and lead a battalion of young men such as this one. To this day, this officer must be blamed for never for a single moment having commanded and exercised the battalion entrusted to him, from the day it was mobilised until the day of battle. The men had never heard their commander's voice. If the battalion preserved its honourable name on the day of battle, it was not his, but rather to the battalion officers' merit, and theirs only.[5]

As we have heard, Major von Weyhers had fought in Spain with the 2nd Nassau Regiment, but the unfortunate implications of his failings at Waterloo will become clear later.

The troops

Providing no cavalry or artillery, we have already seen how the Nassau infantry formed three distinct groups. The two-battalion 28th Orange-Nassau Regiment and three-battalion 2nd Nassau Regiment, which were both formally part of the Netherlands army, under Netherlands' command, and fought together in the 2nd Brigade of the 2nd Netherlands Division; and the independent 1st Nassau Regiment which was under Nassau command and formed part of Wellington's reserve corps under his direct command. A large company of rifle armed volunteer jägers were attached to the Orange-Nassau Regiment.

As we have heard, the 2nd Nassau Regiment went straight into Dutch service when it had defected to the allies at the end of 1813 having been transported to the Netherlands by the Royal Navy. Efforts were then made to bring it back up to strength to serve with the Netherlands army which was then also being raised. After the abdication of Napoleon, recruiting was given a boost when many prisoners of war that had been taken in Spain returned to the regiment. At the end of 1814 the regiment was quartered in the fort in Maastricht, but its integration into the Netherlands army did not go smoothly. Firstly, the rumour spread that the regiment was to be sent to the East Indies, an unpopular posting, which, although it did not turn out to be true, did not get things off on the right foot. It got worse; Private Leonhard, who served with the 1st Battalion, complained:

> In the fort of Maastricht all new recruits received new clothes, but this was followed by an indescribably hard life in the barracks, in which the men were treated like slaves. The deprivation of personal liberties, bad food and vermin – rats and mice – led to fights with the Dutch and in the end to rebellion, which resulted in dead and wounded. Thirteen Dutch hussars were thrown by the Nassau troops over the bridge into the river Maas and were killed by the fall. As a punishment the Nassau troops were deprived of all leave, our meagre pay was reduced, and we had to contend with ice-cold billets. Many of the men fell ill, and some men even became blind.[6]

Needless to say, the men were pleased when they were sent forward to the border in March 1815 with the prospect of war, but it had not been an experience that was likely to endear them to their new masters and comrades-in-arms. Indeed, some doubted their adherence to the cause as Major Friedrich von Gagern, a staff officer in the headquarters of the 2nd Netherlands Division, expressed:

> Our troops were generally very willing, however, having insufficient time to know their commanders on the field of battle, there was not the mutual trust and self-assurance that one can see in experienced armies. Indeed, several of the commanders mistrusted the Belgians, and even the Nassau troops, who had served under Napoleon in Spain.[7]

After their long association with the French and with their new army having no new national organisation or doctrine, the Nassau troops retained their French-style green uniforms with French rank badges, French battalion organisation (each battalion having six companies, in contrast to the British ten, with one of grenadiers, one of *flanquers* (light infantry) and four fusilier, or centre, companies) and French drill. They were also equipped with French muskets, although in April these were exchanged for British muskets. However, none of this fundamentally affected their employability; they were not the only ones to retain French organisation and drill, and their experienced cadres and the time they had been together helped to bond them into a combat-ready force.

Late in April 1815 Wellington carried out a round of inspections of his various units. Having inspected the Nassau contingent that was then with the army, the Orange-Nassau Regiment and the 2nd Nassau Regiment, he wrote to the British Secretary of State for War and Colonies, Earl Bathurst, 'The Nassau troops are excellent'.[8] However, this inspection had taken place before the arrival of the very young and only partially trained 1st Nassau Regiment and, perhaps presupposing that the 1st Regiment would be of equal quality, he considered forming a Nassau division; a plan that was effectively stillborn as the Netherlands army relied on Nassauers to complete their own order of battle and were never likely to hand over command of an organisation they were relying on to make up their own numbers. The newly raised and less well-trained 2nd Battalion of the Orange-Nassau Regiment had also still to arrive with the army.

During 1815 the individual battalions that were present had been drilled often at battalion level, but the whole army had found great difficulty in finding sufficient open space in Belgium to drill and manoeuvre at formation level, giving them the inability to manoeuvre in mass on the battlefield in such a way as the British and French were able to do and did so as a matter of course.

Compared to the other two Nassau regiments, the 1st Nassau Regiment was a different prospect altogether; the regiment had only been put on a war footing at battalion strength in April 1815 and was officially put under Wellington's direct command on the 24th.[9] The decision to bring it up to a regimental strength of three battalions required drastic action. The then Captain Weiz (who later rose to major general), who served with the 1st Battalion, wrote of it:

> Except for the staff officers and captains, the great majority of subalterns and more than nine tenths of the rank and file had never faced an enemy or fought a battle. Of the 2,900 men that this regiment consisted of at the day of marching off from Wiesbaden, which was on the 20th May, more than 2,000 were raw recruits who had *left their homes only four to five weeks earlier* [my emphasis].[10]

It appears that the 1st Nassau Regiment did arrive in Belgium fully armed, uniformed and equipped. Perhaps what made them most distinctive was their white shako and ammunition box covers. However, at about 3pm at Waterloo, fearing that these made them more visible targets for the French artillery, General von Kruse gave the order for them to be taken off.[11]

The 3rd Battalion was a landwehr (militia) battalion; the landwehr were normally raised to serve solely within the borders of Nassau in a home defence role, although many countries, perhaps most notably Prussia, routinely deployed them beyond their own borders. As we have heard, along with the rest of the regiment they had only been put on a war footing in April 1815, were largely raw recruits with little other than the rudiments of training, and were frankly not ready to be thrown into combat. Captain Weiz makes the following comments on their training:

> The training of these men in such a short time had, of course, to be limited to that absolutely necessary. It was indeed a most challenging task due to the small number of experienced officers and NCOs. However, the active cooperation and the good will, which inspired all men, overcame all difficulties in a manner which should never be forgotten in the history of the Nassau regiments. There was no question of parade ground drill; to assure staying in the ranks and the effective use of weapons were the most important objectives. That this was achieved by all company commanders has been proven in the outcome… from the day of marching off from Wiesbaden until arrival in the Brussels vicinity, besides the six to seven hours of marching a day, several hours of exercises were put in…[12]

We see that the few experienced officers and non-commissioned officers of the regiment clearly did their best in the less-than-ideal circumstances and Weiz tries to put as positive a spin on it as possible. But the fact remains that the regiment arrived in Brussels less than two weeks before Waterloo and so lacked the concentrated training conducted by the Hanoverian troops, many of whom had been in the Netherlands for many months. The limitations in their ability to change formation and manoeuvre on the battlefield will become clear as we look at their performance at Waterloo.

Despite the emphasis Weiz claims was put into ensuring the recruits could handle their firearms confidently, even he later commented on their inability to do this, as well as their suspect discipline, at Waterloo:

> With every moment, the threatening storm was moving closer to our front the battalions were ordered, and warned, not to open fire too early at the attacking cavalry. Our young soldiers were still unfamiliar with using their weapons effectively. To prevent them from starting to fire unless ordered, the officers of our first line units moved in front of their companies…[13]

It is interesting that he should also describe how it should be done by describing a next-door British battalion, and this serves to show the advantages of Wellington's policy of mixing experienced and less experienced troops:

> The cuirassiers approached in three echelons on a two-squadron front spaced not too far apart. It was probably a fortunate circumstance

> for the 1st Battalion that the enemy's most advanced echelon first attacked the English regiment to our right. By exemplary behaviour, it fired its first volley when the riders were at a distance of 60 to 80 paces. The effect was spectacular, many riders and horses fell, and the remainder of the squadrons scattered like chaff. But as soon as the muskets were reloaded, the next echelon attacked. It was received in the same successful manner as the first assaulting wave... These examples in our immediate vicinity were of the highest significance for our young soldiers.[14]

Lacking their own artillery and cavalry had serious implications; they had to rely for both on their allies. This support could not be guaranteed and such a lack could have serious consequences; on several occasions during Waterloo, the availability of either would certainly have helped them and probably reduced their casualties.

The 1st Nassau Regiment only arrived in Brussels on 7 June, less than two weeks before Waterloo. However, they were not the last troops to arrive with the army before the campaign opened. This 'honour' went to the 2nd Battalion of the Orange-Nassau Regiment and the company of volunteer jägers. The dire state of the latter is well-illustrated by the following letter written by Captain Bergmann, the company commander:

> Following the call to arms from the king, the volunteers were able to enlist only until the 3rd May, so that we could march from Dillenburg on the 26th May. However, at this time we had an insufficient number of serviceable weapons, as part of those we should have received in Köln and Lüttich were not available. I only received fifty rifles from Köln and none whatsoever from Lüttich. In addition, there was insufficient ammunition, and in Dillenburg I could only secure a thousand rounds of lead shot, which remained from the previous jäger company. When we arrived in Maastricht, I used the presence of the king to request further rifles, but my applications for ammunition were in vain. The day after we received the outstanding rifles, we were consoled by an order to march to Genappe, to obtain a quantity of ammunition from the depot there. My first priority was to urgently ask Prince Bernhard von Weimar, under whom I served, and the Chief of Staff, Colonel Zuylen van Nyevelt, for powder, flints and lead shot. But here I only received promises and before any decision had been made by the authorities, the French crossed the border on the 15th.[15]

An earlier inspection of these troops found that their clothing was in a poor state and their training 'weak'. They were also short of campaign equipment, a shortage that could not be made good before they were called into action for the first time. As we shall see, the problems of the jägers and the 2nd Battalion of the Orange-Nassau Regiment would soon be felt on the battlefield.

This battalion had arrived with the volunteer jägers and also had a problem with their armament. At the time of mobilisation, the Netherlands army had three different types of musket; Dutch, English and French. On 22 April, all the French muskets were collected in and replaced by English muskets. However, the battalions that arrived after that date, which included the 1st Nassau Regiment and the 2nd Battalion Orange-Nassau Regiment, retained their French muskets throughout the campaign. For the last to arrive, the 2nd Battalion Orange-Nassau Regiment, this posed a particular problem at Quatre Bras; Colonel Saxe-Weimar, who was now the brigade commander as well as the regimental commander, wrote:

> The 2nd Battalion [Orange-Nassau] was placed as much as possible in reserve, as they had arrived from Dillenbourg only a few days before the outbreak of hostilities, and while some French muskets had arrived, nearly no ammunition was available, and I was unable to secure English muskets for them.[16]

An officer of the battalion, Captain Eberhard, wrote:

> When on 16 June fighting started with the arrival of daylight, the battalion was unable to take part in the skirmishing with the rest of the brigade due to the low supply of ammunition for its French muskets.[17]

Luckily for them, on the day of Waterloo, they were able to get a supply from the 1st Nassau Regiment who were also carrying French muskets. However, the supply only arrived when, 'the battalion was already facing the enemy, and his tirailleurs were engaged with our skirmishers.'[18]

The impact on morale of starting an engagement with the enemy with only a few rounds in your ammunition pouch is not hard to assess.

Deployment and actions

Frasnes

The 2nd Battalion of the 2nd Nassau Regiment, commanded by Major Normann, was to have the honour of being the first unit of Wellington's army to meet the French in the afternoon of 15 June. Posted at Frasnes and Villers-Perwin, covering the main road from Charleroi, where the French had crossed the frontier, to Brussels, this battalion was to be engaged by no less than the famous *chevau-légers lanciers* of the Imperial Guard, ironically, once a predominantly Dutch unit of the French army.

Having concentrated his battalion around Frasnes as the sounds of fighting to his front between the French and Prussian outposts intensified, Major Normann prepared to observe French activities and then to be ready to retire to Quatre Bras where the rest of the brigade were concentrating. Having initially resisted the French cavalry advance, Normann saw that the lancers were attempting to fix him in position with a central column while trying to outflank him and cut him off with columns to right and left. Leaving a small detachment in Frasnes, the rest of the battalion, under cover of a Netherlands battery, conducted a very effective fighting withdrawal back towards the important crossroads of Quatre Bras.

This was a trying first exposure to action for this relatively inexperienced battalion, but it was conducted with calmness and aplomb and with minimal casualties given the circumstances; a number of charges by a very capable enemy had been repulsed. The detachment that had been left behind was captured, though most of them later escaped and returned to their unit; casualties for the day totalled thirty-three. The Nassauers had given a good account of themselves in their first engagement and had remained steady in what must have been a potentially disastrous situation; this reflected very well on the commanding officer of the battalion, Major Normann.

Quatre Bras

Thanks to the foresight and understanding of the developing situation by Generals Perponcher, commanding the 2nd Netherlands Division, and Constant-Rebecque, the Netherlands Quartermaster-General, the whole of the Netherlands 2nd Division, against Wellington's orders, concentrated at Quatre Bras. The first full brigade there was the all-Nassau 2nd Brigade (consisting of the 2nd Nassau Regiment and the Orange-Nassau Regiment), now commanded by the young Colonel Prince Bernard of Saxe-Weimar, until then the commander of the Orange-Nassau Regiment.

While awaiting the arrival of the 1st Brigade who were marching from Nivelle, Saxe-Weimar deployed his Nassau brigade to try and impose on, and thus delay, the advancing French. To this end the 2nd/2nd Nassau was left in position to the right of the main road at the southern edge of the Bossu wood and was reinforced by two companies of the 1st/2nd Nassau. The remaining companies of the 1st/2nd Nassau were positioned in reserve at Quatre Bras. The 3rd/2nd Nassau were also split up; half were sent to line up with the 2nd/2nd, with the other half remaining in reserve at Quatre Bras. It seems a little odd that two battalions were split in this way when a single, full battalion could have been allocated each task (one supporting the 2nd/2nd and the other providing the reserve); this would have maintained each battalion under the hand of their commanding officer with obvious command and control advantages. The Nassau Volunteer Jäger Company was sent to the southern tip of the Bossu wood. The Netherlands artillery battery was split across the whole front, attempting to cover all approaches. The deployment was weighted heavily towards the Bossu wood which dominated the main road while providing cover for the troops and camouflaging their true strength.

It seemed as if Saxe-Weimar was set to hold the crossroads until the remainder of the division and other allied forces were able to arrive; however, in his report on the action at Frasnes to his divisional commander (Perponcher) written that evening he finished:

> By the way, I need to confess to Your Excellency that I am too weak to hold out here for long. The 2nd Battalion of Orange-Nassau still has French muskets and is down to 10 cartridges per man. The Volunteer Jägers have carbines of four different calibres, and every man is likewise down to 10 cartridges. I will defend the post entrusted to me as long as possible. I expect to be attacked at daybreak of the 16th. The troops are in the best spirit… The artillery has no infantry cartridges.[19]

During the early morning of the 16th, the 1st Brigade of the division marched to support the Nassauers of the 2nd. The divisional commander arrived early and was soon followed by the Netherlands quartermaster general. It was now clear that the crossroads of Quatre Bras must be held to allow Wellington's army time to come to the rescue and to keep open communications with the Prussians at Ligny; the Nassauers were to sustain the first shock of the French advance.

Having identified that the French force in front of them was still quite weak in numbers, in order to impose on them and perhaps delay the concentration of a stronger force, Constant-Rebecque and Perponcher agreed to a tentative advance, to be led by Normann's 2nd/2nd Nassau supported by two companies from the first of the troops to have arrived from the 1st Brigade of the division, the 27th Jägers. Moving forwards with a line of skirmishers, supported by the rest of the battalion formed in column, Normann's men pushed the French vedettes back towards Frasnes. The arrival of the Prince of Orange put an end to this successful action in which the 2nd/2nd Nassau again showed their morale and capabilities.

From 9am the first units of Bijlandt's brigade began to arrive, relieving the pressure on the Nassau units. It was about 10am when Wellington also arrived at the crossroads. By this time, most of the 2nd Netherlands Division was deployed and the Prince of Orange had been able to extend the line across his front with the farm of Gemioncourt, which was close to the main road, serving as a useful bastion.

The French force immediately available to Marshal Ney, who had been given command of the left wing of the French army by Napoleon, was part of the 2nd Corps, consisting of the infantry divisions commanded by generals Bachelu and Foy, and the cavalry division of Piré. These did not come into sight of the Nassau troops until around 1pm. Ney had failed to get his troops in movement until late morning and they would not be joined on the battlefield by the final infantry division of 2nd Corps, that of Prince Jérôme, until well into the afternoon, thus giving the allies the time to organise their defence with the troops available and for reinforcements to get closer to the battlefield to support them.[20]

The first main French advance took place to the east of the main road. Therefore, with the forward Nassau troops deployed just outside the southern edge of the Bossu wood this phase of the battle only saw them under artillery fire and watching the French cavalry patrols attempting to identify the allied positions. By this time the Nassau deployment had altered somewhat; there were now three full battalions of Nassauers in this position, supported by a single battalion of Dutch militia; they were lined up from east to west in the following order; the 8th National Militia, the 1st/28th Orange-Nassau, the 3rd/2nd Nassau and the 1st/2nd Nassau, each with skirmishers to their front and supported by two Dutch artillery pieces commanded by Lieutenant Winssinger. These units were commanded by Colonel Saxe-Weimar, who was present with them. The 2nd/2nd Nassau, having retired from their forward position of the morning, had been placed in reserve at Quatre Bras. The 2nd/28th Orange-Nassau had also been left in reserve due to the shortage of ammunition for their French muskets[21] and could not be expected to hold a position in the front line.

The Nassau troops on the southern tip of the Bossu wood were under the fire of the two horse artillery batteries of the Imperial Guard that were attached to the Guard light cavalry brigade which had led the French advance the day before. Although at extreme range, all four battalions were suffering from the fire. Although this fire must have been unnerving, it could not explain a sudden ripple of disorder in the Dutch militia battalion and the battalion of Orange-Nassau. Lieutenant Colonel de Jongh, commanding the 8th Militia Battalion, reported:

> The right wing was against the left wing of an Orange-Nassau Battalion, which was already arranged in battle order [in line]. Having been here with them for some time, and under fire from an enemy artillery battery which consisted of three pieces, I saw the Orange-Nassau Battalion move to the rear, as a panic spread among them. I was in front of the centre of my battalion and my right flanker company became mixed up with the Nassau battalion… I discovered the Nassau men had been frightened by His Royal Highness the Prince of Orange, who rode in front of our line of battle accompanied by members of his staff...[22]

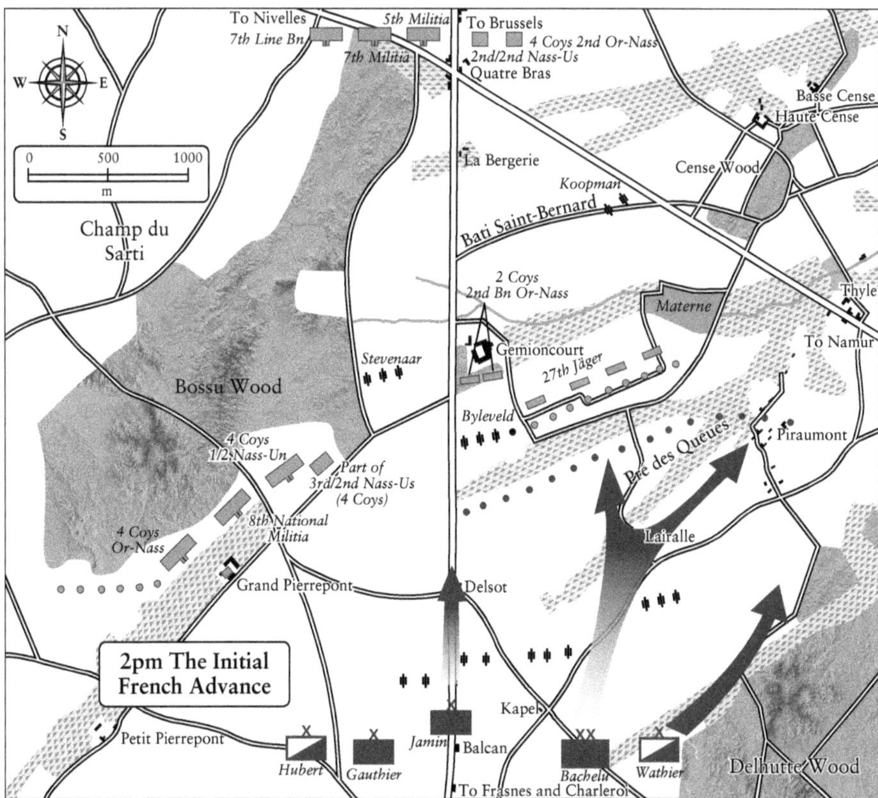

Map showing the initial deployment of the Nassau contingent at Quatre Bras.

The Orange-Nassau battalion had been spooked by a handful of friendly horsemen which can be interpreted as it having suspect morale, despite having been under artillery fire which had caused few casualties (see the casualty returns below) and not having been attacked at all.

As a result of this disorder, the Prince of Orange directed that the four battalions should fall back into the protection of the wood. Even this withdrawal was not conducted smoothly. Colonel Saxe-Weimar, perhaps angry at the disorder of his own battalion, later wrote:

> A battalion of militia commanded by the late Colonel de Jongh, which belonged to the 1st Brigade, was being positioned at a point in the wood ahead of my left, but it retreated from here a little too quickly and not in the best order. I entered the wood at the head of the 1st battalion of my regiment.[23]

As we have seen, de Jongh blamed the hurried withdrawal of the Orange-Nassau battalion for this disorder!

Saxe-Weimar decided to defend the wood with a line of skirmishers with the main body of each battalion held further back in support. The 1st/2nd Nassau held the western edge of the wood, and the 1st/28th Orange-Nassau and 3rd Nassau fell back to the north, almost as far as the Nivelles road and certainly too far away to get involved in any French attack on the southern tip of the wood. This new deployment is difficult to understand and effectively left what had been considered as the key to the allied position protected by just a few companies deployed as skirmishers. The 8th Dutch Militia were ordered to fall back through the wood to the north and to take up a position level with the 7th Line Battalion, which stood closer to Quatre Bras. Apart from the 1st/2nd Nassau, the bulk of the Nassau battalions were now stretched along the Nivelles road just to the north of the wood.

During the French advance, the Netherlands troops were forced back from the line of Gemioncourt; their withdrawal was covered by the arrival and charge of the Netherlands cavalry of General van Merlen, but both the 5th Militia and 27th Jäger Battalions suffered heavy casualties. Although this charge was unsuccessful in throwing the French cavalry back, it gave time for the exhausted and disordered infantry to reach the safety of the allied reserves deployed around the village of Quatre Bras. As Löben-Sels admits, 'This moment [the arrival of Picton's division] seems to have coincided with the check of the charge of the Netherlands cavalry. With some small exceptions, we have to admit that the Netherlands troops took no further active part in the action.'[24]

About four o'clock, the French launched their main attack to the east of the main Brussels *chaussée*; this was met and defeated by Picton's 5th British Division, which had taken over this part of the front line. All the Netherlands troops had now been withdrawn from the frontline and were re-forming to the north of the Quatre Bras to Nivelles highway. Despite the fighting they had experienced and their success in holding up the French advance along the Brussels road, this was a clear move by Wellington to preserve what fighting power and cohesion they had left and is a good example of how he managed his less-experienced troops to ensure they remained battleworthy. The only exceptions to this move were the more experienced 2nd Nassau Regiment and the 1st/28th Orange-Nassau Regiment, which were ordered by the Prince of Orange to recapture the Bossu wood; this they were unable to do due to the strength of the French forces holding the wood and it took the arrival of Cooke's division of British guards to finally wrestle possession from the French.

General von Kruse reported that the 1st Nassau Regiment finally arrived at Quatre Bras 'towards eight o'clock', where they met the 3rd/2nd Nassau 'that had been taken out of the firing line due to its losses.'[25] By this time Wellington, who had now received further British reinforcements (von Alten's 3rd Division), had no doubt also decided to save the Nassauers further losses, as despite what von Kruse states in his report, the 3rd Battalion had only suffered one man killed and thirty-four wounded from a start state of around 850 (just 4 percent); hardly a level of casualties that was likely to break their morale. The 1st Nassau Regiment was not engaged and suffered no casualties at Quatre Bras.

The Nassauers had been given a vital role in the early fighting of the day and had been instrumental in holding the wood of Bossu which protected the right flank of the allied position and protected the important approach road from Nivelles, along which many allied reinforcements were rushing to join the action, but also along which the French could have moved to threaten the concentration of the allied troops there. The 2nd/2nd Nassau Regiment had taken a very creditable part in the initial clash near Frasnes on the 15th and the withdrawal to Quatre Bras which the French had tried hard to crush. On the 16th the Nassauers had had time to catch their breath as the first French pressure came along the centre of the allied position, on the axis of the Brussels *chaussée*; the first concerted French effort to take the wood started at about 3pm with the arrival of Prince Jérôme's strong division. With this force the French were able to slowly, but surely, push the Nassauers both west and north through the wood without meeting determined resistance. Like the Netherlands units, the Nassauers had effectively been withdrawn from the fight on the arrival of British reinforcements; a clear and sensible decision made by Wellington to keep his young and inexperienced allies from the thick of the fight so that they would be able to fight again another day.

Although the Nassauers had been spared the heavy fire of the powerful French artillery, daring cavalry attacks and the close combat in open ground against massed French skirmishers and columns, much of their own combat had been at close range in the bewildering and disorientating environment of the Bossu wood. The fighting here had dragged on for several hours without either side being able to exploit whatever gains they had managed to achieve. The fighting was marked by the limited visibility and short engagement ranges caused by the trees and undergrowth. Such open order, close-range fighting, was usually marked by heavy casualties and the descriptions of the protagonists would suggest that this was indeed the case. In fact, the casualty rates among the Nassau units that fought here were relatively light (see casualty rates below). Saxe-Weimar's order to withdraw the main bodies of the battalions to the north of the wood left only a few skirmisher companies to contest the wood with the French, and these fleeting targets, combined with the cover offered by the trees and the difficulties of manoeuvring large formations of men through such difficult terrain, probably account for the slow French advance. Nassau units that left the wood, to west or north, were able to reorganise and reorder their ranks and were then able to feed fresh men into the skirmish fight among the trees without suffering heavy casualties from getting decisively engaged.

The truth is, the Nassauers were unable to hold the wood and prevent the French from closing on Quatre Bras using this axis; only the attack of Cooke's guards was finally able to rid the wood of Jérôme's men and the guards units that fought there suffered some of the heaviest casualties of the day in significant contrast to the light casualties of the Nassauers.

Despite the need for the intervention of the British guards, the Nassauers had still been able to contest the wood with the French for several hours and given the circumstances they fought in, they had probably done all that could be expected of them. What's more, their low level of casualties, and limited exposure for the rest of the battle, had ensured that they would be ready to fight again two days later.

Nassau casualties at Quatre Bras

Although British and Hanoverian (including the KGL) casualties were carefully recorded and reported, the same was not so true of the other allied contingents. Different sources record different levels of casualties, sometimes with considerable divergence. We have already discussed the difficulties of interpreting casualty states, but even so, they do give some interesting insights, especially where the descriptions of the fighting are not reflected in the casualty returns. The following casualty list comes from Pflugk-Harttung's work[26] in a report dated 26 February 1825.

Unit	Killed		Wounded	
	Officers	Men	Officers	Men
1st/2nd Nassau	-	3	-	40
2nd/2nd Nassau	-	10	1	19
3rd/2nd Nassau	-	1	2	32
Volunteer Jäger	-	-		17
Total	-	14	3	108

The strength of the 2nd Nassau Regiment before the battle is given as:

Staff:	12 officers and 33 ORs
1st Battalion:	23 officers and 847 ORs
2nd Battalion:	24 officers and 842 ORs
3rd Battalion:	24 officers and 853 ORs
Total:	83 officers and 2,575 ORs[27]

Therefore, from a regimental strength going into the battle of eighty-three officers and 2,575 men, this represents a casualty rate of only 4 percent. It must also be remembered that the 2nd/2nd Nassau had suffered thirty-three casualties during the action on 15 June.

Muilwijk gives much lower casualties for the 2nd Nassau Regiment at Quatre Bras, totalling none killed, thirty-two wounded and six missing, with another one killed, five wounded and eleven missing from the volunteer jägers. For the 2nd Nassau Regiment this gives a percentage casualty rate of less than 1.5 percent; hardly the casualties of a hard fight, especially when compared to the losses of the British guards who also fought in the Bossu wood. Muilwijk claims that earlier returns offer no explanation of where the figures actually came from and are therefore unreliable.

The Orange-Nassau Regiment would have sent their casualty return up their own (Netherlands) chain of command and so are not recorded in the above state. Netherlands' casualty returns are particularly difficult to ascertain with any accuracy and even modern Dutch and Belgian historians, such as Erwin Muilwijk, have hesitated to commit themselves to providing any for the battle of Waterloo. However, Löben-Sels, writing in 1849, claims to be quoting 'official states' when he records the Orange-Nassau casualties as only sixteen in total from a starting strength of 1,581 (1 percent). However, it must be noted that his casualties for the 2nd Nassau Regiment are considerably lower than those given above. It is also evident that there were many men officially recorded as 'missing' and it is impossible to know how many of these returned to their unit in time to fight at Waterloo and how many were actually dead. Muilwijk avoids allocating a casualty rate to the Orange-Nassau Regiment.

Waterloo

Having arrived too late to contribute to the fighting at Quatre Bras, the 1st Nassau Regiment spent the night after the battle to the north of the Bossu wood. In the morning of the 17th they did not form up until ten o'clock and then marched off through Genappe without incident, though they had to wade across the Dyle River, as the road had been reserved for use by the artillery and train. Having reached the ridge of the Mont Saint Jean position the regiment took position to the west of the Brussels *chaussée* just a little further down the slope from where they were to fight the next day. In his report, General von Kruse wrote that, 'The retreat was conducted with perfect calm and in good order.'[28] However, for many soldiers, the retreat and the torrential rain clearly had an effect on their morale; Sergeant Johann Doring, of the 1st/28th Orange-Nassau Regiment, wrote of that night, 'Still, all this adversity and the past hardships had taken their toll on our spirits. But this must have equally been the case with the enemy, with the same kind of sky overhead, the same roads and bottomless fields to pass over. There was this vast difference, however, that he was advancing, and we were on the retreat, which deeply affects the soldiers' morale.'[29]

Captain Weiz of the 1st battalion explained how the officers tried to take their soldiers' minds off the coming battle:

> Drying wet clothes and putting equipment, uniforms and ammunition back in shape were the other duties this morning.
>
> In this way, what appeared to be impossible was achieved through the officers' efforts, and another purpose was served, that of leaving the young men no moment for reflection by keeping them busy all the time, which might otherwise have badly affected their fighting morale…[30]

The 2nd Brigade at Smohain, la Haye, Papelotte and Frichermont Château

After the casualties of Quatre Bras are taken into account, the Nassau units of Saxe-Weimar's 2nd Brigade, 2nd Netherlands Division, had the following approximate strength:

2nd Nassau Regiment:	78 officers and 2,400 men.
28th Orange-Nassau Regiment:	39 officers and 1,400 men.

It should be noted that some troops had either been detached (for any number of legitimate reasons) or had otherwise left the colours, as these figures do not accurately reflect the regimental strengths before Quatre Bras minus the casualties of that engagement. Some of the less well motivated, after their experiences at Quatre Bras, had evidently chosen not to stay with their units for what promised to be a cataclysmic battle in the next few days and this would be true of all national contingents, as we shall see.

The brigade was deployed on the extreme left of Wellington's line, looking down from the ridge into the close country around the hamlet of Smohain. However, the 1st Battalion of the 2nd Nassau Regiment, under the command of Captain Büsgen, was detached at nine o'clock in the morning of the 18th to provide part of the garrison of Hougoumont on the extreme allied right. We will return to them shortly.

The remainder of the 2nd Nassau Regiment and the Orange-Nassau Regiment were responsible for securing the left flank to stop the French outflanking Wellington's army to the east, but more specifically to facilitate the arrival of the Prussians that Wellington was expecting during the day. This was a vital role and one that was crucially aided by the ground on this side of the battlefield. As we have heard, Wellington had been impressed by what he had seen of the Nassau troops during his inspections prior to the opening of the campaign, and this high opinion of their troops no doubt convinced him to give them such an important role. No doubt he also felt that the strong defensive ground where they were deployed would further add to the security of this flank and improve their chances of holding it successfully.

The ridge that marked the allied line was rather less pronounced and steep on this flank, but just to its front was an area of broken ground that made the manoeuvre of large masses of troops, which the French tended to adopt for offensive operations, very difficult if not impossible. This was very close country, cut by sunken lanes, thick hedges, orchards, scattered houses, hamlets and a number of very strong building complexes which served as bastions, focal points and pivots for the manoeuvre of troops. Papelotte and la Haye (the latter not to be confused with la Haye-Sainte in the centre of the allied line) can be likened to Hougoumont: large farm complexes with high walls and limited access, while the château of Frichermont was similar, but actually designed to offer a strong defence. Due to the battery allocated to this brigade having been overrun at Quatre Bras, there were only three Dutch guns remaining to support the defence of this part of the line.

The vicious fighting around and in the villages and broken ground at the battle of Ligny two days before had shown what kind of fighting could be expected here. While hand-to-hand fighting in open areas was quite unusual in this period, the same was not true of fighting in the close terrain of farms and villages, where soldiers who were well protected by buildings, walls and thick hedges were reluctant to give up the cover that protected them and which gave them strong fighting positions. What's more, men were far more likely to come across each other suddenly and without warning; fight or flight were the only options and flight had the disadvantage of presenting your back to an opponent who might be only a few yards away. The tactics for fighting in this type of country were also well known; the ground was held by a relatively small number of men in skirmish order whose task was to delay the enemy by causing casualties and breaking up his formations by drawing him into the close country. The main body of the defending force would be held in column behind the area being defended with the options to move against outflanking attacks, counterattacking into the broken area against a disrupted and disorganised enemy or just feeding reinforcements to the skirmishing companies that were already deployed. Wellington's high regard for these troops made them an ideal choice for such a task and yet did not expose them, without integral cavalry or artillery support and still with a high proportion of troops with little or no combat experience, to intense, force-on-force combat.

The fighting around the farms of Papelotte and la Haye, the hamlet of Smohain and the château of Frichermont has perhaps been the most neglected of the battle. This is partly because no British forces were directly engaged there and also because the fighting there has not been considered as a crucial part of the battle or vital to its success. The Nassauers who were involved in this part of the battlefield were certainly less prolific writers than their British comrades.

Despite reports of large French columns facing this area, it is clear from French accounts that they intended no serious attack; General Durutte, commanding the 4th Infantry Division on the extreme right of the French line, does not mention any attack on the area of Smohain and although some fighting did take place there, it is impossible to know for sure which French units were involved. Like the Nassauers, the French deployed thick lines of skirmishers who were best suited to fighting over this kind of ground, with columns supporting them on which they could rally if necessary, or from which they could feed reinforcements forward as required. Although the fighting over the key buildings was almost continuous throughout the battle, with success passing from one side to the other and then back again, the French made no concerted attempt to capture the area and try to disrupt the junction of the Prussians with Wellington's army. Indeed, Colonel Zuylen van Nyevelt, chief-of-staff of the 2nd Netherlands Division, suspected as much; in his post-action reports he wrote, 'The attack on our left wing was actually only a reconnaissance in force to determine if we were in contact with the right wing of the Prussians, or whether a turning movement was possible around our left flank by way of Frichermont.'[31]

Captain Rettberg (not to be confused with an officer of the same name that commanded a Hanoverian artillery battery who we shall meet later), a veteran of the war in Spain (twice wounded and recipient of the *Légion d'Honneur*) wrote the official report on the actions of the 3rd Battalion of the 2nd Nassau Regiment at Waterloo. He well describes the type of fighting that has been discussed above.[32] The main bodies of each of the four remaining battalions of the brigade (the 1st/2nd having been deployed to Hougoumont) were deployed on the ridge above and to the rear of Smohain, while a company of the 2nd/2nd Nassau Regiment occupied la Haye and the *flanquer* company of the 3rd Battalion occupied Papelotte. Throughout the day, these were reinforced by further companies from the battalions when required for a particular mission, or when battle casualty replacements were required.

The Orange-Nassau Regiment covered the left flank of the brigade; four companies of the 1st Battalion and the volunteer jäger occupied Frichermont, while another company occupied the hamlet of Smohain. The final company of this battalion remained in column further back and to the right of Papelotte to maintain communications with the 2nd Battalion held back in column on the ridge.

Behind the Nassauers, and sheltered in the dead ground behind the ridge, were two brigades of British light cavalry to give support if required. The brigade relied on artillery support from their parent division, but few guns were allocated to support them. These came from the sad remains of Stevenart's foot battery that had suffered so heavily at Quatre Bras. At that battle Captain Stevenart had been killed and a number of guns captured by the French. Although most of these had been recovered, the battery's heavy losses meant that only two guns could be manned. At Waterloo, the section was reinforced by a howitzer from Bijleveld's horse battery. These three pieces were commanded by Lieutenant Winssinger and were positioned on the crest of the ridge just north of Papelotte

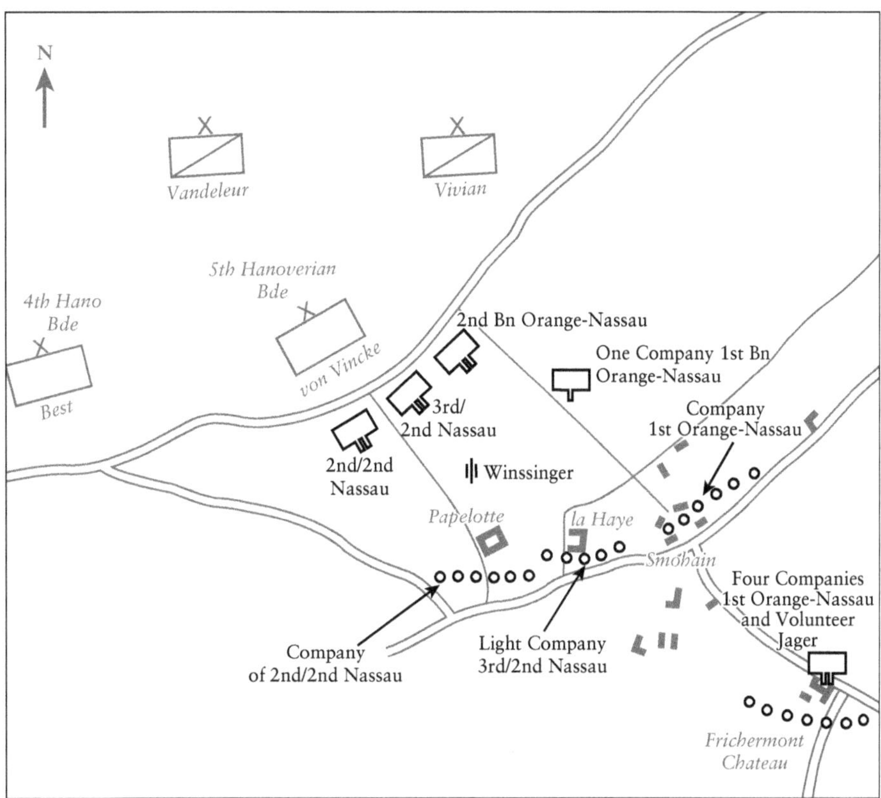

Map showing the initial deployment of the all-Nassau 2nd Brigade of the 2nd Netherlands Division at Waterloo.

from where they were able to fire onto the approaches to the hamlet of Smohain and the twin farms of Papelotte and la Haye. Having their own artillery available would certainly have offered them valuable support.

Captain Rettberg, who was deployed on the right of the brigade line, near Papelotte, describes how the first French attack was launched by a line of skirmishers which, after making some headway, were finally driven back by the Nassau light troops. One of the first French artillery shots mortally wounded Major Hegmann, the commanding officer of the 3rd/2nd Nassau. The next attack, by a stronger line of skirmishers supported by an infantry column, moved forward 'between three and four o'clock.' Once again, these made some gains before being stopped by Rettberg's company and three companies of reinforcements that had been sent forward from the ridge and then driven back by a bayonet charge which nevertheless brought them into range of a French battery firing case shot. From this point he says, 'the enemy no longer attempted a serious attack and only kept up a vigorous musketry fire.'

The final French attack came at about six o'clock when they suddenly appeared on Rettberg's left flank, having taken possession of Frichermont, part of Smohain and la Haye, but his position around Papelotte was so strong that they were easily repelled, not having a support column. An hour later the French appeared to have disappeared and he was surprised to be suddenly attacked by a strong force coming from his left flank and rear. He was driven back before he became aware that they were Prussian troops and the error was recognised. Many of his men joined the Prussians when they continued their advance.

The other Nassau troops in this area of the battlefield had similar experiences; the action was generally one of strong forces of skirmishers firing from, and manoeuvring around, the various cover, without coming into close contact. This dispersed, short-range fighting in close country could easily absorb large numbers of men; Captain von Reichenau of the 2nd/2nd Nassau Regiment wrote 'Towards evening, our entire battalion was posted there [la Haye] as skirmishers…' It could also result in heavy casualties; by the end of the action, Rettburg's company had 'shrunk to about thirty men…'.[33]

However much the left flank was deemed to be something of a sideshow compared to the close quarter slaughter in the centre, the Nassauers could only fight the fight they had been given, and this they had done with great credit. The biggest setback they suffered, in fact, was not a failure in the direct fight, but the loss of the colour of the 3rd Battalion, 2nd Nassau Regiment. Perhaps unsurprisingly, given the shame such a loss generally brought on a regiment, this is not mentioned by any of the Nassau accounts or reports of the battle and we might never have been aware of the capture of this flag had it not ended up in the possession of General Durutte, who commanded the French division whose troops were involved in the skirmishing around Papelotte and Smohain.[34]

The Frichermont château, more isolated and further forward than the other strongpoints, was occupied by men from the 1st/28th Orange-Nassau Regiment; this fell to the French and the battalion was forced to fall back into the hamlet of Smohain to continue the fight there. Some reports claim that Papelotte also fell, albeit temporarily, but others deny this.

We have already heard from Captain Rettberg how he had an engagement with the newly arrived Prussians before the mistake was realised. Lieutenant Colonel von Reiche, General Zieten's chief-of-staff, also described this event and exposes the difficulties presented by the Nassauers' French style uniforms:

> The Nassauers who were leaving the village fell back in open order towards our advancing troops. As the Nassauers were dressed in the French style of that time, our men took them to be the enemy and fired at them. Their commander Prince Bernard of Saxe-Weimar rushed up to General Zieten to clarify the misunderstanding, which he did in no uncertain terms. The general, not knowing the prince, made no excuses and calmly replied, 'My friend, it is not my fault that your men look like the French!'[35]

Writing to his father from Genappe the day after the battle, Colonel Saxe-Weimar narrated the events of the previous days. His description of the fighting is concise, but he finishes his letter with an account of the engagement with the Prussians:

> The victory was still in doubt when, towards 4 o'clock, the Prussians under the orders of Generals Bülow and Zieten, came up on our left flank and decided the issue of the battle. Unfortunately, the Prussians, who were to support me in my village, took my Nassauers, still uniformed in French style, but with true German hearts, for the French, and opened a terrible fire on them. This routed them, and I rallied them a quarter of an hour from the battlefield.[36]

This report, from the brigade commander no less, clearly states that the Prussians routed the Nassauers and he was only able to rally them some distance from the battlefield. Unfortunately, the letter was published in the *Journal de Francfort*, and unsurprisingly generated outrage among the Nassau officer corps (bearing in mind that Prince Bernard was not a Nassauer himself). It was not long before a refutation appeared in the same newspaper, written by three Nassau officers, including the acting commander of the 2nd Regiment at Waterloo, Major Sattler, accusing Prince Bernard of 'attacking the honour and reputation of the regiment that had been so dearly bought.' The claim that the regiment had been routed by the Prussians was strongly denied. The article said:

> At six o'clock, the corps of the Royal Prussian army of Bülow and Zieten advanced towards la Haye along the road from Wavre; their skirmishers, that advanced on both our, and the enemy's flank, fired on both them and us. Our companies, who did not know of the arrival of the Prussians, returned their fire, until the moment that, after a short time, they realised their error, and Captain von Rettberg took a few men with him, went towards the Prussians and revealed their mistake. Both sides ceased firing on each other and then turned their combined fire on the enemy.
>
> Such was the rout that his Highness the Prince of Saxe-Weimar pretends to have seen and to have rallied a quarter of an hour from the battlefield. So here is our account, that we defy the prince and those who were in our vicinity, to contradict. We appoint the public as our judges to decide whether we did our duty or if we have covered our names in shame.

The arrival of the Prussians put an end to the battle for the Nassauers of the 2nd Brigade. Saxe-Weimar wrote:

> The few troops that I had left retreated from the combat. I led them towards a wood which was part of the *Forêt de Soignes* a few hundred paces behind and to the rear of the position where the 2nd and 3rd Battalions were stationed; the other battalions having remained at the posts they had occupied during the battle. The section commanded by Lieutenant Winssinger… retreated with me as he had expended all his ammunition. Just as I had arrived at my new position, I suddenly heard the fire of the battle cease…[37]

The controversial episode aside, the Nassauers had clearly showed great offensive spirit and the initiative and courage to fight in these low-level, close-range engagements, but it is also true that the French seemed to have made no serious attempt to capture the area. Colonel Best, commanding the 4th Hanoverian Brigade a little further to the east, wrote in his report, 'I cannot state if it was the enemy's intention to overthrow our left wing, because even though the enemy attacked furiously the division did not appear strong enough to achieve this task…'[38]

According to Löben Sels[39], the casualties suffered by the four Nassau battalions that fought on the left wing are shown here:

Unit	Killed + Missing		Wounded		Total
	Officers	Men	Officers	Men	
1/28th O-N	1	24	3	33	4+57
2/28th O-N	-	58	4	42	4+100
2/2nd Nassau	1	58	9	86	10+144
3/2nd Nassau	-	21	8	105	8+126
Volunteer jäger	Not	recorded	Not	recorded	26 + 427

The total number of casualties for the two battalions of the 2nd Nassau Regiment which fought around Papelotte and Smohain was therefore 288, or about 18 percent, while for the two battalions of the Orange-Nassau Regiment it was even less at 165, or 12 percent.

At the first roll call after the battle there were 122 men missing from the second and third battalions of the 2nd Nassau Regiment, although the table above shows that some eventually returned to their battalion. There appears to be no record of missing men from the Orange-Nassau Regiment or the volunteer jägers.

These casualty rates are not particularly high, but it must be considered that the Nassauers here fought almost exclusively under cover in a skirmish fight, albeit one which lasted most of the battle. Given that the French deployed relatively few men here, their attacks were more to tie the allied defenders down than a determination to capture the area.

The day after the battle, Saxe-Weimar wrote to his father, 'My brigade then [on the 15th] had a strength of 4,000 men; today I have hardly 1,200 left.'[40] The casualty returns above do not reflect this; however, as we shall see, this was not an unusual phenomenon; many regiments of all nationalities finished the battle with many men separated who were quick to rejoin in the following hours and days.

The 1st Battalion 2nd Nassau Regiment at Hougoumont

The defence of Hougoumont has generated perhaps more British eyewitness accounts than on any other aspect of the battle. It is therefore interesting that in the many British accounts of the defence of Hougoumont, nearly all by members of the British Guards, virtually none mention the 800 or so Nassauers that were also there and actually outnumbered them for the early stages of the battle.

As we have already heard, the 1st Battalion of the 2nd Nassau Regiment was taken from its parent regiment and deployed to the château and farm of Hougoumont, which Wellington considered a vital post if the French were to try and force his right flank; it also served as an obstacle if the French were to attempt to outflank the allied position on this flank. The fact that Captain Büsgen's battalion was selected for such an important role reflects the high opinion Wellington had of this Nassau regiment. Their vital role in helping to maintain this position throughout the battle has been grossly overshadowed by Anglo-centric accounts which generally credit the British Guards alone with this achievement. For much of the battle, this strong battalion of around 800 men considerably outnumbered the British guardsmen that were initially deployed there, and was only overtaken as ever-greater numbers of guardsmen were drip-fed as reinforcements into the château and its grounds as the day progressed.

Büsgen writes[41] that on the morning of the 18th he was still with his brigade on the extreme left of the allied line, but that at about half past nine he was led by an aide de camp to Hougoumont. On his arrival at Hougoumont he claims that the farm complex was prepared for defence but unoccupied, with only a company of 'Brunswick Jäger'[42] on the furthest edge of the wood facing the French. However, British accounts record the Nassauers relieving them in their positions. Büsgen deployed his six companies as follows: the grenadier company in the buildings, two companies (1st and 3rd) in the garden, which was to the west of the farm complex, nearest the French lines, one company (5th) behind the hedge on the southern edge of the orchard, the light company (*flanquers*) in line with the Brunswick Jäger and the final company (the 7th) also remaining in the wood behind them as a formed reserve. General Byng, commanding the 2nd Guards Brigade, was put in charge of the defence of Hougoumont by Wellington and he continued to feed reinforcements into it from his two battalions until virtually the whole of his two battalions were deployed there. However, the Nassauers continued to provide a significant proportion of the garrison throughout the day, although with little recognition for the vital part they played in its defence.

Despite this lack of recognition, Büsgen roundly praises the actions of the British Guards in helping his battalion to repulse the early French attacks. However, he is less candid about the disorganised withdrawal of his two companies that were deployed in the orchard, and we can presume that this was the result of a combination of the light company, and its supporting company, retiring in the face of French pressure and a French assault on the hedge line.

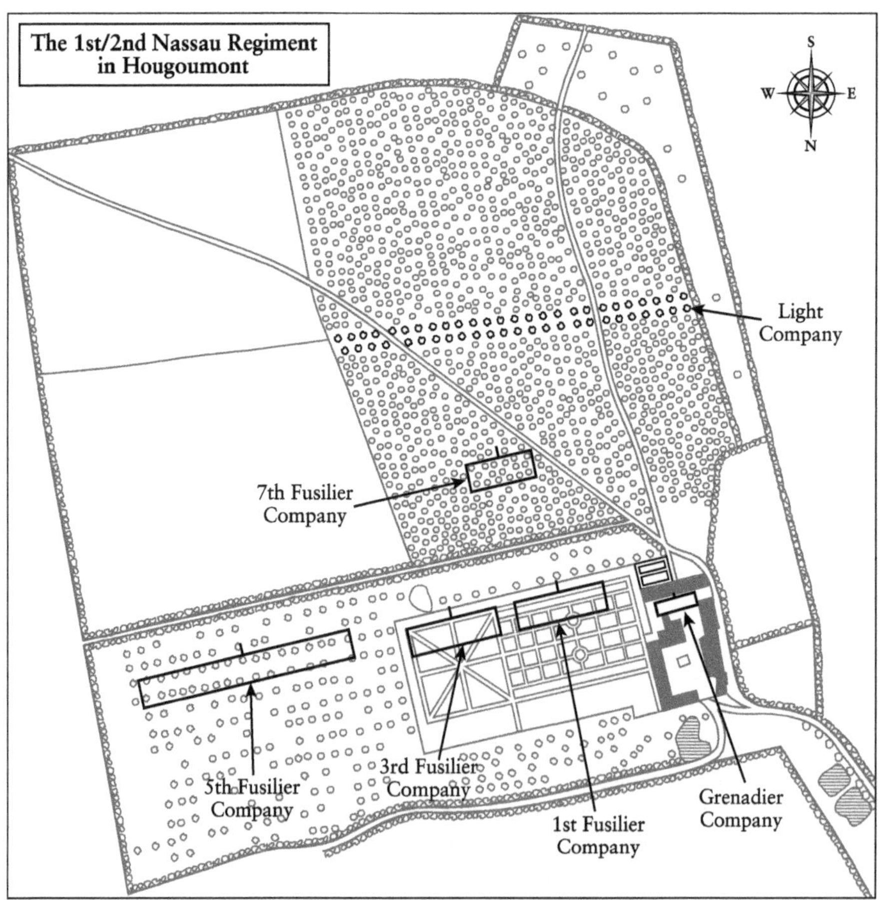

Map showing the initial deployment of the 1st Battalion of the 2nd Nassau Regiment at Hougoumont based on the description by Captain Büsgen.

General Constant-Rebecque, the quartermaster general of the Netherlands army, in his official report[43] wrote that the Nassau force in the orchard was, 'overwhelmed and forced to give way; it retreated, and the enemy captured the hedge which fronted the orchard', admitting that Wellington was forced to send in more British Guards to retake it. The senior Nassau officer at the battle, Major-General von Kruse, was not at Hougoumont with this battalion, but in his report on the battle written in 1836, he wrote about this episode:[44]

> The story spread by the Spanish General Alava and repeated by several writers that the Nassau battalion had abandoned the Hougoumont farm is not true. It apparently originated from the fact that the battalion had returned its colours at the beginning of the action because its commander felt that they could not be properly protected in the expected dispersed order of fighting.

It is logical to assume that these were the light company and the company held in reserve in the wood, though we have no proof for this. The casualty states for each company suggest that the two companies that were deployed in the wood at the beginning of the battle, the *flanquer* and 7th companies, had the highest casualties in the battalion, reflecting the fact that the fighting in the wood was intense and close range and the companies did not have the cover of the walls and buildings that were available to the other companies.[45]

Lieutenant Colonel Home of the 3rd Foot Guards, who was still up on the ridge behind Hougoumont at this moment, later wrote 'They [the French] got possession of the wood but were chased out by an attack & charge by the light companies under Colonel MacDonnell. In this many officers were wounded; then the Nassau troops gave way and were never seen afterwards excepting a few stragglers.'[46] Even Wellington claimed that he had seen the Nassauers run and tried to rally them, but, 'by God, they were so frightened, they fired upon *us* [his emphasis].'[47]

Unhappily, it appears these two companies took no further part in the battle; they certainly fell back onto the ridge behind and Gareth Glover states that it was this rather hurried withdrawal that prompted Wellington to say to Count Pozzo di Borgo, the Russian attaché on his staff, 'It is with these scoundrels that a battle must be won.' Muilwilk, who is prone to find a more positive reason for a withdrawal that continued onto the ridgeline behind, speculates that they had run out of ammunition and were looking for a resupply.[48]

This episode serves to remind us how accounts of what is apparently the same event can be interpreted in different ways. In this case Captain Büsgen's detailed account does not refer to either the disordered withdrawal of the two companies concerned (indeed he says the first attack on the orchard hedge was repulsed), the sending back of the battalion's colours or a search for extra ammunition.

Another example of the Anglo-centricity of the accounts of the fighting at Hougoumont is to be found in the next key episode that Captain Büsgen relates in his report. British accounts describe in great detail what they present as the only French ingress into the farm complex through the main gate in the northern wall. However, Büsgen describes a second that is otherwise ignored by British eyewitnesses of the fighting there. In his report he writes:

> The enemy now for the third time made a rash attack, which was mainly directed at the buildings. Aided by the smoke and flames, his grenadiers forced their way into the upper courtyard through a small side door; they were however, driven out again by the fire from the building windows and the advance through the lower gate and courtyard by a detachment of the already mentioned English battalion [of the Guards]. Some intruders were taken prisoner, but seven of our grenadiers were also captured by the enemy during this action.[49]

Büsgen concludes his account of the fighting that his battalion was involved with at Hougoumont by writing, 'This attack [described above], which ended about half past three o'clock, was the enemy's last serious attempt on the Hougoumont position; the skirmish fire, however, lasted with hardly an interruption until the end of the battle.'

In Gareth Glover's *Archive* series, an official return on casualties that was published in Pflugk-Harttung's book[50] reports that the 1st Battalion 2nd Nassau regiment suffered a total of seven officers and sixty ORs injured (killed: one officer and fourteen ORs). These figures seem surprisingly low for the amount of close action they saw. However, John Franklin found more dependable casualty figures in the Hessisches Haupstaatsarchiv, Wiesbaden, which give the following totals:

Killed:	one officer and nineteen ORs
Wounded:	six officers and ninety-two ORs (two officers and ten ORs subsequently died of their wounds).[51]

Although these figures are higher, they still only represent just under 15 percent of the starting strength of about twenty-two officers and 800 men, though the officers suffered proportionally more. In contrast, the two British Foot Guards battalions involved in the defence of Hougoumont suffered more heavily:

2nd/2nd Foot Guards:	308 of 1,039 = 30%
2nd/3rd Foot Guards:	239 of 1,120 = 21%

Although the level of casualties suggests that the Nassauers did not get as involved in the close combat as the British Guards, this cannot be conclusive. It must be remembered that only four companies remained at Hougoumont throughout the battle (the other two having returned to the ridge) and these were mostly deployed within the buildings and garden where most would have been protected by the walls. The guards did indeed fight within the buildings and garden, but also in considerable numbers in the orchard, the small garden to the west of the farm, in the wood and around the outside of the buildings. Apart from the two companies who appear to have left the battle, the rest of the 1st/2nd Nassau must be credited with playing a vital role in the successful defence of Hougoumont and fully played their part in the repulse of concerted French efforts to capture it.

The 1st Nassau Regiment

We must now turn to the newly formed and only partially trained 1st Regiment. Having not arrived with the army until 7 June, they were to have the most traumatic experience of all the Nassauers present at the battle. To help understand their terrible initiation to battle we have some detailed descriptions of their experiences written by close eyewitnesses.

As we have already heard, the 1st Nassau regiment was part of the Army Reserve Corps, which was personally commanded by the Duke of Wellington. On the 16th, it had only arrived at Quatre Bras at about eight o'clock and although the fighting had not quite finished for the night, it was not engaged and suffered no casualties. The following day it had retreated to the Waterloo position 'with perfect calm and in good order', according to General von Kruse.[52] The night was spent 100 metres behind the road that ran along the crest of the ridge to the west of the main Brussels *chaussée*.

On the morning of the 18th, the regiment numbered sixty-six officers and 2,834 men. It did not stand to arms until almost midday. Von Kruse describes their deployment:

> The battalions are marched off, the 1st Battalion in closed column to the right, the 2nd and third to the left. After a roll call, all battalions turnabout, move down the gentle slope on this [north] side of the plateau and take up position about 200 paces to the rear of the second line.
>
> A short time later the 1st Battalion was drawn forward into the 1st line, at about 300 to 400 paces to the right forward of the 2nd

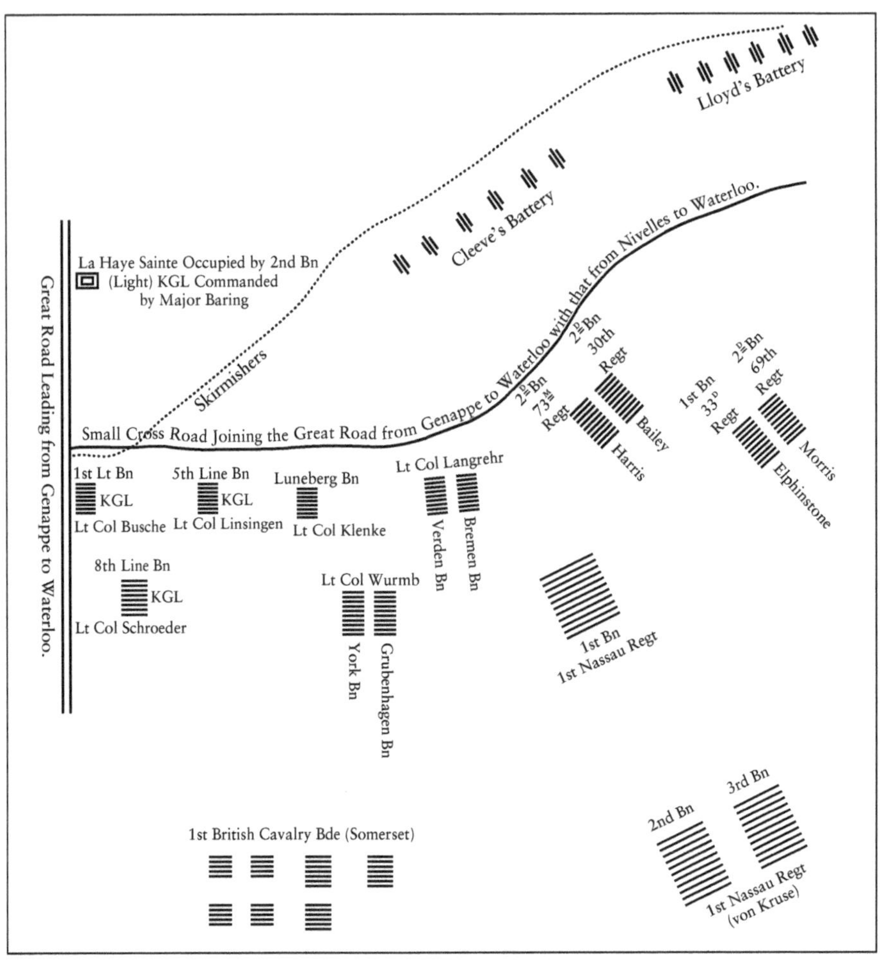

The initial deployment of the 1st Nassau Regiment at Waterloo based on the sketch by Captain Shaw (later General Sir James Shaw-Kennedy).

> Battalion. The cavalry of the army was deployed in several lines at about the same distance to the rear, in the plain before and to the side of the Mont St Jean farm and village.[53]

In this position, they would be sheltered to some extent from the heavy artillery fire that could be expected early in the battle and from where Wellington could choose the best time and point to engage them, given the expected brittleness of their morale and lack of tactical flexibility inevitable in a unit of such limited training and experience.

The regiment remained in this position until about 1.30pm, while the heavy French artillery fire raged on; casualties were minimal. However, at this time the second and third battalions were moved forward, still in column, until they were closer to the crest of the ridge. The first and second battalions now began to suffer heavy casualties from the artillery fire and in a short time almost a hundred men were hit; for some reason the third battalion suffered little. About four o'clock the light company of the 2nd Battalion was sent forward to reinforce the garrison of la Haye-Sainte.[54] Its remains returned to its unit when the farm finally fell to the French about six o'clock.

The lack of training and the inexperience of at least some of the officers became evident at this point, as Captain Weiz explains:

> The 2nd and 3rd Battalions, in the second line were formed in attack columns. The 1st Battalion stood in the first line and, inexplicably, was formed in column of divisions, with the right wing *in front* [his emphasis] that is, every two companies at that time formed a division, or two pelotons; of 160 men per company [so the 1st Company and the Grenadier Company were at the front, who would normally be at the rear]. The pelotons were too strong and unwieldly. This formation of the 1st Battalion was retained through most of the day; its serious disadvantage was that, due to the depth of the column, it suffered heavy losses from the incessant artillery fire, and that, during the cavalry attacks, only the two companies in front were able to fire. Many of the soldiers passed the day or were killed without having fired even once. There can be no worse situation for young soldiers or honourable officers.
>
> The [allied] battalions in the first line to the immediate right and left of the 1st Battalion, each at a strength of about 600 to 700 men, were kept moving at all times by their commanders through ployments and deployments [moving between line and column formation]. Under the exposure of well-directed artillery fire, these were conducted with great competency. These commanders should be commended for always knowing the right moment when to put their force in best defensive order. They had their battalions deployed [in line] if exposed to heavy artillery fire; they ordered them to form hollow squares whenever threatened by cavalry attacks. This procedure had the advantage that the men paid less attention to any danger, busy as they always were, and that their losses were much less in comparison to those of the 1st Battalion. In its case, not even a single attempt was made to follow a similar procedure, even though there was no reason not to do so. All that was thus left to the battalion was to face death-dealing gunfire for hours on end…
>
> Between two and three o'clock, the firing by the enemy artillery slackened off; it had caused terrible losses among our battalions, even though nobody had yet come face to face with the enemy…

> At the time when the firing of the artillery had ceased and the infantry [including them] had advanced to the plateau, everybody was filled with an all-encompassing, vitalising, uplifting and even solemn feeling. Morale was at an all-time high...[55]

The regiment stood and faced the numerous French cavalry attacks, although there is some confusion whether they did this in square or closed column. Although Nassau squares are often mentioned by eyewitnesses, closed column, where each rank of the column closes up the one in front to form a solid square, was a common tactic against cavalry in a number of continental armies, particularly the Austrian, and was a much quicker and simpler evolution for a poorly trained battalion, and would therefore make sense; Captain von Scriba, of the nearby Hanoverian Bremen Field Battalion, wrote:

> To the right of us were Nassau troops (800 men in my estimate). Throughout the battle, they stood in closed column. They never formed square.[56]

Captain Weiz, who was a member of the 1st Battalion and therefore well placed to describe the experiences of his battalion in particular, describes the French cavalry attacks and how the inexperience of his young troops was exposed, but also their courage:

> With every moment, the threatening storm was moving closer to our front the battalions were ordered, and warned, not to open fire too early at the attacking cavalry. Our young soldiers were still unfamiliar with using their weapons effectively. To prevent them from starting to fire unless ordered, the officers of our first line units moved before the front of their companies... All our battalions on the plateau were now attacked at the same time, but none wavered. They all stood like rocks...[57]

General Constant-Rebecque, the quartermaster general (effectively the chief-of-staff) of the Netherlands army, described the lack of steadiness of the Nassau troops in the face of the repeated French cavalry charges:

> I was regularly required to go some distance to the left from the Prince [of Orange] to rally the three squares of the Nassau contingent, which were composed of young soldiers who were under fire for the first time and often retired. I brought them back several times. At one point, one of these battalions was put into complete disorder when a shell exploded amidst their ranks. I rode ahead of them and fortunately managed to bring them back.[58]

Captain von Scriba, of the nearby Hanoverian Bremen Field Battalion, also commented on the wavering Nassauers:

> When the artillery fire started again, we saw to our great consternation our neighbours to our right, the Nassauers, begin to yield in disorder. However, by virtue of their brave officers' efforts, who gave their men an outstanding example, the men were brought to a halt and were returned to their former position. This misfortune recurred, later, one or two times under similar circumstances. Their heavy losses were clear to see for, as mentioned earlier, they stood in very close column...[59]

After the cavalry attacks, Weiz describes the continuing artillery duel which lasted for about half an hour, before the battle went into a new phase. The French now brought forward a number of artillery pieces, which are mentioned by other units in this part of the line. These were able to unlimber, covered by a force of cuirassiers, and open fire with case shot at short range from the Nassauers. Weiz vividly describes what happened:[60]

> In the next attack against the defenders on the plateau, several horse artillery batteries moved up, accompanied by strong cavalry formations. Soon, one could quite clearly see that two sets of guns were spaced at a considerable distance from one another, the reason being, as it turned out, to enable each of them to fire case shot at every one of our battalions with greatest effect. Their cavalry moved up behind their artillery and also to the sides of their guns.
>
> Two guns unlimbered in front of the 1st Battalion at a distance of 200 to 300 paces and started at once to cover us with case shot... The cavalry stationed at the side of the guns gradually moved closer, yet stayed at enough of a distance from these to avoid obstructing their line of fire. The 1st Battalion's situation became ever more perilous with each moment, and extremely so, on its front the two murderous guns, and finally on its right side, 100 paces away at the most the cuirassiers who waited for signs of disarray in our ranks to charge at the battalion; that disarray threatened to happen any minute now under the increased cannonade of case shot.
>
> The first rounds from the two guns went too high and caused no losses to the battalion; all the more terrible were the following ones. From now on, so many men were levelled by each shot that it took superhuman efforts by the officers to have the dead removed and to close the ranks to keep them closed. At this time, the three officers of the No.1 Company... had been wounded, and its sergeant had

been killed, and all it had left were some young inexperienced NCOs. What must be repeated here is that the battalion was formed in right marched off division column and that therefore, the Grenadier and No.1 Companies were at the head. The fate of the battalion depended more or less on the steadfastness of these two companies; No.1 Company could therefore not be left without a leader. Major von Weyhers put Captain Weiz [the author of this report] in charge of that company, whose own No.5 Company stood behind No.1 Company…

That moment of greatest danger just mentioned occurred when Major von Weyhers, the battalion commander, decided to have his men rush at, and disable, the two guns which threatened to annihilate the battalion. Captain Schuler, who was the battalion's most senior officer and well recognised for his bravery in battle, made the most strenuous representations against such a move, and with good reason, because it impaired the other battalions' defensive stance, but primarily because it was likely to fail in view of the closeness of the threatening enemy cavalry. Major von Weyhers could not be dissuaded from his decision and gave the order to attack. After the battalion had advanced some 40 to 50 paces, it received two more rounds of case shot which levelled the major and his horse and many soldiers. The resulting disarray and gaps in the ranks caused an unforeseen halt before order could be restored and the ranks be closed, one of the Duke of Wellington's ADCs hurriedly rode up with the strict order for the battalion to move back to its former position at once…

This retreat to the original position could have been executed if one of our cavalry detachments had faced the enemy cavalry in a way that the latter would have been unable to attack our battalion on the move. However, this was not the case; the seriousness of the situation either had not been observed or evaluated, or there was no cavalry of our own at hand. This was a grave mistake or failure on the part of the general in charge of this sector. Even though Major von Weyhers had made the wrong decision by moving out of the battle line, without an order but still with the best intentions, the absence of any effort to rescue was a much graver mistake.

With the wounded Major von Weyhers out of action, Lieutenant Colonel von Hagen [of the regimental staff] assumed command of the 1st Battalion and at once ordered its retreat to the main line. The rearmost four companies turned around and marched off; however, the two in front held their place. In the general turmoil they either did not hear or understand the order to retreat, or kept firing and were too concerned about the approaching enemy. Not the slightest blame can be laid against the two companies.

> Barely had they found themselves separated from the others when they were already surrounded and attacked by the cuirassiers. By this time, the fighting strength of the two amounted to 130 to 140 men at most. There now started a severe and bloody battle. Pressed together, this cluster of soldiers defended itself in the bravest manner, as was confirmed by all who observed the action. How long this struggle lasted, can no longer be determined, but at least long enough for any allied cavalry to free the embattled detachment from its attackers. That this did not happen, can be considered another great mistake which is all the harder to understand, since not far off a dragoon regiment of the legion [King's German Legion] had taken up position. Those riders certainly lacked neither courage nor prowess; their inaction was a case of absence of decisive leadership at this moment.
>
> Since the cuirassiers received reinforcements all the time, the defeat of our detachment was a foregone conclusion, yet in the hope of relief it fought on to the last. Captains Schuler and Weiz, as well as Lieutenant Wollmerscheid were the only officers with this detachment that was left to its fate. The grenadier company still had 30 to 40 older intrepid soldiers whose bravery made it at all possible that our resistance lasted as long as it did… In a final thrust this little troop was totally overrun and dispersed. Some of the men managed to reach the remainder of the battalion; many however, were to feel the full wrath of the cuirassiers. Still others became prisoners, Captains Schuler and Weiz among them, the former having been wounded in three places…
>
> …the remainder of the four companies had resumed its position in the line, but, severely weakened, could no longer serve as an independent unit. It was replaced from the reserve and General von Kruse combined the remainder with the 2nd Battalion before the four battalions of the Imperial Guard advanced to the attack…

Here again we see a situation where having some of their own artillery and/or cavalry under command could have either prevented such a crisis arising or could have offered a less costly way of dealing with it.

Weiz also introduces us to the grand finale of the battle; the attack of the French Imperial Guard. The 1st Nassau Regiment had one last test to pass before their initiation to battle finally ended. About seven o'clock, Napoleon, having stalled the advance of the Prussians against his right rear, decided to make one last effort to break the thinning and exhausted allied line, committing his final reserve in a last desperate attack on the allied centre. What exactly happened in this phase of the battle has been rather lost as many allied units, mostly British, vied with each other to claim the laurels of having routed the much-vaunted Imperial Guard. This controversy has centred on the British Guards of Maitland's brigade and the

52nd Light Infantry of Adam's brigade. However, the Nassauers, Brunswickers, Hanoverians and the Netherlanders all claim to have played a role in this critical phase of the battle and we shall have the opportunity to look at each.

For the role taken by the 1st Nassau Regiment, let's first hear from General von Kruse:

> Much weakened by this noteworthy action, the French cavalry retreated and the élite infantry, Napoleon's Guard, moved up instead. It took possession of the plateau, from which our infantry withdrew, but only for 100 paces. A heavy small arms fire now broke out. The Crown Prince [of Orange] who had commanded on the plateau throughout the battle and had displayed much courage and judgment, now attempted to end it with a bayonet charge and bestowed this honour upon the Nassauers. I then brought up the 2nd Battalion and advanced with it in column, it was joined by the remainder of the 1st Battalion. This attack was undertaken with much courage. I already observed a flank of the French Guard's square beginning to waver. Caused perhaps by the fall of the wounded Crown Prince, our young men panicked at the moment of their most splendid victory; the battalion fell into disorder and retreated. The remaining battalions of the first line soon followed, and the plateau was then held by only small bodies of brave men. I joined them with the Landwehr [3rd] Battalion and the remainder of the 2nd Battalion, in a position that the enemy fire could have little effect on them.[61]

Perhaps rather inevitably, von Kruse glorifies the failure, blames it on the fall of the Prince of Orange and ignores the efforts of others that we shall come to examine later. The end result was the same: the Nassauers were forced back out of contact with the French.

For a lower level view of this action, we turn to Second Lieutenant Heinrich von Gagern of the 2nd Battalion. He gives a slightly different account in a letter to his mother dated 26 July 1815:

> This immense artillery fire lasted from twelve until after seven o'clock, interrupted only by some cavalry charges, which, however, were repulsed by the brave English cavalry. It was then that our battalion was ordered to make a bayonet attack against a battalion of the French Guard… The major drawback was that our artillery was completely out of ammunition and that we were not supported by a single gun. We attacked two times and were repelled each time. The brave Crown Prince of Orange rode by the side of our square during the first time and encouraged our soldiers, but was also wounded next to our

square… We had to pause quite a while between each attack, partly in order to re-group the soldiers, partly to allow them some rest.[62]

While Gagern tries to find different reasons for the failure of their counter-attack, the key difference is that he suggests that two attempts were made. Once again, we see the contradictions between first-hand accounts; von Kruse led the attack and so it would seem he is a dependable witness; however, Gagern also took part in the attack and although young and in his first battle (he was aged just sixteen and had only volunteered on Napoleon's return from exile), it is hard to believe he would mention two attacks if there had only been one.

The war diary of the regiment, while generally following von Kruse's account in mentioning only one assault, is perhaps more honest in acknowledging the reason for the failure, 'Most of the enemy mass wavered upon being attacked, in spite of its earlier effective and murderous fire, but failure to press it further kept the attack from turning into a success.'[63] This makes clear that the regiment had shied away from coming into close contact and did not have the necessary firepower or willingness to cross bayonets with the Imperial Guard.

Standing behind the 1st Nassau Regiment during this final phase of the battle was Sir Hussey Vivian's 6th British Light Cavalry Brigade, which had earlier been ordered by Wellington to reinforce his centre from the left flank on the approach of the Prussians. Sir Vivian himself wrote:

> A battalion of foreign troops, with white covers to their shakos, fell back *en masse* against the horses' heads of the 10th [Hussars] and undoubtedly, had this regiment not been formed where it was, would have retreated. This was shortly after our arrival on the position. Captain Shakespeare [*sic*], of the 10th was then standing with me in front of that regiment, and we both endeavoured to halt and encourage them; but it was their coming against the horses' heads, and being unable to pass through the files, that did check them. I must, however, do their officers the justice to say I saw many attempt to stop them, and one seized a drummer by the collar, and made him beat the rally. When halted, they faced about, moved twenty or thirty yards forward, and again began firing, which they kept up until the advance took place.[64]

In a letter to Sir Vivian (and later published by Siborne),[65] Captain Shakespear also mentions the white shako covers, but it is possible that he was following Vivian's letter that had been published before his own. These descriptions of the white shako covers suggest that he was indeed speaking of the Nassauers, and yet von Kruse mentions that he had ordered these to be taken off so as not to provide an obvious target for the French artillery. However, Captain Taylor of the 10th Hussars, in his own letter to Siborne, has them as Brunswickers, 'from their dark uniforms.'[66] In fact, to confuse things even further, neither the Nassauers nor the Brunswickers mention this incident, but the Hanoverians of Kielmansegge's 1st Hanoverian Brigade do admit to being stopped by 'English' cavalry formed up behind them. Given the location and size of Vivian's brigade it may well have been possible for it to have been all three at slightly different times given the confusion of events at this stage of the battle, but it is perhaps more likely that it is Vivian, and so also Shakespear, who got it wrong.

The Nassau accounts are clear that they faced units of the French Imperial Guard in their counterattack led by the Prince of Orange.[67] This phase of the battle, often described as 'the crisis', was much discussed and debated after the battle by those British units that claimed credit for their part in the repulse of the Guard and many officers wrote accounts of their involvement. In none of these accounts are Nassau troops mentioned and even most modern historians do not credit the Nassauers as having faced Guard units. This conclusion appears to be based mainly on where they stood on the battlefield, being further to the east of where the easternmost units of the Guard struck the allied line. If this is true, then it was the troops of d'Erlon's corps advancing in support of the Guard from the area of la Haye-Sainte that drove back the Prince of Orange's counterattack. With the evidence available at the time of writing, it is impossible to be sure either way and the Nassau accounts, while stating categorically that they were of the Imperial Guard, give us no evidence as to why they believed this was the case. Von Kruse's report was written on 21 June, just three days after the battle and perhaps too soon to have concocted a story that was not true. The second account quoted above, from Second Lieutenant von Gagern, was written in a letter to his mother dated 26 July, a month later.

The War Diary of the 1st Regiment records that after their unsuccessful attack led by the Prince of Orange:

> Several battalions on both sides in the first English line were retiring so that the plateau was now only held on both sides by some weak troops bodies. General von Kruse joined one of these with the 3rd and the remainder of the 2nd Battalion at the left flank of the centre near the highway (where there was a shack built of brick). The 1st Battalion, by now almost completely wiped out, remained in the second line. These troops returned as best they could, the fire of the French infantry now spreading out on the plateau. Sounds of firing from the left flank and the rear made it appear as if the extreme left flank of the army had been considerably pushed back.[68]

This did not mark the end of the regiment's contribution to the battle, as after the rout of the French army the second and third battalions followed the allied advance as far as Rosomme where, meeting advancing Prussian troops, they stopped. They bivouacked for the night near where Napoleon's headquarters had been established during the battle (la Caillou). Interestingly, the War Diary states that by this time the regiment had only five to six hundred men still with the colours out of the almost 2,500 officers and men that were present when the battle started.[69] The official Waterloo casualty rate for the 1st Nassau Regiment was reported by General von Kruse as:

> Killed: five officers and 249 men.
> Wounded: nineteen officers and 370 men.
> A total of 643 all ranks or 22 percent.

It will be noted that no prisoners or missing are mentioned. We know that when the two companies were overrun by cuirassiers, many prisoners were taken. We must assume that in the following days these were released or escaped and are not included in the numbers and most of those missing had also rejoined their battalions; it is inconceivable to believe that there were no missing from a regiment of young and barely trained recruits that had just experienced their baptism of fire. Certainly, the numbers of men remaining with the colours at the end of the battle suggest this.

Total Nassau Casualties at Waterloo

We have already discussed at length the difficulties of accurately assessing casualties. Using the figures given above, total casualties for the Nassauer troops at Waterloo are as follows:

> 1st Regiment: 643 all ranks.
> 2nd Regiment: 406 all ranks.
> Orange-Nassau Regiment: 165 all ranks.
> This gives a total of 1,214 all ranks of 7,139[70] or 17 percent.

The problems of assessing casualties were highlighted by General von Kruse in his report on the actions of the 1st Nassau Regiment; he writes:

> I am unable to provide an accurate listing of the regiment's losses as, due to the disorder that prevailed for some time at the rear of the army, many men had gone back with the wounded as far as Brussels.[71]

Official reports and later histories by Dutch or Belgian authors such as Löben-Sels and de Bas have given various casualty returns, but these are often contradictory. Erwin Muilwijk's recent research casts doubt on the veracity of all figures quoted in various histories and he refuses to give any in his own volumes. Those given in official returns were no doubt accurate on the day they were taken, but would not necessarily have taken into account detachments, returning casualties and those missing.

Pflugk-Harttung gives the following initial casualty list for Waterloo:

Unit	Killed		Wounded		POW	Missing
	Officers	Men	Officers	Men		
1/28th O-N	NR*	NR	NR	NR		
2/28th O-N	NR	NR	NR	NR		
1/1st Nassau	-	60	11	163		163
2/1st Nassau	3	34	4	142		132
3/1st Nassau	1	11	2	83		92
1/2nd Nassau	-	3	-	40		40
2/2nd Nassau	-	10	1	19		19
3/2nd Nassau	-	1	2	32		66
Volunteer Jäger	NR	NR	NR	NR		
Total	4	109	20	479		**512**

* NR – Not Recorded

The very high number of missing is noteworthy, although the majority unsurprisingly came from the young, inexperienced and roughly handled 1st Regiment.[72] After the battle, most of the missing apparently rejoined their battalions; those that did not were presumed dead (though some may well have deserted). Reflecting the return of some of those missing and those who were initially reported as wounded but later died in hospital, his final casualty figures for the contingent were:

Unit	Killed		Wounded		Total	%
	Officers	Men	Officers	Men		
1/28th O-N	NR	NR	NR	NR	-	-
2/28th O-N	NR	NR	NR	NR	-	-
1/1st Nassau	-	112	11	157	11+269	29%
2/1st Nassau	4	96	3	132	7+228	25%
3/1st Nassau	1	39	2	82	3+121	13%
1/2nd Nassau	2	27	6	46	8+73	9%
2/2nd Nassau	1	13	7	45	8+58	7.5%
3/2nd Nassau	1	27	7	62	8+89	11%
Volunteer Jäger	NR	NR	NR	NR	-	-
Total	9	314	36	524	883	12.4%

This is considerably different from the unit returns – 12.4 percent against 17 percent – but probably better accounts for the return of those missing. While bearing in mind the need for a balanced consideration of what these statistics tell us, we must not ignore the fact that large numbers of missing immediately after a battle could have a significant impact on following operations. Having won the battle, and the French being in such disorder, the allies had time to rally their missing, reorganise and rest their units, at least to some extent. If the allies had been forced to retreat, or if the French had been able to rally and resume the offensive, the implications of high numbers of missing, even in the short term, could have been significant.

Summary/conclusion

The first engagement of Wellington's army in this campaign was borne by the 2nd/2nd Nassau at Frasnes on the evening of the 15th. After their first contact with the Imperial Guard lancers, their withdrawal to the Quatre Bras position was performed calmly and professionally and they coordinated their move well with Bijleveld's battery that supported them. This operation was much to the credit of Major von Normann, the battalion commander.

Despite what some first-hand accounts suggest, the Nassau troops were not heavily engaged at Quatre Bras. That is not to say they did not have an important role to play in the battle, the defence of the Bossu wood, but it appears they did not show the resilience and cohesion that fitted them for the disorientating and loose-order combat that fighting in densely wooded areas demanded. They did suffer from some artillery fire in the early stages of the battle, though without serious casualties, and showed rather shaky morale when the mounted staff of the Prince of Orange approached and seem to have given up the wood without very determined resistance. This is a little surprising given that the 2nd Nassau Regiment was a light regiment and contained the experienced soldiers which had had sufficient time for training that should have made them ideal troops for this type of fighting. This being their first major action of the campaign may go some way to explaining this, as did the impression of French numerical superiority, but in the skirmish battle and in the woods where columns could not manoeuvre, they did an undistinguished job of delaying the French advance.

Throughout most of the battle, the three battalions of the 2nd Nassau Regiment had been held back in reserve near Quatre Bras. Here also was the 2nd/28th Orange-Nassau, who could not be committed to the fight due to the shortage of ammunition for their French muskets.

The French had failed to exploit the relatively half-hearted defence of the Bossu wood, meaning that the Nassau battalions that fought there suffered light casualties and were left with the morale and cohesion to fight again at Waterloo; it had been a fairly easy introduction to battle for those who were in action for the first time.

At Waterloo, the performance of the Nassau battalions generally reflected the experience of the units. The young, inexperienced and barely trained 1st Nassau Regiment had a torrid time in the very centre of the allied line where much of the French fury fell. Their apparent inability to form square, the intense fire they had to endure, facing the repeated French cavalry attacks and then the counter-attack led by the Prince of Orange at the crisis of the battle, all reflects rather well on them and they were generally able to hold their position throughout the battle. Although they required rallying a number of times, each time they returned to the fray.

The role of the 1st/2nd Nassau at Hougoumont has been almost scandalously ignored by British historians, until quite recently. They clearly gave a good account of themselves in the defence of the farm complex throughout the battle. Although the behaviour of the two companies that seem to have left the line of battle to retire onto the ridge does not reflect so well on them, this is more likely to be a failure of leadership (or ammunition) than a lack of courage or willingness within the ranks; after all, the losses show a hard and close fight in the wood against the initial French attacks.

The other battalions of the 2nd Nassau and the Orange-Nassau Regiments gave a good account of themselves on the extreme left of the allied line. Although they were only involved in a skirmish battle and had the advantage of good defensible terrain, the loss of this part of the line would have diverted Wellington's attention from more important points. His confidence in their ability to hold their own here proved to be well-founded and he was able to deploy only the smallest of artillery resources to this flank, redeploying the two brigades of British light cavalry into the hard-pressed centre relatively early in the battle.

During the march to Paris, Wellington finally organised a Nassau division as he had originally proposed before the campaign opened. This should be taken as an endorsement of his satisfaction with their performance at Waterloo.

Perhaps the last word on the performance of the Nassau contingent should be reserved for General von Kruse, who wrote three days after the battle:

> The courage and steadfastness of the [1st] regiment was much to be admired, of which its losses in killed and wounded bore ample testimony. Regrettably, it was well proven here that in critical moments courage alone will not suffice and that unskilled troops will become victims of their inexperience. I am convinced that, if both regiments had been united, their defeat of Napoleon's Guard on this important day would have brought immortal glory to the Nassau troops. The officers' conduct was faultless; many distinguished themselves...[73]

Chapter Three
The Brunswick Contingent

'The Brunswick infantry are some of the finest troops that ever were'[1]

Background

It was only after Napoleon's defeat in 1814 that the old principality of Brunswick-Wolfenbüttel became the Duchy of Brunswick. In the early years of the Napoleonic wars, Brunswick-Wolfenbüttel had been aligned with Prussia, but having defeated Prussia in 1806, Napoleon seized the principality and incorporated it into the new kingdom of Westphalia, giving the crown to his brother Jérôme (who was later to command a French division at Waterloo). The Duke of Brunswick, Friedrich Wilhelm, moved to Austria to carry on the fight against the French. After the Austrian defeat at Wagram, he fled mainland Europe with many of his troops and was transported to Britain by the Royal Navy. The Duke remained in London while his troops fought in Spain under Wellington, but he finally returned to the new Duchy of Brunswick at the very end of 1813, after the French had finally been thrown out of his old homeland by the allies. He immediately began to raise a new army, which was only fully organised in 1814 as the fighting came to a close. In 1815 the Duke led it back into the Netherlands to join Wellington's army after Napoleon's return to France.

Contingent size

In many histories, the Brunswick contingent is often described as the Brunswick Corps. In fact, the contingent had the strength of a strong division. De Bas, a Dutch historian of the 1815 campaign, gives the total for the Brunswick contingent as 6,808 men in a headquarters, eight infantry battalions, five cavalry squadrons and two artillery batteries (10 percent of Wellington's 68,000 men).[2] The eight infantry battalions were divided into an independent light battalion, the Avantgarde (literally 'advance-guard'); a light brigade, containing the Leib Battalion and three light battalions and a line brigade containing three line battalions. The cavalry consisted of a hussar regiment and a single, large squadron of *uhlans* (lancers). The artillery consisted of a foot and a horse artillery battery. The order of battle and strengths are given in Lieutenant General August von Herzberg's 'Detailed Report on the Corps of Troops of His Serene Highness the

Duke of Brunswick from the 15th to and including the 18th June of 1815 with two plans'.[3] The battalion strengths below are the full establishment strengths rather than their true strength; it would be most unusual for all battalions to have a full establishment while on campaign.

Staff
Hussar Regiment – four squadrons (Major von Cramm – 690 men).
Uhlans – one squadron (Major Pott – 232 men).

Horse Battery (Captain von Heinemann – 240 men).
Foot Battery (Major Moll – 240 men).

Avantgarde Battalion (Major von Rauschenplat – 672 men).

Light Brigade (Lieutenant Colonel von Buttlar):
- Leib Battalion (Major von Pröstler – 672 men).
- 1st Light Battalion (Major von Holstein – 672 men).
- 2nd Light Battalion (Major von Brandenstein – 672 men).
- 3rd Light Battalion (Major Ebling – 672 men).

Line Brigade (Lieutenant Colonel von Specht):
- 1st Line Battalion (Major Metzner – 672 men).
- 2nd Line Battalion (Major von Strombeck – 672 men).
- 3rd Line Battalion (Major von Normann – 672 men).

In a letter to the Duke of Brunswick, dated Brussels, 10 April 1815, Wellington requested the duke to set his troops off on their march to Antwerp 'immediately';[4] they were to be expected in Antwerp between 10 and 18 May.[5]

The Leaders

Commanding the Brunswick contingent was Duke Friedrich Wilhelm, Duke of Brunswick, who was famously killed at Quatre Bras trying to rally and inspire some of his young troops when they were under intense fire. He was therefore not present at Waterloo, where command of the contingent had passed to Colonel Olfermann, the duke's adjutant general.

Friedrich Wilhelm was born in 1771; his mother was the sister of Britain's King George III. He joined the Prussian army in 1787 as a staff captain. His father, Karl Wilhelm Ferdinand, was to become the commander-in-chief of the Prussian army. Although the young Friedrich Wilhelm had an uneasy relationship with his father, he enjoyed his patronage through some uncomfortable times in his military career. He fought against the French during the war of the First Coalition (when he received his first wound), but despite a series of scandals, his promotion was quick and by 1801 he was a major-general commanding the Thadden Infantry Regiment of the Prussian army. In the 1806 campaign against the French he remained in reserve at the battles of Jena/Auerstedt and then joined Blücher's troops in the defence of Lübeck. He took an active part in the defence of the city but was captured and blamed for its fall for disobeying orders; his military reputation with the Prussians was tarnished and the consequences were to linger on. He resigned from the Prussian army but, his father having died from his wounds, he found himself the new Duke of Brunswick. Unfortunately, he was the ruler of a principality that no longer existed.

Friedrich Wilhelm eventually moved to Austria to continue the struggle. He raised and financed his own *freicorps* in 1809, but after the Austrian defeat at Wagram he successfully extracted his troops across the whole of Europe and was evacuated with his men to Britain by the Royal Navy. In this long and tricky movement he fought a number of successful engagements against Westphalian army units which helped to re-establish his military reputation, particularly with his own countrymen. Although his troops were taken into British service and deployed to Spain, Friedrich Wilhelm remained in London until the end of 1813 when the French were forced from his hereditary lands and he returned to Brunswick.

He immediately raised a new army and looked to lead them against the French. However, by the time the small army was ready to march, the 1814 campaign was over and Napoleon had abdicated. Keen to show he had made a contribution, Friedrich Wilhelm marched his men into Belgium, but the allied chain of command rather ignominiously ordered him back to Brunswick.

As commander of the Brunswick contingent in 1815, he unfortunately had little opportunity to show his command credentials before his death, but all the eyewitness accounts describe him as a calm and inspirational commander who clearly understood the needs of his young and inexperienced troops. His loss was a great blow to the morale of his men; an aide de camp to General Hill, Captain Digby Mackworth, wrote in his diary:

> Among others who fell on this occasion we have to regret particularly the Duke of Brunswick Oels, who fell gallantly fighting at the head of his own infantry, and died the death of a soldier. His troops, outraged by his loss *gave* [his emphasis], and swear they will *give* [his emphasis], no quarter to the French who fall into their hands, and I have no doubt they will keep their word.[6]

Colonel Elias Olfermann was born in Brunswick and in 1795, aged eighteen, he travelled to England to join the British army as a musician. He joined the 90th Foot, the Minorca Regiment, but three years later became a soldier in the 97th (which was to become the Queen's Own Germans in 1805). He was commissioned ensign in 1800 and later became adjutant. In 1801 he took part in the campaign in Egypt in which he was badly wounded at the battle of Alexandria, but was also decorated for his bravery. From 1808 he was in Spain, becoming aide de camp to Edward Packenham in whose brigade some of the Brunswick troops served. He was present at the battle of Fuentes d'Onoro as a captain, where his decisive action saved his regiment from heavy losses. After returning to England due to illness, he met the Duke of Brunswick. Returning to Brunswick with the duke after it was overrun by the allies, he resigned from the British army in 1814 and became part of the Brunswick forces which he helped to raise. To the anger of a number of more senior and experienced Brunswick officers, he became the Duke's adjutant general in 1815. In this post he was effectively the second in command and therefore took command of the Brunswick contingent when the duke was killed at Quatre Bras. Olfermann commanded the Brunswick contingent throughout the battle of Waterloo until he was shot in the right hand around seven o'clock (according to his own account) and had to hand over command to his assistant, Lieutenant Colonel von Heinemann (who was killed just a little later). Olfermann was therefore a very experienced officer, conversant with the British army's way of doing things and well placed to lead the young and inexperienced Brunswick troops. However, despite continuing to command the contingent after Waterloo, Olfermann was later the target of a plot by more veteran officers and left the forces in 1817.

The more junior officers (and senior NCOs) of the contingent came from a variety of sources.

Luckily, a study of the archives, conducted in 1912, gives us exact figures for those who served in the infantry in 1815.[7] This broke down the officers as follows:

- Those who served in the Brunswick army before the French took over the country and did not serve again until 1813 – 2
- Those who had served in the Westphalian army (some of these also had experience in the old Brunswick army) – 56
- Foreign officers – 10
- Those who served under British command in the Brunswick Oels – 47
- Volunteers – 43
- Allies – 11

Those described as 'volunteers' had no previous military experience, and no doubt filled the most junior appointments. Some of these were unsuitable, and often commissioned through nepotism rather than any sort of qualification or aptitude. At least one young officer was court martialled for absconding from the battlefield. Those described as 'allies' had served in the former contingents of the smaller German states (that had previously been in French service) and wished to fight against the common enemy.

It is therefore clear, given the number of infantry battalions that made up the contingent in 1815 (eight), that three-quarters of them had some previous experience, even if this did not necessarily include combat. Certainly, we can expect that all those who had served in the Brunswick Oels had served on campaign and in battle. In 1814 Friedrich Wilhelm asked the British army to release eleven officers from the Brunswick Oels for him to use to organise and start to train the new army, but as the campaign against the French was continuing in the south, only five were allowed to return to Brunswick.[8]

It was a similar picture in the cavalry and artillery, where the majority of officers had some previous service. A number of senior NCOs also came from the same sources.

Accounts of the contingent during the Waterloo campaign tend to single out the regimental officers and non-commissioned officers for particular praise in keeping their young and inexperienced troops in line, as this exert from Chevalié Mercer shows: 'Every moment I feared they would again throw down their arms and flee; but their officers and sergeants behaved nobly, not only keeping them together, but managing to keep their squares closed in spite of the carnage made amongst them.'[9] The strength and value of the experienced cadre present in all the new armies was fundamental to these young and inexperienced troops maintaining their cohesion and places on the battlefield.

But not all was well among the contingent's leadership; Friedrich Wilhelm, having not served in the Peninsula, had built up his own clique of officers and was prone to promote them over more experienced officers, both those who had served in Spain with the British and those who had served in the Westphalian army. Olfermann was a good example of this when he was appointed adjutant general over more senior officers such as General von Bernewitz, an experienced veteran.[10] It also appears that the Duke did not trust those officers who had served in the Westphalian army and passed them over for promotion. Such decisions caused some resentment in the officer corps and a number of middle-ranked officers resigned just before the campaign opened, some only four days before Quatre Bras.

The troops

When Duke Friedrich Wilhelm returned to Brunswick in December 1813 after the expulsion of the French, he immediately set about raising a new army. This was no doubt later aided by the return of the Brunswick Oels. However, these did not arrive back in Brunswick until late in December 1814, so could not have been used to help train the many volunteers and new recruits that initially flooded into the depots. These veterans no doubt later provided a welcome backbone of very experienced men who could provide ideal NCOs for the fledging army. However, how many of these were volunteers or still in a state to serve should not be over-estimated, as in order to maintain their strength in Spain, they had recruited a wide variety of nationalities (mainly from prisoners of war) who returned to their own homes straight after the end of that war.

Some of the recruits had been conscripted into the Westphalian army in 1813 after most of it had been destroyed in Russia. However, these new units, of little combat value, spent their time on garrison duty, saw little action, and certainly no major battles, before the cities they garrisoned surrendered to the advancing allies. However, although they may not have seen any action, at least they had some experience in uniform.

The units of the new army consisted of a mix of both volunteers and conscripts. The volunteers represented about 50 percent of the Leib Battalion (presuming that these included the returned Brunswick Oels) and Avantgarde, and between only 10 percent and 40 percent in the line and light battalions; the higher number of volunteers being in the senior battalions which had been raised first. For example, the 1st Line Battalion had about 60 percent conscripts, the 3rd Line Battalion about 85 percent.[11] The electorate having lost so many men in 1812 serving with the Westphalian army, the pool of men available for conscription was smaller than might otherwise have been the case; it seems almost a whole generation of young men had been lost to Napoleon's wars. Some volunteers were as young as sixteen. Almost all of the most junior ranks who fought in 1815, therefore, had been in uniform less than eighteen months and had no previous combat experience, in contrast to the officers and many non-commissioned officers, who could claim to have seen battle.

The Brunswickers had their own drill regulations, the *Exercir-Reglement für die Herzoglich Braunschweigische Infantrie,* printed in Brunswick, which seems to have been an unusual mix of British and Prussian drill. No doubt influenced by British tactics, at first it was decided to form line in only two ranks. However, as three ranks were considered more secure for inexperienced troops, and many of the officers and senior NCOs were more familiar with this formation, it was reintroduced.

The Brunswick infantry, both line and light, had an unusual battalion organisation; although the established strength of a battalion was 672, they had only four large companies, without the élite grenadier and light companies of most other European armies. Without their own skirmisher company or skirmisher trained troops, the line battalions relied on the Avantgarde and light battalions to provide their skirmishers, a rather inefficient and inflexible system and one almost unique in armies of the time.

Although the Avantgarde Battalion had four companies like the other infantry battalions, they consisted of two companies of Grey Jägers, who were rifle-armed and wore distinctive grey uniforms, and two companies designated Light Infantry, who were clad in black and armed with muskets. Each company consisted of a captain company commander, three subaltern officers, a sergeant major, six sergeants, six corporals, five buglers and about 140 jägers. The Grey Jägers, recruited among game keepers and skilled hunters from the ducal estates, were good shots and, although newly raised, considered themselves the élite of the army.

It has generally been believed that the Brunswick Oels, who had fought as light infantry for the British in Spain and Portugal, were all incorporated into the Avantgarde on their return to Brunswick, but this is not true. Although Carl Pöhling, who had served in the Brunswick Oels, described the Avantgarde as 'the most experienced troops within the Brunswick contingent',[12] the Brunswick archives show that the majority of the Brunswick Oels manpower was incorporated into the Leib Battalion, which at first, and probably for this reason, was part of the Light Brigade and trained as light infantry.[13] The Leib Battalion were the closest the duke had to a designated élite battalion.

The Brunswick contingent was famous for their black uniforms and skull and cross-bone cap badges, which were commented on by many eyewitnesses:

> Brunswick troops passed us to the front. Ah yes and to look at them marching forwards as proud as a Spaniard on sentry, or a turkey cock in a farmyard, dressed in dark uniform, something like a horse's tail in their helmets with the shape of a scalped face and man's shin bone…[14]

Some stories state that the black uniforms were mourning for Duke Friedrich Wilhelm's father, Duke Ferdinand, who was mortally wounded at the battle of Jena; others that it was mourning for the dismemberment of Brunswick by the French in 1806. However, there seems to be no evidence for either of these claims and the sinister look may simply have been the cheapest and most practical colour, or an attempt to appear intimidating.

The Brunswick line battalions had originally carried captured French muskets, but these were later replaced with British ones. However, it appears that the light battalions continued to carry French muskets, which had been shortened and rebored to British calibre to relieve the logistic problems of having to supply different calibres of ammunition; it seems likely that these too were exchanged for British muskets, but it is not clear when this took place. Brunswick also produced its own muskets at a factory in Herzberg, but it is possible that only the Reserve Battalion, which remained in Brunswick in 1815, carried these.

The two artillery batteries, one of foot and one of horse, each had six guns and two howitzers. This was an unusual mix; the British had five guns and a howitzer in both foot and horse batteries, while the French had six guns and two howitzers in a foot battery, but only four guns and two howitzers in a horse battery. The Brunswick ordnance was a mix of both captured French pieces and pieces manufactured in Westphalia. In 1814 the Duke was able to buy the guns for these two batteries at an auction of equipment that had been captured at the battle of Leipzig; these consisted of twelve French 6-pounders and four Westphalian 7-pounder howitzers of Prussian design, along with the necessary caissons and other equipages.[15]

Although largely lacking combat experience, the troops had at least had time to get used to military life and to become well practised in their drill. This allowed them to manoeuvre competently on the battlefield. Accounts from Brunswick soldiers and officers describe changing various formations on the battlefield while under fire, suggesting that their drill and discipline were sound.

Accounts of the Brunswickers from British officers vary, but many British units had served alongside the Brunswick Oels in the Peninsula and had something of an affection for them; indeed, many British accounts of 1815 continue to refer to the Brunswick contingent as the Brunswick Oels. Lieutenant Colonel Home of the 3rd Foot Guards wrote of them, 'Of the foreign levies the best soldiers in discipline as well as courage, were those of the Brunswick Oels', while Ensign St John of the 1st Guards was even more impressed: 'the Brunswick infantry are some of the finest troops that ever were, they were next to us.'[16] Captain Tomkinson, who served in the 16th Light Dragoons, wrote that Nassau and Brunswick troops 'also behaved well, and must be considered effective…'.[17]

On the basis of their own accounts, the morale of the Brunswickers was high at the start of the campaign and no doubt boosted by the presence of their sovereign Duke Friedrich Wilhelm, an experienced and apparently inspirational leader. The nucleus of all the units had been together for over a year and it can be expected that there had been plenty of time to establish unit cohesion and some understanding and confidence between the officers, non-commissioned officers and men, reinforced by at least some level of campaign experience among the unit cadres. Unlike some of the other contingents, whose predecessors, and even some of those still serving, had fought for the French, there was little to bind the Brunswickers to their current enemies. Indeed, their country having been occupied and incorporated into the newly established kingdom of Westphalia, there was plenty of reason for the new army to fight with determination against their former oppressors.

However, there were also reasons for their new allies to have doubts about the robustness and resilience of the Brunswick contingent. By their own admission, the troops were very young,[18] although this was not unusual among the new levies raised since the liberation of their homelands from French occupation or the first abdication of Napoleon, but their youth is mentioned frequently in their own accounts and those of their allies. Chevalié Mercer of the Royal Horse Artillery often described them as 'lads' or 'boys' in his journal.[19] It is also true that they suffered from desertion, although this was common enough in armies of the time, even the British. However, no fewer than 200 men were reported as missing after Quatre Bras; a very high number given the size of the contingent. There is no suggestion that all these men had deserted, and like many from all contingents, a large number of men found reasons not to remain in the front line during the battle but later returned to their units.

We will see examples of a reluctance to engage and the loss of morale in action during the battle of Quatre Bras later, but Mercer also gives two clear examples which, if he is to be believed, suggest that the morale of the Brunswickers was brittle. In the first, he describes coming upon the contingent during the withdrawal from Quatre Bras to Waterloo:

> The infantry had made so little progress that we again overtook the rear of their column, composed of Brunswickers – some of those same boys I used to see practising at *Schäpdale* in my rides to Brussels. These poor lads were pushing on at a great rate. As soon as their rear divisions heard the sound of our horse's feet, without once looking behind them, they began to crowd and press on those in front, until at last, hearing us close up to them, and finding it impossible to push forward in the road, many of them broke off into the fields; and such was their panic that, in order to run lighter, away went arms and knapsacks in all directions, and a general race ensued, the whole corps being in the most horrid confusion. It was to no purpose that I exerted my little stock of German to make them understand we were their English friends – a frightened glance and away, was all the effect of my interference, which drove many of them off.[20]

Mercer was also posted close to the Brunswick troops at Waterloo and once more describes their shaky morale as they stood in square near his battery during the French cavalry charges; we shall read about this later.

However, it must be taken into account that Mercer also refers disparagingly to other allied contingents, so it is quite possible that he harboured some sense of arrogance and superiority over the troops of his allies, although the detail he goes into in these cases suggests that there was at least an element of truth in them. In fact, like many of the national contingents, even those who had previously fought for the French, there appears to have been much enthusiasm for the cause; Ensign Lindwurm of the 2nd Line Battalion described the 'joyful enthusiasm and wild shouts of 'hurrah' at Quatre Bras[21] and Olfermann's report spoke highly of their courage and confidence.

Deployment and actions[22]

During the campaign, the Brunswick contingent formed part of the Reserve Corps which came under Wellington's personal command. It is probable that Wellington chose this option because the Duke of Brunswick maintained direct command of his own men, which did not give him the flexibility to integrate the Brunswick brigades into British divisions as he was able to do with the Hanoverian troops in order to mix them with the more experienced and disciplined British and KGL brigades. This also allowed him to choose the moment to commit these young and inexperienced troops, keeping them sheltered for as long as possible until he absolutely needed them. He was unable to do this at Quatre Bras because of the exigencies of the moment and he was to see how they wavered under pressure. The desertion of numbers of men, as well as the number of missing after Quatre Bras and the death of the Duke, must also have given Wellington cause for concern about their level of morale.

In the run-up to the campaign, the Brunswick contingent were stationed to the north of Brussels, with their headquarters at Lacken, immediately north of the city. The units stretched from Brussels up to Mecheln, nearly twenty kilometres from the centre of the city and on the opposite side to the French advance; they would have a long and arduous march to reach Quatre Bras.

Quatre Bras

The march of the Brunswick troops from their concentration areas around the north of Brussels to Quatre Bras was chaotic at times (see Mercer above), but given the demands of the moment, this was true of many of the formations rushing to join the battle and many men were left behind, unable to maintain the pace. The force reached Quatre Bras about three o'clock.

Only part of the Brunswick contingent fought at Quatre Bras, led by the Duke himself; the 1st and 3rd Light Battalions, and more significantly both artillery batteries, did not reach the battlefield in time to take part in the fighting. The absence of the latter was to be keenly felt. The remainder of the Brunswick troops arrived at a critical time in the battle; the 2nd Netherlands Division was under increasing pressure from the French combined arms attacks and the charges of the Netherlands light cavalry had been repulsed.

Following Picton's 5th British Division onto the battlefield, the Duke of Brunswick had little time to rest his troops before he was ordered to send the Leib and 1st Line Battalions to fill the gap that had opened between the Charleroi road and the Bossu wood forward of the Bergerie farm. The Avantgarde battalion covered their right flank and stretched into the wood itself. The 2nd Light Battalion was sent to the allied left, to support the 95th Rifles of Picton's division to try and hold open the road that led to Ligny, along which Wellington would have to advance if he was to have any chance of supporting the Prussians, who were fighting Napoleon's main army there. The 2nd and 3rd Line Battalions were left in reserve next to the village of Quatre Bras itself.

It will be remembered that the Brunswick contingent was part of the Reserve Corps under Wellington's personal command. It is therefore extremely unlikely that Wellington would have wanted to deploy any of his reserve, let alone the

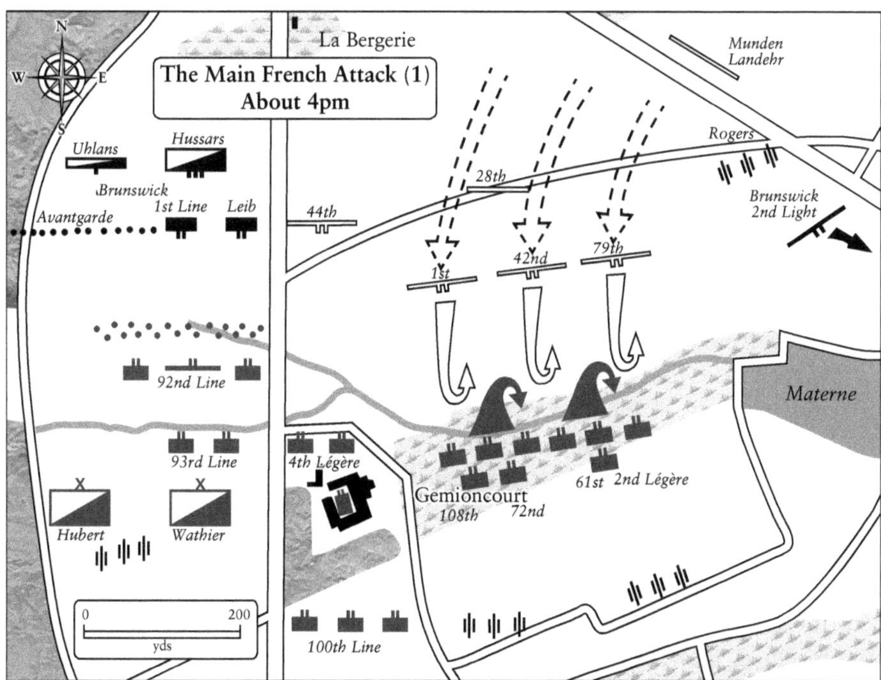

Map showing the initial deployment of the Brunswick contingent at Quatre Bras.

young and inexperienced Brunswick troops, straight into the front line. However, with the Netherlands' troops beginning to show signs of exhaustion, he no doubt felt that he needed to pull them out of the fight to give them time to resupply and reorganise, and to rest them before he might need to use them again. Once more we see Wellington trying to measure the exposure to fire of his allied contingents, as he no doubt expected to fight a decisive battle sometime in the following few days.

It is quite unusual for a battalion to be deployed away from its parent brigade during battle, though we shall see it again at Waterloo, and it must have been quite disconcerting for the Brunswick 2nd Light Battalion to be sent off to the left flank to link up with the British Rifles of a division of which they were not a part. It is therefore not entirely surprising if they felt somewhat isolated and unsure. Their apparent unwillingness to come to grips with the French did not impress the 95th Rifles when they first arrived. Captain Kincaid recalled:

> We were presently reinforced by a small battalion of foreign troops, with whose assistance we were in hopes to have driven the enemy a little further from it [the Cense wood]; but they were a raw body of men, who had never before been under fire; and, as they could not be prevailed upon to join our skirmishers, we could make no use of them whatever.[23]

Given that the battalion had been thrown straight into the front line without any previous experience in battle and having just completed an exhausting march without time to catch their breath or prepare for the fight, perhaps their reluctance should be forgiven, or at least understood. To their credit, having acclimatised to battle, Kincaid was prepared to acknowledge their participation in the final advance:

> In justice to the foreign battalion, which had been all day attached to us, I must say that, in this last movement, they joined us cordially, and behaved exceedingly well. They had a very gallant young fellow at their head [the commanding officer, to whom we must presume he was referring, was Major von Brandestein]; and their conduct in the earlier part of the day, can, therefore, only be ascribed to its being their first appearance on such a stage.[24]

The truth is, that while they may have contributed little to the fight beyond their mere presence, and were eclipsed by the far more experienced Rifles, their contribution must be assessed as being as good as could be expected in the circumstances and that while not lacking courage, they betrayed their lack of experience. Wellington would no doubt have preferred not to have given them their first experience of a fight by being thrown into the front line without a chance to gain a feeling for the sights and sounds of battle.

While the 2nd Light Battalion fought on the left of the allied position, the remainder of the Brunswick contingent, under the command of the Duke of Brunswick, had advanced into position on the centre right, leaving the 2nd and 3rd Line Battalions in reserve defending the hamlet of Quatre Bras. The Leib and 1st Line Battalion formed in closed columns with their left on the main road with the uhlans and hussars forming a second line behind them. Quickly noticing the Brunswick movement, the French brought forward a battery onto a small height almost level with the farm complex of Gemioncourt and only 500 yards away and advanced their skirmishers to harass the two forward battalions. The Brunswick losses quickly mounted, not helped by the fact that the battalions remained in column so they could form square quickly if threatened by cavalry. The reluctance of the Duke to deploy them into line, or to adjust their position in order to reduce their exposure to artillery fire, is unfortunately unexplained; perhaps we can conclude that the Duke was aware of the significant impact on morale of this fire and preferred the intimacy and solidity of a column, rather than the more fragile and less intimate embrace of being in line. The situation these two battalions found themselves in soon became a terrible test of endurance and the Duke sat calmly on his horse smoking his pipe in front of his men to set an example of calm courage.

A Brunswick officer, Heinrich Köhler, wrote of this time:

> The enemy now deployed an artillery battery close to Gémioncourt and unleashed a relentless barrage against the Brunswick column. The losses sustained by the Brunswick battalions, who maintained their positions for a considerable time in the face of this terrible onslaught, were appalling.[25]

The heavy artillery fire continued for close to an hour and without their own artillery, which had still not come up, the Brunswickers had nothing to reply to the fire of the French guns which were close enough to fire cannister. The commander of the hussars was killed and that of the Avantgarde was wounded. Colonel Olfermann reported on this phase of the battle:

> We had no artillery to respond because our corps' artillery had not yet arrived due to its remote cantonments. The cavalry suffered in particular at this point. However, it closed its ranks with great *sang froid* from time to time, that had been taken out by howitzer or canister fire, as did the infantry battalions near there. The Duke was here also, almost during the whole time that the heavy cannonade lasted, and by his presence instilled the utmost intrepidity and calm in his soldiers…[26]

The Duke clearly understood the strain the French artillery fire would be having on his young and inexperienced troops and made a point of setting an example; a Brunswick report on the battle described him at this time:

> The duke himself remained in this place, and even though many a ball struck close to him, he kept casually smoking his pipe, and calmly issued any necessary orders to instil courage and fearlessness in his inexperienced young warriors through his own example.[27]

Eventually, a large French infantry formation in line and column was seen advancing supported by cavalry. With little room to manoeuvre in their current position, the Brunswick hussars were sent to the east of the main road, while in order to try and hold up the French attack the uhlan squadron was ordered to charge the advancing French infantry. Although a strong squadron (around 250 men), the uhlans had insufficient strength to seriously threaten the French, who quickly formed square and threw them back with their fire. Their casualties do not suggest they closed with their enemy (see casualties below).

With the repulse of their uhlans and facing a concerted combined arms attack, the two battalions felt they had no option but to retire to the village of

Quatre Bras. Still under heavy artillery fire and threatened by French cavalry emboldened by their retreat, the infantry withdrawal, in the words of the official report, 'resulted inevitably in some disorder among the inexperienced troops'.[28] Most historians have considered that if this was the description from an official Brunswick report, the reality was rather more of a rout. While attempting to restore some order, the Duke of Brunswick was shot and mortally wounded by a French skirmisher. The impact of such an event on the inexperienced troops, in the midst of such confusion, can be imagined. In an effort to cover their disordered infantry, the Brunswick hussars charged across the road towards the French infantry, who, with sufficient warning, were able to form square and drive them off in their turn. Under cover of the infantry units at Quatre Bras the Leib and 1st Line were able to reach the village without further mishap.

Having re-established order, the Brunswick contingent were no doubt heartened by the arrival of their artillery and towards the end of the day the Leib and 2nd Line Battalion took part in the advance which pushed the French back to their start line of the morning. Although little recorded, this advance at the end of the battle must have been conducted under intense skirmisher and artillery fire, given that it was the only time of the day that the 2nd Line were heavily involved, and they suffered considerable casualties (a total of 191 men killed and wounded).

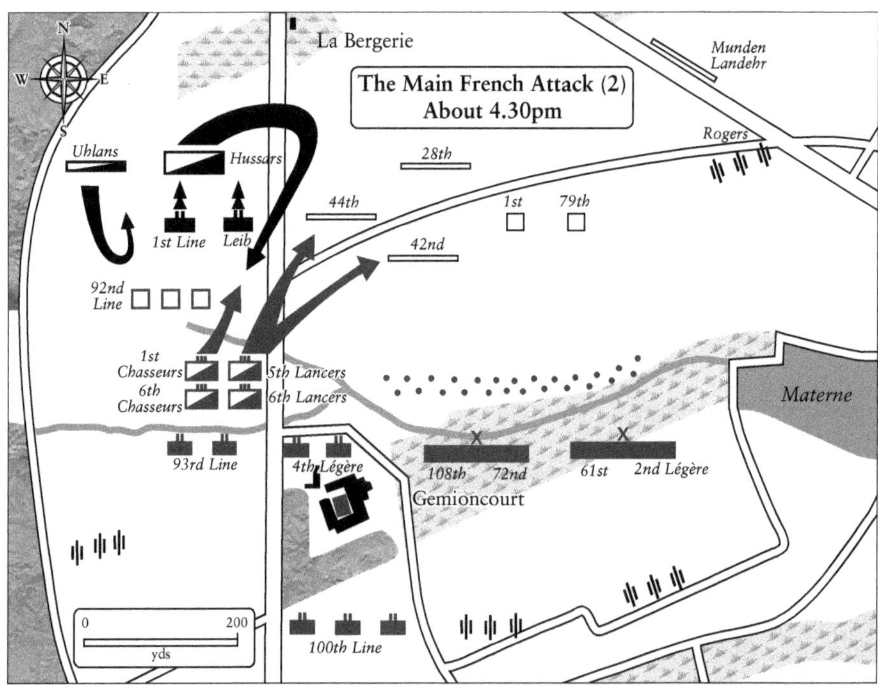

Map showing the charges of the Brunswick cavalry at Quatre Bras and the retirement of the Leib and 1st Line Battalions.

Quatre Bras had been a traumatic baptism of fire for a number of Brunswick units; they had been deployed into an unenviable position with a thankless mission which they had apparently faced with fortitude and courage, but had been unable hold and engage in close combat. They had faced intense skirmisher and artillery fire and suffered heavy casualties. It is also true that many men chose to slip away during the fighting. The Leib, 1st and 2nd Line Battalions had suffered particularly; two of these (the Leib and 1st Line Battalions) had been thrown into disorder and both cavalry units had been repulsed for little or no return. They had shown courage, but also the tactical shortcomings of green troops. Although they had stoically faced a fire to which they had no reply and had seen their comrades falling about them, they had held their ground. However, seeing the repulse of the uhlans and the defeat of the hussars, they were unable to maintain their discipline and determination when ordered to conduct a demoralising retrograde movement, even though it was too much to ask of them to meet the overwhelming attack of the advancing French. In a fitting contrast, the 2nd Line, having been held in the second line for much of the battle, giving them time to acclimatise to the sight and sounds of fighting, clearly conducted a successful advance, albeit against a withdrawing enemy, despite the earlier loss of their Duke and the heavy casualties they suffered.

The contingent had contributed to a successful action and had been blooded in battle for the first time. It was not the time for a brutally honest tactical assessment of the performance of the troops; a more positive spin was required. In his report to the Privy Council, written the evening after the battle, Colonel Olfermann wrote:

> All in all, these mostly young troops have conducted themselves in the bravest manner, and even more so as they were led by the Duke himself against the enemy and by his presence he filled them with unlimited confidence.

The action at Quatre Bras showed once more that inexperienced troops do not generally lack courage or, at times, enthusiasm, but that they do lack endurance under fire. At Quatre Bras, their battlefield value lay more in the ability to occupy a piece of ground than their tactical flexibility. Their ability to manoeuvre on the battlefield is called into question by their employment and performance, although in the case of the Leib and 1st Line Battalions their ground-holding mission gave them little opportunity to do much more than provide a target for the French artillery.

Casualties at Quatre Bras

The following casualty return for Quatre Bras comes from the report of Colonel Olfermann:

The total loss at Quatre Bras was therefore twenty-seven officers and 822 soldiers; 12.5 percent of the total (although the whole contingent were not engaged). Although almost a quarter of this total were listed as 'missing', it is not possible to be sure why this was. However, for many of the contingent this was their first experience of combat and it is not unreasonable to assume that a relatively high percentage of these chose to slip away or felt obliged to help wounded friends to the rear. An unknown number no doubt rejoined their units in time to fight at Waterloo. Friedrich Cappel, an officer in the Leib Battalion, wrote after the battle, 'That night there were only 223 men left out of the 600 men from our battalion who had entered the fray; many men were missing, although some returned later.'[29] As can be seen, this does not tally with the official figures given below, but this phenomenon of a unit finishing a battle far below the strength the official casualty states is quite common during this campaign (and presumably others) among allied units, including the British.

Unit	Killed		Wounded		POW	Missing
	Officers	Men	Officers	Men		
Staff	1	-	-	-		
Hussar Regt	2	15	2	27		
Uhlan Sqn	-	4	-	10		
Horse Bty	Not	Present	-	-		
Foot Bty	Not	Present	-	-		
Avantgard Bn	-	9	4	43		
Leib Bn	-	15	5	106		
1st Light Bn	Not	Present	-	-		
2nd Light Bn	-	18	3	49		
3rd Light Bn	Not	Present	-	-		
1st Line Bn	1	16	2	86		
2nd Line Bn	2	23	4	162		
3rd Line Bn	-	4	1	19		
Total	6	104	21	502	16	200

Although Heinrich Köhler had described the casualties of the Leib and 1st Line Battalions as 'appalling', this may have appeared true to someone in his first battle, but as the casualties for both battalions across the whole battle were about 17 percent, they were well below the totals considered heavy for those times. To put this into perspective, the British 42nd (Black Watch) suffered 55 percent casualties at Quatre Bras and two other battalions of their brigade over 40 percent; all three then fought in the front line for all, or virtually all, of the battle of Waterloo.

Accounts of the fighting at Quatre Bras suggest that the Avantgarde, Leib and 1st Line Battalions were most closely engaged in the fighting and bore the brunt of the French artillery fire, and although this is generally reflected in the casualty lists, the losses suffered by the 2nd Line Battalion, who were in the second line and apparently not directly attacked, were actually the highest of any single battalion. This cannot be reconciled by either Colonel Olfermann's report or the accounts of individual officers and soldiers; indeed, in the single account from this unit, by Ensign Lindwurm, he wrote that despite the French cannister fire, 'only a small number of men were casualties.'[30] Perhaps it was from this battalion, standing largely unengaged throughout the battle, that a large proportion of the men recorded as 'missing' found the opportunity to slip away. Losses among both hussars and uhlans seem astonishingly low given the unsuccessful charges they were involved in, suggesting there may have been some reluctance to press their attacks; this is supported by the eyewitness accounts.

As night fell after the battle of Quatre Bras, the 3rd Light Battalion provided at least some of the screen in front of the allied army, as the following morning their troops were attacked by the French. This engagement was clearly more than just an exchange between the outposts as the battalion suffered one man killed and two officers and twenty-six men wounded.[31] Along with the 2nd Light Battalion they provided some of the allied army's rearguard as the rest of Wellington's army marched back to Waterloo. As these battalions withdrew themselves, they were covered by a cavalry screen and saw no further action that day, although it was at this time that Mercer came upon them and later described their apparently shaky morale.

Waterloo

On the evening of the 17th the Brunswick contingent bivouacked behind the right of the allied line with their right flank resting on the hamlet of Merbe Braine and their left on the Nivelles to Brussels *chaussée*. Their state of morale seems to have been somewhat rocky at this time and Mercer's comments give us the first clue. Their Duke had been killed the day before, two of their battalions and both cavalry units had suffered reverses, they had just taken part in a hurried retreat and now they bivouacked in heavy rain; perhaps it is unsurprising that spirits were a little low.

They remained in position in the third line during the first half of the morning of the 18th and only took up arms when the sound of artillery fire announced that the battle had started; von Herzberg's official report states that this was at eleven o'clock. Although some French overshoots reached them, they suffered no casualties.

It was only at one o'clock that the Brunswick contingent were ordered to move forwards; although the report says that they moved into the first line, they actually moved into a position on the ridge behind Hougoumont. They formed in battalion columns and appear to have filled the gap caused by the deployment of almost the whole of Byng's brigade to Hougoumont. The Avantgarde battalion was sent down into the Hougoumont 'garden', probably meaning the orchard, to support the Nassauers who were occupying it. The Leib and 1st Light Battalions also moved down in direct support, leaving the remainder of the contingent in the protection of the reverse slope of the ridge in line with British battalions to their left.[32] The Brunswick cavalry were formed up behind their infantry with the foot artillery battery deployed on the ridgeline, able to fire on the French attacking the farm and château. Although most of the Brunswick troops were sheltered behind the ridge, many French balls fell among them and the report records that casualties from these were 'significant.' Only the Avantgarde Battalion were in the front line and the report describes their defence as 'tenacious.'[33]

The Brunswick battalions were charged several times during the French cavalry attacks, but the squares stood firm and repulsed the attacks. However, Chevalié Mercer of the British horse artillery was clearly concerned that they would not hold; in his journal he famously wrote:

> These were the very boys whom I had but yesterday seen throwing away their arms, and fleeing, panic-stricken, from the very sound of our horses' feet. Today they fled not bodily, to be sure, but spiritually, for their senses seem to have left them. There they stood, with recovered arms, like so many logs, or rather like the very wooden figures which I had seen them practising at in their cantonments. Every moment I feared they would again throw down their arms and flee; but their officers and sergeants behaved nobly, not only keeping them together, but managing to keep their squares closed in spite of the carnage made amongst them.[34]

While it is generally accepted that Mercer rarely had a good word for the foreign contingents he encountered, his description of them looking uncertain at this time is endorsed by a member of the Dutch 1st Carabiniers, who described how, 'At one time his commander ordered his corps to advance to support a contingent of Brunswickers, who notwithstanding the prayers and the pleas of their officers wanted to withdraw, and which his commander had threatened to cut to pieces in German if they did not maintain their ground.'[35]

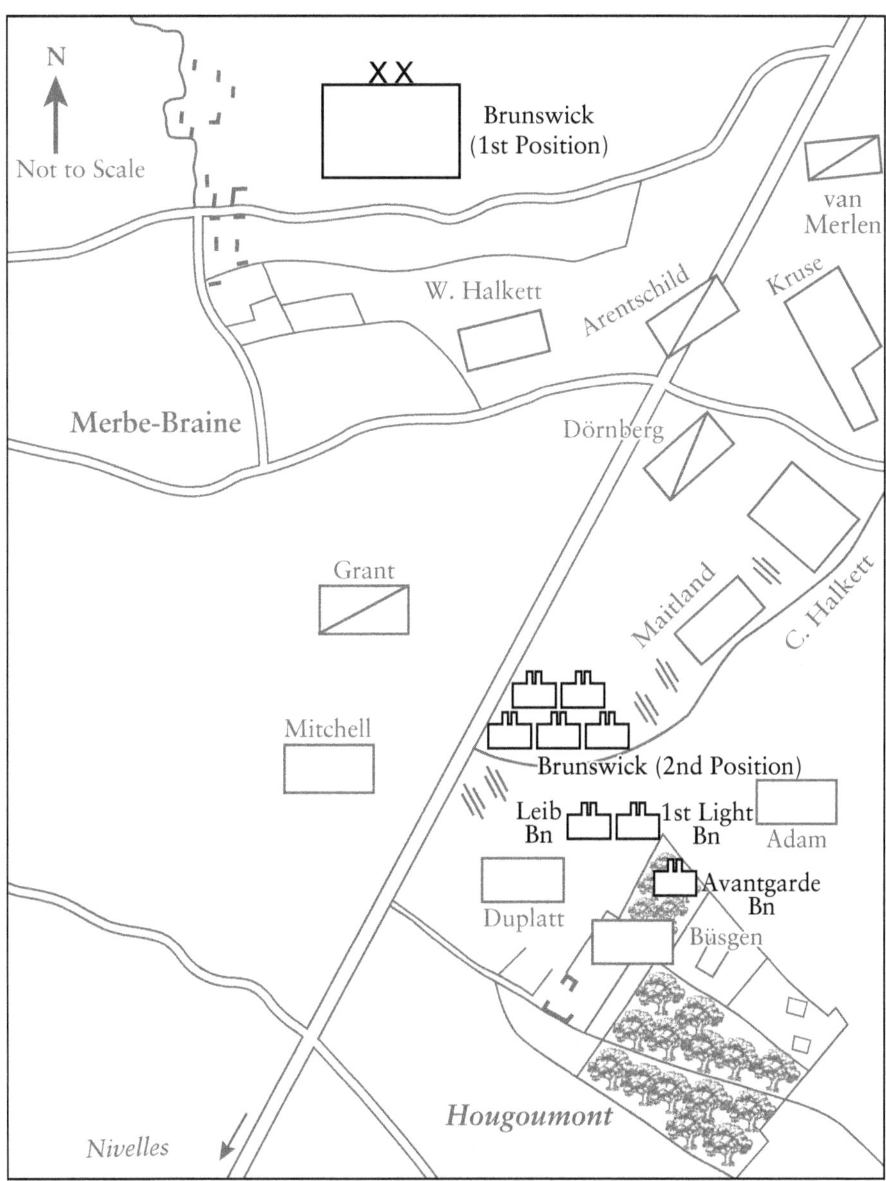

Map showing the initial deployment and second position of the Brunswick contingent at Waterloo.

Von Herzberg's report is one of the few allied accounts which specifically describes the French infantry assault of Bachelu's division and Jamin's brigade of Foy's division at the end of the great French cavalry attacks and he says that Wellington ordered the Brunswick infantry to move forward onto the crest of the ridge and form square. In his own report, Colonel Olfermann wrote:

> the Duke of Wellington ordered me to have three battalion squares advance and move over the ridge. This movement was calmly commenced by the battalions, although it was on everybody's mind that heavy cannister and infantry fire was awaiting us on the other side of the ridge. That expectation unfortunately turned out to be true enough. Hardly had we passed the ridge when entire ranks of the battalion were shot down in quick succession. The enemy soon became aware of the effectiveness of his fire and began to support the cavalry attacks with his horse artillery. It was impossible to hold out there any longer.
>
> I gave the order to return to our earlier position. Soon thereafter, we were here also most violently attacked, but at no gain to the enemy. The 2nd and 3rd Jäger [Light] Battalions and the 3rd Line Battalion stood like rocks. The Duke of Wellington was still near us, and again sent orders to advance. An attempt was made. But the enemy moved up with a stronger force, particularly in artillery, and the losses in our infantry battalions became even greater. The three just mentioned battalions nevertheless occupied repeatedly the slope on the far side of the ridge but were forced to return each time to the former position.[36]

Twenty-two-year-old Lieutenant Theodor Rudolphi was the adjutant of the 3rd Line Battalion. In a previously unpublished letter to his parents, written on 4 July 1815, he describes this action:

> It is not possible for me to describe these various attacks now. Just this much: soon we advanced with lowered bayonets. The grapeshot, bullets and bombs raged in our squares. During an advance, Ensign Kudel was shot in the leg close to my side and the blood and brains of a number of soldiers splashed into my face. We withdrew a little. English cavalry flies past us, withdraws after a short battle. French attack columns of cuirassiers and grenadiers on horseback pounced on our squares. They receive a rain of bullets as thick as hail. They rush back. We push forward again, are pushed back again, the whistling of the balls in our ranks did not cease and many men were struck. Major Normann was killed with his horse, struck in the body, and Ensign Kaiser was shot in the knee. Our soldiers fell the most.[37]

Von Herzberg's report also mentions this advance and like Olfermann, infers it was an impossible mission. To their credit, the Brunswick troops advanced as ordered, but were unable to maintain their position in the face of the French fire. Adam's British brigade were also deployed forward of the ridgeline about this time but were able to reduce casualties by using folds in the ground to give them some shelter from the fire. Whether the ground allowed the Brunswickers to do the same, but they did not choose to use it, or whether the ground was not as kind to them in their position, is unknown. Olfermann's report states 'entire files were mown down in no time at all',[38] and 'they were again forced to withdraw to their former location due to the most violent fire from the enemy.'[39]

There seems to be little information on the employment of the Brunswick artillery during the battle. Certainly, one battery was ordered forward to join the line of guns on the high ground above, and to the north, of Hougoumont, who defended that post throughout the day. Whether both batteries were employed there is not clear.

During the French cavalry charges, the Brunswick cavalry were engaged in counterattacks after their charges on the allied squares had been repulsed. It was around this time that Colonel Olfermann was wounded and forced to hand command over to the acting quartermaster general, Lieutenant Colonel von Heinemann. Several other Brunswick senior officers were also wounded. As the advantage of the fighting in the Hougoumont orchard swayed back and forth, the Leib Battalion was also deployed there and fought alongside the British guards, though no account from the guards mentions them. By this time, the action around Hougoumont had become little more than an exchange of an intense skirmish fire, with the French making no further serious attempt to capture the buildings after about 3.30pm.[40]

As Napoleon was preparing to launch his last desperate attack with part of his Guard against the centre right of the allied line, Wellington rushed to reinforce this part of the line with whatever uncommitted troops he had available. These included much of the Brunswick contingent; 'the 2nd and 3rd Light and the 1st, 2nd and 3rd Line Battalions at once marched off by the left.'[41] Von Herzberg then claims that these were followed by the battalions deployed around Hougoumont, which must be a mistake as these took part in the final allied advance by clearing through the Hougoumont area and finishing the battle there.

Having redeployed to the allied centre, von Herzberg's report describes the Brunswick contribution to meeting the final French attack of the battle:

> The corps, after arriving at the decisive point, had hardly begun to deploy and form at the proper distances when the enemy skirmishers had already climbed up the steep slope and were only a few paces away from the troops. Their unexpected nearness, the all-enveloping dense clouds of powder smoke, the men's exhaustion, the partial disorder of the still incomplete deployment and, lastly, the powerful thrust of the attack caused several battalions to hesitate at first and fall back a little. However, the 3rd Line Battalion under Major von Normann quickly formed up again, took a stand against the enemy and received him with such well-directed fire that he ceased his advance. By virtue of the officers' strong efforts, the other battalions had fallen in again,

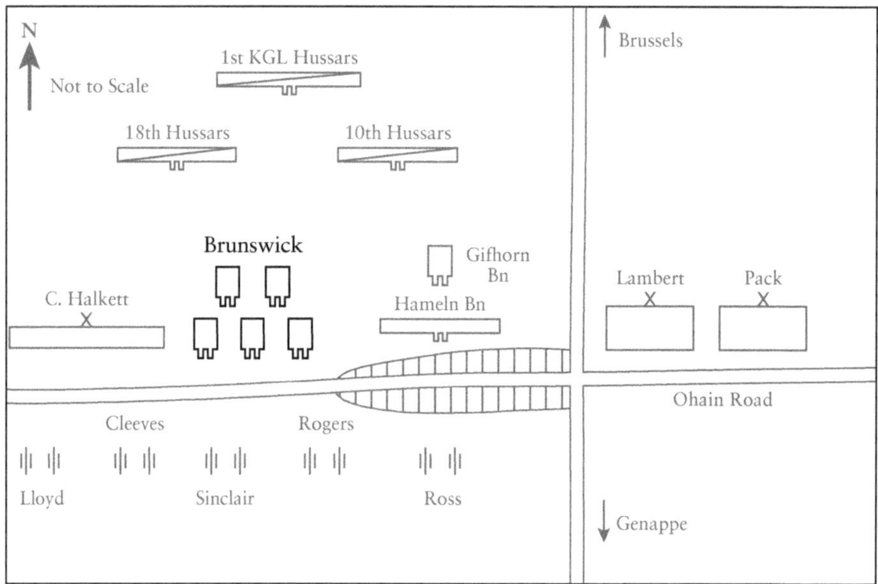

Map showing the deployment of the Brunswick infantry on the attack of the French Imperial Guard.

> closed up, and, together with the Netherlands Aubremé Brigade [this should read Detmer's brigade] and the Nassau brigade [the 1st Nassau Regiment], advanced upon the enemy. This, as well as the murderous fire of the English artillery, a few splendid charges by the English cavalry under Lord Uxbridge, and the powerful forward pressing of the Prussians forced the enemy to retreat. This turned into a total rout, as the army now moved forward at all points.[42]

It is interesting that the report does not mention the Imperial Guard by name, although we can be sure that this is the attack of which he speaks. In the above paragraph, he admits that the Brunswick battalions were forced to fall back; the Nassauers also admit that their attempt to counterattack the French Guard ended in failure and that they were also pushed back, although without joining the final advance as von Herzberg suggests the Brunswickers did.

The claim that it was Brunswick fire that stopped the Guard and that they subsequently took part in the final advance is uncorroborated and flies in the face of the many other allied accounts of this specific phase of the battle. See Appendix E for a more in-depth look at the contribution of the allied contingents to the repulse of the Guard.

The other battalions of the contingent (the Avantgarde, Leib and 1st Light Battalions), which were deployed around Hougoumont, took part in the final advance through the orchards and woods around the château and farm, clearing it of the remaining Frenchmen who had not yet joined the rout of the rest of the army. An officer of the 4th Line KGL also comments on the Brunswick cavalry taking part in the pursuit.[43]

Von Herzberg's report states that after the repulse of the Guard, the Brunswick battalions advanced along the Charleroi road and met Prussian troops near la Belle Alliance. Around ten o'clock they bivouacked near the hamlet of Maison du Roi, about a kilometre further on.

Losses at Waterloo

Unit	Killed		Wounded		Missing
	Officers	Men	Officers	Men	
Staff	1	-	4	-	
Hussar Regt	1	27	5	45	
Uhlan Sqn	-	-	2	13	
Horse Battery	1	2	-	6	
Foot Battery	-	-	-	18	
Avantgarde Bn	-	7	1	20	
Leib Bn	-	14	1	36	
1st Light Bn	-	4	3	41	
2nd Light Bn	2	37	2	73	
3rd Light Bn	1	35	5	75	
1st Line Bn	-	9	-	46	
2nd Line Bn	1	2	1	6	
3rd Line Bn	-	10	2	51	
Total	7	147	26	430	50

The Brunswick losses at Waterloo, taking into account those lost at Quatre Bras, represent approximately 11 percent; actually lower than at Quatre Bras, despite the whole of the contingent being present. However, the latter figures include the 200 men that were reported as missing at that battle, many of whom may have rejoined their battalions.

The Brunswick Hussar Regiment get little mention during the battle, and yet they took relatively heavy casualties. As their only action seems to have been in counter-charging the French cavalry during the latter's charges, it is quite possible that, as light cavalry, they struggled to impose upon the powerful men and horses of the French cuirassiers. Even Lord Uxbridge, commander of the allied cavalry, admitted, '[Our] light cavalry was not always successful.'[44]

The 2nd Line Battalion appear to have taken very few casualties despite having taken part in the advance down the forward slope which the Brunswick report records took heavy casualties. We have also seen that the von Herzberg report states that the Avantgarde Battalion fought in the grounds of Hougoumont; however, their level of casualties suggest they were not heavily engaged, particularly when their casualties are compared with the British guards battalions which also fought there.

The difference in the numbers recorded as missing in each of the two battles is interesting. It is quite possible that those whose heart was not in the fight (or on a battlefield) had disappeared during Quatre Bras, and thus there were fewer men inclined to go missing at Waterloo. It may also be true that many had returned and that having had their first experience of battle and survived, some were more willing to stand firm the second time.

The Brunswick contingent had not spent the whole battle in the thick of the fight and we can be quite sure that Wellington had no intention of them doing so after their rather traumatic introduction to battle at Quatre Bras. Wellington had kept them back in the third line, away from the worst of the French artillery fire, until they were needed. There, they did not operate as a single division but were split into two components; one that operated around and in support of Hougoumont and another in facing down the French cavalry attacks. We can speculate that this allowed each of them to operate with more experienced troops, and Wellington may have calculated that he had more freedom to do this after the death of the Duke at Quatre Bras. Under intense fire when ordered forward of the ridge, they were driven back twice, but however well-founded Mercer's suspicions of their staying power in the face of the French cavalry charges, they stood their ground courageously. They appear to have played down their involvement and repulse during the attack of Napoleon's Old Guard at the end of the battle by not mentioning the Guard at all; however, whether it was actually the Guard or men of d'Erlon's 1st Corps advancing from la Haye-Sainte that drove them back is unclear.

Conclusion

The truth is that the Brunswick contingent had a traumatic campaign; thrown straight into the front line at Quatre Bras, lacking the support of their artillery, the two battalions stood heroically under heavy fire without the means to retaliate. It is little surprise that their cavalry's attempt to cover their withdrawal was overwhelmed and their infantry broken. The loss of Duke Friedrich Wilhelm must have had a stunning impact on their morale. Many appear to have absconded. Wellington tried to shield them at Waterloo by initially holding them back in the third line, sheltered from the French artillery until they were needed. Drawn forward to a position behind Hougoumont, their squares held impressively against the French cavalry attacks, despite what Mercer has to say. This was probably the highlight of their battle. Their attempts to advance were then inevitably thrown back and their move to shore up the centre towards the end of the battle also resulted in their repulse.

Despite evidence of inexperience and rocky morale, the Brunswickers were not lacking in courage; they serve as a prime example of the limitations of young and inexperienced troops. It is impossible to judge how the loss of their Duke affected their performance at Waterloo. Despite Mercer's disparaging recollections, it is telling that despite their reverses they seem to have maintained the respect of their allies, and the efforts of their officers to keep their men at their duty were much admired.

Chapter Four
The Hanoverian Contingent

'The landwehr stood like lions.'[1]

Background

Hanover had been a principality within the Holy Roman Empire before being elevated to an electorate in 1708. Its close ties with Britain dated from when the Elector of Hanover, George Louis of the House of Hanover, became King George I in 1714. Although the two states were joined as a Personal Union – two states with the same monarch – their armies and foreign policy remained separate. However, even before this, Britain and Hanover had enjoyed close ties and Hanoverian troops had fought alongside the British under Marlborough's command. After the breakdown of the Treaty of Amiens between Britain and France in 1803, Hanover was occupied by French and Prussian troops and after Napoleon's victory over the Prussians in 1806 the Treaty of Tilsit laid down that it was to be incorporated into the satellite Kingdom of Westphalia the following year. Many Hanoverians fled and made their way to Britain to continue the fight against the French. The state of Hanover was only restored after Napoleon was forced out of northern Germany after the battle of Leipzig in 1813. After Napoleon's first abdication, the Congress of Vienna elevated the former electorate to an independent kingdom, with its Prince-Elector, George III of Britain, as its king. The new kingdom also saw an expansion of its territory, becoming the fourth-largest state in the German Confederation behind Prussia, Austria and Bavaria.

Hanover immediately began to raise a new army, regular units at first, but soon followed by a militia, or landwehr, early in 1814. But Hanover's most famous military contribution to the Napoleonic Wars was the King's German Legion (KGL), raised from those Hanoverian exiles who had fled the electorate when it was dissolved by the French. Units of the KGL fought as part of the British army throughout the Peninsular War and in the various British expeditions in the Baltic and Mediterranean. It had soon proved itself in combat and was eventually seen as the equal of British troops. It was fully incorporated into the British army. The new Hanoverian army advanced into the Netherlands in 1814.

Contingent size

A Hanoverian subsidiary corps had remained in the Netherlands from the end of hostilities in 1814, but these had been augmented under the leadership of General von der Decken to a total of eight regular battalions and fourteen landwehr battalions, as well as three cavalry regiments and two artillery batteries, although not all of these were to fight at Waterloo. However, when calculating the contribution of Hanover to Wellington's army it should be borne in mind that the King's German Legion were also Hanoverian and when they are taken into account, the Hanoverian contribution to Wellington's army was second only to the British, and greater than the Netherlands (although the Netherlands army was considerably larger in total, it was also responsible for defending the full extent of their frontiers and the major fortresses and cities).

As a sizeable force, and with a number of senior officers that had served with the British army in the Peninsula, many in the contingent hoped to serve as a full Hanoverian corps. However, as many of the battalions were militia units with few experienced officers or soldiers, Wellington had no intention of allowing this, despite the blow to morale this generated. While he could not incorporate the inexperienced Brunswick or Nassau contingents into British divisions, because of the British links with Hanover, he could do this with the Hanoverian formations. Thus a Hanoverian brigade was attached to each of the 3rd, 4th, 5th and 6th British divisions, although at Waterloo, the 6th Division not being fully present, the 4th Hanoverian Brigade (that of Colonel Best) was attached to the 5th Division and fought next to its sister brigade, the 5th (von Vincke).

The Hanoverian contingent present at the start of the campaign was as follows.

1st Hanoverian Brigade: 3,315 – Maj-Gen Friedrich Count Kielmansegge
Duke of York's (Osnabrück) 1st Field Battalion (Major Baron Bülow) (632)
Grubenhagen Field Battalion (Lt Col Friedrich von Wurmb) (643)
Bremen Field Battalion (Lt Col Wilhelm Langrehr) (533)
Verden Field Battalion (Maj Julius von Schkopp) (559)
Lüneburg Field Battalion (Lt Col August von Klencke) (617)
2xcoys Field Jäeger (331)

3rd Hanoverian Brigade: 2,541 – Col Hugh Halkett
Bremenvörde Landwehr Battalion (Lieutenant Colonel Friedrich von der Schulenburg) (655)
Osnabrück Landwehr Battalion (Major Ludwig Graf von Münster) (633)
Quackenbrück Landwehr Battalion (Major Clamor Wilhelm von dem Bussche-Hunefeld) (609)

Salzgitter Landwehr Battalion (Major Friedrich von Hammerstein) (644)

4th Hanoverian Brigade: 2,669 – Colonel Carl Best
Verden Landwehr Battalion (Maj Christoph von der Decken) (642)
Lüneberg Landwehr Battalion (Lt Col Ludwig von Ramdohr) (647)
Münden Landwehr Battalion (Maj Ferdinand von Schmidt) (680)
Osterode Landwehr Battalion (Maj Claus von Reden) (700)

5th Hanoverian Brigade: 2,604 – Colonel Ernst von Vincke
Gifhorn Landwehr Battalion (Maj Georg von Hammerstein) (640)
Hameln Landwehr Battalion (Maj Julius von Strube) (689)
Hildesheim Landwehr Battalion (Maj Georg von Rheden) (640)
Peine Landwehr Battalion (Maj Ludolf Graf von Westphalen) (635)

Duke of Cumberland's Hussars: (Colonel Adolf von Hake) 516
Artillery: 475
Rettberg's Company (attached to the 5th Division (Picton)): 5x9 pounders, 1x5½ -inch howitzer.
Braun's Company (attached to 5th Division): 5x9 pounders, 1x5½ -inch howitzer.

Total: 12,120 (18 percent of 68,000)

There was a further Hanoverian infantry brigade (the 6th) and two regiments of Hanoverian cavalry (the Prince Regent's and the Bremen and Verden Hussars), which formed part of the 4th British Division, and which, with the 1st Netherlands Division and the Dutch Indian Brigade, were detached from the main army to cover the approach to Brussels from Mons in the area around Hal and Tubize.

But this was not all the Hanoverian troops deployed to the Netherlands; there was also a Reserve Corps. This corps, under command of Lieutenant General von der Decken, was composed of newly formed battalions that were not yet fit to take the field; they were used as garrison troops in Belgium and totalled around 9,000 men.

The leaders

Lieutenant General Sir Karl Alten was the senior Hanoverian officer at Waterloo and commanded the 3rd British Division. He was born in Hanover but fled after the French and Prussian invasion of 1803 and joined the KGL. He campaigned in Copenhagen, Sweden, in the Walcheren expedition and in the Peninsula. He fought at Albuera as a brigade commander and even commanded the famous Light Division between 1812 and 1814. He was sent to the British force in the Netherlands in 1814, but although the fighting was over, he remained with the

British forces there which were to form the nucleus of Wellington's army in 1815. He was wounded at Waterloo and forced to hand over command to Major-General Kielmansegge.

Major General Count Friedrich Kielmansegge was a member of a distinguished Hanoverian family. At Waterloo he commanded the 1st Hanoverian Brigade of the 3rd British Division and took over command of the division when von Alten was wounded. He originally joined the army of Hessen-Cassel in 1793 and fought in the campaign in the Netherlands. He fell ill and withdrew from the army. In 1803 he entered the army of Brunswick-Lüneburg, but his short service came to an end with the 1803 Convention of Artlenburg, the surrender of Hanover to the French army, which signalled the dissolution of Hanover and its occupation by the French. Withdrawing to the family estate, he did not serve again until, in the wake of Prussia's re-entry into the war against France, the eastern areas of Hanover also rose against Napoleon in 1813. He volunteered his services and was appointed colonel, raising a corps of jägers, the *Korps der Kielmannseggeschen Jäger*, at his personal expense. He commanded his jägers against the French in Mecklenburg and Lüneburg, including at the battle of Göhrde, as well as the defence and then siege of Hamburg. He then moved to the Netherlands, but the fighting there was over and his unit was disbanded in 1814, although the men were later used as the core of the newly raised Field Jäger Corps. Kielmannsegge was promoted to major general in 1815 and appointed to command the 1st Hanoverian Brigade, which he led at Quatre Bras and Waterloo. Although he had some service prior to 1803 and in 1813–14, he had no previous experience of brigade command on a major battlefield and his experiences of the latest tactics and procedures must be considered limited.

Colonel Hugh Halkett was the brother of Sir Colin Halkett and commanded the 3rd Hanoverian Brigade in the 2nd British Division at Waterloo. He was born in Scotland and had served initially in the British army, into which he was commissioned aged just eleven. He served as a lieutenant in India from 1798–1801 but joined the KGL in 1803 to join his brother who was in the 2nd Light Battalion. He served in the Baltic and North Germany in 1807–08 before moving to Spain, from where he was evacuated after fighting at Corunna. He then served during the Walcheren expedition before joining the 2nd Light Battalion KGL in the Peninsula in 1811, fighting at Albuera (in von Alten's brigade), Salamanca and the siege of Burgos (the latter two as commanding officer). After returning sick to Britain, in 1813–14 he transferred to the new Hanoverian army and served as a brigade commander with Wallmoden's corps in Germany against the French and Danes, fighting at the battle of Göhrde, and finally entered the Netherlands. Commanding his brigade at Waterloo, he is probably best known for the capture of General Cambronne, when the Osnabrück Battalion of his brigade engaged the French Imperial Guard at the end of the battle. He was clearly an officer who thrived in combat, distinguishing himself on many battlefields, but proved less enthusiastic seeing to his duties when not on campaign. His divisional commander during the Waterloo campaign was General Clinton, a general with a penchant for inspections and exercises and a keen eye for detail. Clinton's reports were less than complimentary about Halkett; writing after his inspection of the Osnabrück Landwehr Battalion, he commented 'their equipment was in good order… but anything which depended upon the commander of the brigade has been entirely neglected, this battalion is no more expert in their movements than it was when I saw it last…'[2] And it appears things had not improved when Clinton later wrote to his brother, 'Since I last wrote to you I have been very busily employed in striving to get my division in some order, I have two excellent men in Adam [3rd British Brigade] and du Plat [1st KGL Brigade] at the head of two of my brigades, the Hanoverians are not so well commanded by Colonel Halkett, a zealous man would have perfected them, but under him they have made no progress in the last seven months…'.[3]

One wonders if Clinton changed his opinion after Waterloo.

Colonel Carl Best was an experienced KGL officer and commanded the 4th Hanoverian Brigade (part of the 6th British Division but attached to the 5th during the campaign) at Waterloo. He was born in Hanover and after time as a cadet he was commissioned into the 15th Hanoverian Infantry Regiment Prinz Friedrich in 1781. He went with his regiment to India and was wounded at the siege of Cuddalore (1783) fighting with the British against the French. Returning to Europe, he served as a captain in the 12th Hanoverian Regiment. In 1803 he was promoted to major in the 2nd Light Battalion of the KGL and served with them in the Baltic in 1807 before moving to the Peninsula. Evacuated after Corunna, he fought during the abortive Walcheren expedition. In 1812 he was promoted to lieutenant colonel in the 8th Line Battalion KGL and served with them in northern Germany. In March 1814 he was promoted colonel commanding the Münden Landwehr battalion until appointed to command the 4th Hanoverian Brigade in 1815.

Colonel Ernst von Vincke commanded the 5th Hanoverian Brigade (of Picton's 5th British Division) at Waterloo. He was born in the small German state of Berg and educated at a military school in Strasburg. He was commissioned into the Hanoverian Leibgarde Regiment (a cavalry regiment) in 1784. Promoted captain ten years later he campaigned in the Revolutionary wars in the Netherlands (1793–95) and northern Germany. After the French occupation of Hanover in 1803 his regiment was disbanded, and he left the army. He did not serve again until 13 March 1814, a gap of eleven years, when he became colonel of the Hanoverian Regiment Herzog von York (Field Battalion Osnabrück), serving with them in the Netherlands in 1814 and 1815 when he was made the commander of the 5th Hanoverian Brigade.

The commanders of the four Hanoverian brigades therefore had widely different breadths of experience, reflecting the shortage of experienced senior officers in the newly re-established state. To give at least two of the brigades experienced commanders, Halkett and Best were attached from the King's German Legion. Both Kielmansegge and von Vincke had long gaps in their military service, and one wonders how they coped with embracing the tremendous evolution of warfare that had taken place over the ten or so years of almost continuous campaigning that they had missed during their sabbaticals; no doubt highlighted by many of their junior officers having fought throughout that period in one army or another. Kielmansegge's appointment to command the brigade of regular units was based purely on seniority and once appointed it would have been surprising for Hanover to have allowed him to be superseded in command by a more junior, but more experienced, officer from the KGL.

This disparity or lack of experience was even more pronounced in the commanding officers of the Hanoverian battalions. This is well illustrated by the commanding officers of the battalions of Hugh Halkett's 3rd Hanoverian Brigade. Lieutenant Colonel Friedrich von der Schulenburg, commander of the Bremenvörde Landwehr Battalion, was the only commanding officer of the four in the brigade that had *any* previous military experience at all, having served some time with the Prussian Guard. More representative was the commanding officer of the Salzgitter Landwehr Battalion, about whom Clinton wrote, 'The commanding officer Major Hammerstein seems very little acquainted with his business.'[4] Clinton's impatience with the inexperienced commanding officers in his brigade features in his correspondence, but with the need to recruit, train, equip and administer over 600 men, this lack of any experience must have made it a huge challenge, even putting aside the need to command them on campaign and make significant tactical decisions on the battlefield.

Perhaps unsurprisingly, the most experienced commanding officers were to be found in Kielmansegge's 1st Hanoverian Brigade, which contained all the regular units (those recruited from volunteers in the early months after the re-establishment of Hanover as an independent state after the ousting of the French). Two (Langrehr and von Klencke) had experience in the late eighteenth-century Hanoverian army, both of whom later joined the KGL and got further experience under British command. Another (von Wurmb) joined the KGL and had four years' experience before retiring, and another (von Schkopp) served with the Brunswick Oels in Spain for four years before leaving to join the new Hanoverian army. Only one commanding officer appears to have had no previous military experience at all (Major von Bülow of the Duke of York's (Osnabrück) Battalion).

Of the eight commanding officers in the 4th and 5th Brigades, three (von der Decken, G. von Hammerstein and von Westphalen) have no recorded previous military experience at all, and three (von Ramdohr, von Reden and von Strube), had military experience with the Hanoverian army that ended in 1803 and had not served again until 1814. One (von Rheden) had previous service with both the Hanoverian and Prussian service, while Major von Schmidt, commanding the Münden Battalion, had the most varied experience of them all, having served in the Dutch navy, the Prussian army, the Westphalian army and finally the Hanoverian Kielmansegge's jägercorps.[5]

None of these officers had any previous campaign or combat experience commanding a battalion. Commanding officers in most armies would have worked their way up through the officer ranks, learning their responsibilities, and hopefully gaining operational experience, along the way. They would thus be able to train and supervise the younger officers below them, while preparing themselves for the next step up the chain of command. An inexperienced commanding officer would normally lean heavily on more experienced subordinates in key positions in the battalion, but in the fledgling Hanoverian army these too were lacking. The one commodity that was available was time; the new regiments had been formed during 1814, so many had been in existence for many months before the campaign opened, and significantly, many battalions had been in the Netherlands for more than six months and had therefore had time to complete their equipment and train under the supervision and direction of senior British officers. Some of the regular (field) battalions did have some limited combat and campaigning experience from 1813 and 1814.

At subaltern level, the problem was not so much that the officers had no experience, even in uniform, as this was to be expected of junior officers, but the fact that there were too few of them; the battalions did not have their full establishment. This was exacerbated not only by the shortage of experienced Non-Commissioned Officers (NCOs), but also by the fact that under the German system, it was officers, rather than the NCOs, as it was in the British army, that were responsible for teaching soldiers their drill. One of the first requirements was to train the officers to know and understand their responsibilities in both the administration and care of their soldiers and their instruction (drill); but this could not be done if they were not there to train. The shortage of officers in the Hanoverian battalions features repeatedly in senior officer correspondence of the time; even Wellington wrote, 'The whole of the Hanoverian contingent is deficient in officers, and it is very desirable that measures should be taken to remedy this evil immediately.'[6]

We shall see later how Wellington was keen to augment the manpower of the KGL by encouraging Hanoverian landwehr soldiers to volunteer to transfer from their units into the KGL, but the rejection of this idea led to a solution to the problem of Hanoverian battalions having insufficient officers. General Clinton had proposed an option in April 1815 when he wrote:

> It seems that some arrangement here, advantageous to our cause might be made for drafting some of the battalions of Hanoverians

> into the Legion, or else forming the Legion of three battalions and applying the officers of the other five battalions to the Hanoverian army, the great deficiency of which is in officers and these are deficient no less in numbers, than in expertise, if however measures of this kind be not resorted to we shall miss an opportunity of doubling the number of our officers...[7]

In fact, by reducing the establishment of the KGL battalions, from five to eight officers were freed up from each battalion and posted to each of the landwehr battalions, often with promotion. This meant that each landwehr company received at least one experienced officer; a considerable enhancement. Drawing officers from the KGL was a good compromise, as not only did the landwehr battalions get a full complement of officers, but the officers (and NCOs) that they received from the KGL also provided them with a firm backbone of campaign and combat experience, which must have proved invaluable to the commanding officers and company commanders of the battalions that received them. Clinton was of the opinion that without this influx of experience and expertise, the Hanoverians were 'hardly in [a] state to take the field...'.[8]

It wasn't just relatively junior officers that were taken from the Legion; given the lack of experienced Hanoverian senior officers, as we have seen, two of the Hanoverian brigade commanders, colonels Halkett and Best, were also drawn from battalion command in the KGL.

Although the Hanoverian artillery branch was small, providing just two batteries for the army, both the battery commanders, Karl von Rettberg and Wilhelm Braun, were very experienced ex-KGL battery commanders. Both had campaigned for long periods in the Peninsula; Rettberg had been present at Talavera, Busaco and Badajoz, while Braun had fought with Portuguese units.

The only Hanoverian cavalry unit at Waterloo was the Duke of Cumberland Hussars, an all-volunteer unit. It was commanded by Lieutenant Colonel Adolph von Hake, who had joined the KGL 1st Dragoons in 1804, reached the rank of captain and campaigned in Hanover in 1805 and the expedition to the Baltic in 1807–08 before retiring in 1809. He re-entered Hanoverian service in 1813 with the rank of major before taking command of the Cumberland Hussars as lieutenant colonel. The second in command, Major de Meltzing, had eight years of service and it is likely that other officers had also previously served. It appears that von Hake was not trusted by his officers, and it probably came as no surprise to many that he was to earn infamy at Waterloo.

From the brigade command level to the most recently commissioned ensign, the officers of the Hanoverian contingent had the full range of experience from considerable to none. While Wellington could have been content that the regular field battalions could be depended on, given their experiences over the previous eighteen months, the large number of inexperienced recruits in the landwehr battalions, even if of high quality, needed strong leadership to make them truly combat effective. The lack of experienced brigade and battalion commanders was clearly a worry to Wellington, who did what he could to bring a campaign-hardened core of middle-ranked officers to each of the landwehr battalions by posting in the surplus officers from the KGL. This relative lack of experience, particularly in the battalion commanders, was to manifest itself in some significant incidents at Waterloo.

The troops

The Hanoverian army had been disbanded after the French occupation in 1803 and was only resurrected in 1813 as the French hold on Hanover was loosened by the arrival of Cossacks preceding the allied armies pushing the French from northern Germany. The first battalions raised were regular units (Field Battalions) and formed from volunteers recruited in the initial enthusiasm of the uprising against the French. These regular units, some of which were to make up the 1st Hanoverian Brigade at Waterloo, had therefore been in existence for nearly two years prior to the 1815 campaign opening. These were therefore quite experienced troops; the Lüneburg and Bremen battalions, as well as Kielmansegge's Jägers (which later formed the core of the Field Jäger Corps), had all fought at the battle of Göhrde and along with the Grubenhagen and Osnabrück battalions had further campaign experience in northern Germany and the Netherlands. All were part of the Hanoverian Subsidiary Corps, which had remained in the Netherlands after Napoleon's abdication.

Early in 1814 thirty battalions of militia (landwehr) were raised, drawing on volunteers and conscripts, and requiring all former members of the Hanoverian army to return to duty. In February 1815 each field battalion was linked to three landwehr battalions to form a regiment, although on campaign each battalion remained an independent entity. Not all these battalions formed part of Wellington's army.

The battalions raised in 1813 seem to have all been classified as light battalions, but as the army grew in size and reorganised, particularly with the raising of landwehr battalions, only two light battalions were officially designated: the Lüneburg and Grubenhagen battalions. The uniforms of all the Hanoverian battalions were British in style as some drew their uniforms from KGL depots and many more were sent over from Britain. The two light battalions and the Field Jäger Corps were dressed in green like the British rifle battalions. However, the other field battalions that had also worn green uniforms when they were raised as light troops were to be re-uniformed in red. However, it is unclear if this transformation was complete before the campaign opened and it is possible that there was a mix of uniforms within the battalions. It is clear that the senior British chain of command wanted the Hanoverian troops in red, General Clinton writing, 'their being clothed in red is something…'. Wellington too was keen for them to be in red, but we can only speculate why this should be; perhaps it was an effort to present a higher proportion of the army as British, or to raise morale by making them feel a more integral part of the army, uniformed like the experienced troops. Although the Hanoverians used the British black cockade, officers wore yellow sashes in place of the British crimson, and some Hanoverian troops, certainly the Bremen Battalion, had British knapsacks painted yellow.

During their time in the Netherlands the Hanoverian contingent were organised into a Hanoverian corps with their own national chain of command. However, Napoleon's sudden landing in France and his seizure of power presented the prospect of a quick return to hostilities that was probably inconceivable before this dramatic turn of events. The situation needed a quick assessment of how the force gathering in the Netherlands should be organised for war. General Clinton wrote to Horse Guards:

> the…infantry of which this army is composed, consist more than one half of the Hanoverian levies and although these are excellent materials for forming an army, weak as they are in officers of any experience, they certainly are not in a state to take the field as a separate corps. The most advantageous manner of putting this infantry together appears to be, by forming the divisions, of a brigade of British, one of the Legion and one of Hanoverians, but as so large a proportion of British are now necessarily employed in Antwerp and Ostend, the divisions will consist of a considerable majority of Hanoverians. In the present state of the Hanoverians, they would not, without injury to the consistency of the army, bear to form more than one third, the divisions ought therefore to consist of two brigades of British, and one of Hanoverians, at least for the present such a disposition seems indispensable.[9]

Given Clinton's experience under Wellington in the Peninsula, there is little doubt that he had a good understanding of what Wellington would have wanted; in the Peninsula, the Duke attached a Portuguese brigade to some of his British divisions in order to have them operate with experienced and dependable troops. It was not difficult to predict that given his inability to do this with the Nassau and Brunswick contingents, he would certainly have wanted to achieve it with the inexperienced Hanoverian landwehr battalions.

It is interesting to consider why the Hanoverians did not choose to include a mix of regular and landwehr battalions within a brigade to the same end; the Netherlands were to do this in their own brigades. This was presumably a Hanoverian decision, and it may have been considered that it would have been a step too far to reorganise the brigades as well as reassigning them to different divisions; after all, they had had the time to establish a rapport with the brigade commander, brigade staff and the other units in the formation.

The attaching of Hanoverian brigades to British divisions was to go ahead in April (1815) and it appears that although the reasons for the move were understood, it was still a bitter blow to Hanoverian morale, as Captain Jacobi of the Lüneburg Field Battalion described:

> Regrettably, we Hanoverians soon lost much of our willingness to serve and of our feelings of pride in our independent status, although hopefully not our courage. By the terms of a General Order from the duke [Wellington] of 26th April, the Hanoverian brigades were assigned to various English divisions. Until now, the so-called Subsidiary Corps had existed as a separate corps… under the command of Lieutenant General von Alten. This status was eliminated with the stroke of a pen; we no longer would appear on the battlefield as Hanoverians; we were now individual components of English divisions. Lieutenant General von Alten was still a kind of commander in chief of the Hanoverian troops; but this was only in relation to internal matters (organisation, recruiting, advancement, equipment, higher judiciary etc.). With regard to the order of battle, discipline and provisions, the troops were completely subordinated to their English divisional commanders.
>
> ...here were substantial military considerations that justified this step; the Hanoverian troop complement had only recently been organised; only the field battalions formed in 1813 had proven themselves in battle; and the numerous Landwehr (15 battalions) had no experience. This would, of course, explain the Duke's point of view of the desirability to provide these new units with an example and a firm support by their close attachment to the old and battle tested English regiments. General von Alten assured me later on several occasions that he could not have assumed the responsibility to object to this decision once it was made. To us at least it was a severe blow to our morale. The English generals were totally unfamiliar with the traditions of the Hanoverians; they were therefore unable to appreciate their good dispositions and to connect to the German soldiers' nature. In their eyes, everything was imperfect, even open to criticism that did not conform to English concerns and institutions.[10]

There was another attempt to make the Hanoverian landwehr battalions more resilient which has already been touched on: after the end of the Peninsular War, the King's German Legion that had served in Spain and southern France marched north to the Netherlands to join the other KGL units that were being concentrated there. It was expected that the Legion would be disbanded now that the wars against Napoleon were over. Many soldiers had already left, especially those who were not Hanoverian by birth and had been recruited from the prisoner of war camps or deserted their own units on campaign. This, and the end of recruitment, had left the Legion's units very much understrength in soldiers, although the long-serving and professional officers and NCOs had remained to go through the formal disbandment process. The return of Napoleon had therefore left the battalions and regiments well below their established strength, but their combat experience and numbers still represented a vital resource for the British to try and meet their obligations under the Treaty of Chaumont, which committed the signatory nations to providing a force of 150,000 men each. It was of particular concern for the British army to bring the KGL back up to strength to be able to use their invaluable combat experience in the coming struggle.

The Hanoverian forces were initially under the supervision of General von Alten, who proposed that due to the inexperience of the newly formed units, the recruits should be permitted to volunteer into the King's German Legion to bring their battalions up to strength. Wellington, knowing the value of these units, was quick to support the idea, writing to Earl Bathurst from Brussels on 13 April 1815:

> My Lord,
>
> I enclose a plan for augmenting the numbers in the battalions of the King's German Legion serving with this army.
>
> If His Majesty's Government should approve of augmenting their numbers, no plan can be better than that proposed [drawing volunteers from the Hanoverian contingent], as it will give an immediate increase of good men, and the expense will be limited in amount and in duration of time.
>
> It is necessary, however, that the consent of the Government of Hanover should be obtained to the transfer of the men from the Hanoverian army to the Legion…[11]

Unfortunately for Wellington, the Hanoverian government turned down the proposal and even Wellington acknowledged that the Hanoverian units would object to their men being posted into the KGL. Wellington also admitted that such a plan would take time to implement effectively, just as it seemed that operations would soon begin. Although he was convinced that transferring Hanoverian soldiers into the KGL was the most effective use of the available manpower, he was finally forced to offer an alternative:

To the Prince Regent, dated Ostend, 17th April 1815.

> There remains then, only one scheme; and that is, to reduce the numbers of companies in each battalion of the Legion to the number of six, and to send the officers and non-commissioned officers of the companies reduced to do duty with the Landwehr, which want officers, still keeping their British pay till finally discharged from His Majesty's service.[12]

Wellington had been forced to accept that he would not be able to supplement the KGL units, but the advantage would be that the officer shortage in the landwehr battalions would be made good with competent and experienced officers.

It was originally planned that the regular Hanoverian battalions were to have eight companies, but manpower shortages led this to be reduced to six. The landwehr battalions were also to have six, but a similar shortage of recruits led this to be reduced to only four, lacking the light and grenadier companies employed by many other nations. In the absence of a light company, skirmishers (*schützen*) were drawn from within the companies, every twelfth man being so trained. When in line, the battalion theoretically formed in three ranks, but when the *schützen* were deployed, the weakened third rank was formed up behind the battalion to provide a reserve, leaving the line only two deep. This was a significant departure from British methods and caused some concern; General Clinton, commander of the British 2nd Division wrote in a report that the Hanoverians in his division:

> contain materials for forming a fine army but they have everything to learn, the circumstance of their having a system of exercise completely different from that of the British army is attended with great inconvenience and will prevent the two armies from moving in the field with that precision which is desirable in all cases and in some circumstances to avoid confusion.[13]

Clinton was later to remark that a lack of common drill regulations not only presented the problem of operating together, but also prevented experienced British officers and NCOs helping to train the newly raised and inexperienced Hanoverian battalions.

Our understanding of the young Hanoverian units of the landwehr has been greatly increased by the correspondence of General Clinton. Clinton had been posted out to the Netherlands to act as the second in command of the forces gathering there under command of the Prince of Orange. As such he oversaw the concentration and training of the various contingents and acted as an inspecting officer, as well as trying to curtail the excesses of the prince. He was later to be nominated as the commander of the 2nd British Division, a division that included the 3rd Hanoverian Brigade commanded by Hugh Halkett. Although perhaps overly demanding and a stickler for the minutiae of regulations, Clinton has given us a detailed study of the Hanoverian units under his command, and we can safely assume that they were representative of all the Hanoverian landwehr battalions.

In his various communications and inspection reports Clinton's key messages are repeated over and again. The initial impression he had of the Hanoverian units was that the level of training was low, but the quality of the manpower was high and, although young, and in some cases very young, the men were keen to learn and clearly wanted to do their best. This willingness to improve soon reaped benefits and although there is little doubt that General Clinton was not a popular man in the 2nd Division, it is also without doubt that it was thanks to his attention to detail and determination to train his units that the capabilities of the Hanoverian troops improved exponentially, and his later reports display the progress made by the battalions under his command. Indeed, Clinton predicted that, with a little more time, the Hanoverian landwehr would equal the KGL troops.

His later concerns remained the lack of experience among his commanding officers, a lack of some vital campaigning equipment and the lack of opportunity for the brigade (and his division) to practice their drill as a complete formation.

While the Bremervörde Battalion was making quick strides in its training, thanks, at least according to Clinton, to the experience of its commanding officer, the lack of experienced commanding officers held back other battalions. Of the Salzgitter Battalion he wrote, 'The commanding officer Major Hammerstein seems very little acquainted with his business and… the movements of this battalion are slow, unsteady and incorrect…' But this battalion had been the last Hanoverian battalion to arrive with the army (early May) and had not enjoyed the benefits that Clinton's tough regime had had on the rest of his division. Indeed, the Salzgitter Landwehr Battalion had clearly been scraping the bottom of the recruit barrel, Clinton reporting that it, 'is probably of the whole army the most backward in point of military instruction. The men are young, many even too young to bear fatigue and undersized.'[14]

Clinton worked hard to get his Hanoverian brigade issued the necessary campaign equipment that they were lacking. By constant complaints and appeals, by the time the campaigned opened, the equipment shortages had been made good.

But Clinton continued to be worried about their ability to manoeuvre as a complete brigade. As we have already heard, he was concerned that the differences in drill between the British and KGL battalions, and the Hanoverian battalions, would make it difficult to manoeuvre the division in battle. In late May, Clinton moved his units to an area where the whole division could exercise together. These exercises did not go well, and he complained that the battalions 'are quite ignorant of the principles of moving in any larger body than a single battalion even to the extent of not knowing the distance at which one battalion should be from another.' This problem was exacerbated by the lack of ground available for such exercises, a problem shared by the whole army, and it is perhaps a great relief for Clinton that his three brigades were required to manoeuvre independently of one another at Waterloo.

The artillery

The artillery of the 'new' Hanoverian army of 1813–14 consisted of three foot batteries manned mainly from gunners of the KGL. However, for the 1815 campaign only two artillery batteries deployed, the third having been amalgamated with the other two to bring them up to strength in May of that year. The 1st Hanoverian Battery was commanded by Captain Wilhelm Braun and the 2nd Hanoverian Battery by Captain Carl von Rettberg. As we have heard, both were experienced commanders from their time with the KGL and both had been given a strong cadre of experienced officers and NCOs drawn from the KGL artillery, but also drew manpower from the landwehr artillery, which had been disbanded, and even some men who had served with the Westphalian artillery. Each battery had five guns (9-pounders) and a single howitzer (5.5in) of British manufacture and wore British uniforms. Braun's battery had only received their 9-pounders on 9 June, so had only had a short time to learn how to use them effectively; an officer and some NCOs from the KGL were sent to train them just days before they were to use them in action for the first time.

The Hanoverian cavalry

There were three cavalry regiments in the Hanoverian contingent, although only one served at Waterloo. All three were raised in 1813; the first two, the Bremen-Verden and Lüneburg Hussars were raised in March of that year and were a combination of volunteers and conscripts, but the Duke of Cumberland's Hussars was raised only at the end of 1813 and was exclusively of volunteers; each volunteer was responsible for purchasing his own uniform and horse and so came from wealthier families. Just as some of the officers had some campaign experience, it is quite possible that some of the NCOs and troopers did too. Raised in 1813, it took its title from Prince Adolphus, Duke of Cumberland, who was the son of George III and the Military Governor of Hanover. The regiment was not present at Quatre Bras and numbered about 500 at Waterloo. Made up as it was of wealthy young men who could afford to uniform, equip and mount themselves, it was looked down on by the rest of the army; 'The Cumberland Hussars was the regiment which would not fight, they were farmers sons and private gentlemen, who had equipped themselves at their own expense, but did not think they were to fight.'[15]

When writing to Wellington just before the campaign opened, the Duke of Cambridge pointed out that the Cumberland Hussars were all volunteers and had had very little time for drill and manoeuvre exercises. At the beginning of the campaign the regiment was brigaded with the Bremen and Verden Hussars and the Prince Regent's Hussars under Colonel Baron von Estorff, but the rest of the brigade had been detached to form part of the garrison at Hal and at Waterloo the Cumberland Hussars were attached to General Dörnberg's 3rd British Cavalry Brigade.[16]

Summary

By the time the campaign opened it seems that in most respects there had been sufficient time to get the Hanoverian units up to a standard that would allow them to give a good account of themselves on the battlefield. Most had now been in uniform a sufficient time to have established unit cohesion and were well trained, equipped and armed and their morale was high enough to face their age-old enemies the French with confidence. However, to one man at least, there were still fundamental problems. We have already heard from Captain Jacobi, who served with the Lüneburg Field Battalion, of the disenchantment of the Hanoverian contingent caused by the breakup of the Hanoverian force among the British divisions, but his complaints did not end there; in his account of the campaign that he wrote for his family, he was to say:

> There was no camaraderie among the allied troops, not even among the officers. The ignorance of the others' language, on both sides, the major difference in pay and the resulting great difference in lifestyles prevented any close companionship. Our compatriots in the King's German Legion did not even associate with us; the fifteen-year-old ensign with the red sash proudly looked down upon the older Hanoverian officer [with the yellow sash]. In the course of the campaign, these disparities often became unbearably more pronounced, and it rebounds to the troops' honour that they did not waver in their dedication and loyalty.[17]

It is impossible to say how widespread such opinions were in the Hanoverian contingent and no other of our eyewitness accounts mention any such bad feeling. What is true to say, as we shall see, is that the actions and performance of the Hanoverian officers and soldiers do great credit to them and so we must conclude that although there may well have been some feelings of unhappiness with the way they were treated, it does not appear to have manifested itself in their performance.

Deployment and actions

QUATRE BRAS

Of the Hanoverian troops, only the 1st and 4th Hanoverian brigades and Rettberg's Hanoverian artillery battery were present at the action of Quatre Bras; the 3rd and the 5th Hanoverian brigades, as well as Braun's artillery battery, were too far from the battlefield to arrive in time for the fighting and were directed straight to the position of Waterloo. As Colonel Best's 4th Hanoverian Brigade was the first of the Hanoverian brigades to reach the battlefield, we must start by examining this formation's initiation to the furnace of combat.

4th Hanoverian Brigade

Although it had been planned that Colonel Best's 4th Hanoverian Brigade was to be part of the 6th British Division, this division had not properly formed up and in the night of 15/16 June the 4th Brigade were ordered to march with Picton's 5th British Division, whose own 5th Hanoverian Brigade were quartered too far away to join them before the division was to march. Picton's division set off from Brussels at three o'clock in the morning of the 16th and after only a short rest in the forest of Soignies, arrived close to the battlefield twelve hours later. As the battle was already raging, Best's brigade deployed short of (north) and to the east of the village, behind the rest of the division, with the Lüneburg and Osterode battalions in the lead and skirmishers deployed. They advanced until they reached the Namur road, along which the forward British brigades had deployed in line. The brigade seems to have occupied a rather unusual position; the Lüneburg Battalion had its right resting on Quatre Bras with the Osterode and Münden battalions extending the line, having a small meadow between them and the road that was enclosed by tall hedges. Thus the men were hidden from view but could not see anything themselves; the hedge to their front also formed an obstacle to movement. As will be seen, the Verden Battalion was ordered forward.

As the British brigades advanced to meet the main French attack, the Hanoverian battalions moved forward in line to the road, remaining in reserve and sending out a chain of skirmishers across their whole front.

Despite being able to throw back the French infantry, the British brigades were themselves pushed back as they attempted to pursue the French and were counterattacked by French lancers and chasseurs. Several British battalions were mauled as they attempted to deploy into square and French squadrons approached the Namur road where Best's men lay. Here the brigade came under artillery fire and the skirmishers were engaged with the French *tirailleurs*.

Around four o'clock, Best was ordered to support the skirmish line with one of his battalions. The Verden Landwehr Battalion was designated for this task. The 1st Company were sent forward as skirmishers, but when they were relieved by 2nd Company, these men showed their inexperience and over-enthusiasm

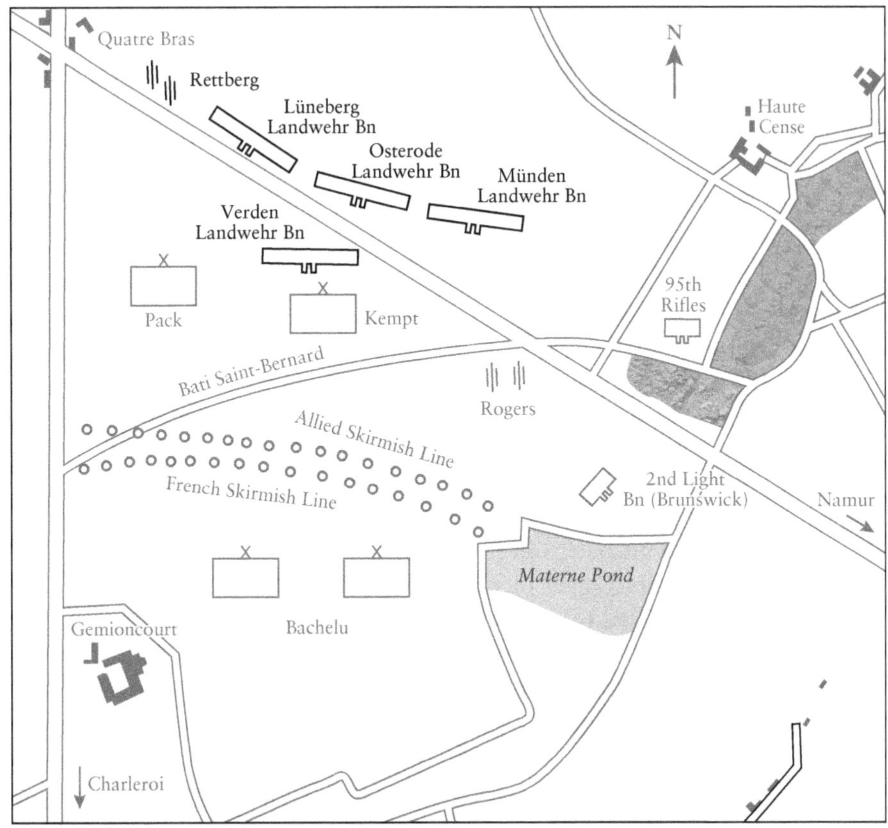

Map showing the deployment of the 4th Hanoverian Brigade at Quatre Bras.

by advancing too far and having three officers, a number of sergeants and sixty-three men taken prisoner. One of the officers of this company, Lieutenant von der Horst, later wrote to describe this action which he commanded:

> From what I saw glittering, I estimated the number of [French] bayonets at 50. I thought I could overpower them and make prisoners some part of them… I saw the soldiers were burning for a fight. My decision had been made, I addressed them for a few seconds and concluded with the appeal: "Whoever is a brave soldier will follow me!" At the head of a platoon, I considered myself strong enough to take on 50 Frenchmen… I was certain of a favourable outcome, in my imagination I already visualised myself with a small group of prisoners that I handed over to my superior. I did not hear the bullets that whistled past myself. The sight of some of my men falling even raised my spirits; I felt as if I was floating between death and life, and both were like a game to me… Now I had the enemy before my

> bayonets. My companions stormed in on him… I was certain of our victory when suddenly we were surrounded in an ambush by a French tirailleur regiment, which had risen out of the corn.[18]

In his report on the battle, Colonel Best quotes the following account of the next phase of the action by Major von der Decken, who commanded the Verden Landwehr Battalion:

> Lieutenant Hurtzig was deployed with his sharpshooters, men of No.1 Company, against the enemy tirailleurs who, from behind a hedge intermingled with trees, poured a deadly fire into our line, which stood on an open plain without any cover. Nobody dared attack this fire-spitting hedge, even though troops of all types, English, Scottish and Hanoverians were facing it. Lieutenant Hurtzig then ordered his sharpshooters to charge at the hedge, with support of the attack promised by Lieutenant von Hinüber with part of No.1 Company. These two officers placed themselves at the head of their men who were at first deterred by a shower of bullets but then, encouraged by the words of their officers, rushed at the hedge and, backed by their support, drove off the enemy. Lieutenant von Hinüber was wounded, later dying of his wound.[19]

At about five o'clock the French cavalry advanced against the line of the Namur road, in the ditches of which lay the Lüneburg Landwehr. Under the control of the former KGL adjutant, the battalion stood and opened fire when the cavalry were only thirty paces away, unsaddling many and driving the remainder away. It was the single most significant engagement of the brigade during the battle; the Osterode and Münden Battalions were not committed and consequently suffered few casualties; there were no further actions from the brigade until the fighting died out around nine o'clock, by which time the skirmishers had run out of ammunition.

Some modern authors have the brigade advancing at the end of the battle in support of the final allied advance that pushed the whole French line back to their start positions. However, in his account of the battle, Best does not mention this and it is possible that only the Verden Landwehr Battalion moved forwards of the Namur road.

1st Hanoverian Brigade

General von Kielmansegge's 1st Hanoverian Brigade concentrated with the rest of General von Alten's 3rd British Division in the village of Soignies on the evening of 15 June and early the next morning started their march to Nivelles via Braine-le-Comte. Here the 2nd KGL Brigade was detached to observe the Charleroi road while the other two brigades force-marched towards Quatre Bras. The march was a hard one and numbers of men dropped out unable to maintain the pace; they only rejoined their battalions after the fighting was over on the 16th.

The two remaining brigades of the division arrived on the battlefield at about five o'clock and at a critical time of the battle. Sir Colin Halkett's 5th British Brigade was sent to the west of the crossroads to fill the gap that had been caused by the hurried retirement of the forward Brunswick battalions, while Kielmansegge's brigade were immediately sent to reinforce the extreme left wing of the allied position where the 95th Rifles and the Brunswick 2nd Light Battalion were struggling to hold their own against the French on this flank. Approaching along the Nivelles road, their advance along the entire allied front attracted the attention of the French artillery; although at extreme range their casualties were light.

As the brigade arrived on the left the main French infantry attack in the centre had only just been repulsed, having broken the first line of Brunswick troops and the French light cavalry had caused havoc among Picton's 5th Division. The feared French cuirassiers had not yet been committed. It was a pivotal moment when the result could still swing either way; whoever was able to commit their reserves first was most likely to snatch the victory.

The brigade took position between the Namur road and the Materne pond with the Lüneburg Field Battalion leading and the two companies of Feldjäger in skirmish order covering the front. Coming under skirmish fire they deployed and with the Lüneburg Battalion pushed the French tirailleurs back, supported by the Grubenhagen Battalion. These two battalions advanced against the hamlet of Piraumont with the British Rifles and Brunswickers to their left. The other two battalions of the brigade, those of Bremen and Osnabrück, followed up in support, but with the Materne pond between them. The Lüneburg and Grubenhagen battalions pushed the French out of Piraumont and back into the Delhutte wood, where they rallied. The ground this advance took place over was anything but ideal, as described by Captain von Scriba of the Bremen Field Battalion: 'the intervening fields were crossed by numerous hedges and ditches and the terrain was not suited to a close combat…'.[20] This resulted in the various units getting mixed together. Captain Carl Jacobi of the Lüneburg Field Battalion wrote:

> While passing through the many hedges and the fields with the corn a man's height, and from the fighting in the wood, there was a mixing of the troops so that officers would lead detachments composed of men from different companies. In the end, the English, the Brunswickers and the Hanoverians became completely intermingled. At the same time, many men had remained in the area to the rear, partly from

> exhaustion, partly from their unwillingness to expose themselves. As a result, the foremost line had become very weak. The officers, on their part, were too much in need of rest upon the break in the action to force themselves to rally the men in the wide expanse of the field of action and to restore order.[21]

Having taken the hamlet, the Lüneburg Battalion were close to capturing a French battery, but a Brunswick signal to halt allowed it to escape. The French then made a number of efforts to retake Piraumont, but were thrown back each time, partly by the Bremen Battalion and also by elements of the Feldjägers who skirmished with the numerous French tirailleurs throughout the action. The Hanoverians even advanced against the Delhutte wood, but although they reached the edge of the wood, they could not establish themselves there, as Jacobi explains:

> When the French advanced with superior force we attempted in vain to hold the edge of the wood. One by one the men fell back when they found themselves deserted by their neighbours. Those more to the rear had lost their senses and started firing. This compounded the confusion, and the entire skirmish line retreated. The French advanced ever more vigorously. The courageous example of our officers and their shouts had no effect; there was no spot to serve as a rallying point where the retreating men could be brought to a halt. All our hold on the wood had been lost.[22]

The Hanoverians had successfully conducted an offensive manoeuvre against capable opponents, although the strength of the French forces on this part of the battlefield is somewhat exaggerated in the Hanoverian accounts. However, it was an ideal initiation for these battalions. As night fell the forward battalions retired on Piraumont and sentries were posted for the night. As it began to get dark the Verden Field Battalion replaced the Lüneburg and Grubenhagen battalions in Piraumont, and together with the Feldjäger and detachments from the Bremen and Osnabrück battalions formed the front line.

2nd Hanoverian Battery

Rettberg's 2nd Hanoverian battery was to have been part of the 4th British Division (Colville), but had been attached to Picton's 5th British Division during the night of 15/16 as the 4th Division was too far away to be able to take a part in the actions of the following two days. It arrived at Quatre Bras with Picton's division at about three o'clock, having been ordered to hurry its move from Genappe. On arrival at the crossroads, it deployed to the east of the village

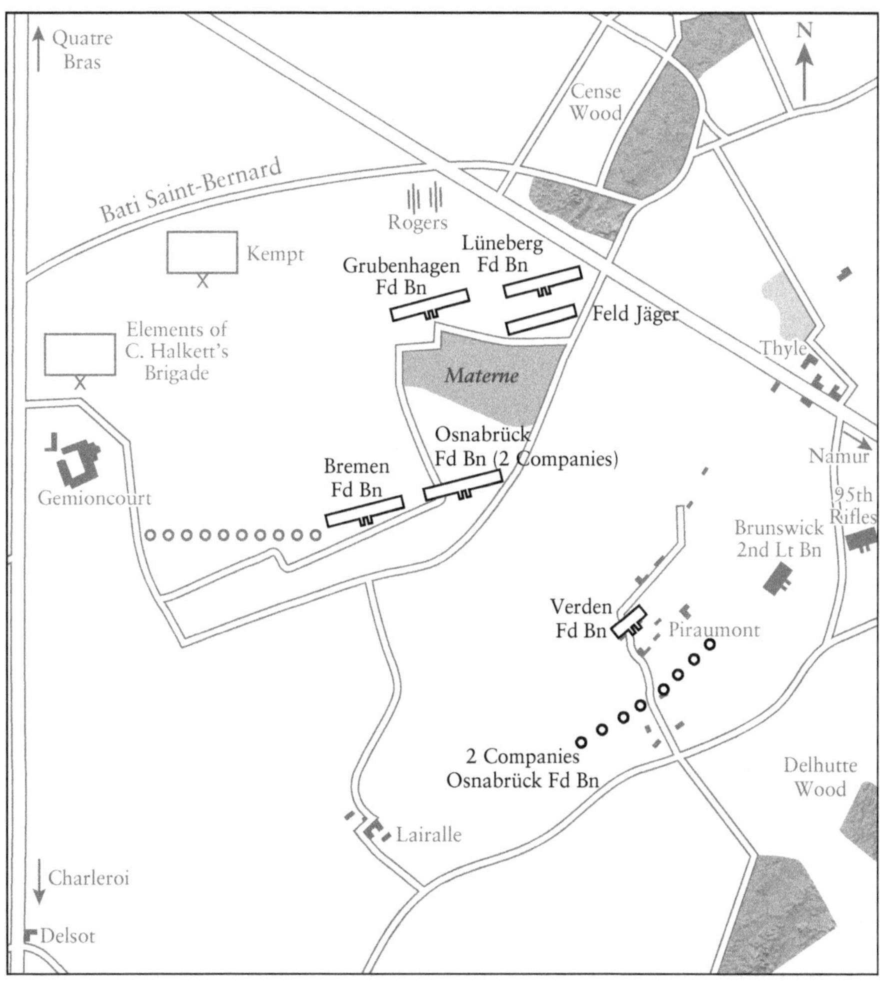

Map showing the final position of the 1st Hanoverian Brigade at Quatre Bras.

and to the north of the Namur road, and immediately came into action against the French infantry, which was pushing the British line back. Having helped to repel a French cavalry attack that approached close to the village, between five and six o'clock it was ordered to move further to the left to join a battery of the KGL (Cleeves') that was already deployed there. Rettberg sited his guns and ammunition wagons with care, covering them with the lie of the ground and keeping non-essential crewmen under cover. From there it exchanged fire with the powerful French artillery opposed to it until dark and was able to maintain its position having only suffered casualties of two men killed and three wounded thanks to the care of its commander, who wrote, 'The enemy cannon fire was very strong, but the young and inexperienced officers and men displayed proved their courage on this occasion'.[23]

Casualties

As has already been discussed, it is impossible to be accurate when assessing casualties; brigade official returns, unit returns, and totals given in individual accounts, all vary to a greater or lesser extent. The official campaign casualty returns for the Hanoverian troops cover losses by unit for the whole period from 16 to 18 June, so we cannot be sure of those on any single day. However, in the 'Report on the participation of the Hanoverian Troops and the German Legion in the action at Quatre Bras', the brigade casualties are reported as:[24]

1st Hanoverian Brigade

Killed: one officer and thirty-six men.
Wounded: nine officers and 129 men.
A total of 175 men, or about 5 percent of brigade strength.

4th Hanoverian Brigade:

Killed: one officer and forty-three men.
Wounded: four officers and seventy-nine men.
Missing: two officers and ninety men (nearly all captured).
A total of 219 men, or about 8 percent of brigade strength.

The Hanoverians at Quatre Bras – summary

Both Hanoverian brigades had initially been deployed into reserve in their first battle giving them at least some time to get used to the sights and sounds of battle before they became decisively engaged. Some inexperience was shown, particularly when half a company of landwehr were taken prisoner; a sure case of courage and enthusiasm, but also a lack of a cool and calculating head in command. However, the regulars of Kielmansegge's brigade showed considerable determination and aggression in the attack on Piraumont and acquitted themselves well, showing that they could deploy under fire and manoeuvre aggressively on the battlefield. The two brigades generally showed a bold front and were fully committed to the final counterattack that pushed the French back to their original start line of the morning. Quatre Bras was a good introduction to battle for both brigades and would have boosted their morale prior to a more challenging test two days later at Waterloo. It will also be seen from the accounts how the Hanoverian officers distinguished themselves in motivating their men and their courageous leadership in action.

17 June

From daybreak on the morning of the 17th, the French sent forward small detachments which opened a heavy and almost constant fire against the forward battalions of the 1st Hanoverian Brigade. Although these did not seriously threaten the position held, they caused a steady drip of casualties and several times the battalions were forced to push men forward to drive them off. However, as the morning progressed, this skirmishing reduced until it stopped altogether at about ten o'clock. The Hanoverian accounts describe French columns, but it is clear the fighting was an almost continuous skirmish. It is probable that this was an armed reconnaissance by which the French were trying to establish whether the allies were planning to hold their positions or retreat, perhaps with a view to launching a more serious attack, but this did not materialise. The forward battalions were beginning to run short of ammunition when they were finally ordered to withdraw. Although the action was minor, the Bremen Field Battalion lost six men killed and fifty-two wounded,[25] a virtually pointless loss of men.

Colonel Best's 4th Hanoverian Brigade were not engaged in the French attacks in the morning and, leaving the battlefield at about ten o'clock, were one of the first brigades to leave Quatre Bras. As no casualties are given for the brigade for the 17th, we can safely say that their casualties were insignificant and quite possibly nil.

About 11.30am, the 1st Hanoverian Brigade marched off towards the north. After a short rest just north of Genappe, the brigade set off again and soon found itself marching in pouring rain. Captain von Scriba of the Bremen Field Battalion described the march:

> The retreat proceeded quite fast, but nowhere did I observe the least bit of disorder… Several men had been left behind on this retreat, exhausted from slogging through the mud of the country roads and became prisoners.[26]

On arrival at the Waterloo position, two British brigades and the 5th Hanoverian Brigade were already occupying the position. By about eight o'clock, all the Hanoverian troops were in their designated positions on the ridge of Mont Saint Jean.

The 4th Hanoverian Brigade appear to have lost no men on the retreat; having been one of the first formations to move, much of their march was conducted before the heavy rain fell and it is possible that stragglers had the opportunity to catch up before they were overtaken by the pursuing French cavalry. This was not true for the 1st Brigade who departed sometime later; they reported eighteen men missing for the day who had fallen behind and been picked up by the French. Casualties for the 1st Hanoverian Brigade on the 17th were:

Bremen Field Battalion: six killed and fifty-two wounded (probably including the eighteen missing men.)

Verden Field Battalion: twenty killed and wounded.

Osterode (Duke of York's) Field Battalion: one killed and eleven wounded.[27]

Waterloo

1st Hanoverian Brigade

The 1st Hanoverian Brigade had spent the night 500 metres to the rear of their allocated position in the allied line of battle. At eleven o'clock they were ordered to break camp and advance forward into their position in the first line with its left 200 paces from the Brussels road. This intervening gap was filled by Colonel von Ompteda's 2nd KGL Brigade. To the right of the brigade was Major General Sir Colin Halkett's 5th British Brigade. All three brigades were part of General von Alten's 3rd British Division; von Alten had placed the Hanoverians between his two most experienced brigades.

Kielmansegge's brigade were deployed in battalion close columns in two lines in order to allow sufficient space between each to give them room to deploy into line without interfering with the battalion next to them. In his report written the day after the battle, von Alten wrote to Wellington:

> In compliance with your Grace's orders, and those of His Royal Highness the Prince of Orange, to form the division for the attack in two lines of contiguous columns, I placed them in columns of two battalions together at quarter distance, the right regiment on its left company, the left on its right company, so as to deploy right and left into line, or to form squares as necessary; the columns composing the 1st and 2nd lines chequered.[28]

Throughout the allied army, and no doubt at Wellington's direction, who knew of the strength and power of the French cavalry, much thought had been put into forming square quickly and efficiently. For the 1st Hanoverian Brigade, it had been decided that because of the numerical weakness of each of the battalions, two battalions would combine to form a single square. The Bremen and Verden battalions were to form one square and the Grubenhagen and Duke of York's the other. The odd battalion, the Lüneburg Field Battalion, would stand alone and operate as dictated by circumstances. One of the Feldjäger companies would provide the skirmish screen in front of the brigade and the other was sent down into the Hougoumont wood to strengthen the allied light troops already deployed there; it was joined by 100 trained marksmen, fifty from each of the Lüneburg and Grubenhagen battalions.[29]

In the early part of the battle, between 12pm and 2pm, the brigade had sheltered from the intense French artillery fire by lying down in the shelter of the dead ground behind the ridge. Although some casualties were suffered, these were not significant.

When Count d'Erlon's 1st French Corps launched its main attack on the centre left of the allied line, its 1st Brigade (Colonel Charlet) of the 1st Infantry Division (Quiot), was ordered to attack the farm of la Haye-Sainte, which lay

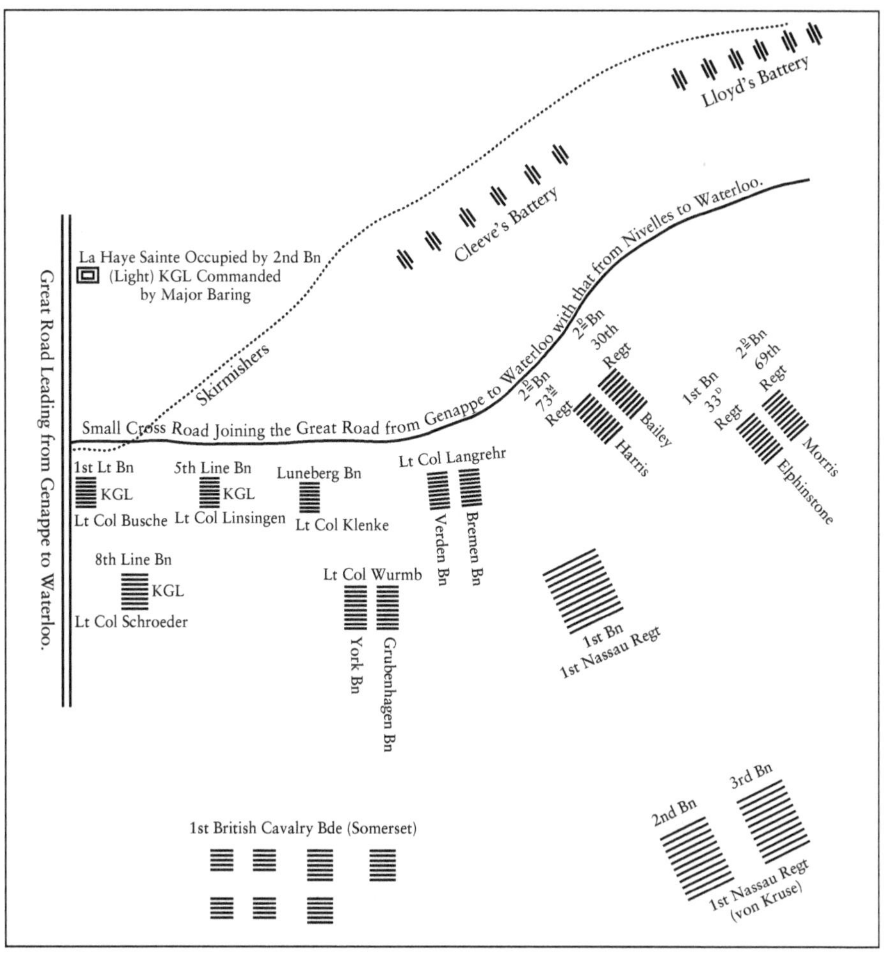

The initial deployment of the 1st Hanoverian Brigade at Waterloo based on the sketch by Captain Shaw (later General Sir James Shaw-Kennedy).

just to the forward left of Kielmansegge's brigade. The farm was defended by the 2nd Light Battalion of the KGL commanded by Major Baring. Baring's men quickly lost control of the orchard which lay on the French side of the farm but maintained a strong defence of the farm itself. However, on the allied side of the farm was a small garden, and when this also fell to the French, Baring was surrounded and cut off from resupply and reinforcements. Seeing this, Colonel von Klencke, commanding the Lüneburg Field Battalion, was ordered by the Prince of Orange to launch a counterattack and re-establish communications with the garrison.

There are a number of accounts of this attack available from eyewitnesses, but we shall restrict ourselves to that of Captain Carl Jacobi of the Lüneburg Field Battalion:

> after two o'clock a vigorous attack was launched against the farm of la Haye Sainte which was located immediately in front of us, our lieutenant colonel led us down from our position to confront the enemy. Full of determination and in good order we advanced and threw ourselves upon the enemy who fell back. Part of the battalion, including also my company, was sent into the orchard of La Haye Sainte; the remaining part spread out across the open against the French tirailleurs. In the beginning we successfully defended the orchard; but then the enemy moved up with formed columns against whom the enclosure of sparse hedges offered no protection. We were forced to yield, without any time left to again rally the men. Outside we fell in with the other scattered parts of the battalion, in the midst of the French cavalry, which at this moment carried out its first bold attack against the position. The battalion was completely dispersed. Some of the fleeing men found refuge behind the squares of the brigade, myself included, although French cuirassiers had trotted past myself, 10 to 12 paces away. Nobody among us really knew how we had escaped the horse's hooves or the horsemen's swords… This was the sudden and sad outcome of our action; our losses were considerable, but most depressing was, the evidence that at this moment the Lüneberg Battalion had ceased to exist; not even the smallest gathering of its troops could be found anywhere.[30]

Jacobi says that after the disaster he was able to rally five other officers and about fifty men, though he later gives the battalion's casualties as two officers and eighteen rank and file killed, 137 wounded and forty-seven missing.

In a footnote to his account Jacobi gives an interesting insight into the jealousy that existed between KGL officers and the ex-KGL officers now serving with the Hanoverian landwehr:

> The unfortunate outcome of our bold advance has since provoked considerable criticism. Lieutenant Colonel von Klencke was deeply envied by many in the legion. At the end of the year 1811 he had left that corps as one of the more junior captains, and now was met by his former comrades as one of the more senior lieutenant colonels. They later expressed the opinion that von Klencke had tried to outshine others in front of the army by his bold sortie, without fully considering the adverse situation. The lieutenant colonel, on his part, affirmed later to have received the order to attack from an adjutant of the Prince of Orange, the commander of our corps. General von Alten later told me that he had admired the cold courage with which the battalion had advanced, but had also noticed the riskiness of the undertaking;

> he had been unaware of any order from the Prince of Orange. A further clarification of the circumstances has never occurred.[31]

Having gathered up the remains of the battalion, Jacobi, who was now the senior officer (von Klencke having been wounded and Major von Dachenhausen captured), returned them to the brigade. However, they were then ordered by General Kielmansegge to march back to Brussels with what remained and to try and gather up as many others of the battalion as possible. Jacobi comments that 'if the general had had more war experience, he probably would not have given this order'[32] which removed vital men from the battlefield.

D'Erlon's infantry attack against the allied centre-left having failed, the next hammer blow was to fall on the centre right where Kielmansegge's brigade were formed in their two squares; the square of the Bremen and Verden Field battalions on the right and the square of the Grubenhagen and Duke of York's battalions on the left. The first wave of cavalry consisted of the French IV Cavalry Corps commanded by General Milhaud and consisted of over 3,000 of the famed and feared cuirassiers. This was to be the most significant challenge the brigade had yet faced. Although they had seen action at Quatre Bras and suffered from the heavy artillery fire, this was to be on a much grander scale, and it was to become clear what their first challenge was to be.

Although the brigade's report states that the first charges were met 'with the utmost calm',[33] personal accounts do not support this. Captain von Scriba of the Bremen Field Battalion wrote, 'All officers in the square made the greatest efforts to keep the men from prematurely firing single [individual] shots.' Major Julius von Schkopp of the Verden Field Battalion, who commanded the square, observed, 'The French cavalry was fired at in the first attack at a distance of 120 to 180 paces, and not 30 to 40 paces, which I recollect absolutely as I was so discontented I ordered the officers of the Verden Light Infantry Battalion in a loud voice to kill anybody who fired too early without an order.'[34] However, after this initial show of inexperience, the battalions repulsed the repeated cavalry charges with stoicism and accurate fire, showing commendable composure.

Captain von Scriba makes a number of interesting observations during the cavalry attacks, apart from the efforts to stop the men from opening fire too early. At one stage a formation of cuirassiers passed just six paces from the flank of the square, but few fell when they were fired on; von Scriba noting that the men were firing too high, and the officers reminded the men to aim lower. Firing high was a common mistake in inexperienced troops before proper weapon sights and marksmanship training. It also becomes clear how after each unsuccessful cavalry attack the morale of the squares went up as the soldiers realised that as long as they held their nerve and their formation the cavalry could do them little harm.

Von Scriba also writes of the problems of losing men to the transport of wounded men to the rear:

> We lost many men from the artillery fire, particularly from howitzer shells, and we strove all the time to fill the gaps. I must remark, by the way, that for transporting each wounded man, one, sometimes two, left the ranks. This circumstance reduced our strength considerably. At first, the bearers ended at the nearest houses of [Mont] St Jean, but, later on, always farther to the rear to a point that the majority of the bearers did not return until after the battle had ended.[35]

The 1st Brigade accounts list five attacks by the French cavalry, noting that by the last the flagging morale of the French cavalry was evident.

It was only towards the end of this phase of the battle, with the French and allied cavalry increasingly exhausted and incapable of further great efforts, that the brigade perhaps faced its greatest challenge of the battle. By this time the original commanding officer of the square, Lieutenant Colonel von Langrehr, had been mortally wounded and both majors had also been wounded. Not surprisingly, this phase of the battle gets the most attention from our eyewitnesses and, but for minor details, they are all in agreement. We shall therefore follow just one of them, Lieutenant Wilhelm von Tschirschnitz of the Bremen Field Battalion, in a report dated 16 November 1824:

> At approximately five o'clock, the command of the square was given to Captain von Bothmer of the Verden Light Infantry Battalion; the regular form of the square had been lost because of the terrible fire and the fact that few healthy soldiers remained, and the men fell and were transported to the rear by their comrades. The whole formation became a triangle which despite this unfavourable situation was fortunate enough to repel the fourth attack by the French cuirassiers; they thought to profit from our momentary hesitation. However, our square was finally forced to give way to an attack from enemy infantry formed in square which had cannon in its middle, and which was supported by strong musket fire. Our loss of men at this time was very great; more than this, several soldiers who had taken an injured comrade out of the line returned to the combat; but unfortunately, not every man had this sense of duty and this is why that at the conclusion of the battle the battalions were very weak, and the following morning, almost half the men who had begun the battle returned.

The officers' calm and exemplary behaviour enabled the retrograde movement of the square to be stopped in front of the English cavalry and they started to put the battalion in order, which had been terribly mixed up by the incessant fire.[36]

Von Tschirschnitz states that the forced withdrawal of the square was only stopped by the line of British cavalry formed up behind them; Major General

Sir Hussey Vivian, who commanded the 6th British Cavalry Brigade, wrote in a letter to William Siborne, 'I arrived in the rear of the infantry just at the time that several small squares of foreign troops were giving way. In fact, my wheeling into line in their rear and cheering them actually halted two of these, and gave them confidence…'.[37]

But the remaining four battalions of the brigade were not yet finished; Tschirschnitz tells us that it was due to musket fire that the square had been forced into a triangle, yet both General Kielmansegge and Major Müller talk of two guns being brought forward by the French. The official report of the 1st Hanoverian Brigade says:

> In front of the left square the enemy manoeuvred two light cannon to within a few hundred paces, which were covered by infantry and cuirassiers. We had no means to oppose the murderous canister fire, for our artillery had expended their ammunition and had been sent to the rear. A counterattack by two weak battalions was futile… At this moment another cavalry attack was repulsed, although the violent canister and musket fire had overpowered almost the entire flank of our square, which had become a triangle.[38]

It will be remembered that the 1st Nassau Regiment also described suffering from these guns and that their first battalion lost many men in charging them. The report mentions the withdrawal of the Nassauers and blames them for the withdrawal of Kielmansegge's brigade:

> The two battalions which stood on the right advanced in square with some Nassau battalions, and they forced the enemy cavalry to retire. However, the violent canister and musket fire from the advancing column which met them caused the General commanding the 1st Corps[39] and the remaining staff officers belonging to the two battalions, to be wounded.
>
> The retreat of the Nassau squares made it impossible to maintain the ground we had won, and it was necessary to retire to a position further back.[40]

Major Müller also blames the withdrawal of the Nassauers for this movement.

Despite the long and often bitter arguments among British officers as to which regiment was responsible for the repulse of the attack of the French Imperial Guard, although there is some acceptance that Netherlands troops may have made a contribution, there is no mention of any Hanoverian troops having played any role in it; indeed, in British accounts of this phase of the battle, the Hanoverians get no mention at all. However, a number of Hanoverian accounts make clear that they, at least, believe that they were involved and the fact that their open and honest accounts accept that they were beaten back only strengthens their case. Others may argue that their accounts were influenced by or even drawn from each other and that there is insufficient evidence to conclude that it was indeed the Imperial Guard they faced rather than some other supporting unit of the French army. The allied contribution to the repulse of the Imperial Guard is examined in detail in Appendix E, so here we will only look at what the Hanoverian accounts tell us.

Perhaps the most graphic account of this phase of the battle comes from Captain von Scriba of the Bremen Field Battalion, whom we have already met. His account coincides neatly with French accounts which describe the attack taking place in a number of battalion squares accompanied by sections (two guns) of artillery; most British accounts describe the Guard attacking in column. Von Scriba describes the attack thus:

> Not far from us, I saw a strong column of enemy infantry moving at the *pas de charge* and with beating drums towards the English brigade of Major General Sir Colin Halkett. General Halkett advanced against them and very calmly met them with levelled bayonets and brought them into such disorder that they made off singly in full flight. During this time period (half past seven o'clock), as a decision was nearing, a strong square of French Guards with several guns also advanced towards us, and immediately started firing at a heavy rate. Our small troop could not withstand this strong assault for very long. At first, our men, full of fury, returned the fire but, unfortunately, were running short of ammunition… The gallant battalions (Bremen and Verden) yielded, but slowly and calmly. The officers' efforts and encouraging words brought the men to a halt some 300 paces, at most, behind the original position, and still before the cavalry columns in the rear. We were just in the process of reforming and had succeeded to some extent when His Royal Highness, the Crown Prince of the Netherlands came up to us, praised the battalions' conduct and promised to remember us, but at the same time insisted on a quick advance. He could not even allow the completion of our reforming because, as he said, the enemy was already in disorder and had been beaten. Our brave troops, unformed although compact, advanced again, with the Prince at its head, shouting 'Long Live the Prince of Orange!' At our former position we were received by case shot from not more than 200 paces away. The men bravely stood fast as before, but all resistance ceased due to a lack of ammunition. For a time the men helped themselves to that of the dead that were lying about. The remnants of both battalions retreated slowly. In response

to some officers' remonstrances they pointed out the lack of ammunition, even urgently asking them for fresh ammunition, and that they would willingly fight to the last. Both the officers and the men of the two battalions continued to be inspired by the best of will. Most were physically exhausted, but this did not diminish their morale...[41]

Von Scriba's account is in complete agreement with that of his regimental comrade Lieutenant von Tschirschnitz, though it is quite possible that there was some collaboration. Other officers support them; their brigade commander, General Kielmansegge, and Major Müller and Lieutenant von Bülow of the Bremen Field Battalion do not mention the Guard by name, but their description of the action at this time of the battle is also in general agreement with them.

Von Tschirschnitz's account is more candid about the final retreat, admitting that the soldiers 'started to panic' when ordered to retire, and in Jacobi's account of the Hanoverian contribution to the battle he describes the final retirement as taking place 'in disorder.'[42]

Both the 2nd KGL Brigade and the 1st Hanoverian Brigade, having been repulsed in this final action, were ordered to retire by General Kielmansegge, who had succeeded to the divisional command after General von Alten had been wounded. According to von Alten's report on the battle:

The squares by this time had been so much reduced in number by the continued fire of cannon, musketry and ultimately grape shot of the enemy, that they had hardly enough men to remain in squares, and therefore were withdrawn from the position by Count Kielmansegge; and the remains of the Legion and Hanoverian brigades, and part of the British brigade, reformed on the high road in rear of the village of Mont St. Jean.[43]

Although von Alten was not then present with his division, having been evacuated wounded, these two brigades reformed a full thousand metres behind the front line. On receipt of von Alten's report, Wellington initially disapproved of over two brigades being taken out of the line at such a critical point in the battle, and on 20 June ordered Kielmansegge to put himself under arrest. However, after an appeal from von Alten[44] he was later absolved of any wrongdoing. Luckily, this incident took place as the whole French army disintegrated and fled from the battlefield, so there was no danger to the integrity of the allied position. Although the troops took no part in any further fighting, having re-formed, the brigades were led forward once more by General Kielmansegge into their former positions where they bivouacked for the night among the dead and wounded.

As a result of von Alten's appeal, Kielmansegge was reinstated to command of the division and survived with his reputation intact. However, there can be little doubt that he had exposed his inexperience in high command, and it is likely that Wellington, in the aftermath of a great victory, as in other incidents we shall explore, chose not to investigate too closely an unfortunate decision that might in other circumstances have had serious consequences. The detail of this incident is examined in more detail in Appendix E.

The 1st Hanoverian Brigade had suffered terribly; the official casualty returns do not reflect the condition of the battalions at the end of the battle. On top of the killed and wounded, many men were missing; Lieutenant von Bülow of the Bremen Field Battalion states that on returning to their position, 'Our battalion strength was 80 men.'[45] Two battalions had lost their commanding officers; Lieutenant Colonel von Wurmb, of the Grubenhagen Field Battalion, was killed and Lieutenant Colonel Langrehr, of the Bremen Field Battalion, was mortally wounded. Many men and officers were missing; even Captain Jacobi, who had been sent back to Brussels by General Kielmansegge with the fifty men he had been able to rally after the Lüneburg Battalion had been dispersed by cuirassiers, admits that he abandoned his men there to sleep in a comfortable billet with a friend. Having heard of the victory, he took some more rest and then wrote home before he left to find his men and lead them back to the battalion; he finally found them on the 20th when the battalion was able to muster about 200 men.[46] On 22 June Jacobi's company consisted of forty-one men of the 138 it had contained on the 16th.

The 1st Hanoverian Brigade had been deployed in the front line in the vital centre of Wellington's position. It had been fiercely engaged almost throughout the battle. The almost total loss of the Lüneburg Field Battalion in the ill-fated counterattack on la Haye-Sainte may well have shaken the morale of this relatively inexperienced brigade. However, although it showed some inexperience in the battle, it also showed a bold front and high morale during the French cavalry attacks, and although forced from its position a number of times, thanks to the efforts of its officers and enthusiasm of its men it was able to rally and return to its position in the line until finally ordered to retire by General Kielmansegge.

3rd Hanoverian Brigade

Colonel Hugh Halkett's 3rd Hanoverian Brigade, as part of General Clinton's 2nd British Division, had taken no part at Quatre Bras, having left its cantonments near the town of Ath in the morning of 16 June and with the rest of the division it arrived behind the ridge at Waterloo on the evening of the 17th, joining the troops that were already concentrating there.

On the morning of the 18th the brigade took position to the west of the Nivelle road close to the hamlet of Merbe Braine. This was a considerable distance behind the allied right to the northwest of the farm and château of Hougoumont, forming a link between the main line and the 3rd Netherlands Division that was deployed at the small town of Braine l'Alleud. Du Plat's 1st

KGL Brigade was deployed in front of Halkett's and Adam's brigades. When the French attacked Hougoumont, Adam's brigade moved forwards to the main ridge, leaving Halkett in reserve. However, even this far back many cannon balls, having flown over the ridge, caused casualties within the battalions.

The brigade was left in reserve until approximately 4pm, when it was ordered to move forward. It took position behind the road that marked the allied position between the main roads from Charleroi and Nivelles, helping to fill the gap left by Byng's brigade, most of which had deployed into the area in and around Hougoumont. Here, the number of casualties suffered from the French artillery increased considerably. Du Plat's and Adam's brigades moved forwards of the ridgeline and formed square to break up the French cavalry attacks, but Halkett's Hanoverians remained behind the ridgeline in reserve. The brigade formed square but were not charged by the French cavalry, remaining in dead ground.

In its new position the brigade split into two wings. The Bremervörde and Quakenbrück battalions moved to the right to stand in the corner of the line behind Hougoumont, while the Osnabrück and Salzgitter formed squares on the ridgeline to protect the artillery. Here they were beyond the road and deployed under heavy artillery fire, which prompted the commanding officer of the Salzgitter Battalion to write in his post-action report 'a deployment which reflects a particular honour on the battalion in having executed it in outstanding order while exposed to a heavy fire.'[47] It seems that General Clinton's drilling was paying off. For the rest of the battle the brigade operated as separate wings; until now none of the battalions had faced an attack at close quarters, though there is no doubt that the constant loss of casualties from artillery fire must have been very trying for the young soldiers. Halkett positioned himself with his two forward battalions.

No doubt their lack of participation in the battle, at least to some, was very frustrating; the attacks on Hougoumont and the great French cavalry charges had been repulsed without their involvement. However, as they approached the final phase of the battle, at least two of the battalions were now to be given their opportunity to come to grips with the French.

Although the Osnabrück and Salzgitter battalions were working together as a wing of the brigade, what happened next suggests that they were not deployed next to each other. Sometime after seven o'clock, the French Imperial Guard advanced in Napoleon's final desperate attempt to force the allied line. The main effort of the attack fell along the allied line from close to la Haye-Sainte to close to the fields to the west of Hougoumont; that is to the left of the leading two battalions of the 3rd Brigade. The final battalions of the French Guard were defeated by the famous flanking attack of the 52nd and the advance of Adam's brigade. Halkett himself describes what happened next in a letter to the famous historian of the battle, Captain Siborne:

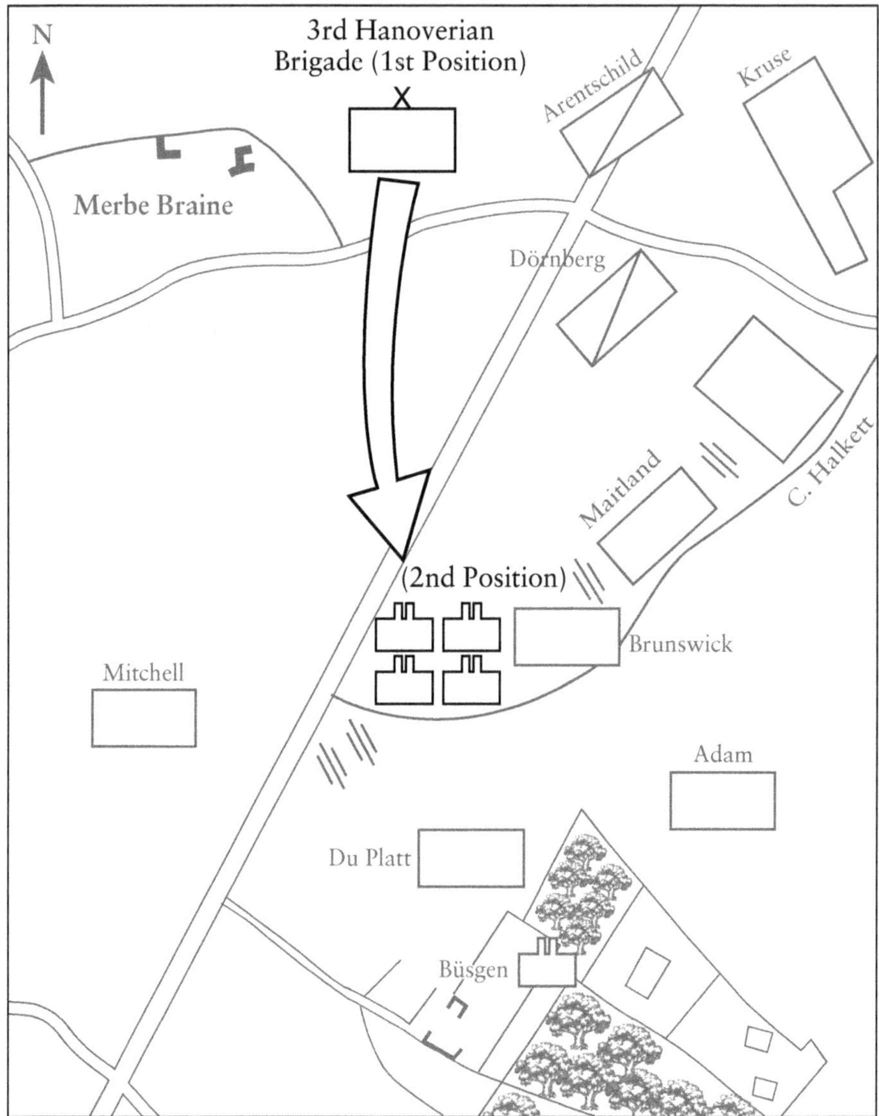

Map showing the initial and second positions of the 3rd Hanoverian Brigade at Waterloo.

The moment General Adam's Brigade advanced, I lost no time to follow with the Osnabrück Battalion (2nd Battalion, Duke of York), then on the left of Hougoumont, of which post I was in command, one of the Battalions of my Brigade occupying the wood and two others in the ditches in the rear, other troops occupying the enclosures, etc.

During the advance, I sent my Brigade Major, Captain v. Saffe, to bring up the two Battalions posted in rear of Hougoumont, but

> neither he nor the Battalions showed themselves. Next day I found that Captain Saffe was killed before having delivered the message. The Osnabrück Battalion soon got in line and on the right of Adam's Brigade. During the advance we were much annoyed by the Enemy's Artillery. The first Company of the Osnabrück Battalion broke into platoons, and supported by the sharpshooters of the Battalion, made a dash at the Artillery on our right and captured six Guns with their horses...
>
> During our advance we were in constant contact with the French Guards, and I often called to them to surrender. For some time, I had my eye upon, as I supposed, the General Officer in command of the Guards (being in full uniform) trying to animate his men to stand.[48]

As Halkett had followed the French Guards to his front, Adam's brigade had veered off to the left, leaving the Osnabrückers dangerously exposed. The battalion was eventually faced by a square formed by the 2nd Battalion of the 1st Chasseurs, commanded by *maréchal de camp* Cambronne. This was one of the most senior and experienced battalions of the French Guard, commanded by a veteran of all the major campaigns of the French army, who had served in the Guard since 1809. Covering the flight of the battalions that had launched the failed attack, Cambronne was spotted trying to rally his men and encourage them to stand; Halkett recalled:

> The enemy continued to retire. Their commanding officer was at first on horseback and urged them energetically to stand fast, but in vain. I saw him somewhat later with two aides de camp about 150 paces behind the column, but now on foot after the loss of his horse.[49]

Cambronne had indeed had his horse killed beneath him and been wounded above his left eye; Halkett determined to capture him: 'I ordered the sharpshooters to dash on, and I made a gallop for the General. When about cutting him down he called out he would surrender…'.[50]

With Cambronne sent to the rear, the battalion now continued to the left to the Brussels high road, having driven off the crews of some French guns which were left abandoned. French resistance had effectively ended, and the battalion continued along the main road driving the fugitives before it before coming to a halt at about ten o'clock deep in the French rear. Here they encountered the Prussians and halted so they would not impede their advance and because they were too exhausted to go on.

The Salzgitter Battalion found itself with a different role; the battalion was tasked with clearing the Hougoumont wood in cooperation with some Brunswick units.[51] The commanding officer of the battalion, Major Hammerstein, wrote:

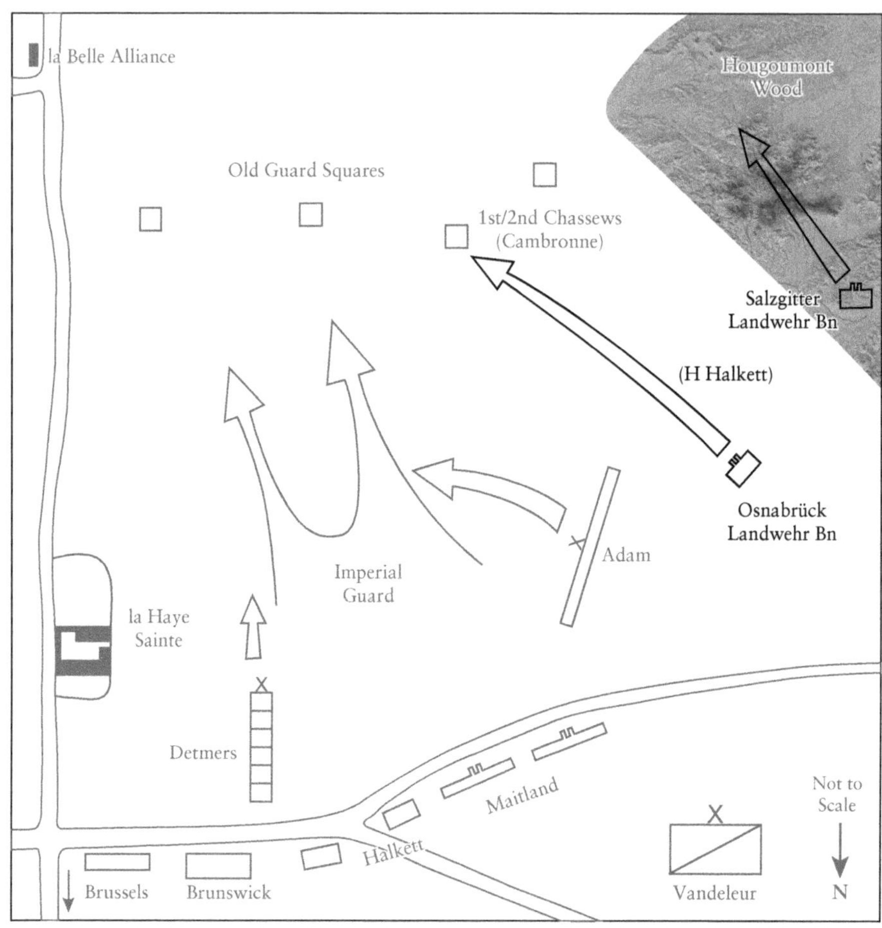

Advance of the Osnabrück and Salzgitter Battalions at the end of the battle.

> The enemy held on most tenaciously. We moved forward by companies; my men had also run out of ammunition and began using the enemy's cartridges... Our advance was made extremely difficult by the enemy who had protective ditches on both of his flanks. Under these circumstances, and because dusk was setting in, nothing seemed to be more effective than an attack with the bayonet. Shouting "Hurrah!", we were quick and fortunate to gain possession of the wood, certainly an important position. The battalion rallied immediately upon leaving the wood and advanced up the elevation in closed column. It was night by this time.[52]

Unsure which direction to take, Hammerstein headed for the main road and, meeting other allied units there, decided to bivouac for the night. Despite facing a demoralised and retiring enemy, at least they had finally crossed bayonets with the French. The same could not be said for the Bremervörde and Quackenbrück battalions, which had remained in the same position from three o'clock until evening. At the end of the battle they did follow the advancing line to the edge of the Hougoumont wood, although they ended the battle without having faced the enemy. They spent the night on the edge of the wood.

Although restricted in the role they were destined to play, the inexperienced battalions had done everything that could have been asked of them and the Osnabrück Battalion had displayed high morale and offensive spirit in their pursuit of the French Guard. Colonel Halkett, who had not impressed General Clinton before the campaign opened, showed that if he lacked ability on the drill ground, he was an inspirational and courageous leader in combat. In his report on the battle, Clinton summed up the performance of the brigade neatly:

> I have the honour to report to your Lordship that the conduct of the 2nd Division during the action of yesterday in as such as to entitle it to the approbation of your lordship and to that of the commander of the forces, the steadiness with which the young Hanoverian Brigade under Colonel Halkett sustained the effect of a lasting cannonade during the several hours which that brigade continued to be in reserve, would have been creditable in veteran troops...[53]

4th Hanoverian Brigade

Having arrived from Quatre Bras in the evening of the 17th, the battalions of the 4th Hanoverian Brigade passed la Haye Sainte farm at about seven o'clock, climbed the ridge and then turned right towards what was to be the left of the allied line. At first, they remained on the high ground as it was believed that the French might attempt to seize the position, but after a short and ineffective cannonade the guns fell silent. The brigade therefore continued its march and bivouacked in the fields close to the hamlet of Mont St Jean, to the north of the ridge line. The brigade was to remain part of Picton's 5th British Division throughout the battle.

At ten o'clock in the morning of the 18th the brigade was ordered to move forward up the slope to just short of the ridgeline and to deploy; Colonel Best described the position his brigade took up in his report of 1824:

> The 4th Brigade under my command received the order to deploy on a nearby height, to the left of the high road leading to Genappe. Having arrived at this point I encountered the 5th [Hanoverian] Brigade under the command of Colonel von Vincke. Major Heise[54] of the Hanoverian artillery had deployed a battery in front of my brigade in order to be able to fire immediately. All of the troops began so to occupy the most

> advantageous positions the terrain at Mont St. Jean offered, and to deploy and to prepare for the forthcoming battle. On the right of my brigade stood the 9th English Brigade commanded by Major-General Sir Denis Pack, consisting of the 1st Battalion of the 42nd Regiment, the 1st Battalion of the 92nd (Highland) Regiment and the 2nd Battalion of the 44th Regiment.[55] On the left was a Nassau brigade in Belgian service, commanded by Prince von Sachsen-Weimar, consisting of the 1st and 2nd Battalions of the Orange-Nassau regiment, together with the 2nd and 3rd Battalions of the [2nd] Nassau-Usingen Regiment. This brigade formed the extreme left wing and occupied the village of Smohain with the farm of Papelotte in its front.[56]

As the battle began with the French attack on Hougoumont, the manoeuvring of cavalry to his front made Best believe that they were about to be attacked by that arm. Heise's battery opened fire on the French horsemen, who probably belonged to General Jacquinot's 1st Cavalry Division which was attached to d'Erlon's 1st Corps.[57]

In light of the cavalry threat, Best claims to have liaised with Colonel von Vincke and agreed that the two brigades should join to form one large square.

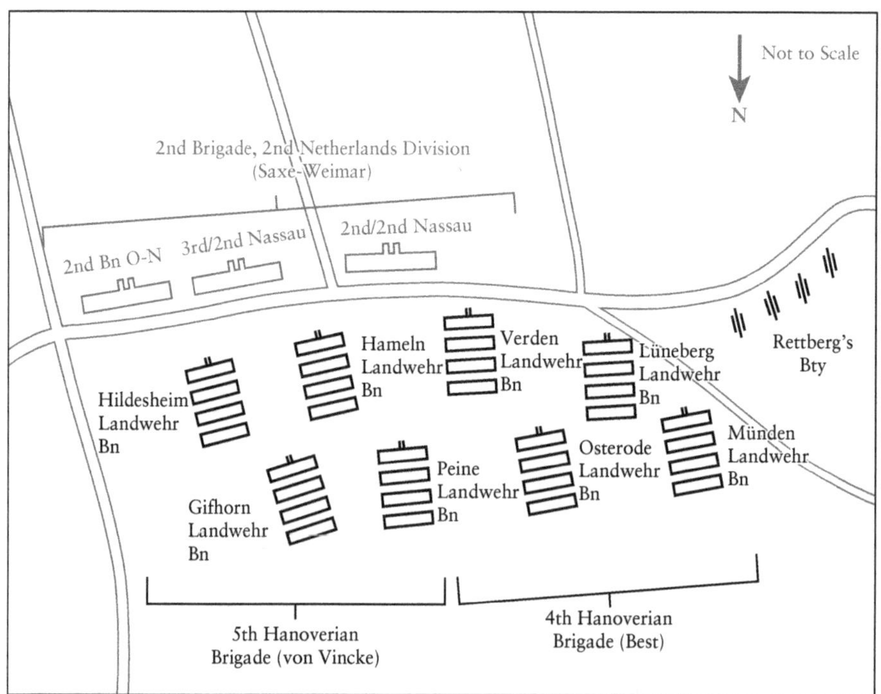

Map showing the initial deployments of the 4th and 5th Hanoverian Brigades at Waterloo.

In his post-action report, written just four days after the battle, Best wrote to General von Alten, 'I came to an agreement with Colonel Vincke, whose brigade was on my left, to form a solid square, composed of the two brigades, which was then arranged.'[58] Although Best was far more experienced than Colonel von Vincke, the latter, as the senior officer, must have had the final say in this formation, which will be described in more detail when we look at the activities of the 5th Brigade. A chain of skirmishers was deployed across the front of the brigade, and these were soon engaged with the French *tirailleurs*.

When d'Erlon launched his major infantry attack on the centre left of the allied line, it seemed as if his right column would strike Best's line. However, the attack was launched in echelon and this column did not come within range of the Hanoverian line before the attack was repelled by the charge of the Union Brigade of heavy cavalry, and Best's men remained spectators of the drama unfolding before them.

Around two o'clock, the 5th Hanoverian Brigade were re-deployed to the centre of the allied position and Best's brigade was now left to cover the frontage that had been the responsibility of von Vincke's battalions as well as its own; Wellington had clearly concluded that there was no longer any threat to this part of the line. Colonel Best described their deployment as follows.[59] The Verden Battalion was deployed in line on the left flank of the brigade, behind the hedge of the Ohain road; it maintained contact with Saxe-Weimar's brigade. This battalion was deployed in line and supported the actions of the Nassauers, engaging the numerous French skirmishers. Rettberg's battery was deployed to their right and to the right of this battery were deployed the Osterode and the Lüneberg Battalions; both in line. The battalions changed formation as dictated by circumstances. Towards five o'clock in the evening, two companies of the

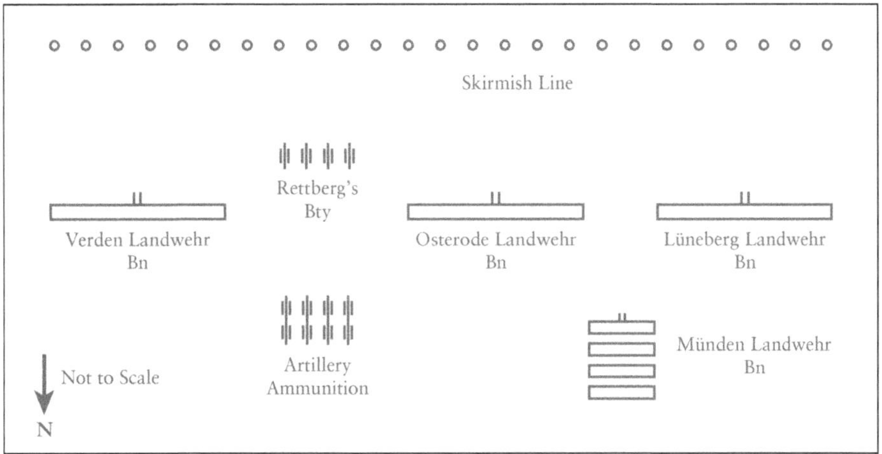

The second deployment of the 4th Hanoverian Brigade based on a sketch by Colonel Best.

Osterode Battalion were sent forward in open order to reinforce the skirmish line, which was under considerable pressure. Although there was no attempt by the French to force the line here, the skirmishing lasted throughout the battle and the skirmishing companies used up all their ammunition.

The Münden Battalion was deployed in the second line behind and to the right of Rettberg's battery and formed the brigade's reserve. After taking up this position, there were no serious attacks on the left wing, but they continued to take casualties from both artillery and long-range skirmisher fire. This frustrating lack of action when still taking casualties is well described by Ensign Opperman in a letter to his parents, 'If we had never been under artillery fire, we now found out what it was like. Men were falling by files, particularly in our No.4 Company. At this horrible place where one faces combat but cannot loose off a single shot we stayed until after 5 o'clock.'[60]

Around this time the first Prussian cavalry arrived near the battalion and gave them the news that Blücher was coming with his whole army. This news was soon followed by an easing of pressure by the French skirmishers, who began to fall back in face of the Prussian advance.

However, with the capture of la Haye Sainte by the French about six o'clock, the pressure on the centre of the allied line was increased as swarms of skirmishers moved forward from the farm and engaged the exhausted British and Netherlands troops who still held this part of the line. The action here became intense, and the Münden Battalion was sent to support the 92nd Highlanders. The battalion stood less than 100 paces behind the 92nd, but to their immense frustration were not needed in the front line. As Lieutenant von Berckefeldt, adjutant of the Münden Battalion, wrote in his description of the battle:

> here it was where from the soldiers' ranks the loud request was heard: 'Why don't we go at them and revenge our fallen comrades?' But it was impossible to grant their request. Standing still and with their arms at the ready, the battalion had to remain where it was and at a distance of a few feet had to let the Scots alone fight on in this murderous contest. Our battalion commander was constrained in this regard by the strictest and most definite orders and the splendid opportunity to come to blows with the enemy thus came and went. It hurt deeply that the battalion had been denied here the chance to give proof of Hanoverian bravery in going to the attack and in hand-to-hand combat.[61]

When it became clear that the enemy had been held, the Münden Battalion had to return to its position behind Rettberg's battery. Here it stayed until called forward to join the rest of the brigade near la Belle Alliance.

The brigade was not involved in the repulse of the Imperial Guard at the end of the battle and when the order came for the final advance, Best immediately gave the order to join the move forward. It seems that at this time the Münden Battalion had not returned to its position and that the brigade advanced without it. The advance continued across the valley that had separated the two protagonists and the 4th Brigade were stopped as they reached the former French position where they bivouacked. Here they were joined by the Münden Battalion.

It is interesting to note that soon after the brigade halted and settled down for the night, it was visited by General Kempt, who had taken over command of the 5th Division when General Picton was killed. Having congratulated the brigade on its achievements during the battle, he still felt that it was the occasion to point out that Wellington had noticed that the brigade had opened fire at too long a range and had consequently wasted their cartridges. Although this was interpreted as over-eagerness, it is interesting that a point like this should be brought up on such an occasion.

Hanoverian reports are unusually candid about the men in their formations who did not do their duty, something generally omitted in British reports. In his report to General von Alten, Colonel Best wrote:

> Although, on the whole, I can be satisfied with the conduct of officers and men during this battle, I regret to have to note that several individuals took advantage of the opportunity to stay in the rear, in particular several assistant surgeons and junior surgeons who failed to provide any help…These useless people returned later to their battalions and offered all kinds of excuses… The musicians were supposed to transport the wounded… those men were nowhere to be found and returned to the brigade as late as the third or fourth day after the battle.
>
> Captains Siegner and Ostwald of the Verden Battalion[62], claiming sickness, went to the rear and, allegedly, even as far as Antwerp. Captain von Rauschenplat of the Osterode Battalion also went back due to indisposition. Ensign Schwabe of the Osterode Battalion stayed with the baggage on his commander's order even though the brigade had already given that assignment to Lieutenant Best. Lieutenant Kuhlmann of the Münden Battalion, who is of weak disposition, also went back, feeling unwell. Captain Jormin and Lieutenant Schneider of the Lüneburg Battalion also went to the rear due to sickness, although the latter did return. The QMSgt of the Lüneburg Battalion was the only one who stayed with his unit; all others had retired with the baggage. Several NCOs and privates took advantage of an opportunity to retire with the baggage and went to Brussels and as far as Antwerp, and now return day by day.
>
> Colonel Best recommends the surgeons mentioned for 'appropriate punishment.'[63]

The 4th Hanoverian Brigade probably had the least prominent role of the four Hanoverian brigades present at the battle; none of the battalions had been involved in close combat, but rather had stood under artillery fire and been involved in skirmish fire fights throughout the day. Of particular note is that no fewer than four company commanders unaccountably went missing from across the brigade (out of sixteen) just before Waterloo; although no more than two were from any single battalion, the potential impact of this, not least on the lieutenants who found themselves in command of companies, could have been profound on the morale of the men. But this does not seem to have been the case and to their credit, they had patiently and courageously endured the French fire, held their portion of the line, and not allowed their enthusiasm to get the better of them. This was all Wellington could have asked of them in the circumstances.

5th Hanoverian Brigade

In the night of 15/16 June, the 5th Hanoverian Brigade was ordered to concentrate at Halle and then march to the small town of Waterloo. However, because it was widely spread out in its cantonments it was not ready to march until eleven o'clock in the morning. As they marched, they could hear the sound of gun fire from Quatre Bras. This clearly had a poor impact on the Gifhorn Landwehr Battalion; Ernst Christian Schacht, who was a nineteen-year-old soldier in the battalion, wrote in a letter to his parents, dated 25 August 1815:

> The cannonade became more intense, and now we were told that the attack had begun and that it was the beginning of the battle. What a thought! One thought after another, one sigh after another went up to God. Everybody lost courage and nothing helped. All we could do was search for our courage once again. We remained at Waterloo until half past five and we saw 40,000 Dutchmen retire with many wounded; the word spread that there was no chance against the French who were too strong.[64]

Having reached Waterloo at six o'clock in the evening and having no further orders Colonel von Vincke gave his men some rest before setting off again. Reaching Genappe towards eleven o'clock at night, von Vincke received the order to bivouac in front of that town and to march on to Quatre Bras at dawn the next morning (the 17th). The brigade arrived at the hamlet as the morning's skirmishing came to an end, and in his report von Vincke probably exaggerated a little by writing 'we were only briefly under fire but had no casualties.'[65]

In the afternoon, the brigade retraced its steps towards Waterloo. On arrival at the Mont Saint Jean farm von Vincke was directed to take position on what was to be the left wing of the army (see diagram on p.130).

The following morning the brigade found itself with the 4th Hanoverian Brigade to its right and Prince Saxe-Weimar's all-Nassau 2nd Brigade of the 2nd Netherlands Division to his left; though in his report von Vincke rather surprisingly states, given that it was written just two days after the battle, 'there were no troops on my left flank',[66] although he does not mention Saxe-Weimar's brigade which were to his front left.

In agreement with Colonel Best's report on the 4th Hanoverian Brigade, von Vincke mentions the large force of French cavalry that was observed manoeuvring opposite his brigade. When he believed this force was advancing against him, 'To avoid manoeuvring at this moment, I had all eight battalions of the two brigades [his and Best's] stand next to each other in close column. I then had the rear ranks face outward, the flanks turn left and right, so that, in my eyes, the whole formed an impenetrable mass.'[67]

The 'square' of which he speaks was actually a very large solid column, consisting of all eight battalions of the two brigades. How these battalions were actually deployed is not made clear, but we can safely assume that the battalions were in column and in at least two lines, each of four battalions. This is an extraordinary formation and one unseen anywhere else in Wellington's army; its formation is examined in more detail in Appendix A. Its look must have been very similar to d'Erlon's widely criticised attack columns, and it is surprising that such an unusual formation has not generated more discussion among students of the battle. While *perhaps* an adequate defence against cavalry, it would have proved a costly one if it had faced infantry or concentrated artillery fire, although we must assume that much of it, if not all, was sheltered behind the ridge, and the French artillery at this time was concentrating its fire on the left centre of the allied line where d'Erlon's attack was planned to fall.

Much of the French artillery fire, passing over the ridgeline, went over the heads of the men, but some inevitably fell among the ranks, as Christian Schacht describes:

> We remained in this formation [the closed square] until 2 o'clock. During this time more than 80 balls flew narrowly over our heads. At last some came lower and struck us, killing and mutilating some and wounding others. We witnessed such cruelty in this way, it was butchery. I am trembling as I write… Thousands upon thousands had lost their lives, merely for the sake of their country. Seeing all of this made me lose all sense.

As d'Erlon's attack was repulsed and the French cavalry engaged their British counterparts, the solid square remained unemployed further to the east. However, they were not to remain in that position for long.

Colonel von Vincke wrote two reports on the actions of his brigade at Waterloo; the first was relatively short and dated Le Roeulx (not too far from

Mons in Belgium), 20 June 1815, when things must have been fresh in his mind. The second was dated Ostendwalde (near Osnabrück in Hanover), 7 January 1825, after he had had time to reflect, speak to fellow officers[68] and read other accounts of the battle. Up to this point in the battle, both his accounts agree, but there is some divergence from this point.

In his later account, von Vincke states that his brigade was moved to the centre left of the allied position directly behind the British brigades of the 5th Division to reinforce them in case of need in their defence against d'Erlon's corps. Here, although not directly engaged, they suffered many casualties. This deployment is not mentioned in his first account written four days after the battle. The accounts then once more coincide.

Now that the threat to the centre left had been neutralised, and as Wellington now assessed the threat to his left flank as a weak one, he chose to reinforce his centre and von Vincke was ordered there with his brigade. The time this move was ordered is unclear; Major von Strube, commanding officer of the Hameln Landwehr Battalion, says it was 12.30, but this must be too early; von Vincke only states that it was after d'Erlon's repulse. He has more to say on the move itself:

> In the first position, only a few men were wounded, but we had considerable losses on the march to the new position assigned to me, primarily due to the many contradictory instructions, at first to halt, then to march by files, and then again to march by companies, and eventually again by files. Even so, there was not the slightest sign of disorder, and the conduct of our men left nothing to be desired.[69]

We must presume that the changes of formation were to try and reduce casualties during the march, but it is also unusual for anyone other than the battalion or brigade staff to make such minor tactical decisions. If there was some confusion, it is at least to the credit of the battalions that there was no disorder.

On arrival in the centre, the brigade deployed in two groups; the Hameln and Gifhorn Battalions were deployed further forward than the other two, and to the left, but very close to, the main Brussels road, 'about 300 paces from the farm of Mont St Jean, and 700 paces from La Haye Sainte' according to Captain Hartmann of the Hameln Battalion.[70] At first they deployed in two columns, but when the French launched their great cavalry charges the two battalions formed a single square, four ranks deep. In this new position the two forward battalions lost men to both musketry and close-range artillery fire.

The Hildesheim and Peine battalions formed up further back and to the right of the main road, just forward of the farm of Mont Saint Jean and behind the allied cavalry; they too formed a single square when threatened by cavalry. Von Vincke noted that these two battalions were placed here, 'to detain the very numerous fugitives.' Controversially, at about six o'clock, these two battalions received orders to retreat and marched off the battlefield,[71] leaving von Vincke with just the Hameln and Gifhorn Battalions directly under his command. To his left he identified several British squares (these were presumably of the 5th British Division or of Lambert's brigade).

After the cavalry charges had finished, the Hameln Battalion was sent across onto the right-hand side of the main road and then, at about six o'clock, the Gifhorn Battalion was ordered to follow it. However, each occupied a very different position and did not deploy next to each other. Major von Strube, commanding officer of the Hameln Battalion, described his new position thus:

> The battalion remained in this position [on the left of the main road] until almost half past five, when it received the order to occupy a height on the right of the high road and to deploy there, in accordance with a direct order from the Duke of Wellington, who was positioned on this height. On the right of the battalions stood the Nassau contingent

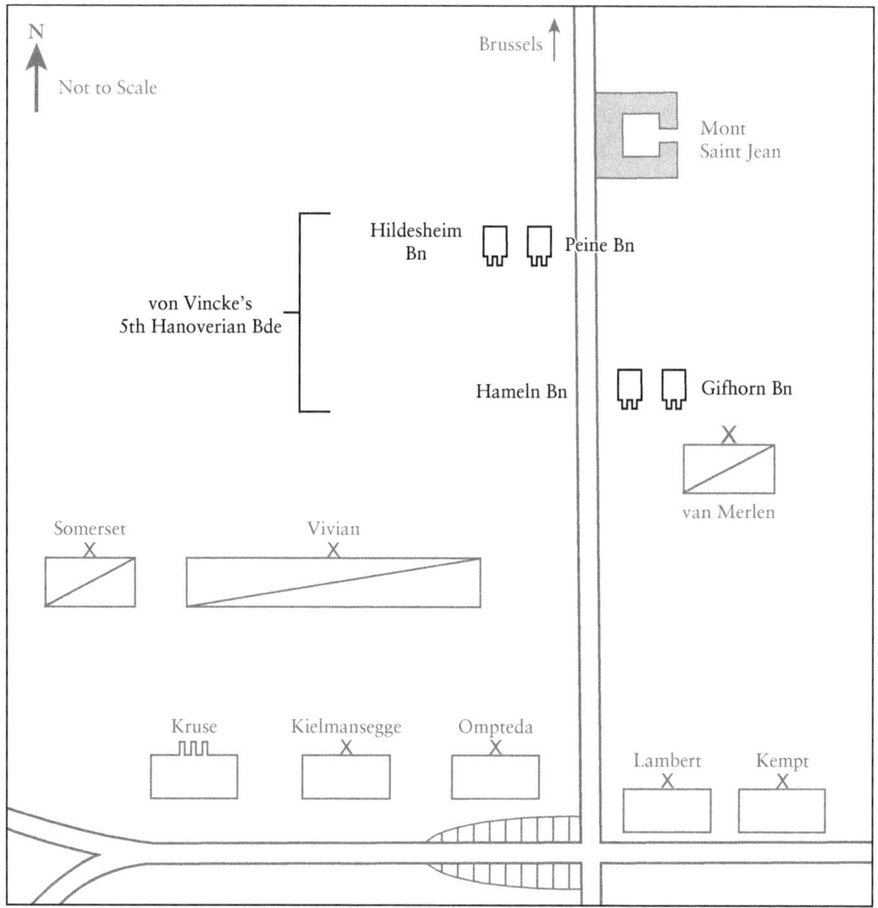

Map showing the second position of the 5th Hanoverian Brigade at Waterloo.

> and on the left were English regiments belonging to the 5th Division, as well as the 8th Battalion of the Legion.[72]

The battalion therefore occupied a position just to the right of the main road, on a small elevation with the Brunswickers (whom he erroneously identifies as Nassauers) just to their right, and the British 5th Division on the other side of the main road. It is not clear where the rest of von Ompteda's brigade were at this precise moment, but their own accounts have the 5th Line Battalion dispersed, the 2nd Light in la Haye-Sainte and the 1st Light in the sunken lane around the crossroads. The 8th Battalion that von Strube mentions were also rallying after having been dispersed by French cuirassiers and the disorganisation of this brigade no doubt accounts for Wellington ordering the Hameln Battalion into what was effectively a gap in the very centre of his line.

> around six o'clock in the evening, I received the order from Lieutenant Colonel Cambel [sic] of the Quartermaster-General's staff, to march with my remaining battalion, the Gifhorn, across the high road as far as our right wing, where I was to take position a little in front of the 1st Hussars Regiment of the King's German Legion, next to the Brunswick infantry, and to order the men to lie down, because the musket fire was extraordinarily severe. This was more or less the same spot that the Grubenhagen Battalion had held previously.[73]

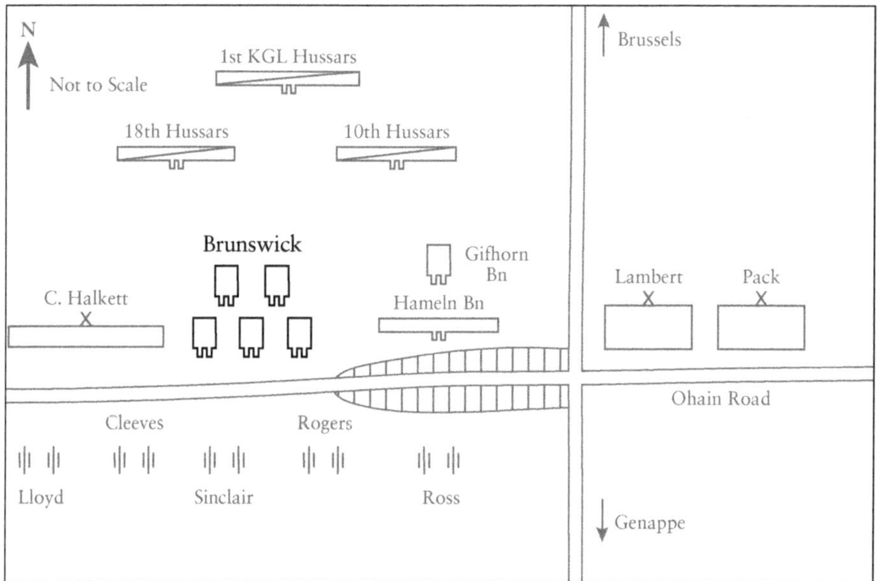

Map showing the final position of the Hameln and Gifhorn Landwehr Battalions at Waterloo.

As the Brunswick infantry was ordered to this position to reinforce the centre just prior to the attack of the Imperial Guard, this helps us to place these two battalions in the front line and filling the gap left by the retirement of the 2nd KGL Brigade, 1st Hanoverian Brigade and the 1st Nassau Regiment (the latter two of which have already been studied).

Although von Vincke has the Brunswick troops to their right, and von Strube the Nassauers, both wore dark uniforms, and in the smoke and confusion of battle might easily have been confused with each other; though it could conceivably have been either, at different times. Despite this slight discrepancy, we can now be quite sure that, contrary to most accounts of the battle, these two battalions appear to have filled the gap left in the allied line after the withdrawal of the Nassau and other Hanoverian troops (both KGL and 1st Hanoverian Brigade).

The accounts of von Vincke and von Strube now have the Hameln and Gifhorn Landwehr Battalions in the front line at the very centre of the allied line towards the end of the battle.

This position was in the thick of the fight and von Vincke admits what an impact it had on the inexperienced Gifhorn Battalion:

> It was here that the commander of the Gifhorn Battalion, Major von Hammerstein, received the wound that killed him. Major Leue, the second major of the battalion, had already been fatally wounded in the 3rd [previous] position. On the move to the second position the senior captain, Wiedenfeldt had also been wounded, although not quite as severely. The resolve of the battalion's men was gravely tested, and it took the active assistance and presence of mind primarily of my Senior Adjutant, Captain von Ludewig, and also of Captain von Wick and Adjutant Schwake, to restore complete order within a few moments.[74]

Von Strube of the Hameln Battalion continues:

> Having occupied the position the battalion fired 30 rounds per man against the enemy's infantry, especially the *Garde Impériale* which was undertaking its final attack...[75]

Thirty rounds per man represents a considerable firefight lasting a considerable time (at such close quarters), though if this is the truth, the Hameln Battalion's casualties (von Stube gives the battalion's casualties for the day as nine killed and sixty-four wounded out of a strength of 400 men present at the battle[76]) do not suggest they were facing a formed and formidable enemy. Von Vincke states that this was the first time the battalions had opened fire.

If the brigade had been immediately to the right of the Brussels road, it is unlikely that it faced the Imperial Guard, who it is generally accepted attacked the line further to the right.[77] But the Guard's attack was supported by the French units that had captured la Haye Sainte and operated from the area around the farm, putting pressure on this part of the allied line. This seems to be supported by the report of Major General Lambert, whose brigade had moved forward from reserve and was in position just the other (eastern) side of the main road. In a letter to Siborne he wrote:

> after the enemy got possession of the Haye Sainte [sic], they kept constantly sending small detachments to a mound close to the intersection of the Brussels road to Genappe, which forced the Hanoverian Brigade of the 6th [sic] Division to fall back…[78]

Although he has the wrong division, the only other Hanoverian brigade in this part of the allied line was Kielmansegge's, which had been ordered to retire by this point in the battle. It is therefore more likely that it was these men that von Vincke's men engaged.

At eight o'clock, by von Vincke's account, the final advance began, and the two battalions moved forwards with the general advance of the allied army. The Earl of Uxbridge was wounded nearby and four men of the Gifhorn Battalion carried him back. The two battalions continued their advance until half past ten at night, although there is no talk of any engagements. They stopped at the farm of Gros Fromage, just north of Genappe; an advance of about four kilometres. They bivouacked for the night in a nearby orchard.

In his own summary, Colonel von Vincke wrote of his brigade:

> The oldest veterans could not have faced the fire with greater calm than that shown by our young men. As soon as one of theirs had fallen or was wounded, another stepped up in his place, without the least commotion. Only the surgeons, musicians and drummers ran away at the first cannon shot, but slowly turned up again.[79]

His comments on his young soldiers reflect those of other commanders of the contingent that the men showed great courage in their first major battle and generally maintained their cohesion throughout the day thanks to the strenuous efforts of their officers. His criticism of his surgeons echoes that of Colonel Best in his report on the 4th Hanoverian Brigade. Von Vincke ordered that each surgeon was to account for their actions on the day of battle by answering some laid down questions.[80] Although von Vincke was generally unhappy with their excuses, the truth is that these were relatively recently recruited assistant surgeons with no previous experience in war, disorientated by the confusion of battle and struggling to find a brigade that moved location on the battlefield a number of times and who were concerned about accounts from fugitives that the French were advancing on Brussels.

Summary

Histories of the battle pay little attention to the actions of the 5th Hanoverian brigade, implying that it had little involvement in the battle. However, the accounts from within the brigade show this to be a false presumption; indeed, the brigade, or at least two battalions of it, were more involved in the various phases of the battle than is generally acknowledged, and if they were not involved in any dirty, prolonged face-to-face fighting that caused them heavy casualties, it is probably true to say they took a far more prominent part than they are generally given credit for. However, the brigade contribution was certainly one of two parts, for while the Hameln and Gifhorn battalions took a very creditable part in the battle, the retreat of the Hildesheim and Peine battalions from the battlefield, although almost certainly ordered, reflects more on the inexperience of their commanders than it does on the potential of their men.

The move of the Hameln and Gifhorn battalions to the right of the main road has had little or no exposure in previous histories of the battle, yet accounts from the 1st Hanoverian and 2nd KGL Brigades, and the Nassau contingent, show that a dangerous gap had appeared in Wellington's line, which was filled by these two battalions. It is not possible to speculate what the full implications would have been if they had not been available and capable of filling this gap, but it is worth noting that it happened at the true crisis of the battle.

Colonel von Vincke's leadership proved to be somewhat suspect, and like the commanding officers of the battalions just mentioned, he displayed his own lack of recent campaign and brigade command experience; perhaps it is no coincidence that two events of particular note in our consideration of the Hanoverian brigades involved the 5th Brigade; the strange formation formed in the early stages of the battle and his loss of control over half his brigade which resulted in its retreat towards the end of it. He was probably lucky that a victory did not expose his performance to too much scrutiny, but reflected the shortage of suitably experienced senior officers in the Hanoverian service prior to the campaign opening.

While the loss of some key officers in the Gifhorn Battalion led to shaky morale for a time, as in the other Hanoverian brigades the soldiers displayed enthusiasm and courage, and although they were generally carefully managed by Wellington, they held the line and were still battleworthy at the end of the fighting. When they left General Kempt's division towards the end of the year to march back to Hanover, the general wrote to von Vincke:

> I cannot permit you to depart without expressing my entire approbation of the conduct of the officers and men since I have had the

> honour to command them. Though very young soldiers, they evinced the greatest steadiness and very best spirit in one of the greatest battles fought in modern times. Qualities which I feel persuaded will never leave them and their general discipline and regularity in camp and quarters has also been highly commendable.[81]

The Hanoverian Artillery

After Quatre Bras, von Rettberg's 2nd Hanoverian Battery continued to operate with Picton's 5th Division, although officially part of the 4th Division which had been deployed to Hal. At Waterloo, it was initially deployed on the ridge just to the east of the crossroads that marked the centre of the allied position, in a strong position; von Rettberg wrote, 'I had the most beautiful position that one could wish for artillery... I stood about 8 to 10 feet higher than the [Ohain] road. Immediately on the other side of the road the terrain ran gently down towards the enemy. I had arranged to cut down the hedge in the morning to have a view.'[82] He maintained that his fine position was the reason his casualties were so low, even though, 'a continuous cannonade took place between us that lasted until evening. The enemy concentrated his fire on the cutting at La Haye Sainte and at our right wing.'[83] Although not directly attacked, the battery continued its fire throughout the battle and was finally forced to reduce its rate due to a shortage of ammunition until it ran out altogether. Due to this shortage, it took no part in the allied advance at the end of the battle. In the evening it was replaced by a Prussian battery but passed the night on the battlefield. Its losses were only one man killed and one officer and ten men wounded.

Having bivouacked on the night of 16 June by the side of the road which ran from its cantonments in Gent to Brussels, Braun's 1st Hanoverian Battery continued its march on the morning of the 17th to the Soignies forest, where it spent the night of the 17th. On the morning of the 18th it continued its march straight onto the Waterloo position, which it reached about midday. It was initially deployed as part of the artillery reserve located near Mont St Jean farm. However, it was not to remain unemployed for very long; at about 3pm it was deployed into the front line to support Major General Lambert's brigade, which was deploying forward to reinforce the left centre that was being attacked by d'Erlon's corps. As it moved, Braun was wounded in the thigh by a cannonball which also killed his horse, and he was forced to hand command over to Lieutenant von Schulzen. As it took position next to Picton's 5th Division the battery's howitzer was destroyed and a number of men wounded before it had fired a shot in anger.[84] The battery's fire contributed to the defeat of d'Erlon's attack.

Shortly after d'Erlon's men were thrown back, the acting battery commander was mortally wounded, and the command passed to the next senior lieutenant, d'Huvelé. He moved the battery forwards of the Ohain road in order to improve its field of fire and remained there for the rest of the battle, often under skirmisher fire, which caused considerable casualties, and always under artillery fire. As the afternoon progressed, because of the increasing number of casualties, there were only enough men to crew three guns and by 6.30pm the battery requested manpower from the unnamed Scottish regiment to their right. Eventually only a single gun could be manned, which by 7.30pm had fired the last of the ammunition and the battery was ordered to the rear by General Kempt. Due to a shortage of horses and the exhaustion of the remaining men, this was a long process. Only two guns were fit for service the next day; one officer and eight other ranks had been killed and two officers and thirty-three other ranks had been wounded; 1,300 rounds had been fired. The battery had displayed considerable courage and endurance, especially having been under command of junior officers for most of the battle.

The Duke of Cumberland's Hussars

The Duke of Cumberland's Hussars were the only Hanoverian cavalry regiment to serve at Waterloo. The other two were with their parent brigade (Colonel Estorff's) which was part of the allied force detached to Hal. Why the Cumberland Hussars were not with them is unclear. Their controversial role in the battle is examined in detail in Appendix C so we shall only give an outline of their actions in this section.

The regiment was initially deployed in reserve behind the centre of Wellington's line, some 400 metres behind the ridge, in line with the other cavalry regiments of Dörnberg's cavalry brigade (the 1st and 2nd Light Dragoons KGL, and 23rd (British) Light Dragoons). Although some way back from the front line, many French cannon balls which flew over the ridge fell among them and their casualties slowly increased; standing inactive under fire from an enemy you cannot see must have been very frustrating and unnerving for such inexperienced troops. Their situation was not helped by the fact that they remained mounted, unlike the brigade next to them, a tactic which would have reduced the steady drip of casualties.

As the French cavalry made their repeated charges on the allied line, regiment after regiment of allied cavalry was committed to countering their charges. The British heavy cavalry, already much reduced from their earlier charges, were so weak and exhausted that an increasing number of light cavalry were committed to this task. Eventually, the Cumberland Hussars were ordered forward from their position in reserve. However, before it received any order to charge, the commanding officer, Lieutenant Colonel von Hake, ordered the regiment to retire and it marched from the battlefield.

This movement did not go unnoticed and a number of aides de camp and staff officers were sent back to order it to return; first to the battlefield and then to take up a position at Mont St Jean where it would be out of danger. Nothing could persuade the commanding officer to stop, and the regiment eventually drew up eight miles from the battlefield in front of Brussels.

It is worthy of note that the regiment had in fact suffered quite heavy casualties despite their lack of action; around sixty killed and wounded – about 12 percent of the whole. It also seems that some officers and men of the regiment, appalled by the behaviour of their colonel and comrades, refused to retire and attached themselves to other regiments in Dörnberg's brigade and served through the battle, and this would explain why a number of Waterloo medals were later awarded to the regiment.

Von Hake was later court marshalled and cashiered and the regiment condemned to the humiliating duty of escorts and other general duties in the rear areas for the advance into France.

Casualties

1st Hanoverian Brigade (Kielmansegge) Casualties on the 18th:[85]

	Killed	Wounded	Missing	Total	%
Fieldjäger	No	Breakdown	-	53	16%
Bremen Field Bn	10	67	26	103	19%
Verden Field Bn	56	100	14	170	30%
Osterode Field Bn	14	48	-	62	10%
Grubenhagen Field Bn	13	54	-	67	10%
Lüneburg Field Bn	20	89	82	191	31%
Total	113	358	122	**646**	**20%**

During the 16th, 17th and 18th, total casualties were thirty-eight officers and 939 men. The brigade started the campaign with 3,315 men; a loss over the three days of 27 percent.

3rd Hanoverian Brigade (Halkett) Casualties on the 18th:[86]

	Killed	Wounded	Missing	Total	%
Bremervörde Landwehr Bn	18	24	48	90	14%
Osnabrück Landwehr Bn	18	87	-	105	17%
Quakenbrück Landwehr Bn	1	9	24	34	6%
Salzgitter Landwehr Bn	21	64	83	168	26%
Total	58	184	155	**397**	**16%**

During the 16th, 17th and 18th, total casualties were 208 men. The brigade started the campaign with 2,541 men; a loss over the three days of 8 percent.

4th Hanoverian Brigade (Best) Casualties on the 18th:[87]

	Killed	Wounded	PoW	Total	%
Verden Landwehr Bn	55	85	89	229	36%
Lüneburg Landwehr Bn	9	72	-	81	12%
Osterode Landwehr Bn	16	103	-	119	17%
Münden Landwehr Bn	13	138	-	151	22%
Total	93	398	89	**580**	**22%**

In 4th Brigade accounts there is no mention of so many men being made prisoner on the 18th and it appears that this figure (eighty-nine) reflects those that were captured at Quatre Bras and were still missing, so not actually lost at Waterloo. This would bring casualties for the brigade on the 18th down to 19 percent.

During the 16th, 17th and 18th, total casualties were 430 men. The brigade started the campaign with 2,669 men; a loss over the three days of 16 percent.

5th Hanoverian Brigade (von Vincke)

There is no breakdown of casualties for this brigade by battalion; the following is from Siborne[88] which covers losses on 15th–18th. However, as the brigade was not present at Quatre Bras, nor in the retreat on the 17th, these must be very close to the casualties suffered on the 18th only:

	Killed	Wounded	Missing	Total	%
Gifhorn Landwehr Bn	15	72	-	87	14%
Hameln Landwehr Bn	9	64	7	80	12%
Hildesheim Landwehr Bn	3	21	-	24	4%
Peine Landwehr Bn	8	42	6	56	9%
Total	35	199	13	**247**	**10%**

During the 16th, 17th and 18th, total casualties were 247 men. The brigade started the campaign with 2,604 men; a loss of 10 percent.

The level of casualties among the Hanoverian contingent generally reflected the extent to which they were drawn into the fighting. The 1st Brigade deployed in the centre of the first line suffered considerably, and the casualties in the 3rd and 5th brigades fell most heavily on the two battalions of each that saw the most fighting, while the other two battalions, which were involved in virtually no fighting, suffered only comparatively light casualties, although the casualties suffered by the Peine Landwehr Battalion (as well as the whole of the 4th Brigade which saw little fighting throughout the day) show that the effect of the French artillery was considerable, even to the battalions in the shelter of the ridge.

In the first chapter of this book, we covered the need to be careful in interpreting the numbers of 'missing' and above we have seen how the number of missing in the Verden Landwehr Battalion of the 4th Brigade from Quatre Bras were brought over into their casualties for Waterloo. The number of missing for the Lüneburg Field Battalion (1st Brigade) can be explained by their having been ridden down by cuirassiers during their doomed counterattack on la Haye Sainte. However, the relatively high number of missing from the Salzgitter Landwehr Battalion (of 3rd Brigade) is interesting; the battalion saw little fighting through the day until it advanced through the Hougoumont wood as darkness fell and with the French fleeing the battlefield. We have no indication how many later returned to the battalion and how many were lost.

Figures from the 5th Brigade (von Vincke) show that by 15 June, before any fighting had taken place, the four battalions had lost on average 10 percent of their original strength. This loss was no doubt due to men absent who were sick and many on 'detached duties' (a regular and frustrating drain on manpower that was a daily duty on campaign), but probably also included a number who were unaccounted for, for less legitimate reasons. This drain on manpower, or 'strategic consumption' as it is often called, saw a steady reduction in available manpower as a campaign dragged on and is well illustrated by the Verden and Bremen Field battalions of the 1st Brigade. The Verden Battalion started the campaign with a strength of about 560 men and the Bremen Battalion with about 530. Major von Schkopp of the former battalion wrote, 'I distinctly recollect that when we arrived and bivouacked in Paris the Bremen had 180 men, and the Verden Light Infantry Battalion 120 men.'[89]

Conclusion

The Hanoverian contingent had made a significant contribution to the victory, although perhaps somewhat tainted by the actions of the few. The 1st Brigade with the most experienced battalions had been trusted to hold a vital part of the allied line, the very centre, and despite being put under substantial pressure and pushed back a number of times they returned to the fray each time and played a significant role in holding it against repeated French attempts to break the line there. The other three infantry brigades saw much less close combat; only two battalions from each of the 3rd and 5th Brigades saw much fighting. The two from the 3rd Brigade took a leading role in the final advance and the two from the 5th played an important reinforcing role in the centre at the crisis of the battle. The 4th Brigade, although it remained in a relatively quiet sector of the battlefield, maintained its position there and allowed the senior commanders to concentrate on other more pressurised sectors. The two batteries maintained their positions and their fire throughout the day and the stamina of the 1st Battery, as damage and casualties reduced them to two serviceable guns, which continued its fire until the very end, deserves particular credit. The name of the Cumberland Hussars will forever be associated with cowardice, but this unit, and the two battalions of the 5th Brigade that withdrew from the battlefield, should not cast a shadow over the accomplishments and high morale of the rest of the contingent, who did more than could have been expected of them.

Chapter Five

The Netherlands Contingent

The Dutch-Belgian troops, from political or other causes, which is unnecessary to inquire into, would not fight the French... the Dutch-Belgians did not fight at all...'[1]

The slanderous quote given above comes from a British officer who should, as the deputy assistant quartermaster general of the 3rd British Division, and a future general in the British army, have been well placed to give a rather more objective and fair interpretation of the contribution of one of the biggest contingents in Wellington's army. Until more recent times it has been the one most maligned in the historiography of the battle and yet has still not been objectively analysed.

The reasons for this are not particularly difficult to find; as we shall see, not only did Wellington himself have his doubts over their loyalty and dependability, but the memoirs and accounts of contemporary British officers and observers also openly shared these concerns and were quick to draw erroneous conclusions from their own 'snapshot' observations of the army of the Netherlands' performance on campaign and on the battlefield.

Background

By mid-February 1815 the two independent states of the United Provinces and Belgium had been combined into the Kingdom of the United Netherlands. Despite this, in most English histories of the campaign the army of the Netherlands continues to be almost universally described as the Dutch-Belgian army as if these two separate countries still existed.

The Belgian provinces

Prior to the French Revolution, Belgium was known as the Austrian Netherlands. It was invaded by the French in the revolutionary campaign of 1794 and immediately incorporated into France. Despite French repression and the mass conscription of Belgians into the French army, uprisings against French rule failed and the country was not liberated until 1814 when the provinces were occupied by the Austrians and Prussians. The nucleus of a new Belgian army, the *Légion Belge,* was raised, but after years of war there was little enthusiasm for military service and recruiting was slow. The Belgians were apathetic to their new rulers; a provisional government established under an Austrian governor-general.

The United Provinces

After their invasion of the Austrian Netherlands in 1794, the following year the French revolutionary armies invaded the Dutch Republic of the United Provinces. Choosing not to incorporate their latest acquisition into France, it was renamed the Batavian Republic and its army compelled to fight for Napoleon. In 1806 the republic was renamed the Kingdom of Holland and Napoleon's brother Louis put on the throne. He ruled semi-independently of France. However, in 1810 the kingdom was incorporated into France and its military forces were made a part of the French army. In November 1813, after the French defeat at Leipzig, Holland was invaded by Cossacks. The Dutch rose against the French and organised a provisional government with pro-royalty leanings. Willem Frederik, the crown prince of the House of Orange-Nassau, landed in Holland from exile in Britain to wide acclaim and was established as the Sovereign Prince. Immediate efforts were made to raise a Dutch army, but there was a shortage of money and experienced volunteers. The last French garrisons only surrendered in May 1814.

As the Congress of Vienna considered the future of a new Europe, the allies wanted a northern buffer zone against France that was strong enough to resist an invasion. The result was the joining of the protestant United Provinces of the northern Netherlands to the catholic Austrian Netherlands to become the United Kingdom of the Netherlands. By mid-February 1815, the Dutch had established control of their new territories in Belgium and on 16 March 1815 Willem Fredrik proclaimed himself King of the Netherlands.

The United Kingdom of the Netherlands

The problems facing the new country should not be underestimated; its systems of government were still establishing themselves. It was virtually bankrupt, its people were fiercely anti-conscription and yet it had most to lose; it was likely to be the first country to be invaded and faced the loss of its recent independence. On this basis, a considerable effort would be expected, but there seemed little enthusiasm for raising a new army in view of the considerable difficulties that it faced.

The new army lacked ethos and part of it at least, a sense of loyalty to the new establishment. Yet this army faced not only providing a contingent for the allied army, but also needed to garrison and police the full borders of the new state while having only those officers and men who had fought for their potential enemy to bring experience and military competence to the new force.

While the United Provinces welcomed their union with Belgium, the same cannot be said of the Belgians, who lost their independence by the decision of the Congress.

It is perhaps unsurprising that the British doubted the motivation of the Belgian troops. The allied suspicion of the Belgians is dealt with in detail in Appendix D, but it is worth quoting a Belgian general, General Renard, who wrote in 1855:

> Above all we must ask if the cause for which we fight is such that it can take the place of powerful ties of a strong discipline in the unit, where neither the time nor the circumstances have permitted them to be bound together. It is just to ask if the Belgians, at this time, fought for a cause that would excite their courage against a hated enemy. For the Belgians in 1815, for what cause were they going to shed their blood? Was it for the independence of their homeland? No, because their hopes on this subject had been disappointed; England itself had robbed them of this independence, to bind their fine provinces to a state that they had learnt to hate and from which, for two centuries, they had received only insults or bad experiences.[2]

Contingent size[3]

2nd Netherlands Division (Lieutenant General Perponcher-Sedlnitsky) – 8,281 (the 2nd Brigade was entirely composed of Nassau troops and is covered in Chapter 2).[4]

1st Brigade (Major-General Bijlandt) – 3,755
27th Jäger Battalion – 835
7th (Belgian) Line Battalion – 716
5th Militia Battalion – 490
7th Militia Battalion – 675
8th Militia Battalion – 558

Horse Artillery Battery (Bijleveld) – 111
Train – 120
(Belgian) Foot Artillery Battery (Stevenart) – 116
Train – 134

3rd Netherlands Division (Lieutenant General Chassé) – 7,146

1st Brigade (Colonel Detmers) – 3,298
35th (Belgian) Jäger Battalion – 605
2nd Line Battalion – 471
4th Militia Battalion – 519
6th Militia Battalion – 592

17th Militia Battalion – 534
19th Militia Battalion – 467

(Belgian) Horse Battery (Krahmer de Bichin) – 123
Train - 162

2nd Brigade (Major-General d'Aubremé) – 3,848
36th (Belgian) Jäger Battalion – 633
3rd (Belgian) Line Battalion – 629
12th Line Battalion – 431
13th Line Battalion – 664
3rd Militia Battalion – 592
10th Militia Battalion – 632

Foot Battery (Lux) – 121
Train – 146

1st Netherlands Cavalry Division (Lieutenant General Collaert) – 3,429

Carabiniers Brigade (Major General Trip) – 1,292
1st Carabiniers – 446
2nd (Belgian) Carabiniers – 435
3rd Carabiniers – 411

1st Light Cavalry Brigade (Major-General de Ghigny) – 1,086
4th Light Dragoons – 647
8th (Belgian) Hussars – 439

2nd Light Cavalry Brigade (Major-General van Merlen) – 1,051
5th (Belgian) Light Dragoons – 441
6th Hussars – 610

Divisional Artillery
½ Batteries of Gey and Petter – 241

Total: 14,571 (21 percent of 68,000)

Of this total, about 10,200 were Dutch troops and about 4,100 were Belgian.

The leaders

Until the Duke of Wellington's arrival in the Netherlands in April 1815, the British, Netherlands and Hanoverian troops in Belgium had been commanded by the young Prince of Orange, the Hereditary Prince of the United Netherlands. British history has not been particularly kind to the prince who, at twenty-two years old, was already a full general in both the British and Netherlands armies. Several recent historians have tried to re-establish his reputation, but perhaps have attempted to push the pendulum too far in the other direction. A truly objective assessment of his experience and performance does not seem to have been attempted.

The Prince of Orange

Willem Frederik George Lodewijk van Oranje-Nassau had received a thorough military education, partly through instruction from his mentor Jean Victor de Constant-Rebecque and partly in the Prussian army, into which he was commissioned aged sixteen. He moved to England in 1809 and spent two years at Oxford University before being commissioned as a lieutenant colonel in the British army in 1811 and being sent to the Peninsula, where he became an aide de camp to Wellington. Although an exacting post, the Prince did not command troops in battle at any level, and so, despite two years of campaign service, the vital experience of this most demanding test of military leadership was denied to him. He had been quickly promoted to colonel and as an aide de camp he was present at a number of battles and sieges, including Ciudad-Rodrigo, Badajoz, Salamanca, Burgos, Vittoria, St Sebastian, Sorauren and Nivelle, and displayed his undoubted courage on many occasions. He left Spain in 1813 and spent a short time in England where he was further promoted to major general in the British army. He returned to the Netherlands at the very end of 1813 as the French were slowly being pushed from his country of birth and became commander in chief of the fledgling Dutch army. In April 1814 he was appointed a general of infantry and Inspector General of All Arms and of the national militias then being raised, and then lieutenant general in the British army in July that year. In the same month he became commander of all the allied forces in the Netherlands, with Constant de Rebècque as his chief-of-staff, and a full general in the British army. His advancement had been meteoric, and, given his age, frankly unwarranted except by the political and diplomatic standards of the day, bearing in mind he had not commanded in battle or even on operations at any level.

Such rapid promotion with such comparatively little command experience was sure to catch up with the Prince. As the build-up of troops began in 1815 his shortcomings began to be exposed. A meeting with General Lord Roland Hill in April did not go well; Hill's aide de camp, Digby Mackworth, wrote:

> It appears that the prince has made himself unpopular in our army, and that the present situation has a little turned his head, nor have flatterers been wanting to make him believe that he is as great a

> general as some of the ancient princes of his house; which, judging from the present state of the army under his command, and from the mode in which everything is carried on by him, does not appear to be the case...[5]

Some contemporary accounts certainly seem to support the notion that he had made himself unpopular with the army. Ensign Macready of the 30th Foot wrote in his memoirs:

> The Prince of Orange kept us hard at work – he prepared for a campaign by filling the hospitals. Twice a week we marched ten miles to the heath of Casteau, near Mons, and we were drilled in corps or divisions. These parades, with our return to quarters, often lasted from three in the morning to six in the afternoon... Here we were drilled out of all patience, and, like the soldiers of ancient Rome, I longed for war, as a release from fatigue. His Royal Highness of Orange continued to annoy us, and increase the sick list by his detestable drills...[6]

Macready's complaints may well reflect those of a young officer who has heard similar from his men without fully comprehending the importance of training prior to a campaign, but it is also probable that, although the prince was well intentioned, his youth and inexperience failed to get the right balance between the troops being sharp and ready for battle and tiring them out by constant repetition.

General Henry Clinton was sent out to act as his second in command, but his experience with the prince left him with a similarly disagreeable impression and he wrote to his brother:

> The impolicy of appointing so incompetent a person to the command of an army had now been made apparent and the authors of this very injudicious measure have left all the mischief which it was calculated to produce, have given the Prince of Orange the rank of general in our service they cannot supersede him but by the person of Lord Wellington, without displacing him and so the army is exposed to all the danger of his inexperience, or to what is hardly less objectionable to the direction of people at home, who cannot be acquainted at the time they issue their orders, with what is to be the state of things at the time when their orders can be obeyed, but we have often seen that our present ministers show more activity in endeavouring to repair a mischief, than in sagacity in guarding against it. They are warned that the Prince of Orange is extravagant in his ideas for disposing

> of his army, they wait until he has done that of which they disapprove and perhaps with reason and then they issue their mandate for remedying the evil, by making him undo what he has done… It is impossible for more to have been done to harass the troops, to excite the contempt of officers and to destroy the confidences which all were at first disposed to feel in the presence of our army. Our good fortune has been that the enemy has not been in a state to take advantage of our calamities and the arrival of the Duke of Wellington will be considered as now applying the remedy, as if he was not only the only general fit to command an army, but the only one capable of keeping it from falling into confusion.[7]

Having taken over command of the army in March, it was only on 5 May that Wellington was officially nominated as the supreme commander of the Netherlands field troops. To his credit, the prince handed over command of the army to Wellington without complaint, although, as he wrote himself, he would have been reluctant to hand over to any other general despite his own considerable lack of command experience:

> Having heard today from Lord Bathurst that your Grace is to take over command of this army, which I will be happy to give over to you, although I cannot deny that I would under the present circumstances do it with reluctance to anyone else…[8]

Perhaps he rather arrogantly believed that he was better qualified to command an army than the many British generals who had commanded in battle and on campaign throughout the Peninsular War.

The Prince's initial tactical deployment at Quatre Bras, designed to hide his true strength and impose on the French, was creditable and Wellington made no changes when he first visited the battlefield. Despite this, given that he was to fight a delaying action to give time for reinforcements to arrive, the Prince chose not to fight a classic delaying action by trading ground to buy time and withdrew from his most advanced positions without fighting. He was therefore forced to fight at Quatre Bras with little ground to trade and some of his units lost heavily. He was certainly helped by Marshal Ney's apparent timidity. Once the French looked like launching a concerted attack, he might well have done better to concentrate his troops rather than allowing them to become isolated in small actions in which the French could deploy superior forces. The real credit for a Netherlands' stand at Quatre Bras lies squarely with de Constant-Rebecque, his chief of staff, and Perponcher-Sedlnitsky, commander of the 2nd Netherlands Division, who chose to ignore Wellington's orders and concentrate at, and defend, the vital crossroads.

The Duke of Wellington had appointed the Prince as the commander of the allied 1st Corps for the campaign, although to Wellington, who had rarely organised his army into corps, this was more an administrative post than tactical. Indeed, at Waterloo, the divisions of the 1st Corps were split across the whole front of the battlefield, and we can only speculate as to why Wellington chose to do this. It is quite possible that because he knew the Prince well he had identified both his strengths and weaknesses. His lack of experience at every level of command and his relative youth made him unsuitable for a high-level formation command, such as corps or even divisional level (contrast this with Napoleon's employment of his brother Jérôme). But Wellington had clearly identified the Prince's true worth: his courage, energy and sense of duty. Having effectively stripped him of his corps command at Waterloo, by breaking up the 1st Corps, he was given command of the 'centre' where his courage and inspiration saw him repeatedly encourage the men, personally lead several counterattacks, and rally wavering troops of all nationalities. However, his time in command at Quatre Bras and at Waterloo also exposed his lack of command experience at the tactical level, and his interventions in a number of well-documented tactical decisions resulted in many deaths. However, despite this, it is fair to conclude that an assessment of his value at Waterloo remained in credit when the victory was finally won.

Other senior officers

Within the Netherlands war ministry, two key men were lieutenant generals Janssens and Tindal. Janssens was the minister for war and Tindal was made inspector general for the southern provinces (Belgium), the most likely theatre of war. Both were Dutch but had served in the French army for considerable periods and reached general officer rank. Tindal had served as a battalion and then brigade commander in the Imperial Guard and had been promoted to *général de division* after being seriously wounded at the battle of Dresden in 1813. Janssens had seen considerably less campaigning than Tindal but had served in the French army since 1810 and commanded a brigade-sized force during the 1814 campaign in France.

In the *Memorandum Relative to the Dutch Army*, dated 2 April 1815, the presumably British author wrote:

> The Ministry of War, at the head of which is General Janssens, is poorly composed. The past conduct of this general does not inspire great confidence, particularly as he is so poorly surrounded. All the heads of the different offices are known to be men attached to the Revolutionary system and to France. The military administration in Belgium under Lieutenant General Tindal is no less bad… I repeat, it is essential to keep these [men] far from the army.[9]

Perhaps the most significant senior military staff appointment in the Netherlands army was Jean Victor de Constant-Rebecque, who was the quartermaster general. He started his military career in a Swiss regiment in the service of France but did not serve under Napoleon and left their service in 1791. Having taken part in the defence of the Tuilleries and escaped, he entered the Dutch army. After the French invasion in 1795, not wishing to serve the Batavian Republic, he transferred to the Prussian army and stayed with them until 1805 when he was appointed as governor to the Prince of Orange and accompanied him to his studies at Oxford University and on his tour in the Peninsula as aide de camp to Wellington. Returning to Britain after the battle of the Pyrenees, he became commander of the Dutch Legion which was made up of prisoners of war taken by the British in Spain. He returned to Holland on its liberation and was promoted colonel, then major general, and was made quartermaster general of the Dutch army in 1814. In this important post he oversaw the rebuilding of the Dutch and then Netherlands army and the campaign of 1815. In his long career, he had some campaign experience, but no command experience in battle.

At divisional level, Lieutenant General Hendrik Perponcher-Sedlnitsky commanded the 2nd Netherlands Division. He had joined the Dutch army in 1788 and fought against the French. He then joined in the Austrian army before transferring to British service from 1800, serving in Germany, Egypt, Portugal and Zeeland. He became commander of the Loyal Lusitanian Legion for a short period. He fought under the then Arthur Wellesley before returning to England. He returned to Holland after Napoleon's defeat at Leipzig and was present and instrumental in the return of the Prince of Orange at the end of 1813. He commanded the 2nd Netherlands Division during the Waterloo campaign.

Although Belgian, David Hendrik Chassé joined the army of the Dutch republic in 1775. As a revolutionary he fled to France on the Prussian invasion of 1787 and enlisted in the French army. In 1793 he became lieutenant colonel commanding a demi-brigade and assisted in the French invasion of Holland. He then joined the army of the newly established Batavian Republic. He fought with them against the invading British and Prussian troops and in Germany. In 1806 he became a major general and commanded a brigade. He fought in Spain with the Dutch troops under French command from 1807 and took over command of the Dutch division that was deployed there in 1809. He transferred into French service with the annexation of Holland in 1810 and fought at Vitoria. He was recalled with his division to fight in the campaign of France in 1814. After Napoleon's abdication he returned to Holland and was accepted into the Dutch army as a major general and, despite Wellington's concerns, was appointed to command the 3rd Netherlands Division.

Of the three[10] infantry brigade commanders at Waterloo one, d'Aubremé (a Belgian), had served in the French army. Bijlandt and Detmers (both Dutch) had not served the French and had, indeed, fought against them. However, Detmers, having served for two years, resigned in 1799 and had not served between that year and 1814. Bijlandt also saw a long break in his service from 1802 until 1813. Both therefore lacked recent campaigning experience and familiarity with modern military procedures and tactics. This was a significant lack of command experience at such a critical level of command. At least d'Aubremé had fought through the tough campaigns of 1813 and 1814, but he was to take the least active role of the three brigades at Waterloo.

The 1st Netherlands Cavalry Division was commanded by General de Collaert, a Belgian, who had thirty-five years of military experience. Although much of it was in French service, he did not see much serious fighting until the campaigns of 1813 and 1814. The three brigade commanders had also spent a substantial amount of time in the French army and had much combat experience. De Ghigny and Von Trip van Zoutelande retired from the French army as colonels; de Ghigny (a Belgian) had commanded the French 12th Chasseurs à Cheval in Russia where he was wounded twice. He only transferred from the French army to the Dutch in March 1815. Trip (who was Dutch) had commanded the French 14th Cuirassiers, leading them in Russia in 1812 and during the campaigns of 1813 and 1814. Van Merlen was also Dutch and had been promoted to *général de brigade*. He had been wounded and captured by the Prussians in 1814.

Of the officers we have considered above, eight had fought in the French army and four had not. Perhaps Wellington's suspicion of at least some of these men is understandable. However, those senior officers who had served the French brought a significant amount of campaign and battlefield experience with them that must have made their contribution to a largely new and young army invaluable. For those who had not fought for the French, the opposite is also true; although there was little reason to doubt their loyalty, their level of campaign and battlefield experience was significantly less, and some had little recent military or command experience to bring to the new army.

The *Memorandum Relative to the Dutch Army* goes on to say:

> Chief-of-Staff Constant-Rebecque, the quartermaster-general, is a man not only good for his principles, but very active. He is the best choice for a position of this importance.
>
> What background do we have on General Evers[11], as well as on all the officer corps which were of the French system by choice and by habit?...
>
> Why not send away these useless and dangerous generals such as Chassé, Storm de Grave, Matuscwitz, men without means and of the poorest principles? ...the king could employ them elsewhere, either to command the depots or recruiting. Some may even command militia battalions: anywhere would be better, where they could do no harm,

> than on the frontier of France, where they are at the moment… Too much confidence at the present moment, in people whose way of thinking is or has not always been right, can have the most unfortunate consequences.

While there is certainly some British snobbery exposed here, the plain-speaking tone of this memorandum clearly expresses concern over the loyalty of those senior officers, mainly Belgian, who had a long career in the service of France. Those who might doubt that there was any cause for concern should remember that the Prussians were soon to face a mutiny of their Saxon troops, whose loyalty had been questioned after many years of service to Napoleon. It is also worthy of note that the only senior officer who comes in for praise is the one who had served with Wellington and the Prince of Orange in Spain. The extent to which Wellington, and no doubt much of the British contingent, was right to suspect the loyalty of the senior Dutch and Belgian officers will become evident as we study the latter's performance on the campaign.

After inspections of the Netherlands army units in late April that Wellington conducted with King Willem, Wellington was far more positive than before about the appearance of the Netherlands troops. However, when on 28 April he wrote to the British Secretary of State for War and Colonies, Earl Bathurst, he was still concerned by some of the King's military advisors:

> He [Willem] is surrounded by persons who have been in the French service. It is very well to employ them, but I would not trust one of them out of my sight, and so I have told him…[12]

Lower levels of command

Like the other allied contingents raising a new army, one of the most pressing problems was the supply of officers. The Netherlands had four sources it could draw on:

- Those who had fought in the Revolutionary wars in the armies of the United Provinces or the Austrian Netherlands but had retired when the French had invaded.
- Those who had fought through the last wars, mostly in French service, and had a good level of time in uniform and campaign experience.
- Volunteers from 1813 and 1814 who had joined as their country was being liberated from the French.
- Volunteers who had answered the call on the return of Napoleon.

When King Willem raised his new army even before the final eviction of French forces in 1813, the first officers to step forward were those patriotic men who had served in the Dutch forces before the French invasion and then resigned their commissions or retired rather than serve the French. With the liberation of their homeland imminent, they once more volunteered for service, many raising new units or encouraging volunteers to join the new army. These no doubt contributed much in the early days of a fledgling army, but as the army grew, the need to train the recruits in the field pressed and war threatened, many of these older officers displayed their lack of recent service and up-to-date tactical knowledge. However, as they were older officers, and despite their obvious shortcomings, they expected rank that was commensurate with their seniority and as a reward for their renewed service. This posed a dilemma to the king as many of them were unsuited to high command and many may not have been fit enough for prolonged campaign service.

A similar dilemma faced the new king in how he should treat the men who, with no prior military service, had taken the lead in the uprising against the French in 1813 and who somehow had to be rewarded for their actions. In the enthusiasm of the early days, and as a reward for raising new units, some of these men had been promoted to colonel in order for them to command the unit they had raised, often at their own expense. Once true veteran officers of the wars became available and the French army began to gather on the frontiers in 1815, there was little choice but to replace these men with those better qualified for battlefield command.

Until many Dutch and Belgian officers were released from the French army after Napoleon's abdication, the organisation and capabilities of most of the army was poor; the officers, however well intentioned, were older, less experienced and well behind on their military education. It was not until the truly experienced officers returned from French service that real strides were taken in making the army fit for the field.

As these experienced officers returned, so the older or inexperienced officers could be replaced. This inevitably caused some upset as volunteer officers were pensioned off or transferred to the army's staff or garrison posts in the country's fortresses. By April 1815, all officers with no previous military experience were forced to hand over their commands, and even as late as May 1815, some older and unsuitable commanding officers of regular units were replaced by younger, and perhaps more experienced, commanding officers who had originally been appointed to command the militia battalions.

It was clearly in the best interests of an army that was being raised almost from scratch that it should have officers with campaign experience, and in truth, many were available; but the majority of these had served in the French army and it is unsurprising that senior officers of other contingents questioned their loyalty. It seems, however, that King Willem and his advisors were prepared to take the risk and it is fair to say that such a risk was justified; with so little time to raise, organise, equip and train an army, it would surely have been impossible without the experience many officers brought with them from the French army.

However, not every veteran of French service who returned home after many years on campaign was keen to serve again; no doubt many looked forward to settling down and living in peace. Such was Henri Scheltens, a Belgian, who served in the 7th (Belgian) Line Battalion with the rank of lieutenant during the Waterloo campaign. He had long campaign service in the French army, much of it in the Imperial Guard, which he left in 1814 as a sergeant. In his memoirs he speaks honestly of his feelings of going back to war:

> I must now say frankly that I no longer had the heart for war. I had already experienced enough not to want any more. I arrived in my lodgings feeling unsociable, although I was received with the best possible grace.[13]

However, despite his misgivings, like many other experienced men, Scheltens was quickly commissioned and made his unit's *adjutant major*, becoming responsible for drilling his battalion so they would be able to manoeuvre on the battlefield. He clearly worked hard at this, commenting, 'in four months I managed to train my men and cadre in all the theory and practical manoeuvres in the regulations.'[14] Scheltens also informs us that many of the officers serving in his unit had previous military experience.

It also seems that even many of those who had served in the French armies had no great loyalty to their former masters and the evidence for this comes from the *Memorandum on the Netherlands Army* from which we have already quoted. It also states:

> Many [Dutch] commanders and subaltern officers have in truth served France, but generally they were so badly treated, that the idea of no longer being under a foreign yoke and being an independent nation has produced a good effect on them. I make the exception of some wicked men, such as supported the revolution. The whole army is enthusiastic about Lord Wellington, and also about the Hereditary Prince of Orange. With Lord Wellington taking the general command of all the troops in Belgium, and the Hereditary Prince that of the Dutch army, we can be sure of happy results.[15]

The situation was helped when the union of the United Provinces and Belgium was announced, as once the future of a United Netherlands was clear, Belgians who had formerly served in the French army now came forward in greater numbers. By the start of 1815 nearly all the officers of the 8th (Belgian) Hussars had had experience with the French army and the same was true of the 2nd (Belgian) Carabiniers, in which nineteen out of the thirty officers had served in the French army, nine of them had been awarded the *Legion d'Honneur*, and three others had served in the Austrian army. The commanding officer of the latter regiment, Colonel Jean Baptiste de Bruyn de Basique seems to have considerably exaggerated his experience in the French army to secure the command of this regiment, as no record of his service could be found by André Dellevoet while researching his book on the Netherlands cavalry. He may even have had virtually none, although his performance at Waterloo did suggest he had some command experience, though probably at a lower rank than he claimed.[16]

In most of the allied armies the most junior commissioned ranks were filled by suitable young volunteers from prominent families, and there is no evidence to suggest there was any shortage of young men prepared to step forward. At this time there was no officer academy in the Netherlands, so these young men had to be trained in their regiments.[17] It was therefore common in all armies that the most junior officers had no campaign experience.

The troops

Even during their liberation from the French, both the United Provinces and the former Austrian Netherlands (Belgium) made immediate efforts to rebuild their own armies. Although recruiting was slow at first, particularly in Belgium, it began to improve in autumn 1814 when it was declared at the Congress of Vienna that the two countries were to be combined into a single, new state: the United Kingdom of the Netherlands. Until this point, the efforts of the two states to build their armies were wholly independent of each other. After the declaration, Willem immediately took steps to amalgamate the two different armies into one, with a target of 30,000 men. Up until this point, the effort that was put into recruitment reflected the motivation of the two different states. For the United Provinces, which were generally hostile to Napoleon and France, there was a determination and enthusiasm that was not reflected in Belgium, where feeling against Napoleon was far from universal in those who had once fought for him, and the evidence suggests the Belgian population, who were mostly Catholic, were even more ambivalent; many felt they had more in common with the French than they did with the protestant United Provinces with whom they had a long history of competition and ill feeling.

The martial spirit of the Dutch in particular seems to have been broken by the French occupation and the constant demand for manpower for the French army. The numbers of volunteers for military service in the newly liberated country was insufficient to meet the requirement. The initial target had been 20,000 men, but this was soon increased to 30,000. As the pool of volunteers quickly dried up, there appeared to be no alternative to reintroducing conscription, but Willem wanted to avoid imposing this as it had been so unpopular under French rule. However, in order to meet the target for the army there appeared to be no option and when he felt secure enough to introduce it, he did so only for those forces with a home defence role, the militia. All the regular army were therefore volunteers, with the home defence militia battalions manned by conscripts.

Prior to the Napoleonic wars the army of the United Provinces had exceeded 100,000 men, but now they struggled to raise a field army of 30,000 (not including the garrisons of the many fortresses that protected the country's borders and major cities) that was felt indispensable to ensure the country's security. Yet, once Napoleon had returned, it became increasingly likely that the newly established United Netherlands would be the stage for the first battles. The Netherlands was therefore facing a fight for its national independence and survival and had no alternative but to invest all its energies and resources into a new army, only part of which would come under Wellington's command for the 1815 campaign.

Much as the senior officers of the new army who had served the French were treated with suspicion, particularly by the country's allies, so those soldiers who had also served France raised concerns about where their loyalties lay, even though the vast majority had been conscripted and had no other choice but to serve or desert. A generation of young men had perished in Napoleon's wars; either in Spain or the costly campaigns in Russia in 1812 and Saxony in 1813. Major Friedrich von Gagern, a staff officer of the 2nd Netherlands Division, wrote in a letter to van Löben Sels:

> Our troops were generally very willing, however, having insufficient time to know their commanders on the field of battle, there was not the mutual trust and self-assurance that one can see in experienced armies. Indeed, several of the commanders mistrusted the Belgians, and even the Nassau troops, who had served under Napoleon in Spain.[18]

The Belgian troops were mobilised on 24 March 1815, a week later than the Dutch. On its liberation, the former Austrian Netherlands was split between Prussian and Austrian administration. The Austrians, Prussians and the Dutch all tried to recruit a new military force but there appears to have been little enthusiasm to raise a new army among the population. It had been exhausted from the previous wars and there was an unsurprising shortage of volunteers; many of its young men were still in, or just returning from, French service. The most significant new force that was raised was known as the *Légion Belge*. However, initially at least, it was a small force, poorly manned, paid and fed, and its training left a lot to be desired; it lacked equipment and suffered from high levels of desertion. As recently part of France, Belgium faced a rather uncertain future until the Treaty of Paris determined that it was to be absorbed into a new United Netherlands.

On 1 August 1814 the Austrian-administered territories were handed over to their new rulers and the army was to be absorbed into that raised by the Dutch. When Napoleon returned to France in March 1815, the reorganisation of the Netherlands army was still not complete, and it was not until late in April that the Dutch and Belgian regiments were numbered in a single sequence.

When the new army was to be raised at the end of 1813, the battalions were to consist of ten companies in the British manner, each company of just short of 100 men giving a battalion strength, with a headquarters, of just under 1,000 men. Battalions of the line and the militia were to be organised in the same manner. However, it soon became evident that insufficient men were being recruited and the number of companies in each battalion was reduced to six; the same organisation as French battalions with which the veterans of the army were familiar. A number of battalions were disbanded, and their men sent to bring other battalions up to strength.

In his history of the campaign,[19] de Bas attempts to challenge the notion that many of the Netherlanders had served under the French, stating, 'of the 28,000 NCOs and soldiers, in round figures, which served under the orders of Lord Wellington, hardly 1,200, of which only 29 of the militiamen of the levée of 1814, had previously served on campaign.' However, in his recent study, which included a detailed examination of the regimental records, Erwin Muilwijk states that each unit had between 15 and 25 percent of NCOs and soldiers with previous military experience. Although this may have served to fuel concerns about their loyalty, such a hard core of experienced men no doubt improved the quality of the units.

De Bas also states that the quality of the men in the militia was as good as that in the regulars, the only difference being that the regulars had spent more time in uniform, most having answered the early call for volunteers. The militia had all come from the conscription of 1814 and had on average six months under arms, while those of 1815, although called (in May), had not been sufficiently uniformed, equipped and trained to take part in the Waterloo campaign. Nearly all the battalions and regiments of the Netherlands army were under strength, some considerably so. To give two examples, the 5th Militia Battalion, with an establishment of 571 men, had only 460 on 16 June, the day of Quatre Bras;[20] and the 8th Hussars were able to field just three squadrons instead of four, although the problem was as much a lack of horses as it was a shortage of trained men.

In September 1814 the army received a considerable reinforcement as the French army sent home all foreigners still in French service, many of whom were prepared to continue to serve their own country. However, by 18 March 1815 it was clear that the proposed 30,000 men was still too ambitious. Instead, only some 20,000 could be mustered immediately. In January the Dutch infantry had been organised in a consecutively numbered list of thirty-six battalions, but a reorganisation of April unified the armies of the United Provinces and

Belgium into a single list, which led to the disbandment of some Dutch units (their manpower bringing other units up to strength) and their numbers being allocated to the Belgian battalions. King Willem also increased numbers by drawing on the manpower of Nassau, which we have already studied, and also recruited three Swiss battalions, although these were not ready for the field in time for the campaign.

It was only on 23 March that Wellington was nominated to take over command of the army. No doubt it was shortly after this that a memorandum was written to update Wellington on the situation of the army's condition. This stated:

> The Netherlands army can put 30,000 men in the field, and still keep a reserve to put 15 to 18,000 men in the fortresses. Its effective force is currently 42,000 men. By the King's decree of February 27th, the militia, which lacks seven thousand men, will be immediately completed; as the recruitment of the militia is by conscription, the reserve will be, in a short time, above 18,000 men. The recruitment in the line regiments, being voluntary, goes more slowly, and the composition of the troops of the line is not as good as that in the militia. The spirit of the Dutch army is very good: we can be sure that they will do their duty...
>
> The Belgian troops are poor: we cannot count on them. The best way ahead is to put them in the second line as much as possible...
>
> In general we cannot count on any resources from Belgium; they are raising 20 battalions of militia there.[21] If they are confiding the command to officers leaving the service of France, this formation will only produce trouble. Old officers from the service of Austria and Holland should be placed with them; there are sufficient numbers; and then young men of the country.[22]

As with the other contingents, Wellington wanted to mix newly raised Netherlands units with more experienced troops such as the British and KGL. He therefore discussed the possibility of this happening with Earl Bathurst, Secretary of State for War and the Colonies. In a letter to the Earl dated Brussels, 6 April 1815, Wellington wrote:

> I am sorry to say that I have a very bad account of the Netherlands [left blank in *Dispatches*] troops; and King William [left blank in *Dispatches*] appears unwilling to allow them to be mixed with ours, which, although they are not our best, would afford a chance of making something of them...[23]

Wellington therefore set up a meeting for 11 April with the Prince of Orange in order to discuss the issue. In this meeting he put forward the same argument that he had used with the Hanoverians and for the same reason; to give the inexperienced troops confidence in the troops on their flanks and for them to serve as an example. He no doubt also stressed the point that this is what was happening with the Hanoverian brigades. However, the prince was not to be convinced, although his reasoning was strong; the Netherlands army was just reorganising itself, integrating the Belgian with the Dutch troops within their own brigades, and a second reorganisation would almost certainly lead to confusion and be counterproductive. It is also likely that the prince, like King Willem, would have wanted, for their own national pride, to maintain them under their own chain of command. Wellington had no option but to accept this.

From mid-April 1815, the Netherlands army was in its new cantonments along the southern frontier with France. Now they had to be properly integrated into their brigades and divisions and be put into a state to campaign. Equipment needed to be brought up to establishment (much was still missing) and the units and brigades needed to drill and manoeuvre together so that proper discipline could be established, as well a feeling of trust between units that would be fighting side-by-side. As most units were still under strength, from April to June a continuous stream of reinforcements was sent from the depots to the field army, including a number of officers arriving to take up their new commands.

To ensure that progress was being made in the organisation, equipping and training of the new army, a constant series of inspections was carried out to monitor progress and identify what improvements needed making. At the end of April, Wellington conducted some of his own, accompanied by King Willem. The Duke appeared rather more positive than before about the appearance of the Netherlands troops, when on the 28 April he wrote to Earl Bathurst:

> the Dutch National Militia are a very good body of men, although young. The Belgians young, and some very small. The cavalry remarkably well mounted, but don't ride well. The whole well clothed and equipped for service; and, as far as I could judge, from what I see of their movements, well disciplined. They are completely officered by officers who have been in the French service. It was an extraordinary circumstance that the only corps which cried *Vive le Roi*! were the Belgians, which appears in these good days to be the common cry of treason... He [Willem] is surrounded by persons who have been in the French service. It is very well to employ them, but I would not trust one of them out of my sight, and so I have told him...[24]

As in any army, some units fared rather better than others, but it seems that, given the lack of experience within many of the units, the standard reached was generally satisfactory. Early in May the infantry and artillery were ordered to conduct live fire training and although this was carried out, it was not repeated and no doubt many men entered the campaign without such formal training. From 4 May the Netherlands units were ordered to drill every other day. However, while this was possible at the lower command levels, a shortage of ground that was expansive enough to carry this out above battalion level prevented the brigades from drilling together and practising brigade manoeuvres as they might have to do on the battlefield. This was a significant lack of capability which would affect their ability to coordinate their movements and impose limits on what they could achieve in action. As this lack of suitable training ground affected many of the brigades, there is no doubt that Wellington became aware of it and took particular care over how these units were employed. It can be imagined that a lack of training area would have been a more serious problem for the cavalry regiments and brigades; even on 1 June the Prince of Orange informed Wellington that the cavalry had had very little opportunity to practise their manoeuvres due to the lack of suitable terrain. It appears that only van Trip's brigade was able to practise any brigade manoeuvre before the campaign opened.[25]

Since 1813 the Dutch infantry had used the French drill regulations; there was no official Dutch equivalent. As the majority of the experienced officers and NCOs had served in the French army, this seems reasonable enough, and to avoid confusion, French organisations were adopted by the new army. On 27 April the decision was made that all infantry battalions would deploy in two ranks in the British manner. We can only speculate that this decision was made by the Prince of Orange, who wished to maximise firepower using British tactics with which he was familiar. While this seems to have been accepted readily enough, this thin formation was risky with inexperienced troops and it was generally believed that three ranks, in line with most continental armies, gave the men a greater feeling of security and confidence. This change was to have unfortunate consequences at Waterloo.

But such a late change in tactics was not the only problem the army of the new nation had to face. Some commanders only spoke Flemish or French, but not both. This caused some confusion and some officers required others to give commands in Flemish which they did not speak themselves.[26] The language problem even complicated the workings of the army staff; the chief-of-staff of the 2nd Netherlands Division, Colonel van Nyevelt, was forced to make a copy of the division order book himself in Dutch as none of the other officers in the headquarters spoke this language.[27]

Throughout the weeks following Napoleon's return, the Netherlands army worked hard to supply the units with the campaign equipment that was required, but there were still shortages in the militia by the time the campaign opened. Before Napoleon's return, Netherlands units were issued with whatever muskets were available; these were a mix of Dutch, French and British models.

Recognising that three different calibres would create logistical problems it was decided that all units should be issued British muskets; all other muskets were to be handed in on 22 April. The exchange was quickly completed for all units that were present with the army, but those that reported later, like the 2nd Battalion of the 28th Orange-Nassau and all three battalions of the 1st Nassau Regiment, fought through Quatre Bras and Waterloo with French muskets. The employment of the 2nd Battalion of the 28th Orange-Nassau Regiment at Quatre Bras was severely limited by having only ten rounds per man and they were only effective at Waterloo by negotiating for French ammunition from the 1st Nassau Regiment.

Arming the cavalry also caused considerable concern and the Netherlands army increasingly relied on British supplies for uniforms, equipment and arms. At the end of May, the lack of carbines for the carabinier regiments even resulted in a desperate attempt to collect 400 blunderbusses in the northern provinces, but insufficient were found. As late as 4 June, 500 carbines and 816 English pistols arrived with ammunition, but even with these, the 2nd Carabiniers were still short of 120 pistols.[28]

Desertions were common throughout the army, but particularly in the Belgian units, although it is impossible to compare those of the Netherlands field army with any other nation of this period. However, Napoleon's hopes for mass desertions among the Belgian troops did not materialise. He had ordered a depot for Belgian deserters to be established at Lille in order to raise Belgian units to fight for his own army. However, only 378 men reported to the depot and these included Hanoverians and Saxons as well as Belgians.[29]

On 5 May King Willem finally agreed to give the Duke of Wellington immediate command of all Netherlands forces of the field army in the southern provinces and fortress garrisons along the border with France. This was to leave Wellington with little time to influence preparations before the French attack crossed the frontier on 15 June.

The cavalry[30]

The early recruitment of two light and two heavy cavalry regiments in the United Provinces went quickly, there being no shortage of volunteers. However, the provision of horses, uniforms, weapons and equipment took rather longer, although other than for horses they were reliant on Britain to make up their shortages. Things did not go so well in Belgium; the first Belgian cavalry regiments, unable to gather sufficient recruits, took to recruiting Germans and other foreigners. However, many of these deserted having been paid their bounties and 100 men deserted from one of the regiments in just four months. Although there was a sprinkling of experienced officers and NCOs, the majority of recruits had no experience at all. Perhaps unsurprisingly, the regiments which were raised first recruited better than those that followed. Like the regiments of the United Provinces, much of the equipment and arms came from Britain. When the campaign opened, the Dutch regiments were substantially stronger than those raised in Belgium.

In late 1814 recruitment to the Belgian 5th Light Dragoons had improved and many of the volunteers were experienced soldiers. Out of 421 subalterns and other ranks, 117 had previous campaign experience. The regiment consisted of 80 percent Belgians, with the remainder being Germans and French. Their training had quickly improved when the old and inexperienced commanding officer was replaced by Lieutenant Colonel de Mercx, who had long experience with both the Austrian and French armies. With green coats, their uniform was very similar to the French chasseur regiments and with yellow facings almost identical to the French 6th Chasseurs, with whom they fought at Quatre Bras. This similarity in uniforms resulted in a friendly fire incident when they were fired on at that battle by the British 92nd Highlanders.

The 8th (Belgian) Hussars were poorly recruited and trained at the end of 1814, but early in 1815 nearly all the officers of the regiment had had experience with the French army, although very few of the hussars had any experience at all. The commanding officer of the regiment, Lieutenant Colonel Duvivier, was an extremely experienced officer, having fought in a number of significant campaigns and battles with the French, but apparently only spoke Dutch, while most of his men only spoke French, forcing him to use an interpreter to translate his commands up to the day of Waterloo.[31]

In the ranks of the 2nd (Belgian) Carabiniers, 90 percent were Belgian, the remainder Dutch and German, almost 40 percent of whom had served in the French army. There was, however, considerable desertion, even in March 1815, and much of their early enthusiasm seems to have disappeared. Most of their uniforms and virtually all their equipment came from French stocks left behind in 1813 and 1814.

In an inspection of both light cavalry brigades on 7 May they were reported as well equipped with uniforms and in good spirits, but were only able to manoeuvre at company (half squadron) level because of a lack of suitable ground. The shortage of carbines and pistols had been made good with British supplies. Discipline among the officers of these regiments had to be tightened, partly due to lieutenants commanding companies instead of captains.

Even by the middle of May, the cavalry regiments were not up to full strength and during this month reinforcements were still being received from the depots. On 13 May the 8th Hussar Regiment was reinforced with another 100 men and two days later a full squadron of recruits for the 2nd Carabiniers left for the army; the 1st and 3rd Carabiniers also received reinforcements.[32] None of the regiments went on campaign at full strength. Although great efforts had been made to meet the requirement, the rushed sending of reinforcements just a short time before the French invasion ensured the regiments faced real difficulties in integrating so many new recruits into their squadrons. In general, the Netherlands cavalry went on campaign with a strong cadre of very experienced officers and NCOs, but with a high proportion of enthusiastic, if raw recruits.

The artillery[33]

Having been appointed as the sovereign of an independent Netherlands during the expulsion of the French from the northern Netherlands in 1813, Willem's decree of 6 December 1813 allowed for an artillery arm of 4,000 men. Although this was followed by further decrees laying down the organisation of the new army, early recruiting efforts fell woefully short. His aim was to have six batteries of foot artillery and two of horse artillery in the field army. Progress continued to be slow until men became available as the French army collapsed and prisoners of war held by the allies were released after Napoleon's abdication in 1814. Once these experienced officers and NCOs became available, the army was able to release those who were out of date, too old or too inexperienced and the artillery that was to serve in 1815 began to take shape.

Since the creation of the new armies in 1814, the artillery batteries that were raised were garrisoned in the fortified towns. Many guns had been left behind by the French as their garrisons had surrendered or left, so there was no shortage of ordnance. Unfortunately, many of the batteries that were established did not have train units to move them and the necessary direction to make the artillery batteries mobile was not implemented until March 1815, on Napoleon's return, when the army was ordered to deploy to the frontier with France. The shortage was not just of limbers, caissons and manpower, but most crucially of trained horses; of the sixteen batteries, only seven had a train available. The aim was that each infantry brigade was to have a battery attached, the cavalry division was to have two half-batteries attached and there was to be an artillery reserve. The efforts were enhanced by the activity and determination of the battery commanders who had experience with the French army.

The last artillery batteries only arrived with the army during the first week of May, giving them little time to integrate with their divisions. By the time the campaign opened, although the artillery had not quite reached its target number of batteries, it was the 1st Netherlands Division that was a battery short, so those Netherlands divisions serving with Wellington's army had their full allocation. The *Memorandum* noted that, 'The corps of artillery is very good, very well composed…'[34] Of the six artillery battery commanders that served in Wellington's army, two were Belgian (Krahmer de Binchin and Stevenart) and the other four were Dutch (Bijleveldt, Gey, Lux and Petter). Five had served in the French army and accumulated considerable campaign and battle experience (three having won the *Légion d'Honneur*); the only one to have avoided French service was Lux, who had retired in 1809 but rejoined the fledgling Dutch army in 1813, and who thus had the least campaign experience. The Netherlands artillery was therefore commanded by experienced artillery officers, most of whom fought in at least three major campaigns. Stevenart was to be killed at Quatre Bras. The Netherlands artillery was well organised and well placed to do itself justice during the campaign.

Summary

Much has been written about the lack of trust that many of the allies had in the Belgians in particular, but also the Netherlands leaders and troops in general. Despite many officers and men of the Netherlands army having served with the French, this was conscripted service, certainly for the other ranks, and as this was compulsory service there little doubt that the majority of these troops were glad to see the back of the French and the restoration of an independent Netherlands. Whilst many first-hand accounts may question the effectiveness of the Netherlands troops, their officers all speak clearly and convincingly of their courage and enthusiasm and the account of their actions that follow will allow the reader to judge for themselves.

Like many of the allied contingents, it is only fair to remember that the units and formations of the Netherlands army were relatively new; even the most experienced had only been organised a little over twelve months and most had a high proportion of very young and hastily trained recruits. The time available to establish a sense of ethos and discipline was insufficient and the training of the day gave them only a rudimentary feel for what combat was like. It is entirely unreasonable to expect them to have performed to the standard that was taken almost for granted of the British troops whose regiments were long established, highly experienced for the most part and inculcated with the confidence that they were superior to the French.

Deployment and actions

Quatre Bras[35]

Of the Netherlands contingent, only the 2nd Netherlands Division and van Merlen's 2nd Light Cavalry Brigade fought at Quatre Bras. Despite this, it is not difficult to argue that Quatre Bras was perhaps the Netherlands' army's 'finest hour' during the Waterloo campaign. When Wellington was informed that the French had crossed the frontier, he ordered his army to concentrate at Nivelles, believing that the Prussians were covering the main road that ran from Charleroi to Brussels on which Quatre Bras lay. At this time, the crossroads was occupied by the all-Nassau 2nd Brigade of the 2nd Netherlands Division, which was commanded by the young Prince Bernard of Saxe-Weimar. The nominated commander was Colonel von Goedecke, who, as we have seen in Chapter 2, was unable to assume command having been kicked by a horse.

The greatest significance of the battle fought at Quatre Bras was not the conduct or result of the fighting, but the fact that it was fought at all, and for this the credit lies squarely at the feet of the senior Netherlands commanders. If these had obeyed their orders, the battle would not have been fought and the consequences for the allied cause could have been significant. It is therefore important, when assessing the contribution of the Netherlands contingent, to spend a little time looking at the situation on the evening of the 15th and the morning of 16 June.

The Prince of Orange was visiting his forward troops on the morning of 15 June when the first roar of cannon marked the crossing of the frontier by the French. Although this could possibly have been the sound of artillery training, with the advice of some experienced senior officers he was quick to appreciate its true meaning and wasted no time in sending off preliminary concentration orders to some of his subordinate formations. As the Prussian advanced posts withdrew towards Gosselies, eleven kilometers south of Quatre Bras, the gunfire drew closer to the Netherlands advanced posts and put units on alert. The Prince returned to his headquarters at Braine-le-Comte at about 10am and decided to ride to Brussels to confer with Wellington; he was content that the French offensive was directed against the Prussians to the east and did not directly threaten his own corps. He left strict instructions for any further intelligence to be forwarded to him in the capital and left de Constant-Rebecque, the quartermaster general, in charge.

By the early afternoon, information had been trickling in and de Constant-Rebecque was now confident that the French were attacking at Charleroi and the Prussians were withdrawing towards Gosselies and even Fleurus, leaving the Netherlands' front exposed. Soon after 2pm one of the Prince's aides de camp was sent to Brussels to inform him of the latest developments. In the absence of the Prince, at about 3pm, de Constant-Rebecque issued the orders for the Netherlands' troops to move to their allocated concentration areas.

On his arrival in Brussels, the Prince briefed Wellington on the situation at the border and the preliminary orders he had given. Wellington, wishing for more information before committing himself to ordering a concentration of the whole army, directed the Prince to send an order back to his headquarters in Braine-le-Comte, to send the men back to their cantonments. This order did not arrive with de Constant-Rebecque until 9pm, but in the meantime the Prince's aide de camp arrived in Brussels at 5pm to inform the Prince and Wellington that the French had certainly crossed the border, had attacked the Prussians and that there was no report of any French troops threatening the border opposite Mons. An hour later, news arrived from the Prussians of the French offensive and the Prussian intention of concentrating near Fleurus, thus exposing the front of Wellington's left, and leaving open the Charleroi to Brussels *chaussée*.

The Prussian news prompted orders for the concentration of the allied army, though the preparation of orders was no small task. At about 7pm, the Prince of Orange received his orders for the concentration of his corps. These orders were immediately sent off to Braine-le-Comte, but rather surprisingly the Prince, having been invited to the Duchess of Richmond's ball, felt there was no requirement for him to return to his own headquarters.

In the late afternoon of the 15th, General Perponcher, commander of the 2nd Netherlands Division, received news from the 2nd Nassau Regiment that heavy firing appeared to be approaching their position in the village of Frasnes. Shortly after, and before he had had sufficient time to decide what he should do, he received the order from General de Constant-Rebecque (written at 3pm) to deploy his division with one brigade at Quatre Bras, and the other at Nivelles. Perponcher immediately gave orders for his two brigades to concentrate at their allocated positions; the 1st Brigade (Bijlandt) at Nivelles and the 2nd (von Goedecke) at Quatre Bras. On receipt of the news that the forward troops had been attacked, Perponcher, quickly and correctly realising the strategic importance of Quatre Bras, ordered that in case of attack, it was to be held for as long as possible. In the absence of Colonel von Goedecke, Prince Bernard Saxe-Weimar decided, without awaiting orders, to concentrate the brigade at the crossroads. This was a brave decision given his sudden ascension to command and lack of orders and ensured he had concentrated his brigade at least three hours earlier than would have been possible if he had waited for orders. As his troops arrived, he ordered them into defensive positions in front of the village.

Through the evening of the 15th, Perponcher received increasingly disturbing intelligence of the French offensive and its progress up the *chaussée* from Charleroi towards Brussels. He was now aware that there were no longer any Prussian troops covering his front and that there was nothing therefore between the French and his single brigade at Quatre Bras. He sent this information to General de Constant-Rebecque with one of his most trusted staff officers. While awaiting further events he sent an order to Saxe-Weimar to take command of the brigade and to hold Quatre Bras unless attacked by overwhelming numbers. Perponcher also gave orders directing all baggage and unnecessary equipment to be sent to the rear.

It will be remembered that it was only at 9pm that de Constant-Rebecque received the order from the Prince of Orange to send the troops back to their cantonments; this would have reversed all the good work that had been done in the preceding hours. What was he to do? It was rather late to execute this order, yet it was unequivocal. However, it was at this moment that he received the news of the attack on the Nassauers at Frasnes. Instantly realising the importance of this information, de Constant-Rebecque chose to ignore the latest order from the Prince and ordered Perponcher to be prepared to reinforce Saxe-Weimar at Quatre Bras. Soon after he sent of one of the Prince's aides de camp to explain to him the actions he had taken and to pass on the latest situation; the time was about 10.30pm. Shortly after the aide had been sent off, the orders for the concentration of the 2nd and 3rd Netherlands Divisions at Nivelles arrived. Perhaps unsurprisingly, orders had passed each other *en route*, but the latest orders were out of date, having been despatched before news of the attack at Frasnes; the importance of maintaining a force at Quatre Bras was clear. These latest orders would have seen Saxe-Weimar's brigade join that of Bijlandt at Nivelles, leaving Quatre Bras and the road to Brussels completely unguarded. The chief-of-staff of the 2nd Netherlands Division, Colonel van Nyevelt, wrote:

> General de Perponcher assessed that His Royal Highness [the Prince of Orange], who was in Brussels when he gave these orders, did not know as well as himself the movement of the French and Prussian armies and that he also did not know that Charleroi had been evacuated and that the Prussians were rallying close to Fleurus.
>
> His Excellency the divisional general, who was well informed of the true state of affairs and understood the importance of covering Brussels to block the gap which had occurred between the Prussians and ourselves and to prevent the enemy from penetrating up to the route through the Soignies forest, where the enemy could have been able to stop the arrival of all support, thought that he could take upon himself the decision not to execute these orders [to concentrate at Nivelles] but to continue, on the contrary, to defend the position at Quatre Bras with the greatest energy. To this end he repeated the order to remain there and had His Royal Highness informed of the decision he had taken.[36]

On the evening of the 15th, Wellington remained convinced that the main French offensive would be directed on Mons, but his decision to concentrate on Nivelles was taken in order to be able to support the Prussians in case of attack; although at this time he still did not believe the main French effort was against Brussels up the Charleroi road. Wellington was only convinced this was the case when the Prince's aide de camp, who had been sent by de Constant-Rebecque at 10.30pm, arrived at the ball at about midnight. The information detailing the French attack on Frasnes could not be ignored.

Confusingly, and due to the conflicting orders that arrived because of the long distances that had to be covered, events had been moving more quickly than the orders could be despatched. Around 2am on the morning of the 16th, the orders to concentrate the 2nd Netherlands Division at Nivelles arrived from corps headquarters; these contradicted the orders to hold and be prepared to reinforce Quatre Bras. Perponcher made the conscious decision to ignore this latest order and to reinforce Quatre Bras immediately, leaving three battalions to hold Nivelles until the 3rd Netherlands Division arrived to relieve them. Perponcher marched towards Quatre Bras with the 27th Jägers and the 8th Militia Battalion; on the way he met fifty Prussian hussars who were separated from their unit and convinced the commander to remain with him. Perponcher rode ahead of the infantry and arrived at the crossroads at 3.30am.

About the same time, the Prince of Orange arrived at his headquarters at Braine-le-Comte where he was met and briefed by de Constant-Rebecque. The Prince endorsed de Constant-Rebecque's decision to reinforce Quatre Bras and directed him to leave immediately to move there; he would follow shortly. De Constant-Rebecque departed Braine-le-Comte at 3.45am; Nivelles lay 12km to the east and Quatre Bras another eight.

Before the first serious engagements of the campaign, the senior staff officers of the Netherlands army had made a number of crucial independent decisions, without endorsement from their superiors and therefore contrary to standard operating procedures. Like Napoleon, Wellington did not encourage initiative among his subordinate commanders, preferring blind obedience to orders. De Constant-Rebecque, Perponcher, and even Saxe-Weimar risked incurring the wrath of the army commander for the decisions they had made. Yet these decisions were to make a vital contribution to the success of the campaign and the credit due to these men can hardly be exaggerated as they denied the French an unopposed occupation of Quatre Bras and an opportunity for Marshal Ney, commander of the French left wing, to intervene decisively at the battle of Ligny that was fought on the 16th, just ten kilometres to the east.

The first two battalions of Bijlandt's brigade, the 27th Jägers and the 8th Militia Battalion, arrived at Quatre Bras at 5am. The 27th were immediately sent forward to cover the front between the large farm of Gemioncourt towards the small hamlet of Piraumont. The 8th Militia Battalion was sent down to the southern tip of the Bossu wood to reinforce the detachments of the 2nd and 3rd Battalions of the 2nd Nassau Regiment that were already guarding that important point.

At Nivelles, de Constant-Rebecque found the remaining battalions of Bijlandt's brigade occupying the town as ordered. He hastened off the 5th and 7th Militia and Stevenart's artillery towards Quatre Bras. This left just the 7th Line to guard the town until Chassé's division arrived.

De Constant-Rebecque arrived at Quatre Bras just before 6am, followed shortly afterwards by the Prince of Orange, who, escorted by all the general officers present at the crossroads, conducted a reconnaissance of the position. As the Netherlands position did not extend much beyond Gemioncourt, the Prince of Orange ordered an advance to occupy the Balcan heights on which the Delhutte wood stood; this would allow them to dominate the approaches to the position from the village of Frasnes, around which the French seemed to have concentrated a force, though apparently with little infantry. Indeed, on the morning of the 16th, only the French vanguard was at Frasnes; the main body was still around the town of Gosselies, six kilometres further south.

Given the relatively weak Netherlands force that was deployed around Quatre Bras, the Prince's aim should surely have been to identify the strength of the French force facing them and then, if it was superior in strength, to delay its advance for as long as possible to give time for allied reinforcements to arrive. The general tactic for a delaying force was to impose upon the enemy, force him to continually deploy and then to withdraw to a subsequent position to repeat the tactic without getting decisively engaged. This was to give up ground to gain time; therefore, the more ground that could be disputed, the longer the enemy could be delayed. An attempt to push back the French outposts therefore made good tactical sense. However, the Prince also needed to protect his line of retreat, which was to the west, towards Nivelles, as this was where the remainder of his corps was concentrating. It is both clear and understandable that he had no thought of protecting the Namur road which provided Wellington's communications with the Prussians.

To the east of the main road the 27th Jägers were chosen for the advance and two companies were ordered forward. The jägers were supported by the small force of Prussian cavalry. To the west of the road the advance was conducted by the whole of the 2nd Battalion of the 2nd Nassau Regiment with the objective of occupying the farm of Petit-Pierrepont which was just over a kilometre northwest of Frasnes. Having succeeded in pushing back the French outposts, the Netherlands troops now dominated the approaches out of Frasnes and Bijleveld's battery was brought forward to the Balcan inn, to make best use of an excellent field of fire. At 6.30am there was still no apparent movement in the French lines and the Prince of Orange still had no idea of the force he was facing. The Prince ordered the light cavalry brigade of van Merlen to move to Quatre Bras.

At 8am, Wellington and some of his staff left Brussels for Quatre Bras. At the same time the French had still not stirred themselves from Frasnes, leaving the Prince of Orange increasingly convinced that the French had no great strength there.

The 5th and 7th Militia Battalions, accompanied by Bijleveld's artillery, arrived at Quatre Bras at 9am after a tiring march. Such was the lack of threat that they were left at the village to cook some breakfast.

At 10am, Wellington also arrived at the crossroads where he joined the Prince of Orange and Perponcher. Conducting a reconnaissance forward, on reaching the Balcan heights, he too was of the impression that there was no significant French force in front of them and, turning his intention to what the Prussians were up to he returned to Quatre Bras without making any changes to the Prince's deployment.

With the arrival of the 7th Line from Nivelles, where it had been relieved by the arrival of units of the 3rd Division, the whole of General Perponcher's division was concentrated at Quatre Bras by midday. The skirmishing at the outposts had continued since the early morning advance, but now the 2nd/2nd Nassau were running short of ammunition, and they were relieved by the 3rd Battalion.

At 1pm, Wellington left Quatre Bras to meet up with Marshal Blücher at Ligny. It was only shortly after his departure that the Prince of Orange was informed that the French seemed to have awoken from their slumbers and were intent on action. The Prince immediately moved to the advanced posts. Columns of infantry and cavalry were seen in movement and artillery could also be seen moving forwards.

By this time, the Prince of Orange's deployment was as follows: Bijleveld's battery was deployed on the heights of Gemioncourt, while that of Stevenart was level on the opposite side of the main road. Two of Stevenart's guns, under Lieutenant Winssinger, had been detached to the allied right supporting the battalions deployed on the southern tip of the Bossu wood. Two guns and a howitzer of Bijleveld's battery, under the command of Second Lieutenant Koopman, were deployed on the extreme left, covering down the Namur road. The 1st Battalion of the Orange-Nassau Regiment, four companies of the 1st Battalion, 2nd Nassau Regiment, 8th Militia and 3rd Battalion, 2nd Nassau Regiment were drawn up in line with them with a detachment in the Grand Pierrepont farm and the Volunteer Jäger Company protecting the extreme right of the line. The line was drawn up outside the wood. The skirmisher line was advanced into a sunken lane which gave them good cover. The 5th and 7th Militia remained at the village of Quatre Bras to the north of the Nivelles road, facing the Bossu wood as a reserve. They were joined there by Major Normann's 2nd Battalion, 2nd Nassau Regiment, after it had been withdrawn from the outposts. The 2nd Battalion, Orange-Nassau Regiment, lacking ammunition for their French muskets, were also kept back in reserve to the east of the main road. The other two companies of this battalion temporarily occupied the Gemioncourt farm. To the east of this farm, along the line of the Gemioncourt stream that ran down to the Materne pond, the 762 men of the 27th Jägers held a long line, nearly all spread out in skirmisher order with only two companies of formed-up men acting as a reserve. The extreme left of the 27th lay opposite the farm of Piraumont. The 3rd Battalion, 2nd Nassau Regiment were now withdrawn from the high ground overlooking Frasnes and were redeployed to the west of the gunline, the skirmishers forward to offer some protection to the gunners.

Out of the ten infantry battalions available, four were initially kept in reserve. Keeping a third of your force in reserve was considered sound military practice, allowing the commander to reinforce a threatened position, launch a counterattack, or to provide a force behind which another force might rally.

But the Netherlands deployment had one fundamental flaw; it was designed to fight the type of battle *they* wanted to fight. This was a battle to delay the French for as long as possible by drawing them into a slow and costly fight for

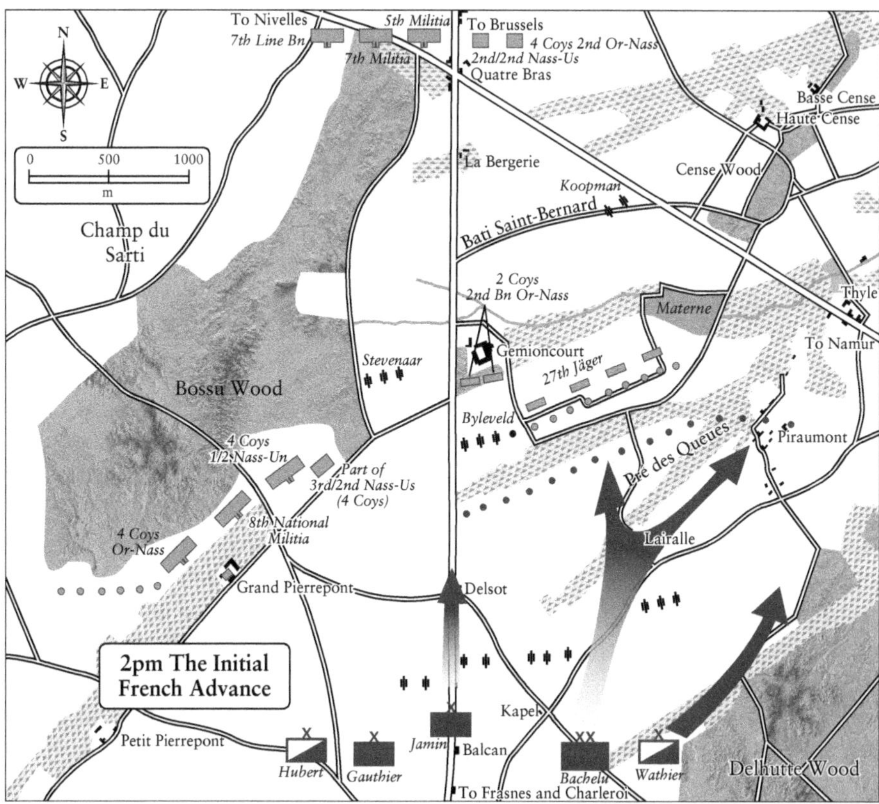

Map showing the initial deployment of the 2nd Netherlands Division at Quatre Bras.

the Bossu wood; difficult terrain, a challenging environment and a close-quarter slog where command and control was difficult. This was not the battle that the French liked to fight; large columns manoeuvring across generally open ground preceded by large swarms of skirmishers and supported by heavy artillery fire. In fact, by deploying a higher proportion of their men in and around the Bossu wood, the Prince of Orange only encouraged the French to advance across the more open ground where they would most benefit from their superior numbers, especially in cavalry and artillery. The Prince had largely left open the quickest route to the vital crossroads. What's more, this axis would keep open the Namur road for the French, which would allow Marshal Ney to send troops towards Napoleon (who was at Fleurus) if required.

Having occupied the Balcan heights the French were soon able to identify the weakness of the allied left; just a single battalion, mostly deployed as skirmishers, supported by a strong farm and a battery of guns. The giving up of these heights without even a skirmish no doubt saved the French much time when every minute counted to the Prince of Orange.

The reasons for such a slow start to the French advance do not need to concern us, but when the advance did start, it came in overwhelming strength against the weakest part of the Netherlands line. At about 2pm, to the east of the Brussels *chaussée*, Bachelu's eleven battalions advanced towards Gemioncourt and the ground between this farm and the Materne pond. He was supported by the four cavalry regiments of Piré's division while Foy's division covered his left flank. The advance was supported by numerous artillery batteries and was preceded by a dense swarm of skirmishers against which the inexperienced jägers could offer little resistance. The Prince of Orange quickly identified that the 27th Jägers had no chance of holding such an overwhelming advance for long and dispatched the 5th Militia down the main road from Quatre Bras into the front line. Coming under French artillery fire they took position to the west of the road, level with Gemioncourt; two companies were deployed into the orchard to the south of the farm and a skirmish screen was sent forwards.

The power of the French artillery was being felt by the Netherlands guns; with much of the infantry hidden by the ground and the high crops, it was the batteries of Bijleveld and Stevenart that were being targeted and they soon began to take significant casualties in men, horses and equipment. Bijleveld's battery was ordered to withdraw, increasing the pressure on Stevenart. Soon one of his guns was unserviceable and it became evident that if he did not move back soon there would be insufficient horses left to drag the guns off. The battery was ordered to withdraw to a position further back, out of effective range of the French artillery. Unfortunately, before the move was completed, Stevenart was struck by a ball and killed, and another gun put out of action.

With the loss of their artillery support, the 27th Jägers were pushed back to the line of Gemioncourt and the stream that ran from that farm down to the Materne pond. The 27th had the farm on their right flank which they occupied with a company, and beyond it to the west was the 5th Militia. These two battalions faced almost the whole of Bachelu's division and, until Stevenart's and Bijleveld's batteries were redeployed onto the high ground behind them, were without artillery support. What's more, the militia battalion were inexperienced in skirmishing tactics and unable to cope with their far more experienced French opponents as Captain Franz Mollinger later described:

> Lieutenant Colonel Westenberg [the battalion's commanding officer] ordered two companies to move into the orchard, while three others, which I had the honour of commanding, were sent further to the front, but in an instant the same were almost completely annihilated, as the men, who despite having been trained to fight in extended order, congregated and were mown down.[37]

The Prince of Orange realised that these two battalions were insufficient to hold up the French advance and at about 2.30pm decided to send the 7th Line Battalion from the reserve to bolster the front line. Although the forward

Netherlands troops looked like being overwhelmed, the undulating ground, streams and thick hedge lines were slowing the French advance. The 7th Line had been deployed north of the Bossu wood, so advanced down its western side and then passed through the wood towards the east to break out into the open ground astride the main road. The battalion now wheeled to the right and came into line between the 5th Militia and the Bossu wood. Three Netherlands battalions now held a line across the open ground from the Bossu wood to the Materne pond. All three faced heavy artillery fire and a growing pressure of French skirmishers.

While the battle for the open ground developed, the battalions deployed to defend the tip of the Bossu wood also came under increasing artillery fire and faced the inevitable swarm of French skirmishers. However, they faced no infantry columns or concerted attack as the French were concerned about how many allied troops were hidden among the trees and correctly felt that the open ground offered them the quickest and easiest route to the crossroads.

In our study in Chapter 2 it was seen that three of the four battalions defending the Bossu wood were Nassau battalions; the fourth was the 8th Militia Battalion commanded by Lieutenant Colonel de Jongh. At first, they only had

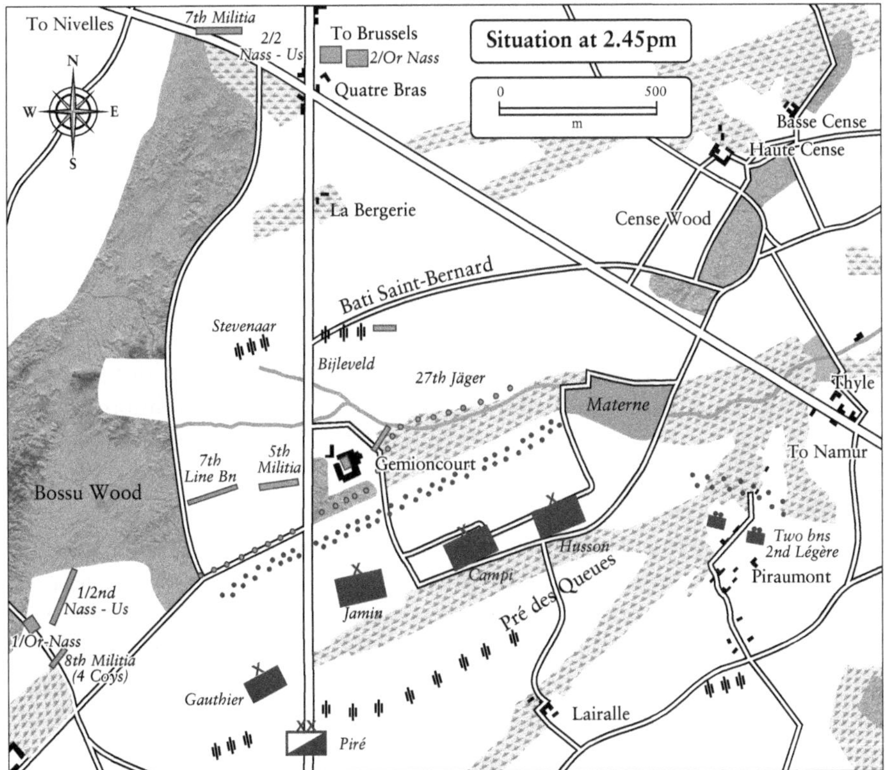

Map showing the Netherlands deployment at 2.45pm at Quatre Bras.

a few cavalry patrols to worry about, but later they came under heavy fire from French artillery which quickly began to undermine morale, resulting in the appearance of the Prince of Orange and his staff, causing two of the battalions to become disordered as they thought they were French cavalry. As we have seen in Chapter 2, each battalion blamed the other for this disorder. To give the four battalions some shelter from the artillery fire and, it seems, to protect their morale as well as their manpower, they were ordered back into the cover of the wood. Companies of skirmishers were left on the edge of the wood and these were soon engaged with their French counterparts. If the Prince of Orange truly wanted to use the wood as some sort of bastion, it is rather strange that he now ordered the Nassau battalions to withdraw through the wood, covered only by some skirmishing companies, and to rally north of the Nivelles road. The 8th Militia were ordered to leave two companies to contest the wood as skirmishers while the remaining four companies were to fall back and then to break out of the wood to the east and support the 5th Militia and 7th Line.

In the initial French advance, Piré's light cavalry division had moved towards the east, supporting Bachelu's division. But as the infantry advanced, it soon became clear that the succession of streams running west to east and the thick hedges that lined them made it difficult cavalry country. It therefore moved back towards the main road, crossed it, and formed up behind the infantry facing the narrow neck of ground between the Bossu wood and Gemioncourt. Although this neck was only 500 metres wide, it presented no obstacles to a cavalry advance.

The Prince of Orange had now established a solid line of troops from the Bossu wood to Gemioncourt composed of the 7th Line and 5th Militia, supported by the 8th Militia, but the gap between this latter farm and the Materne pond was only very thinly held by the 27th Jägers, most of whom were in skirmish order. Only two weakened batteries were able to offer support. They were faced by a thick line of aggressive French skirmishers backed up by infantry and cavalry columns and supported by at least five batteries of artillery.[38] With only open ground behind him, and little enough to deploy the reinforcements rushing to support him, the Prince of Orange felt he must hold this line for as long as possible.

Netherlands accounts of the next phase of the fighting are confused, thin on detail and contradictory. French accounts do not help us. It appears that the French skirmishers were able to overface their Netherlands opponents and push back the formed lines of infantry beyond. But each time the Netherlands troops, encouraged by the Prince of Orange, gallantly formed into columns and pushed the French skirmishers back before being threatened by the overwhelming French columns. There is no evidence to support the direct engagement of French infantry columns, and the detail given in many histories on this phase is clearly largely conjectural, but it seems clear that the French attacks were by thick swarms of skirmishers supported by heavy and effective artillery fire. Some Netherlands accounts describe forming solid columns to resist repeated French cavalry charges.

The front line was under considerable threat. The infantry battalions were being pushed back under the pressure of the French skirmishers and cavalry attacks; Gemioncourt was captured by the French. The Netherlands' artillery, now established further back, although in a position to fire on the French advance, were once more attracting the attention of their French counterparts. It was about three o'clock; the Netherlands troops had just managed to hold their positions, but now the line was in danger of breaking.

As the Netherlands line was looking increasingly fragile, Marshal Ney was to receive reinforcements. Prince Jérôme's strong infantry division, the last of 2nd Corps that was to fight at Quatre Bras, now arrived on the battlefield. Ney immediately ordered Napoleon's younger brother to take the Bossu wood. Soye's brigade marched forwards and into the wood, pushing the line of allied skirmishers back, who were unable to resist such overwhelming numbers.

About this time, Wellington returned to Quatre Bras from his visit to Blücher. Having made a commitment to support the Prussians if he possibly could, his journey back along the Namur road made him apprehensive that this road was in danger of being cut by the French. He therefore made a personal point of ensuring the first British reinforcements that were to arrive on the battlefield would be deployed to this flank. This would have been of little consolation to the Netherlands troops who found themselves desperately attempting to hold onto their positions astride the Brussels road near Gemioncourt. However, just as things seemed hopeless, van Merlen's light cavalry brigade arrived and formed up close to the village along with its accompanying half-battery of horse artillery commanded by Captain Gey. The latter deployed forwards, to the west of the main road in front of the village. Here it was joined by the remains of Stevenart's battery which had been ordered to withdraw to avoid further damage from the French artillery.

The decisive moment seems to have come with a number of French cavalry charges. The Netherlands infantry started a withdrawal; the 5th Militia formed a closed column and started a retreat towards the crossroads, the 27th Jägers attempted to do the same, but in a rather less compact formation as they drew in some of their skirmishers. The 7th Militia Battalion were standing back in reserve, though no effort had been made to use them to hold the French advance and cover the retreat of the rest of the brigade. This job was to be given to van Merlen's newly arrived cavalry.

The situation was getting desperate. The open ground to the east of the Bossu wood was now hardly contested by the Netherlands troops; the 5th Militia and 27th Jägers were both withdrawing back towards the crossroads; to the west of the main road, the 7th Line and 8th Militia stood firm. In the wood itself, the French advance was only being opposed by companies in skirmish order; the main bodies of their battalions had withdrawn out of the wood to the north. The batteries of Stevenart and Bijleveld had been forced back and now stood just in front of Quatre Bras itself, continuing to fire on the leading French troops. The French appeared to be a short advance from attacking the village itself.

Van Merlen's cavalry formed up just to the south of the Namur road, to the east of the village, with the 6th Hussars in the first line and the 5th Light Dragoons in the second. The hussars sent off a squadron to conduct a reconnaissance to the southeast where French cavalry had been reported; the other squadrons of the regiment were allowed to feed their horses after a long and tiring march, although the 5th Light Dragoons remained mounted. Although the first British infantry were now also arriving it would be some time before they would be fully deployed. However, the tactical position was getting critical and in order to cover the disorganised retreat of the 5th Militia and 27th Jägers, the Prince of Orange ordered van Merlen to charge the French cavalry.

The situation was desperate, and haste was required. However, the hussars were feeding their horses when the order arrived and the commanding officer, Lieutenant Colonel Boreel, who had not served since 1795 having resigned as a lieutenant, was to show his inexperience. Choosing not to get his regiment properly formed up, the charge was sounded before the squadrons were ready. The regiment advanced without being in a suitable formation and against an experienced and organised enemy the result was a forgone conclusion. Lieutenant Deebetz described the *ad hoc* nature of the charge:

> The said regiment [6th Hussars], had placed itself in battle order in front of the road from Quatre Bras to Namur when it received the order to take up a new position to the right and come behind the road from Quatre Bras to Nivelles. This movement with platoons to the right had already begun, so that part of the regiment was already near to Quatre Bras, when a staff officer rode along the side of the regiment shouting "Hussars charge!". If this order had been brought to the commander, or been executed in an orderly fashion, it might have ended well, but instead, the platoons wheeled away from the left wing and consecutively formed in line to the left and advanced for the charge, seemingly '*en fourageur*'[39]. The outcome was a general retreat until behind the road of Quatre Bras to Namur, where the regiment reassembled.

Exploiting their success, French cavalry then fell on the 5th Militia and 27th Jägers, who had no defence against the rampaging enemy cavalry, and many were cut down while others threw away their arms and equipment in order to escape. Lieutenant Barre of the 5th Militia later wrote:

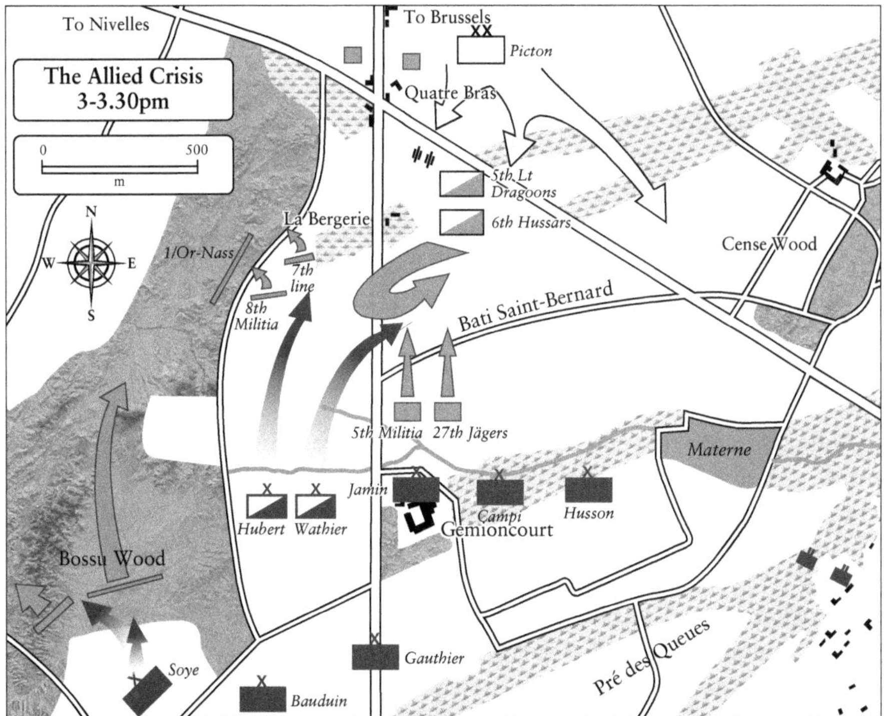

Map showing the final actions of the Netherlands' troops at Quatre Bras.

> The battalion had formed mass against cavalry several times and maintained its position; yet the fourth, or last time the enemy succeeded in reaching several platoons before the formation was completed, as a result of which many men were sabred; this took place about seven o'clock in the evening; one cavalry charge followed another and the battalion was almost entirely dispersed.[40]

While his time is wildly out, he understandably played down the effect on his battalion as a witness shows; Sergeant Johann Doring of the 1st Battalion 28th Orange Nassau Regiment described it as a rout:

> A battalion of Dutch [infantry] was driven back right away, because they had been posted on the main *chausée* in the middle of our line, their falling back put us and the other corps in great danger. These Dutchmen had suffered severely from the enemy's fierce cannonading and musketry and had become completely disheartened. They left their position, some throwing away their muskets.[41]

As we have seen, the 27th Jägers suffered a similar fate, though they were caught in skirmish order with no defence from cavalry apart from what the ground offered. Second Lieutenant Hylckama, of the battalion, described what happened in a letter dated 8 July 1865:

> We produced a heavy musketry fire, and this was followed by a [French] cavalry charge, which our brave hussars tried to stem unsuccessfully. Meanwhile the skirmish line yielding, with subsequent loss of cohesion, rushed to take cover in the terrain, but before they reached it, they were run down by the cavalry, many were sabred whilst others found death under the hooves of the horses.[42]

The nightmare was not yet over; seeing the remaining guns of Stevenart's battery still attached to their limbers that had accompanied the Netherlands cavalry forwards to the west of the *chaussée*, other French squadrons fell on the defenceless guns and cut down the gunners. Fortunately, they had no way of carrying off the guns. Beyond the battery was the 7th Line, which, close to the Bossu wood, rushed to the cover it offered rather than form square or closed column, and although some were cut down, the majority of the battalion was able to reach its shelter; the commanding officer, Lieutenant Colonel de Jongh, admitted, 'it was not possible for me to keep my troops in good order'.[43] The battalion moved north through the wood and rallied in the open ground level with Quatre Bras. As Lieutenant Scheltens of the battalion noted, 'many men were missing'.[44] The 8th Militia Battalion were also able to seek shelter within the wood, though all order was lost, and, like the 7th Line with whom they no doubt got mixed up, the battalion was only able to rally its men north of the Bossu wood. The French cavalry, however, were still not finished: their next target was Gey's half-battery, which, unable to fire on the mass for fear of hitting their own men, was also overrun and their guns left behind. However, Gey gallantly rallied his men, led them in a counter-charge and once more took possession of his guns. In all the confusion and milling horsemen, the Prince of Orange came very close to being captured; one of his aides de camp was seriously wounded and left for dead. Even Wellington was forced to take evasive action.

The flight of the 6th Hussars was covered by a squadron of the 5th Light Dragoons and the regiment was able to rally behind the village, but many men were missing, some of whom made their way back to Brussels. However, the French cavalry were now disordered by their own charge and their mêlée with the 6th Hussars. While they were vulnerable, they were charged by the remaining two squadrons of Colonel de Mercx's 5th Light Dragoons, who, properly organised, delivered an effective counter-charge which, despite a hard fight and being outnumbered, pushed back the French cavalry. During the fighting, men recognised former comrades, but calls from the French for the

Belgians to change sides were ignored. After the initial Netherlands success, the French committed fresh reinforcements, who finally turned the tide against the courageous 5th Light Dragoons who were forced to retire. Although this was attempted in order, it was disrupted by the French and they were forced into a disorderly rush towards Quatre Bras. Unfortunately for them, dressed in a very similar fashion to the French 6th Chasseurs à Cheval, in a final ignominy, they were fired on by the British 92nd and suffered further casualties. The regiment rallied with difficulty behind the village but took pride in their achievement. Adjutant van Doren later wrote:

> The officers, in any case the captains, who were all experienced officers of the former French army and had participated in several campaigns, excellently distinguished themselves, whilst the subaltern officers and troopers, of which half had shared grief and joy with the French, in good spirit and an exceptional bravery, at the end of the fight were greeted by their young prince.[45]

Despite a most gallant resistance, Bijlandt's brigade had effectively been dispersed; the 5th Militia and 27th Jägers were trying to rally north of the village, the 7th Line and 8th Militia had been forced to seek safety in the wood itself and could only rally as groups of their men made their way north and the cavalry were rallying in the same area covered by the reserve. The artillery was in a poor state; the chief of staff of the 2nd Netherlands Division, Colonel van Nyevelt, wrote, 'the artillery, having had three of its guns captured and four others dismounted, several of its ammunition wagons had exploded, and most of its officers and many men killed or wounded, was almost no longer in a state to fight.'[46]

By 4pm almost the entire Bossu wood was in the possession of the French and this threatened the integrity of the allied position. The French needed to be pushed back. The Prince of Orange ordered a counterattack into the north of the wood, but, made with insufficient strength (by the 2nd Battalion of the Nassau Regiment), it was apparently easily repulsed; in his report, Colonel van Nyevelt wrote, 'the enemy had penetrated into the wood. His Royal Highness ordered the 2nd Battalion Nassau with a few Brunswick light infantrymen, to regain possession of the wood. The battalion attacked with courage, but because of the enemy's superior strength, the enemy repulsed them.'[47] This was the last major effort of the Netherlands troops. The British guards were finally able to clear the wood, launching their attack shortly after 6pm and suffering some of the heaviest casualties of any of the allied units at the battle.

With the arrival of increasing numbers of allied reinforcements, and given the inevitable casualties and exhaustion caused by the fighting of the previous two hours, the Netherlands troops were in no state to fight on; even van Löben Sels, whose account sets great store by the performance of the Netherlands troops, admits, 'With small exceptions, we can admit that the Netherlands troops took no further active part in the action.'[48] Wellington clearly believed that if they were to take a viable part in battles to come, it was time to allow them to rally their dispersed men, rest and restore their morale.

Netherlands casualties at Quatre Bras

Of all the contingents in Wellington's army, it is the Netherlands whose casualties are most difficult to state with any degree of confidence; many of the various sources and accounts of the battle give widely different numbers. As we have discussed when studying the Nassau contingent, Erwin Muilwijk has studied the problem of establishing Netherlands' casualties and concludes that it is impossible to be absolutely confident. In his book on Quatre Bras he gives the following figures from the report of Colonel van Nyevelt, chief of staff of the 2nd Netherlands Division:

Bijlandt's Brigade

27th Jägers: K 1/10, W 4/128, M 1/118 (Total: 263). Start state: 25 officers and 786 men.

7th Line: K 1/6, W 1/55, M 0/31 (Total: 94). Start state: 23 officers and 678 men.

5th Militia: K 3/67, W 7/117, M 7/102 (Total: 303). Start state: 22 officers and 460 men.

7th Militia: No casualties recorded. Start state: 25 officers and 651 men.

8th Militia: K 0/5, W 0/6, M 0/14 (Total: 25). Start state: 23 officers and 543 men.

Saxe-Weimar's Brigade

1/28th Orange-Nassau: No casualties recorded. Start state: 28 officers and 865 men.

2/28th Orange-Nassau: No casualties recorded. Start state: 22 officers and 666 men.

1/2nd Nassau: 16 men wounded. Start state 28 officers and 895 men.

2/2nd Nassau: 8 men wounded. Start state: 28 officers and 857 men.

3/2nd Nassau: 3 men wounded, 6 missing. Start state: 28 officers and 871 men.

Nassau Vols: 1 killed, 5 wounded, 14 missing. Start state: 5 officers and 172 men.

As we have already studied the Nassau contingent, we will not consider them further here.

A total of 304 men from the division are reported as 'missing', but it is impossible to be sure how many of these later rejoined their units; some will have been prisoners of war, some would have been separated from their units and others will have been killed.

In contrast, van Löben Sels gives the following figures for the 2nd Netherlands Division, stating that they were 'after the official returns'.[49] While there are some figures that are the same or very similar to those above, the total for the 27th Jägers is significantly different; it appears that the following figure only includes those killed or wounded, but not those missing.

27th Jägers: 144
7th Line: 94
5th Militia: 293
8th Militia: 23
1st/1st Nassau: 16
2nd/1st Nassau: 8
3rd/1st Nassau: 9
Orange-Nassau: 16
Artillery: 63

Löben-Sels notes, 'In this number is included 296 prisoners of war or separated from their unit, but most of whom returned.' It is perhaps no coincidence that this is the same figure that van Nyevelt reports (less officers). For an unspecified reason he does not list the 7th Militia; we must presume that, as with Muilwijk's figures, none are available.

Lieutenant Colonel de Jongh, the commanding officer of the 8th Militia, a man who ought to know the casualties of his unit, records eighty-eight men killed, wounded or missing, a substantial difference from the figures given above. It is possible that de Jongh's total was immediately after the battle before many men who were listed as missing had returned to the battalion.

It is no surprise that it was the 27th Jägers and 5th Militia that had suffered the most, accounting for 566 of the division's 798 casualties; 70 percent. Given that the 7th Line suffered ninety-four casualties, this leaves just 138 losses from the other seven and a half battalions. It is true to say that given three units suffered 82 percent of the division's casualties, the rest of the division suffered very lightly when considering the very risky situation they found themselves in at the beginning of the day. The description of the heavy fighting in the Bossu wood is hardly supported by the casualty figures, but it was mostly Nassau troops that were committed there, and their contribution has already been considered.

These casualties do not include the two cavalry regiments who were hard pressed in the short time they were engaged. In his study of the Netherlands cavalry during the campaign, Andre Dellevoet gives the casualties of the 5th (Belgian) Light Dragoons as 121 officers and men, but gives no figures for the 6th (Dutch) Hussars. Losses are available for this regiment for the whole campaign in which it lost seventy-four men killed or wounded at Quatre Bras and Waterloo, and 131 missing; it is not stretching credibility too far to suggest that most of these were lost as prisoners at Quare Bras. The 5th Light Dragoons were reduced to two squadrons for the remainder of the campaign. While the 6th Hussars had been poorly committed to the charge, showing the inexperience of the commanding officer, both regiments showed great courage and determination and any suspicion over the trustworthiness of the Belgians was surely dispelled by their spirited charge against superior numbers.

We must assume that the men of the 27th Jägers, in their desperation to avoid being cut down by the French cavalry, had discarded both equipment and arms, as the commanding officer, Lieutenant Colonel Grunebosch (who had been seriously wounded by a sabre blow to the head and arm) wrote that even as the battle still raged, the battalion 'received the order from the Prince of Orange to retire to Nivelles and to immediately collect and replenish its weapons etc'.[50] It did rejoin its brigade at Quatre Bras the following day and retired with it to the position at Waterloo.

According to van Nyevelt's numbers, the casualties of the 2nd Netherlands Division were 11 percent of its total strength. This is certainly not catastrophic and is no doubt why it was at this point that Wellington took them out of the fighting before they got so weakened or demoralised that they would be unable to fight again in the following days.

Summary

We have already stated how important a number of key decisions made by the senior Netherlands officers were in making a stand at Quatre Bras which, if they had not been made, would have had a significant impact on the way the campaign would then have played out. The credit for this lies with General de Constant-Rebecque, the Netherlands quartermaster general, General Perponcher-Sedlnitzky, the commander of the 2nd Netherlands Division and Colonel Prince Saxe-Weimar. It is perhaps exaggerating to say that the allies would have lost the campaign without their intervention, but their brave decision certainly made a significant contribution to its success. The Prince of Orange too, although displaying an occasional lack of tactical finesse (perhaps forgivable given his lack of battlefield command experience), is worthy of praise; he displayed exemplary courage throughout the battle, often exposing himself to great danger in order to motivate and inspire his young soldiers.

The eventual defeat of most of the Netherlands units does not reflect poorly on them. These were largely young and inexperienced troops facing overwhelming numbers; the miracle is that they resisted as long as they did. Their inexperience had been particularly exposed by their inability to skirmish as effectively as the French, but they had displayed great enthusiasm and courage against a more numerous (three times) and experienced enemy with a fearsome reputation, and despite their losses they continued the fight in the face of difficult odds. Van Merlen's cavalry, although ultimately bettered, had faced twice their own number and had succeeded in easing the pressure on the Netherlands' infantry and bought time for the first British and Brunswick troops to deploy.

But this valiant defence must also be put into perspective. The French attack did not become serious until two o'clock; before then it had been little more than skirmishing, and the Netherlands troops were relieved from the line at approximately 4pm. They therefore fought in the front line for two hours and not all day as is often claimed. Indeed, it was Marshal Ney's slow start that allowed them to hold their position for so long rather than the fight put up by the Netherlands troops. The battle raged on until almost 10pm; it therefore lasted eight hours, yet most of the Netherlands' troops had fought for no more than two of them; albeit perhaps, the most vital first two hours. By taking them out of the line, Wellington had ensured the Netherlands troops would be able to recover from their exertions in time for the trials that were yet to come; another example of his careful management of his less experienced and battle-tested troops.

There is no doubt that French failings made a dangerous and potentially catastrophic mission somewhat easier than it should have been for the Netherlands' troops, but we must be wary of taking credit from them for something that was out of their control.

During the night of the 16th the Prince of Orange wrote a short letter to his father the king. In it he wrote, 'It is with the greatest satisfaction that I can assure Your Majesty that the troops have fought with much bravery, particularly the infantry and the artillery…'.[51]

It would seem that the cavalry was somewhat unfairly overlooked for praise; despite their defeat, they had fought as bravely and enthusiastically as the other arms.

17 June

On the morning of 17 June the French probed the allied outpost line in front of Quatre Bras, no doubt wishing to confirm that Wellington's army was still in position. Although there was plenty of skirmishing, there appears to have been no serious attempt to attack and to gain ground. As the morning advanced, Wellington learned of the Prussian defeat at Ligny and their retreat to the north. Feeling he had no option but to conform with this movement or face the full weight of the French army, he ordered his own retreat. This started at ten o'clock and was not interfered with by the French.

The men of the 2nd Netherlands Division were no doubt grateful for having had the time to rest, clean their weapons and replenish their ammunition before starting their own move. The 27th Jägers, having marched to Nivelles the previous day to re-equip had returned to join their brigade before the move started. The losses of the 27th Jäger and 5th Militia had now become clear. Lieutenant Colonel Grunebosch, commanding the former, reported that having started the battle with twenty-three officers and 792 men, his reported casualties were one officer and ninety-four men killed, six officers and 123 wounded and seven lost as prisoners, supposedly leaving a total of 584 men if all those wounded were lost to the battalion. However, he also admits that on arriving at the Waterloo position, all that remained to him was 'six officers and between 200 and 300 men'.[52] If we take his strength as six officers and 300 men, this shows a shortfall of sixteen officers and 369 men unaccounted for *above* their casualties; a very high proportion for which he offers no explanation. The 5th Militia had started the previous day's battle with a total strength of 482 and once their casualties are deducted, had only 179 officers and men remaining in the ranks. However, some of the missing may have returned in time for Waterloo, although the commanding officer, Lieutenant Colonel Westenberg, admitted, 'I only had a few hundred the following day [the 17th] when I was deployed with the brigade on the height of Mont Saint Jean…'.[53]

The 2nd Netherlands Division followed the 3rd British Division to the Waterloo position. With no staff officer to meet them, they bivouacked between the villages of Mont Saint Jean and Merbe Braine, though they had not been there long when General de Constant-Rebecque joined them and led them to their new positions; for Bijlandt's 1st Brigade, this was to the left (east) of the main *chaussée*, forward of the Ohain road which ran more or less along the crest of the allied ridge. From here they had a clear view of the ground which was to stretch between the two sides. Saxe-Weimar's all Nassau 2nd Brigade occupied the extreme left of the allied line, standing on the ridgeline overlooking the farms of Papelotte and la Haye, and the village of Smohain (see Chapter 2). Between the two brigades were deployed the 4th and 5th Hanoverian Brigades. Wellington had chosen to split up the two brigades of the division, which must have been very frustrating for the divisional commander, General Perponcher. Wellington gave no reason for this, but we can reasonably presume that having not been given permission to mix Netherlands brigades within British divisions, he had decided to do it anyway in the way they were deployed.

General Chassé's 3rd Netherlands Division, covered by the two remaining Netherlands cavalry brigades (Ghigny and Trip) had spent the 16th occupying and covering the town of Nivelles in case it should be attacked by the French. At about eleven o'clock on the morning of the 17th, Chassé was ordered to march to Waterloo.[54] Reaching the heights overlooking the small town of Braine l'Alleud, they were met by General de Constant-Rebecque who directed them to their new position in front of that town, securing the extreme right flank of

Wellington's army. The town lay in a wide valley which would have offered the French a covered approach around the allied right and the position of Hougoumont. However, General Chassé, having conducted a reconnaissance, redeployed the division with the 1st Brigade (Detmers) guarding the approaches and within the town itself, and the 2nd Brigade (d'Aubremé) in reserve, 'with its front turned obliquely towards the route from Nivelles to Brussels; the right wing a little in the rear'.[55]

The two brigades of cavalry that had remained near Nivelles were ordered to move to Waterloo while covering the 3rd Netherlands Division that moved before them. A small cavalry rear guard consisting of Lieutenant van Uchelen and eight men from the 4th (Dutch) Light Dragoons was pressed by some French hussars and in a skirmish van Uchelen and a few of the men were taken prisoner.[56] The main body arrived at Mont Saint Jean at about 5pm, where it joined van Merlen's brigade that had retired from Quatre Bras. The division bivouacked near the junction of the Charleroi and Nivelles roads with Ghigny on the left, van Merlen in the centre and Trip on the right. The artillery of Petter and Gey bivouacked behind the brigades.

Waterloo

In his history of the campaign, de Bas gives a total of 16,583 Netherlanders at Waterloo. That is:

2nd Division and the 2nd Cavalry brigade: 7,591 all ranks after subtracting the casualties of Quatre Bras.

The remaining cavalry brigades: 2,323.

3rd Division: 6,669.[57]

This represents approximately 25 percent of Wellington's army and a considerable proportion of the whole, although this includes the all-Nassau 2nd Brigade which we have already considered as a separate contingent in Chapter 2.

The Prince of Orange had started the campaign as the nominated commander of the allied 1st Corps. However, before the battle started, a significant change was ordered by Wellington. As the Netherlands troops had been split across the whole front and depth of Wellington's position the Prince was to give up command of this corps and instead was appointed as the commander of the 'centre'. The 3rd Netherlands Division was put under command of the 2nd Corps (Lord Hill) and the 2nd Netherlands Division under command of General Picton, commander of the 5th British Division. The Netherlands cavalry division (Collaert) was put under command of the Earl of Uxbridge, who now commanded all the allied cavalry. It is not clear which divisions and brigades now came under the Prince's new command or what the formal command structure was with the commanders of these formations, although there may have been one which has not been passed down to posterity. How this arrangement was to work therefore, has not been made clear, nor the reasons for it (though we can speculate). It was certainly unusual, and well designed to cause confusion in a crisis, not least because the centre seems to have contained formations from the 1st, 2nd and Reserve Corps. Perhaps it is well that the allies were to win the coming battle!

Deployment

Many less recent histories of the battle describe the deployment of the 1st Brigade, 2nd Netherlands Division as being on the forward slope of the allied ridge, very exposed to French observation and fire, and it is true that as morning broke, this is exactly where they were, as described in the previous section. This deployment is often used as an excuse for a weak resistance to the first French assault, having been exposed to a devastating fire from the French grand battery as they were the only available infantry target for the French guns. This myth has been perpetuated in a number of more recent histories. However, the chief of staff of the 2nd Division, Colonel van Nyevelt, describes the movement of the brigade and the reasons for it:

> At midday, the whole of the First Brigade (van Bijlandt) and the artillery of the right wing made a move to the rear, in order not to block the English guns placed behind them, and also to be less exposed to the enemy's fire. These troops crossed the sunken lane and deployed in the same order of battle as they had been in before, supported to right and left by English and Scottish troops and the guns in line with those of the English.[58]

Different accounts give a different order of the units within the 1st Brigade, so we cannot be absolutely sure of their deployment. However, Erwin Muilwijk, in his recent study,[59] gives the following based on first-hand accounts; the right-hand unit was the sad remains of the 27th Jäger, no more than 300 strong, then the 8th Militia, 7th Line Battalion, and finally the 7th Militia on the left; each of these battalions were deployed in two-deep line. The weak remains of the 5th Militia, a little less than 200 men, were in reserve behind the centre of the brigade's line. Bijleveld's battery, consisting of seven guns, was to the front of the two right-hand battalions. Lieutenant Colonel Grunebosch, commanding the 27th Jägers described his position as 'about 20 paces in rear of a gravel track [the Ohain road] which ran along the height of Mont Saint Jean…'.[60] A line of skirmishers covered the front of the brigade. In contemporary sketches, the Netherlands brigade is shown in front of the front line of British troops, on its own, with the British regiments almost forming a second line; British eyewitnesses describe advancing to engage the French, while the Netherlanders clearly did not. To the right rear of the Netherlands brigade stood Kempt's British brigade and to the left rear, that of Pack; the battalions of these two brigades remained in column in the dead ground behind the ridgeline. It seems that the frontage was too narrow to allow all the battalions that were deployed here to stand in line. When the battle opened, the Netherlands battalions were ordered to lie down to reduce casualties.

As we have heard, on the afternoon of the 17th, General Chassé's 3rd Netherlands Division was deployed at Braine l'Alleud, with the 1st Brigade in front of and occupying the town, and the 2nd Brigade in reserve to the rear.

The Netherlands cavalry occupied the same position in which they had spent the night; in the area of Mont Saint Jean farm between the main roads from Genappe and Nivelles. The regiments stood in columns by squadron with the half batteries of Petter and Gey between the brigades.

After the casualties of men (including the death of Captain Stevenart) and horses, and the losses of guns and equipment suffered at Quatre Bras, the artillery had been reorganised. Of Stevenart's battery, only the section of two guns

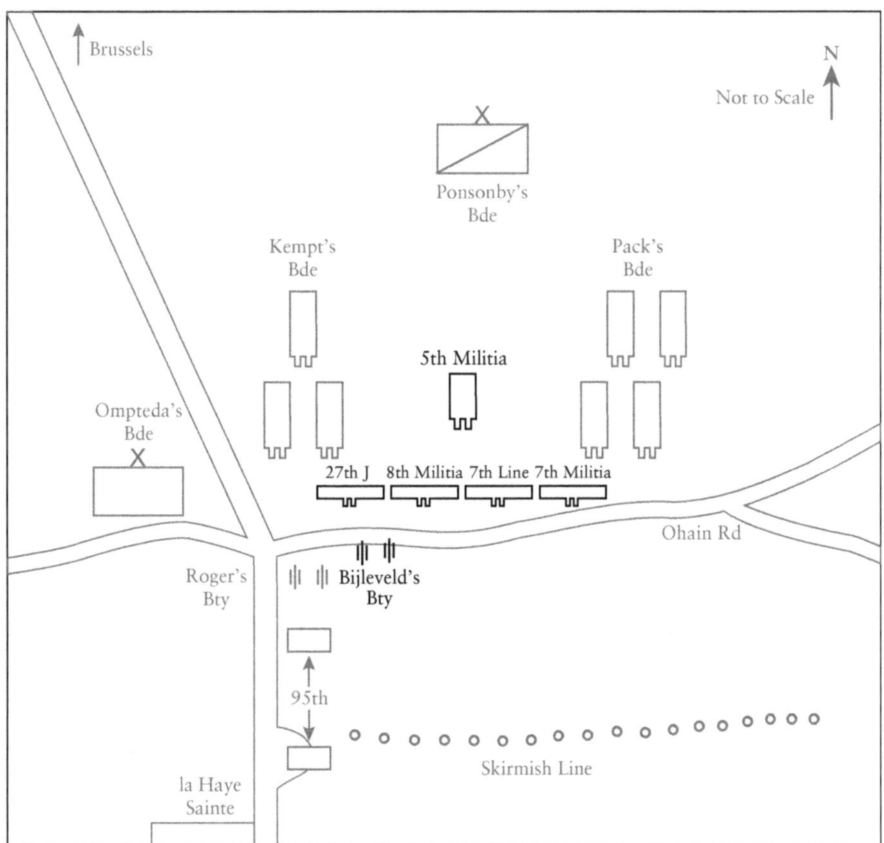

Sketch showing the initial deployment of Bijlandt's 1st Netherlands Brigade at Waterloo based on first-hand accounts.

commanded by Second Lieutenant Winssinger could be deployed, but these were reinforced by a howitzer of Bijleveld's battery. This small battery was deployed on the allied left on the high ground overlooking the farms of Papelotte and la Haye, in support of the 2nd Brigade of the 2nd Netherlands Division. Bijleveld's battery, which at Quatre Bras had supported the 2nd Brigade, switched to support the 1st and deployed in front of its right wing. The remaining seven guns were deployed next to Rogers' British battery, having detached one of its howitzers to reinforce Winssinger's section. As we have seen, the two half batteries attached to Collaert's cavalry division, remained with them in the third line.

Bijlandt's 1st Brigade, 2nd Netherlands Division

It will be remembered that the 2nd Brigade of the 2nd Netherlands Division was the all-Nassau Brigade of Colonel Prince Saxe-Weimar. Their actions at Waterloo have already been discussed in Chapter 2.

Wellington's decision to place Bijlandt's brigade in the front line is an interesting one. The Duke had a clear policy of putting his more inexperienced contingents into the second or even third line to preserve them as much as possible for when they were really needed. It is true that the brigade had British units on both flanks, but it is also true that, although they had had time to recover from their experiences at Quatre Bras, as we have already seen, two of the five battalions had suffered considerably on the 16th and were mere shadows of their former selves and, what's more, two of the other three had had quite traumatic experiences at that battle. We are left to speculate as to whether this was a deliberate policy, or an oversight.

The performance of Bijlandt's brigade has long been used by British authors to illustrate the ineptitude and cowardice of the Netherlands' troops at Waterloo, running in the face of d'Erlon's attack and making no further contribution to the battle. The brigade certainly found itself very much in the front line facing the massive French infantry columns that were launched about 1.30pm. The most detailed account of the attack comes from Colonel van Nyevelt, the divisional chief of staff, and as a start point, we shall look at his report in which he wrote:

> three attacking columns, commanded by Comte d'Erlon, advanced against our position, with the 103rd [105th] Regiment in the lead. The enemy crossed the valley, in which he was fired on by our artillery and pushed back our skirmishers. We did not fire a single shot until they were fifty paces away, but then we could no longer contain the impatience of the soldiers and we opened fire in two ranks under which our opponents continued to march bravely.
>
> The brigade that was attacked [Bijlandt's] was formed in a line of two ranks, which produced a weak and poorly maintained fire. The fall of some files caused an opening of which the enemy took

> advantage to pass its columns through. Everything across the extent of the front was forced to retire while the platoons on the wings coolly closed ranks against the nearest troops.
>
> The enemy passed through the first line and arrived on the plateau; the second line started to move and marched against them while an English Guard cavalry regiment moved forwards to charge them in case of a retreat.
>
> The enemy, having penetrated our line, realised with surprise that there were masses of infantry they had not been able to see from their position because these troops, which were lying on the ground, were hidden from sight by the hedge.
>
> While the enemy tried to hastily reform, the nearest troops of the second line advanced against their flanks, while the Chief of the General Staff [Constant-Rebècque], having rallied 400 men which had retreated, supported this movement. We threw the enemy back beyond the hollow way and chased them with bayonets in their kidneys to their own position while the cavalry, falling on them, caused a dreadful carnage in their ranks.
>
> The Netherlands troops, dragged along by their enthusiasm, had overtaken the English and captured two fanions; but in the meantime, the escaping troops had unmasked their artillery which re-opened fire and the whole line took up its former position.[61]

Van Nyevelt tells us that the French columns got within fifty paces of the Netherlands line before they opened fire. He insinuates that the soldiers did so without orders because of their 'impatience' and this fire was insufficient to stop the column which broke through the Netherlands' ranks and forced those in front of them to 'give way'. Although he states that the units on the flanks maintained their positions and fired into the flanks of the columns, it was the troops of the second line, the brigades of Kempt and Pack, which actually repulsed the French. Their action gave de Constant-Rebecque time to rally 400 men of Bijlandt's brigade which then joined the pursuit of the French.

Van Nyevelt's excuse that the fire effect of the Netherlands troops was poor because they fired in two ranks does not bear scrutiny; the British fire effect was much lauded and feared for this very reason. It seems he was seeking an excuse for the poor marksmanship of his men, which was far more likely to have been the failure of discipline rather than anything else; perhaps an understandable lack of training and of inexperienced troops. Thus, instead of firing a single, concentrated volley, it is likely that the soldiers fired at will or by files, thus lacking the devastating effect for which British firepower was known. Some Netherlands troops may well have held their positions, but other testimony puts this in doubt. General de Constant-Rebecque wrote in his own report:

> The 1st Brigade of the [2nd] division received the first shock and was pushed back… [as the British cavalry attacked…] During this time, I attempted to reform the battalions of General Bijlandt's brigade and to move them forward, and as General Ghigny's cavalry was at hand I led them into the hollow to the right of the enemy so as to support the retreat of the English cavalry which advanced too far… In regaining the position, I also returned with numerous prisoners…[62]

Lieutenant Colonel de Jongh, the commanding officer of the 8th Militia, passes quickly over this key phase of the battle, writing:

> Towards half past twelve the first line of the enemy approached, formed in columns and drove the skirmishers back to the line of battle. They then attacked the line of battle, pushing into it and disordering the weak battalions. The English cavalry charged at this moment and sabred the greatest part of the two columns, which had forced our division back. I assembled the main part of my battalion and marched forward and supported the attack of the English cavalry and we captured many French men, officers and soldiers. After the enemy attack was completely repulsed, the chief of the general staff of the division ordered me to position the battalion in the previous position behind the hollow road in front of la Haye Sainte (part of my battalion was detached to escort the prisoners of war to the rear)…[63]

One of the British officers who were dismissive of the contribution of Bijlandt's brigade was Lieutenant Winchester of the 92nd Highlanders, who, as part of Pack's brigade, were deployed to the rear left of the Netherlanders. In his letter (dated 1834) to Captain Siborne, who was compiling a history of the campaign, he wrote:

> At the commencement of the action, a corps of Belgians from 8,000 to 10,000 men were formed in line in front of the 5th [British] Division, but soon after they were attacked and their skirmishers driven in on their line, the whole of them retired through the 5th Division, and were seen no more during the action.[64]

But not all British officers were so quick to insult the courage or resilience of the Netherlanders; Lieutenant James Hope, who, ironically, was of the same regiment as Winchester (the 92nd), also wrote to Siborne, and stated:

> With loud shouts of '*Vive l'empereur*!' the left column attacked the farmhouse of La Haye Sainte, while the right column, supported by

> the 3rd, moved against the Belgian troops assailed with terrible fury, [who] returned the fire of the enemy for some time with great spirit. But on the approach of the French, they shifted their ground, and retired behind the hedge, which, although it afforded them no shelter from the enemy's fire, yet concealed them from their view. Hence, on seëing themselves well supported, they showed a little more courage, and although exposed to a heavy fire, they maintained their ground with considerable fierceness…
>
> With drums beating, colours flying and eagles soaring above their huge headdresses, the enemy advanced in solid column to the attack. Their progress was considerably retarded by the fire of our artillery, and volleys of musketry from the Belgian infantry, till the enemy having almost gained the summit of the ridge, our allies partially retired from the hedge. At the entreaty of their officers, the greater part of them again returned to their posts, but it was merely to satisfy their curiosity, for they almost immediately again retired without firing a shot. The officers exerted themselves to the utmost to keep the men at their duty, but their efforts were fruitless and at length the whole corps took fairly to their heels.
>
> The post thus abandoned by *Les Braves Belges*, was instantly reoccupied by the 3rd Battalion the Royals, and 2nd Battalion 44th Regiment.[65]

This account, although rather colourful in places, is unusual in its praise, but is also clear that the whole brigade 'took to their heels'. As we have seen in other contingents, it is often the dedication of the officers that caught the eye of their allies.

Lieutenant Colonel Grunebosch, commanding officer of the 27th Jägers, was seriously wounded at Quatre Bras, but appears to have commanded the battalion again at Waterloo, although his description of this battle is less detailed than that of the former. He wrote two letters to van Löben Sels. In the first, he admits that his battalion had been reduced from just over 800 men before Quatre Bras, to only '6 officers and between 200 and 300 men' on the morning of Waterloo, but then admits that after the 'scattering' of the brigade, it was reduced to only 'five or six officers and between 50 and 100 men'.[66] His second letter was written in 1841 and unfortunately describes a very different scenario in which during the attack of d'Erlon's corps, the brigade, 'were able to withstand the French column with their fire, until the 2nd British brigade of cavalry under General Uxbridge cut them to pieces.'[67] This clearly illustrates how even seemingly dependable eyewitnesses change their story over time, usually to make earlier impressions more creditable to their unit or formation (though to the frustration of those historians and enthusiasts who followed).

Although General Perponcher wrote a detailed account of Quatre Bras, he wrote only in very general terms on Waterloo; his must have been a frustrating battle, with his two brigades split by a considerable distance and, each commanded by their own brigadiers, he was left with little to command; that is not to say that he was not in the thick of it, having two horses killed under him during the battle.

General Bijlandt's own account is very thin on detail; he does not mention the retirement of the brigade, and only states that on d'Erlon's attack:

> I personally received the order from the Prince of Orange to move forward and to attack with the bayonet without giving the enemy time to deploy. A Scottish brigade which was placed in rear of my position followed the movement and arrived almost at the same time upon the enemy. The confusion was great, the mêlée horrific, and it was in this confusion that I received a bayonet thrust in my thigh…[68]

None of the other senior officers mention an order from the Prince of Orange and we cannot put much faith in Bijlandt's account that was written in 1841, over twenty-five years after the battle, when he was seventy years old.

Information on the actions of the brigade after d'Erlon's repulse is rather hazy and thin on detail. In this first action, Bijlandt and van Nyevelt were wounded, Perponcher had two horses killed under him, and two battalion commanders, Westenberg (5th Militia) and van der Sande (7th Line), were also wounded. Lieutenant Colonel Gruneboseh wrote:

> because of the scattering of those that remained; for this reason the battalion, having a strength of five or six officers and between 50 and 100 men, moved closer to the 8th National Militia Battalion [of de Jongh], who had maintained its position, having to its left a British regiment, whilst the 5th National Militia Battalion was positioned to the right rear towards the main road, and the 7th National Militia Battalion was deployed as skirmishers on the declivity of the ridge of Mont Saint Jean.[69]

Most of the remaining men of his battalion had been despatched back to Brussels escorting the French prisoners. About sixty men of the 8th Militia had also escorted the prisoners and in the absence of the 27th Jägers, the remains of the 7th Militia Battalion provided the skirmish screen.

But perhaps the clearest picture is painted by Lieutenant Colonel de Jongh of the 8th Militia and who, on the wounding of Bijlandt, found himself in command of the remains of the brigade:

As the brigade general [Bijlandt] was forced to leave the battlefield because of his wounds and Lieutenant Colonel Westenberg, commanding the 5th National Militia, which after the first enemy attack had been repulsed, took a position behind the 3rd line with the debris of his battalion (which was very few) was also wounded, I, as the oldest commanding officer of the brigade took the command upon myself and assembled the three battalions, No.7 and 8 National Militia and No.7 Infantry of the Line [The commanding officers of the 7th Militia and 7th Line were both wounded and had handed over command]. 1st Lieutenant Noot and 2nd Lieutenant Count van Stirum and about 26 or 27 NCOs and Jaegers [of the 27th Jägers] reported to me, requesting to fight under my orders... I had these various troops united with my battalion and placed in this position and during the entire day, supported by the English infantry... repelling all attacks and several times helped to throw the French back into the valley in front of our position...[70]

The picture that is painted is that due to their numerical weakness, the 27th Jägers were selected to escort the many French prisoners back to Brussels, but that a party of that battalion, presumably separated from it, attached themselves to de Jongh's remaining force. Sixty or so men of the 8th Militia Battalion were also used to escort the prisoners.[71] Having lost their commanding officer, the 5th Militia Battalion had remained in reserve. This left de Jongh with the remnants of the remaining three battalions to hold a part of the line of battle with British troops on both flanks, from where they continued to engage the French skirmishers that were active across the front throughout the battle. There is no doubt that on top of the men detached to escort prisoners, many men had drifted away from the ranks. General Perponcher, in his report dated Paris, 11 July 1815, wrote, 'the whole brigade was deployed as battalion skirmishers...'[72] giving a good indication of both how many men were left in the line and the sort of fight that continued on this flank during the afternoon.

Although there were no more significant French attacks in column on this part of the line the pressure continued throughout the day, and even the 5th Militia were required in the front line. Van Nyevelt wrote in his report:

Our losses rapidly increased; already no reserve existed, all had been pushed ahead. The 5th Militia Battalion had moved into the front line... The 1st Brigade, which was stationed on the slope of the ridge without protection and without cartridges, was exposed to the most intense hail of volley fire and was unable to keep the position

> any longer. Under the command of Lieutenant Colonel de Jongh they retreated behind the line.

This retreat took place before the attack of the Imperial Guard, so we must presume it was sometime just before 7pm and the extreme fire came from the remains of d'Erlon's corps which was ordered to pressure their part of the line as support to the Guard's attack. No doubt exhausted, under intense fire and lacking ammunition, they could no longer maintain their place in the firing line and retreated.

The final sad vignette of this brigade is recounted by Colonel Prince Saxe-Weimar, commander of the 2nd Division's 2nd Brigade, who had been fighting all day on the allied left flank. He wrote:

> [After the Prussian arrival] The few troops that I had left retreated from the combat. I led them towards a wood which was part of the Forêt de Soignes a few hundred paces behind and to the rear of the position where the 2nd and 3rd Battalions were stationed… Lieutenant General Perponcher [commander of the 2nd Division]… came and joined me in my bivouac where he spent the night; *his 1st Brigade having been almost entirely dispersed* [my emphasis].[73]

Perhaps 'entirely dispersed' is rather unfair, but by the time of the Imperial Guard's attack, the 1st Brigade's battle was over. De Bas states that the 7th Line and 5th Militia Battalions had less than half the men still in the ranks that they started the day with.[74] The brigade had had a traumatic battle; it had suffered many casualties and many men were missing. It would take some time to gather up those who had taken casualties to the rear and for those who had become separated to return to their units.

3rd Netherlands Division

It will be remembered that the 3rd Netherlands Division, commanded by Lieutenant General Chassé, an experienced general previously in French service, spent most of 16 June in the town of Nivelles, thus not fighting at Quatre Bras. It had therefore suffered no casualties and was reasonably fresh when it arrived at Waterloo on the 17th. Its deployment on the extreme right flank of the allied army in the small town of Braine l'Alleud meant it lay some 1,500 metres to the west of the centre of the allied line and 1,000 metres to the northwest of Hougoumont (see Map 1 on page 22). Although some way from the main position, the town of Braine l'Alleud lay in a shallow valley that led from behind the French front line around the right flank of Wellington's position. It therefore lay in a tactically significant position which offered the French a way to outflank

Wellington's strong defensive position and the opportunity to fight the battle on ground of their choice rather than Wellington's. However, Napoleon did not feel he needed to manoeuvre to defeat Wellington and such a manoeuvre would have taken considerable time, a commodity Napoleon was short of if he was to seize Brussels before having to worry about having to fight the Prussians once more. He therefore chose not to use this approach.

To look at the actions of the division up until its final action in confronting the attack of the Imperial Guard in the evening of Waterloo, the following is based on the report of Lieutenant Colonel Carl van Delen, the division's chief of staff, which was dated 11 November 1815.[75]

In the morning of the 18th the division worked hard to fortify Braine l'Alleud in case of a French attack, but as Napoleon's army formed up before the main allied line, it must have become clear to Wellington that the French emperor was not considering a wide movement around his flank and decided to order Chassé to close in on the main position. Chassé called in all his outlying detachments to concentrate the division at Braine l'Alleud and make them ready to march. Just two battalions of the 1st Brigade were left in defence of the town; the 6th Militia Battalion in the town itself and the 17th Militia Battalion, which had been placed to form a link with the right of the main position. Once the rest of the brigade had formed up, they marched to the left towards the main Nivelles to Brussels road and halted near the hamlet of Merbe Braine. The 2nd Brigade followed and formed up on their left. Shortly afterwards, this brigade moved on, divided into two groups of three battalions each, and formed up next to the 2nd British Division which lay in reserve behind Hougoumont. General Chassé described these moves in a letter to the Prince of Orange dated 4 July 1815:

> Towards three o'clock, the division received the order to take front obliquely along the chaussée from Nivelles to Brussels. The brigades were sometimes formed in columns, sometimes in line, and at other times in square. These manoeuvres were executed with a *sang-froid* which would have done honour to experienced troops, despite a violent cannonade which caused heavy losses in the ranks. The soldiers remained in this painful situation for several hours, fearlessly facing death, and when one of their comrades was struck, they shouted '*Vive le Roi*! *Vive la Patrie*!'[76]

As this move took place during the French cavalry charges it was conducted in square. It can be seen that the division had started taking casualties from French balls that had sailed over the ridgeline to their front, despite being unseen by the French gunners.

Back in Braine l'Alleud, the two battalions that had been left guarding the town found their vedettes being probed by French lancer patrols with which they exchanged fire. These patrols must have come from General Piré's light cavalry division of Reille's 2nd Corps, which was deployed on the extreme French left. However, when Chassé was ordered to take up his new position at three o'clock, the two battalions still around the town were ordered to re-join their brigade. The division was now formed up along the Brussels road, obliquely to the front line; 'the 1st Brigade found itself immediately behind and lining the Brussels road; to the right flank was the 2nd Brigade in two columns by division (with a two-company front). Throughout these moves, and in their positions, the two brigades suffered from a very lively fire from enemy guns and howitzers. They remained there for about an hour.'[77]

The division now stood idle in reserve yet continued to suffer from artillery fire which caused casualties and shook the morale of the young troops. It was not until the early evening that some of them at least were finally called into action. Van Delen describes what happened next:

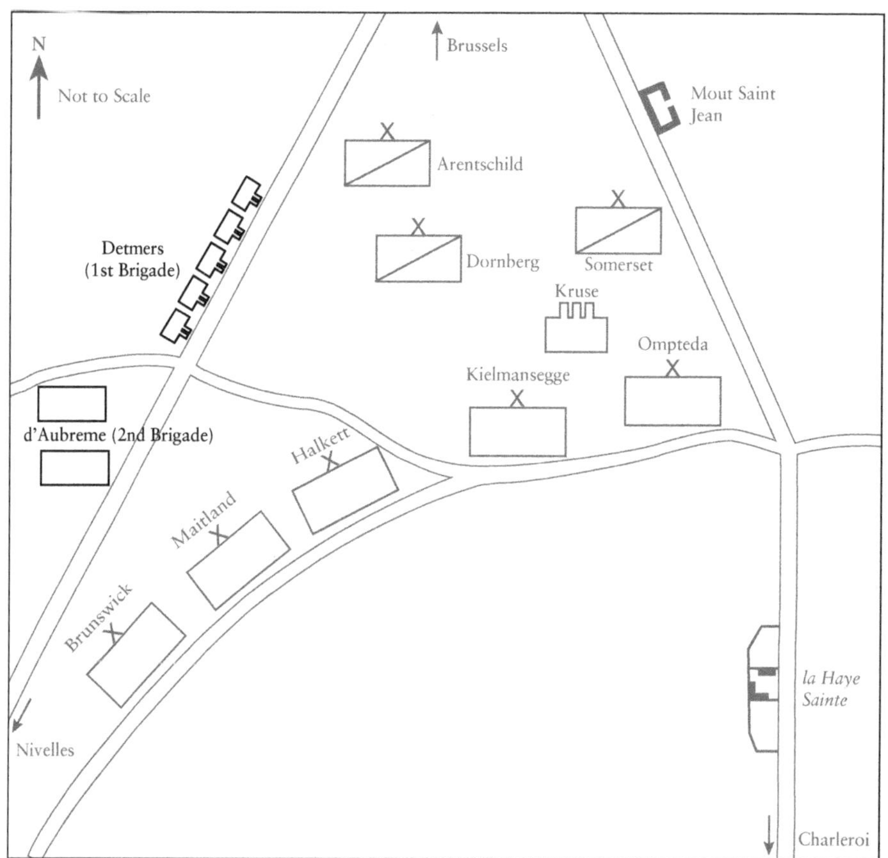

Map showing the second position of the 3rd Netherlands Division at Waterloo.

> Towards evening, General Baron Chassé noticed that the fire from the English artillery, that was on the height in front of us, without ceasing completely, reduced in intensity. He hurried off immediately to find out what the cause was and learnt that these batteries were lacking ammunition. At the same time, noticing that the French Guard was moving to fall on this artillery, His Excellency did not lose a minute to send our artillery, commanded by Major van der Smissen, onto the height and to have him open a violent fire. Betweentimes, an English aide de camp arrived with Colonel Detmers and ordered him to place himself in the front line with three battalions. The colonel formed the 35th Jägers, 2nd Line Battalion and 4th National Militia Battalion into column by division and moved them forwards. These battalions marched on the reverse slope of the heights on which the English army had taken its positions, so that they were, until a certain moment, sheltered from the fire and that only the bayonets were struck by the balls. Finally, Colonel Detmers found a gap into which he could move; he was situated between the left of two battalions that executed a very violent and well-maintained fire by rank and a battalion formed in a triangle in the rear of the position.[78] Our battalions having changed direction to the right, marched immediately to get itself into line. At the same time, the battalion formed in triangle and a unit of chasseurs placed on its left flank started to break up. In the meantime, His Excellency had returned to the division. He made a short, but energetic speech to the three battalions remaining of the 1st Brigade and moved them forwards. Leaving General d'Aubremé in reserve with the 2nd Brigade, the commanding general brought together all the battalions of the 1st Brigade, formed them into a closed column and, putting himself at their head, had the charge beaten and led them towards the enemy. Disdainful of the violent enemy musketry, and ignoring a cavalry attack which threatened his flank, the brigade rushed forwards to shouts of '*Oranje boven! Vive le Roi*!' Suddenly, the enemy Guard against which our attack was directed, left its position and disappeared before us. The brigade continued to follow the enemy until late into the evening; the darkness and the ardour of the pursuit somewhat broke up the troops.'

Chassé's account of this phase of the battle is very similar to that of van Delen; however, as the attack of Detmer's brigade is discussed in considerable detail in Appendix E, we will not go into any more detail here.

Detmer's advance continued after the retreat of the Guard until it became so dark it was of no advantage to continue further. The brigade was ordered to halt at about ten o'clock, although by this time it appears that Detmer's column had split into two, as van Delen writes, 'One part under Colonel Detmers was

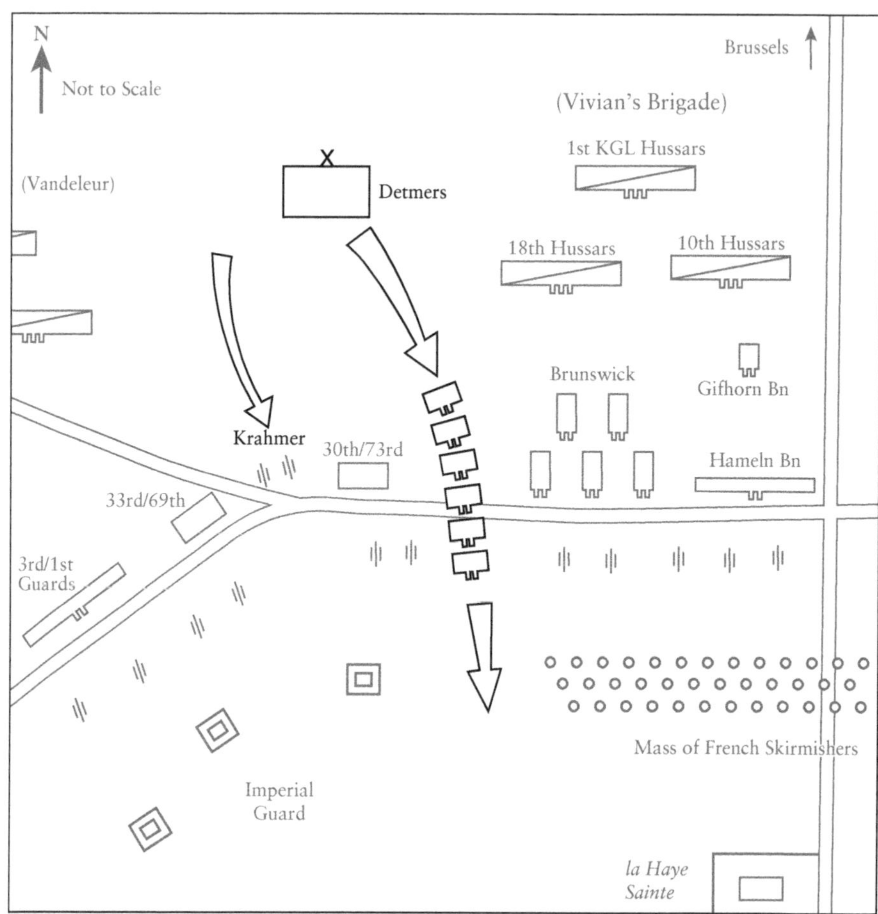

Map showing the advanced position of Krahmer's battery and the attack of Detmer's brigade in the repulse of the Imperial Guard at Waterloo.

ordered by Quartermaster-General Baron de Constant-Rebecque to halt around 10 o'clock in the evening, while another part, with which I was positioned, had already met Prussian troops and was ordered to halt by myself.' Detmers described the place they stopped for the night as, 'to the right of the Namur road [presumably he means the Charleroi road], having in our right rear what has been called the 'observatory'.'[79] Captain van Omphal, aide de camp to Chassé, states that they were at the farm of Rossomme.[80]

Van Delen also explains what happened to the 2nd Brigade:

> The 2nd Brigade remained in its last position, in which it had continued to suffer from a lively cannonade, until the moment when an aide de camp of General Lord Hill [commander of the 2nd Corps] came to inform General d'Aubremé that the 2nd British Division had

> made a forwards movement and that the brigade was to support it, with the result that the brigade, which until then had been fired on from the front, also suffered on its left flank. The two columns of the brigade nevertheless remained in the best order and continued ready to form squares. A quarter of an hour later, the same aide de camp from General Hill returned with an order directing the brigade to make a movement to the right to take the place of the 2nd British Division which had marched ahead. The brigade had arrived in this position when the aide de camp returned to General d'Aubremé with the news that the battle was over to our advantage; at the same time, he gave the order to establish the brigade in two lines to the right of the English artillery, where it passed the night in bivouac.

After what must have been a most frustrating time standing under artillery fire for much of the battle, the 1st Brigade at least had found themselves thrust into the presence of the Imperial Guard solely on the initiative of their commanding general and taking part in the final victorious advance which followed the rout of the French army. Indeed, as they immediately followed up the retreat of the Imperial Guard, it is certain that they advanced in conjunction with Adam's brigade, of the 52nd and 71st British regiments, before the general advance was ordered by Wellington.

Why did Wellington choose to deploy Chassé's division on the extreme right flank? Certainly, it needed defending because it was a vital outpost to deny the French a threatening avenue of approach, largely in dead ground and outflanking a strong defensive position. But he may also have been deployed there because of concerns about his devotion to the cause based on his previous French service. Although the position was an important one, he would have served as a tripwire; a French assault on Braine l'Alleud would have given Wellington time to react, while by not putting the division in the main line of battle, its suspect loyalty did not threaten the integrity of the main line.

However, Chassé's performance certainly showed that any concerns were unfounded. Indeed, his actions of the 18th do him great credit and shows his great experience. The redeployment of his division at Braine l'Alleud to make the position stronger, throwing forward his artillery to reinforce the allied artillery that was running short of ammunition and leading his final attack, were all done without orders, displaying a use of initiative that would certainly not have been encouraged by Wellington.

Chassé's performance and the division's role in the repulse of the Guard has earned them a rightful place in the history of the battle, but it must also be admitted that it was very much a cameo role and one that did not involve the front line, close contact that pushed back Bijlandt's brigade of Perponcher's division and which earned this brigade a rather less renowned reputation.

The 1st Netherlands Cavalry Division[81]

The role of the Netherlands cavalry at Waterloo is certainly one of the least known or acknowledged contributions of the contingent to the battle and what is known is tainted by one regrettable incident, which we will explore later, or over-shadowed by the exploits of the British cavalry in the overwhelming numbers of Anglo-centric accounts of the battle.

Collaert's cavalry division started the day back in the third line in the area of the Mont Saint Jean farm with de Ghigny on the left, van Merlen in the centre and Trip on the right. The artillery of Petter and Gey stood between the brigades. As we have heard, Collaert had been put under Uxbridge's command during the morning.

After the fight for Hougoumont had been raging for some time, it became evident that the next French attack was to be launched against the left centre of Wellington's line. Observing the French preparations, Wellington ordered Collaert to move his division forwards to support the front line. Trip's heavy brigade moved forwards in the centre to cover any French penetration down the main Brussels *chaussée*. De Ghigny initially moved behind Picton's 5th British Division to the east of the main road, but on the arrival of van Merlen's brigade, both moved further to the east, the former to a small wood to the south-east of Mont Saint Jean farm and behind Pack's brigade, and the latter in the third line behind Ponsonby's British heavy cavalry. Both of these brigades lost men to the French artillery fire which dropped over the ridge.

After the stubborn resistance of Picton's division, d'Erlon's attack was broken up and routed by the timely charge of Ponsonby's cavalry. This cavalry having lost its order and continuing its charge far beyond the point it should have rallied, van Merlen advanced his own brigade to support Ponsonby and stopped in the bottom of the valley to cover its eventual withdrawal; it also took the opportunity to gather up many French prisoners that had been left behind by the British. The remnants of Ponsonby's men having straggled back, the Netherlands brigade withdrew behind the ridge having offered a valuable service to their allies. Further to the east, de Ghigny's brigade executed a similar service to Vandeleur's brigade which had moved forward to engage the French chasseurs and lancers that had counter-charged Ponsonby's cavalry and were causing them serious casualties. Having repulsed the chasseurs, Vandeleur's men were themselves disordered by the lancers, who forced them to retire behind de Ghigny's men. The Netherlands cavalry had dispersed some French infantry before the lead regiment, the 8th Hussars, were attacked themselves by lancers and thrown back towards their own lines; they were covered by the 4th Light Dragoons who had followed them in reserve. The two Netherlands light cavalry brigades had carried out a vital role in covering their British allies and generally kept themselves in good order.

As the French prepared to launch their cavalry attacks from four o'clock, the brigades of de Ghigny and van Merlen moved to the west, back across the Brussels *chaussée* to the rear of the allied infantry squares. Trip's carabinier brigade also adjusted its position for the same mission; it was now the only intact heavy cavalry available to Wellington with which to try and counter the famed French cuirassiers.

As the cuirassiers launched their first attack on the allied squares, the 1st Carabiniers were ordered to counter-charge, supported by the 2nd Regiment. As the French cavalry became disordered by the fire of the squares and the need to ride round them, they were confronted by the carabiniers and forced back down the slope; the carabiniers returned to their original position to rally after their successful charge. A second charge by the 2nd Carabiniers, supported by the 3rd Regiment, also succeeded in repelling the cuirassiers as their own formations broke up around the squares.

In the repeated French cavalry assaults and counterattacks by the allied cavalry it becomes impossible to establish a cohesive narrative from the confusing eyewitness accounts. It is clear that not every charge was a success as order was lost and horses became exhausted, the 1st and 3rd Carabiniers were certainly broken by cuirassiers at one point and the survivors were organised into a single squadron (having started the battle with three). During this time the commanding officer of the 1st Regiment, Lieutenant Colonel Coenegracht, was killed and that of the 3rd, Lieutenant Colonel Lechleitner, was seriously wounded (and died several days later from his wounds). The carabiniers had made a major contribution to the failure of the French cavalry attacks and their losses reflect the close combat in which they were engaged.

Perhaps inevitably, and like the British cavalry, the Netherlands light cavalry did not fare as well as the carabiniers. De Ghigny's brigade was standing behind Hougoumont and was ordered by the Prince of Orange to charge some cuirassiers that were to their front; after initial success they were then driven back. A little later the Prince ordered them to charge some heavy cavalry of the Imperial Guard. The 8th Hussars that led this charge found themselves confronted by some French horse artillery that opened fire on them, killing many men as well as the horses of de Ghigny and the commanding officer Lieutenant Colonel Duvivier. Orders to withdraw were misunderstood and resulted in disorder; only a timely counterattack by a small group of the 4th Light Dragoons saved the day. The 8th Hussars were reduced to a single squadron.

Van Merlen's brigade also did not suffer lightly, although due to the death of this commander the tale of the brigade has been largely untold. However, like de Ghigny's brigade, their casualties speak of heavy engagement, and if they were not always successful, they maintained their place in the line and fought until the end of the day. Van Merlen's death was no doubt a great blow to the morale of the men of his brigade; Lieutenant Colonel Boreel, commanding officer of the 6th Hussars, took over command.

In his *History of the Waterloo Campaign*, Captain William Siborne made much of an incident in which Lord Uxbridge, commander of all the allied cavalry, put himself at the head of Trip's brigade and ordered it to charge, but the brigade refused to move. This incident, which doubtless happened, has long been used to denigrate the Netherlands troops and is based on a letter written to Siborne by an aide de camp of Uxbridge's, named Seymour, who wrote:

> as to the question as to the conduct of the Dutch Brigade of Heavy Cavalry, the impression still in my mind is that they did show a lamentable want of spirit, and that Lord Anglesey tried all in his power to lead them on, and while *he* [his emphasis] was advancing, I believe I called his attention to the fact of his not being followed.[82]

Uxbridge himself wrote:

> I have the strongest reason to be excessively dissatisfied with the general commanding a brigade of Dutch heavy cavalry...[83]

We have already seen that many senior commanders, foremost among them Wellington himself, were loathe to criticise any nation or unit in formal reports after the battle, so such criticism is rare indeed. But perhaps we should not judge Trip and his men too harshly on this incident; in the thick of the action, Uxbridge often put himself at the head of a regiment or brigade of cavalry, bypassing the chain of command, and leading them to the charge. While perhaps commendable when the unit was British and knew the man who was to lead them, it must be remembered that the Netherlands cavalry had only been put under Uxbridge's orders that morning, and he knew his new command as well as they knew him; not at all. And, of course, he did not know their language. It is only fair to say that their willingness to charge the French up to this point had been well-illustrated and their casualties stand as a better testament to their courage.

As the French cavalry charges subsided, all the brigades of Netherlands cavalry now stood in the second line behind the ridge, though French balls continued to drop among them and cause casualties. By this time, the accounts of their officers and men show that the regiments were becoming very weak from casualties and men who had moved to the rear. As Boreel appealed to Collaert for permission to move his brigade to shelter, Collaert was wounded himself and forced to retire. Trip took command of the division and ordered Boreel to join his brigade to that of the carabiniers. Unable to find this brigade, Boreel was ordered by Uxbridge to join Vandeleur's brigade. However, the 5th Light Dragoons refused to follow Boreel and moved to join de Ghigny. Whether this was because the very experienced acting commanding officer of the 5th, Major de Looz-Corswarem, had no respect for Boreel who had not served for twenty years, or some ill feeling between Dutch and Belgian, is not clear. As Dellevoet himself admits, 'Effectively, van Merlen's brigade had ceased to exist.'[84]

The Netherlands cavalry, exhausted by their efforts during the great French cavalry attacks, took no part in the repulse of the Imperial Guard, although they followed up the pursuit of Vivian's and Vandeleur's brigades and were involved in the final skirmishing of the French rout. 'Towards midnight, I arrived with the division three quarters of a league [about three kilometres] from Genappe and as I could no longer usefully march as the men and horses were exhausted, I was forced to establish our bivouacs in this area'.[85]

And so the cavalry's contribution to the battle ended. It will be remembered that a very high number of cavalry officers in the Netherlands' cavalry regiments had considerable experience in French service, reflecting those of other contingents in the various arms. Once more, accounts of the battle highlight the dedication and professionalism of these officers and there can be little doubt that without this backbone of experience, many units would not have performed as well as they did. What is particularly noticeable in the Netherlands accounts of their cavalry engagements is the maintenance of order and a reserve, which provides a clear contrast to the loss of control and inability to rally of the British cavalry. Perhaps this more than anything reflects the French experience of many of the Netherlands officers.

The Netherlands Artillery[86]

We have already described the deployment of the Netherlands' artillery at the beginning of the 18th. Winssinger's small battery remained on the allied left throughout the battle, supporting Saxe-Weimar's brigade which had been tasked with holding the farms of Papelotte and la Haye, and the hamlet of Smohain. There is little information available on its activities, although Winssinger's very short report mentions that having initially engaged French lancers, it then fired on French artillery for most of the day, presumably because much of the French infantry on this part of the battlefield were deployed as skirmishers, offering few viable targets.

The first attack of the battle was that against the allied strongpoint of Hougoumont. As soon as the first French advance against the farm became clear, the two half batteries of horse artillery of Gey and Petter were ordered forward from their division and into the allied gunline that overlooked the château. Both these officers were very experienced, having served with the French on numerous campaigns. From a position to the north-east of the château, the two half batteries, commanded by Petter as the senior of the two officers, engaged the French forces around Hougoumont and the French cavalry during its charges against the allied ridge. They seem to have suffered badly from French counter-battery fire; Petter's half battery alone lost twenty-eight horses. For the whole day, Collaert's division manoeuvred and fought without them, though in the charges and counter-charges in which Collaert's division was involved, it is difficult to see how they could have been usefully employed. However, in the final analysis, there is no doubt that they contributed to the successful defence of the strategically important point of Hougoumont.

Bijlevelt was another very experienced officer who had served in the French army; at Waterloo, his horse battery held a rather precarious position in front of Bijlandt's brigade about a hundred paces (according to Bijlevelt) to the left of the key crossroads in the centre of the allied line, where d'Erlon's heavy infantry attack fell. Like the infantry brigade it was supporting, it was withdrawn slightly just before the battle opened using drag ropes. In fact, one of the guns had to be left behind when a rope broke and was only retrieved later in the battle. This gun must have been a big loss just before being confronted by d'Erlon's massive columns. The new position was 'behind an earth bank and a hedge, in which openings were made for our line of sight.'[87] This battery fired throughout the day and although there was heavy loss in horses and wagons, the losses among the gun crews were remarkably light; four gunners killed, and two officers and twelve other ranks wounded.

The Netherlands' battery which took perhaps the most famous part in the battle was that of Captain Krahmer de Binchin. A Belgian with much experience in the French army, he had been captured in 1813 and released to join the Netherlands army the following year. Unfortunately for Krahmer, his battery is most often described as that of van der Smissen, who in fact was the artillery commander on the staff of the 3rd Netherlands Division commanded by General Chassé. It appears that when the division was ordered towards the main position having originally been deployed around the town of Braine l'Alleud, the two batteries (those of Krahmer and Lux) attached to it were sent back to the artillery reserve near the farm of Mont Saint Jean. Here they stood for most of the battle and it was only in the evening that they were called into action. General Chassé described his order for their involvement:

> Towards evening I noticed that the fire of the artillery upon the height in front of us was slackening considerably, although not stopping completely; I immediately went there to enquire the reason and I was told that they were running out of ammunition. At the same time, I saw that the French *Garde Impériale* was moving to attack this artillery, and so I did not hesitate one moment; I ordered our artillery upon the same height and its commander, Major van der Smissen, commenced a heavy fire.[88]

This event no doubt took much longer than Chassé implies as his aide de camp, Captain van Omphal, was sent back to bring the artillery up, but could not at first find it, 'because Major van der Smissen, who commanded this arm, on his own initiative had decided to place them further away from the position he had been allocated.'[89] However, it is now well known that the battery came into action just as a square of the Old Guard attacked the ridge and the battery played a decisive role in its repulse; a role much described and admired by a number of British eyewitnesses, including Captain Macready who describes the position of the battery:

> Some guns from the rear of our right poured in grape among them, and the slaughter was dreadful. Nowhere did I see carcasses so heaped upon each other [Footnote: Craan's plan represents these guns to be Mr. Van der Smissen's. Whosoever they were, they were served most gloriously, and their grand metallic bang, bang, bang, bang, with the rushing showers of grape that followed, were the most welcome sounds that ever struck my ears-until I married].[90]

What is less well known, is that the division's second battery, commanded by Captain Lux,[91] was to have accompanied it, but a leading caisson having overturned in a sunken lane, the battery was held up and did not make it to the front line. Krahmer's battery limbered up after the repulse of the Guard and followed the pursuit of Detmer's brigade, twice unlimbering to engage the retreating French and finally bivouacking with the division near Rossomme. Unsurprisingly, the battery suffered comparatively heavy casualties, losing twenty-seven men dead and twenty-one wounded, but had reserved a special place for itself in the history of the battle.

Casualties

Netherlands unit casualties are not accurately available for the battle of Waterloo. The official casualty states that were lodged in the archives show casualties for the entire period from 15 to 18 June and are not broken down by day or engagement. Accounts by brigade and divisional commanders often included casualty returns, but these often vary considerably with more official returns and are not clear on exactly when they were taken. This is significant because returns made soon after a battle often included large numbers of men recorded as missing who often returned in large numbers during the following days. This was a problem for all nations.

The two most prominent Netherlands's historians of the campaign, de Bas and Löben Sels, present casualty returns, based, as they claim, on the official returns. However, only Löben Sels gives detailed unit returns. The difference between the two is not significant enough to concern us. In the more recent account of the campaign by Erwin Muilwijk, he expresses his doubts over the accuracy of the returns of the more contemporary de Bas and Löben Sels, and in his Waterloo volume chooses not to present any at all. However, in the interests of showing the casualties of all the contingents, below are the figures according to Löben Sels.[92] We have already discussed the problems with trying to assess quality or performance based on casualties and those recorded as missing, but that is not to say they are of no interest or relevance.

When presenting the casualty returns in his own book, van Löben Sels wrote:

> It is very difficult to accurately state the respective losses… we have to say here that the losses that the Netherlands army suffered at Waterloo are not known accurately, for those of the preceding days are included in the general total. According to several official pieces, this army lost from the 15th to the 18th June, 148 officers, 3,928 NCOs and other ranks with 1,630 horses *hors de combat*. But as the losses suffered at Quatre Bras are included in these, and that these, including those of van Merlen's brigade, that we do not know, can be estimated as 750 men, the losses at the battle of Waterloo can be estimated above 3,000 men. However, it should be remembered that a large number of missing, prisoners or separated soon returned to the ranks. Due to historical interest, we have the details of these losses tracked, as far as we could assemble them from official records.[93]

General Headquarters: one officer killed, and five officers wounded.

2nd Division (HQ and 1st Brigade only):

Unit	Killed and Missing		Wounded		Total
	Officers	ORs	Officers	ORs	
Divisional HQ	1	-	2	-	3
27th Jägers	1	170	5	172	348
7th Line Bn	2	100	5	134	241
5th Militia Bn	3	172	7	132	314
7th Militia Bn	1	221	7	57	286
8th Militia Bn	-	87	5	103	195
Arty and Train	1	28	6	83	118
Grand Total					1,505

3rd Division

Unit	Killed and Missing		Wounded		Total
	Officers	ORs	Officers	ORs	
Divisional HQ	–	–	2	–	2
35th Jägers	–	–	2	–	2
2nd Line Bn	–	55	4	34	93
4th Militia Bn	–	44	–	26	70
6th Militia Bn	1	26	1	15	43
17th Militia Bn	–	31	1	24	56
19th Militia Bn	–	51	1	24	76
36th Jägers	–	44	–	10	54
3rd Line Bn	–	57	2	23	82
12th Line Bn	–	10	–	13	23
13th Line Bn	–	40	–	20	60
3rd Militia Bn	–	7	–	26	33
10th Militia Bn	–	10	–	14	24
Arty and Train	–	27	–	21	48
Grand Total					666

Cavalry Division

Unit	Killed and Missing		Wounded		Total
1st Carabiniers	3	25	8	66	102
2nd Carabiniers	1	87	4	64	156
3rd Carabiniers	–	32	2	29	63
4th Lt Dragoons	4	101	8	135	248
8th Hussars	1	132	7	145	285
5th Lt Dragoons	–	81	2	74	157
6th Hussars	3	141	6	64	214
Arty and Train	–	17	1	19	37
Grand Total					1,162

Grand Total: 3,339

It should be noted that those recorded as missing have been included in the 'Killed and Missing' column; this is most unusual. Where the numbers of killed exceed the number wounded (most noticeably in the 7th Militia and 8th Hussars), it can be assumed that these units suffered a high number of missing, as it was generally accepted that for each death there were around five wounded.

In his history, de Bas, who notes that the official casualty states were compiled with 'the greatest care', gives the following figures for 15–18 June, though these include the Nassau troops in Netherlands service which have not been included in van Löben Sels' figures above:

Killed: twenty-seven officers and 446 men.
Seriously wounded: forty officers and 842 men.
Lightly wounded: eighty-nine officers and 1,245 men.
Missing: two officers and 1,581 men.

Total losses: 4,272.[94]

The figure of de Bas is higher than that of van Löben Sels because he has included the Nassauers; if these are taken out (see Nassau figures in Chapter 2), the totals are in broad agreement. It is interesting that de Bas has listed the missing separately; the high number is noteworthy. He concludes that the losses of the contingent (but including the Nassauers of the 2nd Brigade, 2nd Division) was just under 20 percent.

The most high-ranking casualty of the Netherlands contingent was the Prince of Orange, wounded in the shoulder at the height of the action, as he led troops forward and which forced him from the battlefield. But many other Netherlands senior officers were wounded, including de Constant-Rebecque (who several times had to defend himself sword-in-hand), Perponcher, Collaert, van Merlen (who was killed) and Bijlandt; a testimony to their courage and leadership.

Summary

By splitting up the Netherland brigades, Wellington had knowingly undermined the influence of their most senior commanders; not least the Prince of Orange who effectively lost his command on the morning of the battle. De Constant-Rebecque was reduced to little more than an aide de camp and Perponcher effectively lost command of his division. Chassé was initially kept away from the main line of battle and his involvement in the fighting was due to the use of his own initiative. Though his part in close combat was limited, Chassé did more than enough to prove that Wellington's suspicion of him was entirely unfounded.

However well fitted the Prince of Orange was for senior command, and his loss of corps command on the morning of the great battle and his poor tactical decision-making suggest Wellington had his concerns, there was no doubt about his courage and his ability to inspire not only his own men, but those of other contingents as well. He was wounded at a critical time in the battle as the French threatened to break through the centre of the allied line, rushing round encouraging the battered units and organising counterattacks. Rather like his handling of the inexperienced contingents, Wellington knew well how to get the best out of what was available to him and may well have carefully appointed the Prince to a role without a formal command and on a part of the line whose role was going to be static, but where his ability to inspire the men was perhaps more important than his need to make key tactical decisions.

The battlefield performance of the Netherlands infantry generally betrayed their inexperience; they displayed no shortage of courage and enthusiasm but lacked the cohesion and stubborn 'sticking power' of the more experienced British troops.

It is very difficult to arrive at the absolute truth of the contribution of Bijlandt's brigade to the battle; it is unfair to expect too much from the inexperienced units after their tough fight at Quatre Bras where two of the five battalions suffered very heavily and two others sufficiently to have shaken them somewhat before a major battle just thirty-six hours later. At Waterloo it appears they were deployed in the centre of the front line to be used as some sort of 'sacrificial layer' to disrupt a French attack before Wellington could strike with the experienced British infantry of Picton's 5th Division. Though there is no direct evidence to support this analysis, to this author there is no other convincing interpretation. They were certainly broken by one of d'Erlon's columns, but without troops immediately to their flanks and taking into account the inevitable shaky morale of some of the units after Quatre Bras, this could only be expected by whoever, presumably Wellington, but quite possibly Picton, chose to deploy them there. Most Netherlands accounts brush over the incident, or twist it to appear almost heroic, while most British eyewitnesses merely describe them running away having offered little or no resistance.[95] The reality is difficult to establish, and the truth is certainly somewhere in between the two extremes. There is no doubt that the brigade continued in the front line until it ran out of ammunition, but it is likely that by this time the men left in line were only a fraction of its initial strength.

Although Chassé's troops made a telling contribution at the very end of the battle they had not fought at Quatre Bras and were not involved in any hard fighting; their true battlefield value cannot be accurately assessed.

The cavalry contributed much more to the battle than they are generally given credit for, and they certainly played their part in covering the over-extended British heavy cavalry and the counter-charges against the French cavalry. They displayed the courage and determination to close with their enemy and there is little doubt that much of this was due to the outstanding battlefield experience of all their senior officers and many of their middle-ranking officers, who handled them economically and with tight control, timing their charges to avoid going head-to-head against well-ordered cuirassiers.

The artillery performed well in their specialist role, no doubt thanks to the experience of many of their battery commanders. Bijleveld and Krahmer made significant contributions to the battle, but Lux failed to fire a shot all day due to the accident, for which it is impossible to fairly judge if this was purely an unfortunate accident or a reflection of his inexperience.

Conclusion

We have seen that there was much suspicion about the fidelity of the Netherlands troops before the campaign opened, caused largely by the numbers who had fought for France over many years, and this was particularly true of the Belgians who had integrated rather better than the Dutch into French service. However, such concerns were proven to be absolutely unfounded by an analysis of their performance during the campaign, and perhaps even more so of the senior officers who had previously served France and reached positions of high rank in their army. It was these men that had been the subject of Wellington's particular concern in the rebuilding of the Netherlands army and yet their performance exceeded all expectations on the battlefields of 1815.

While their combat effectiveness did not compare to the largely experienced British units, like the other contingents of mostly young, conscripted and inexperienced troops, the Netherlands contingent performed better than could have been expected. Given their inexperience, those who fought and suffered against heavy odds at Quatre Bras deserve much credit for fighting in the front line just two days later at Waterloo. Bijlandt's brigade cannot be blamed for bowing under the first impact of one of d'Erlon's massive columns; and although for many men this marked the end of their contribution, a core of brave and determined men continued to fight throughout most of the day. Chassé's 3rd Division had the morale to confront and help to repulse the Imperial Guard. The cavalry and artillery performed better than might have been expected and far better than they have been given credit for. Much of the credit that is undoubtedly due to the whole contingent stems, perhaps ironically, from the great level of experience in the officer corps that had been gathered in the service of France. From the decision to stand and fight at Quatre Bras, to the motivation and leadership of inexperienced units on an unforgiving battlefield, the officers gave their men the morale and motivation to be able to hold their heads high after a strict analysis of their performance has been carried out.

Chapter Six

Summary and Conclusions

You see the consequences of the battle of June as clearly as myself. Ours is no less glory than the Prussians or the English; everyone has done his share for victory. The Belgians, our brothers, suspected from siding with the enemy, have resolved this issue at once, and in a most honourable way for them…[1]

In Chapter 1 we discussed the issue of military effectiveness and the factors that we need to consider before we can objectively assess the true contribution each contingent made to the victory of the Waterloo campaign. Military effectiveness provides the context in which we must consider the battlefield contribution of each contingent. Merely comparing them to the achievements of the British army is a pointless exercise. The best we can hope for is to assess the extent to which each unit, brigade or contingent fulfilled its potential; did they perform as well as could be expected in the unique circumstances that each of them faced? It is this that will help us assess their contribution to victory rather than to try and construct a league table of achievement in combat, and importantly, it is also this that will determine whether they were correctly handled and managed in order to maximise their effect.

Most of the soldiers that made up the allied contingents during the Waterloo campaign were young soldiers with little or no previous service, and certainly no campaign or battle experience. History shows that regardless of the individual courage and enthusiasm of inexperienced soldiers, while they may achieve some minor advantages, if they meet determined resistance, disorder is most likely to follow. Any unit, formation or army, which must face a capable enemy, and support the fatigues and challenges of war, must possess good cadres, training and discipline; the soldiers must have confidence in their leaders and the leaders know their subordinates. Such units cannot be improvised. It requires time and incessant care to form them; they cannot be raised from thin air. An improvised military organisation is inevitably a poor organisation. Therefore, to judge an army without taking into account the circumstances in which it was raised and prepared will teach us nothing.

When assessing the contribution of the various contingents therefore, we must consider the context in which they were raised and take an objective approach to assessing their contribution, particularly when trying to analyse battlefield performance and achievement.

After French occupation or subjugation, the countries contributing contingents to Wellington's army all had to rebuild their armed forces more or less from scratch at the end of 1813 or into 1814. Only the Nassau and Brunswick contingents[2] had a hard core of men who had served before 1813; the majority of troops, volunteers or conscripts, had been in uniform less than twelve months; few had experience of intense campaigning or battle. Many had been forced into uniform more or less willingly, and while many had been through a reasonable amount of training, almost none had manoeuvred as part of a brigade or division and some, a minority, had received hardly any training at all. They had generally lacked sufficient time to gain trust in their officers, develop true unit cohesion and ethos or got to know their chain of command. What could be expected of these contingents? Certainly not what Wellington expected of the British and King's German Legion soldiers, and how could it have been otherwise?

There is no doubt that Wellington had a clear idea of how he should employ his allies, and although he failed to receive official sanction to mix the Brunswickers, Nassauers and Netherlands troops into his British divisions, he did so in practice by spreading them throughout his front line, or keeping them back in reserve, leaving many of them with dependable British or KGL troops to their flanks or in support. However, whatever shortcomings they may have had, Wellington could not have fought a major battle without them; around 70 percent of his infantry was non-British and 50 percent of his cavalry and artillery.

Throughout the battle, the allied contingents showed great courage and enthusiasm, and the very few that did not, were the exception that proved the rule. However, if maximum effectiveness was to be drawn from these men, then they would need careful battle management; not expecting of them more than they were capable of. This meant timing their commitment so that they were not in the front line in the most intense fighting for long periods and giving them tasks which were, as far as possible, within their capabilities.

Wellington had much experience in carefully handling allied contingents and knew well how to get the best out of them. As many as possible were therefore held back in the second or third line under the comparative shelter of the ridgeline and only fed forward when they were needed, when still fresh and complete with ammunition. Those that got specific missions from the start of the battle, such as Saxe-Weimar's brigade of Nassau troops, including the battalion of the 2nd Nassau sent to Hougoumont, were given defensive missions on ground that strengthened the defence. Others, such as the 4th and 5th Hanoverian brigades, held less threatened sectors of the line, where they were unlikely to be required to manoeuvre. In other defensive roles, the contingents fought well enough, and even in square, none of them were overrun by cavalry; although a number of squares lost their cohesion and retired, they returned to the fray. Even Bijlandt's men should not be too harshly judged given their traumatic experience at Quatre Bras, and that at Waterloo they faced huge columns and were fighting in an unfamiliar and less robust formation.

Offensively, the allied infantry lacked the confidence, cohesion and tactical flexibility to close with a determined enemy. Wellington did not believe they had the determination, morale or confidence for a face-to-face, close-range musketry duel with the ability to outlast the French or close with cold steel. Advances made by the Brunswickers, the 1st Nassau Regiment and some of the Hanoverians were all driven back by French fire. The most offensive movement made by one of the contingents at Waterloo was by the Lüneburg Field Battalion in its counterattack against la Haye Sainte; the battalion was dispersed. Although Chassé's attack at the end of the battle is worthy of mention, it faced no serious opposition.

The same cannot be said for the cavalry, who, excepting the Hanoverian Duke of Cumberland Hussars, showed they had the will and determination to close with the feared French cuirassiers, even if they were not always successful. In their case it is fair to say that their casualties reflected their courage.

The allied contingents did not take the brunt of the tough, close combat, but, carefully managed and sparingly committed, they achieved what was necessary for the victory. Young and inexperienced troops, in newly raised regiments without illustrious predecessors to emulate, or innate confidence to inherit, lacking the cohesion, tactical flexibility, discipline and stoicism of veteran troops, did all that could be expected of them. The Belgians in particular should get a special mention; without the motivation of the other contingents, with the demoralisation that many of them must have felt for the loss of independence of their nation, the Belgian regiments fought well and suffered accordingly. They must surely have surprised Wellington given his suspicions of their loyalty and those of other contingents as well.

The many individual accounts of the battle all seem to agree that the real strength of the allied contingents was the quality of their leadership. Many of the senior commanders and most junior officers performed exceptionally; inspiring and motivating their troops, setting an example and controlling them tightly. The Netherlands senior leadership made excellent decisions at Quatre Bras in particular, and Chassé acted decisively and offensively at Waterloo. The shortage of experienced officers in the Hanoverian contingent illustrates this point clearly and shows why Wellington took measures to try and resolve this problem. Perhaps it is no coincidence that many of the more contentious events of the battle involved this contingent. Kielmansegge and von Vincke were old and out of date; Kielmansegge took most of the 3rd British Division out of the line without informing anyone, leaving a large hole in the very centre of the position at a critical time; von Vincke made some odd tactical decisions and lost control of his brigade when two battalions left the battlefield. The lack of experienced battalion commanders did not help and allowed such decisions to go unchallenged. However, these provide a useful contrast to the officers of the other contingents, many of whom had gained their knowledge and experience with the French. Despite his scepticism of their loyalty for this very reason,

Wellington had cause to be grateful for the experience in French service of many of these officers. Accounts of the Nassau, Brunswick and Netherlands contingents repeatedly praise the officers for courage and dedication in keeping their men together, rallying them when needed and leading them forwards when ordered. For the largely inexperienced soldiers of these contingents, it was the officers that made them combat effective. Without their example, it is quite possible that many would have faded away.

What we can and cannot learn from the level of casualties each contingent suffered, as well as those recorded as 'missing', has already been discussed in Chapter 1. There is certainly interest here, but we must be careful in how we interpret the figures. It is probably clear that those who were most closely engaged suffered the most; beyond that it is left for the reader to make their own judgement.

- British: 6,736 out of 24,000 = 28%
- KGL: 1,666 out of 5,824 = 28%
- Nassau: 1,054 out of 6,987 = 15%
- Brunswick: 660 out of 5,962 = 11%
- Hanover: 2,007 out of 11,218 = 18%
- Netherlands: 2,739 out of 13,361 = 20%

NB: Includes those recorded as 'missing.'

It is not surprising that the British and KGL infantry suffered much more heavily than their allies. But it must also be acknowledged that Wellington had deliberately kept many of his less experienced troops back in order to reduce their casualties, maintain their order and discipline, and keep their morale at a level that they would respond when ordered and still be capable of cohesive action when they were needed. These figures better illustrate the success of Wellington's management of his allied contingents rather than a lack of their courage or capability.

The various contingents offered a vital, but very much supporting role to the combat experienced troops of the British and KGL units who really conducted the face-to-face, attritional, dirty close combat in defence, and cohesive, determined, and aggressive counterattacks. The contingents were generally superbly managed by Wellington; when fed carefully into battle and given limited roles, they performed as well as, or better than could be expected. However, when their commitment could not be so well controlled, either in front line defence or offence, their inexperience was exposed, and they were generally beaten. They showed high morale and a readiness for combat, but on notable occasions exposed their inexperience. Whatever their record of success or failure, the truth is that Wellington could not have defeated Napoleon without them and each in their own way made a vital contribution to the victory.

Appendix A

Von Vincke's Square

Not long after the battle opened, Colonel von Vincke, commander of the 5th Hanoverian Brigade, felt there was a growing threat of a cavalry attack against his brigade. He therefore ordered what must be considered a most unusual formation to be taken up by his and Colonel Best's 4th Hanoverian Brigade that stood to his right. In his own words, he wrote:

> To avoid manoeuvring at this moment, I had all eight battalions of the two brigades stand next to each other in close column. I then had the rear ranks face outward, the flanks turn left and right, so that, in my eyes, the whole formed an impenetrable mass.[1]

This single mass of eight battalions, a total of over 5,000 men, was larger than three of the four divisions that made up d'Erlon's I Corps, whose formation has caused such controversy over the last 200 years. It is puzzling that von Vincke's formation has not generated similar discussion. In fact, the way it was formed is even more perplexing; an officer of the Münden Landwehr Battalion, part of Best's brigade, described how it was organised:

> Colonel von Vincke, commander of the 5th Brigade, now took command of both brigades that he now formed into a compact mass of one large square, of which the front face now stood on the crest of the plateau. The eight battalions that were to form the square could not simultaneously move up to the point of assembly. As each battalion arrived there, it closed up to the battalion that was already in place, so that the battalions of the two brigades became mixed up. The total number of men of the two brigades now in the completed square was about 5,000. Both brigades remained inactive in this position for a good hour. The French artillery failed to direct its fire at this compact mass, to which only a few cannon balls could have inflicted severe losses…[2]

It appears that no effort was made to keep the various battalions within their own brigade structure, but they formed up next to whichever battalion was closest. Apart from the obvious vulnerability to fire, another shortcoming of this formation later became apparent as the same officer of the Münden Battalion describes:

> [After the repulse of d'Erlon's attack] An officer from the staff of the Duke brought an order that the 5th Hanoverian Brigade was to march off to Mont Saint Jean to reinforce the centre, while the 4th Brigade was to hold the position that both brigades had held until then. The resulting breaking up of the square proceeded slowly due to several unfavourable circumstances. As already mentioned, the battalions of the two brigades had been intermixed. The disentangling of battalions took as long as an hour, during which the concentrated mass had to remain in one location, and moreover on unfavourable terrain. The heavy soil was soaked by the rain and had turned into a morass on which the men could not stand but sank in, to an extent that many of those at the centre of the square had their shoes and gaiters removed, remaining stuck in the ground. They now attempted to salvage them as the square was broken up, but not very many succeeded in this. The battalions were drawn out of the square one by one and were marched off immediately.

The exact look of the single, solid, 'large square' is not made clear in contemporary accounts but given that the battalions could not just march straight out of the formation there must have been at least two lines of battalions which were each formed in column. We can only assess that it must have looked something like that shown in the diagram below, or possibly even three battalions deep.

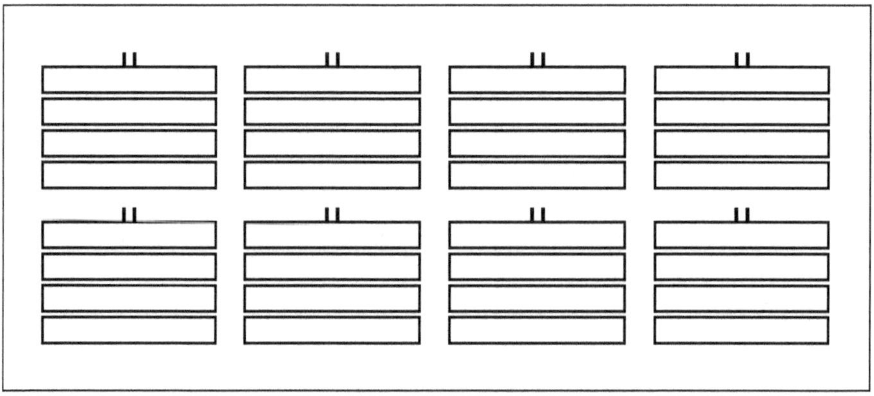

An interpretation of the formation of the 4th and 5th Hanoverian Brigades in the early afternoon of the battle of Waterloo based on first-hand accounts.

The drawbacks of this unusual formation are clear; its depth would have increased casualties from artillery fire; it could not have maximised its own firepower if attacked by enemy infantry; it would not have been able to deploy easily or quickly into a more appropriate formation depending on the threat; it would have been vulnerable to skirmisher fire, forming such an easy target; and one wonders what the consequences could have been if they had needed to redeploy quickly. Although justified as an effective defence against cavalry, the destruction of several of d'Erlon's divisions by the British cavalry suggests that even this is debateable. The close proximity to their comrades may have bolstered the morale of the young and inexperienced men who were in it and perhaps given them a sense of security, but the ravages of enemy artillery fire would quickly have called this into question. Perhaps it was lucky for von Vincke and his men that its effectiveness was not put to the test.

It is possible that von Vincke was displaying his lack of military experience, or certainly combat experience, and one wonders if the very experienced Colonel Best remonstrated with him but was forced to concede to his senior officer. Best wrote to General von Alten, 'I came to *an agreement* [my emphasis] with Colonel Vincke, whose brigade was on my left, to form a solid square, composed of the two brigades, which was then arranged.'[3] Perhaps this was Best using veiled speech to diplomatically suggest he had tried to convince von Vincke that this was not a good idea, but we cannot be sure and, given that there were no serious consequences, it seems the commander of the 5th Hanoverian Brigade escaped a potential catastrophe with his reputation intact.

Appendix B

The Retirement of the Hildesheim and Peine Landwehr Battalions

It may be remembered that after d'Erlon's attack had been defeated and calm restored to that part of the line, Colonel von Vincke's 5th Hanoverian Brigade was ordered to move from its second location to the rear of the British brigades of the 5th Division to the left of the main Brussels road and to take up a new position behind the allied centre astride the road; the Hameln and Gifhorn battalions were in a more forward position to the left of the road and the Hildesheim and Peine battalions were further back, close to the farm of Mont Saint Jean, and to the right of the main road. During the great French cavalry attacks they formed two squares, each composed of two battalions.

Sometime around six o'clock the Hameln and Gifhorn battalions, under command of Colonel von Vincke, were ordered into the front line. It seems that at the same time, the other two battalions were given very different orders, which were to set off a controversial chain of events. Colonel von Vincke's report on the incident stated:

> The Gifhorn and Hameln Battalions formed the square on the left, the Hildesheim and Peine Battalions, under the command of Major Graf (Count) von Westphalen, that on the right. This square suddenly marched back on the highway towards the Waterloo area. According to information I received later, its commander had been given an order by an English Adjutant to take up position at a nearby wood and gather the numerous fugitives.[1]

Major von Westphalen was the commanding officer of the Peine Battalion and being senior to the commander of the Hildesheim Battalion was in command of the two battalions while separated from their parent brigade. In his report on the incident addressed to his brigade commander, von Vincke, he wrote:

> On the 18th an English officer brought me an order to retire. I do not know the officer, nor the commander of the division. Bad weather had kept the latter from visiting his brigade, stationed in and near Halle

and soon to be led to face the enemy, and from familiarising it with his person and his adjutants.

The order was given to me in an overly hurried and awkward manner. The officer addressed me in English, he shouted at me from a distance of about 40 paces, '*Retirez-vous*' [retire!], and pointed at the highway, whereupon he hurried off. I would have liked to ask him who had issued that order and how far I was to retire with the Hildesheim and Peine Battalions. But the bearer of this order must have been more concerned about another matter than this order, since he rode off in such a hurry.[2]

Von Westphalen went on to say that he had no reservations about obeying the order as Colonel von Vincke had earlier informed him that all operational orders would be delivered to him by an English adjutant.[3] He then claims that he sent his own aide de camp to find Colonel von Vincke to inform him of the order he had received, but this officer was unable to find him. Having sent this officer off he ordered the commanding officer of the Hildesheim Battalion, Major Ludewig, to lead the march to the rear with his battalion. As they marched through the Soignies forest, von Westphalen received a written order signed by Lieutenant Colonel Scovell, who was the Assistant Quartermaster General to the 5th Division. In his own statement on the affair, Scovell wrote that the order said:

Sir, I am convinced it is a mistake, the Hanoverian Battalion retiring. You will therefore halt your men on each side of the road where this shall reach you, and the only way you can repair the harm you are doing, is to stop all the stragglers and form them with you in the wood. I promise to take all the responsibility to this order on myself, and to give you timely notice, should the army retreat.[4]

Scovell wasn't the only officer to notice the rearward movement of these two battalions. Lieutenant Collman, who described himself as an orderly officer, rode to catch von Westphalen and to inquire, on behalf of General von Alten, who apart from commanding the British 3rd Division was also the senior Hanoverian officer on the battlefield, and General Kielmansegge, commander of the 1st Hanoverian Brigade, the reason for the movement. No doubt von Westphalen gave him the information requested and we must suppose that this was reported back to General von Alten. On receipt of this information it seems that von Alten chose not to countermand the order or to determine who had sent it. He did not mention the incident in his report to the Duke of Cambridge in Hanover.

Major von Ludewig was the commanding officer of the Hildesheim Battalion, having acceded to command after the wounding of the original commanding officer, Major von Rheden. In his report on the incident dated, 'In camp near Clichy, 5th August 1815' he wrote:

> Colonel von Vincke was ordered to move with two battalions to the highway, and Major Count von Westphalen received the order to have the other two Peine and Hildesheim battalions form square behind the battery of Major Heise [Cleeves]… The two battalions were standing there from four until past six o'clock. Now an order was received to form squares to the right of the highway. We did not stay there for very long when Major Count von Westphalen formed his battalion on the highway and ordered me to form the Hildesheim Battalion in front of the Peine Battalion. The Count told me: "We are retiring, your battalion will stay in front." It was then that I made representations to Major Count von Westphalen against our going back. When I realised that he became touchy on this matter, I told him that I would follow his orders, but that he should keep in mind that he would be accountable for anything untoward, and that I would decline any responsibility in this matter.
>
> I am firmly convinced that Count Westphalen had received the order to retire because I observed an English officer ride up to the count shortly before we formed up on the highway. I was too far away to hear what he said. To me, it remained inexplicable why we were sent to the rear, since the time was already close to eight o'clock, there was no longer any danger, and the outcome of the battle was already as good as assured.[5]

In another letter from Colonel von Vincke about this incident, addressed to Colonel von Berger, the chief of the Hanoverian general staff, von Vincke wrote that he:

> noticed that an English adjutant had given different orders to the other two battalions [Peine and Hildesheim]. I immediately sent off an officer to obtain information about these for me, but, not being mounted, he was unable to return right away. Besides, Count von Westphalen's assertions are correct to the extent that I was able to determine; it is entirely impossible to know all the persons that deliver orders, since some were not even in uniform. On that day, I received several completely contradictory orders, one immediately after another, and I followed always those which appeared to me the most appropriate for the situation. I, moreover, need to testify on behalf of Count von Westphalen that on that day he displayed the greatest calmness and presence of mind while under heavy fire. Other

> units were also said to have received orders to retire to the second line. That was definitely the case with the artillery of Major Heise. Part of it did in fact retire, and the remainder would have done the same if Major Heise had not considered the sending back of everything all at once as most calamitous.[6]

It does not seem to have ever been established from whom the order to withdraw originated and who the aide de camp was that delivered it. However, the circumstances of the incident and the order of events are not in doubt; it seems that there was no dispute that the order to retire had been given to von Westphalen; the key issue became whether he should have complied with the order in the circumstances in which he found himself and in the light of the fighting that was going on around him. We have seen that the commanding officer of the Hildesheim Battalion urged him not to obey the order and even von Vincke wrote that not only had he received what seemed inappropriate orders during the battle, but he had also used his experience and military judgement to decide when to ignore an order that had been given to him.

Major von Westphalen must have understood that his judgement in this matter was under scrutiny and felt he needed to be exonerated of any blame for complying with a direct order. He must have discussed the issue with his brigade commander who agreed the matter required investigation. Von Vincke's report goes on:

> With Major Graf von Westphalian accompanying me, I sought out in Paris the Adjutant General Sir E Barnes and requested a detailed investigation of the occurrence but was given this answer: 'It was the Duke of Wellington's firm intention to let all similar matters sink into oblivion.' I was convinced that Major Graf von Westphalen had acted in conformance with a particular order, or an order as he understood it, given that he had only a limited knowledge of the English language. To us, the names of the officers of the English staff were unknown; on this day they wore neither uniform nor any distinguishing markings of the general staff. They might just as easily have been French officers among us in a similar garb.
>
> For as long as I had Major Graf von Westphalen under my eyes on this day, he did his duty with the greatest intrepidity. On 18 June, Lieutenant Colonel Heise, with the artillery, had also received several orders to retreat but had disregarded them because in his position he could not convince himself that this was necessary, while on the other hand, a retreat might have had some most unfavourable results. The last change in my position was caused, I suppose, by fears of a disastrous outcome from the repeated attacks on our centre and right wing.[7]

Barnes' words on Wellington's policy on the investigation of such incidents are confirmed by the Duke himself, who wrote from Paris on 8 August 1815:

> you cannot write a true history of a battle without including the faults and misbehavior [sic] of part at least of those engaged. Believe me, all those who you see in military uniform are not heroes; and although in the account of a general action, as of that of Waterloo, there are many examples of individual heroism which do not get mentioned, it is better, in the general interest, to pass in silence those parts of history than to tell the whole truth.[8]

No further action appears to have been taken.

Appendix C

The Actions of the Duke of Cumberland Hussars

The Duke of Cumberland's Hussar Regiment joined Wellington's army on the battlefield and was positioned in reserve behind the centre of Wellington's line, 400 yards behind the ridge. Here it was in line with the other regiments of Dornberg's cavalry brigade (comprising 1st and 2nd Dragoons KGL, and 23rd (British) Light Dragoons), to which it was attached, forward of the junction of the two main roads. For most of the day it remained stationary in this position, its inexperience meaning it was kept out of the fighting until it was needed.

Even this far back, the regiment was not protected from French 'overs' and a growing number of casualties were taken since they remained sitting on their horses in the open and, unlike the more experienced cavalry regiments nearby, did not dismount to minimise the risk. It was probably from this exposure that the regiment took most of its casualties, amounting to about sixty killed and wounded – about 12 percent of the whole. For a raw unit, taking such casualties while sitting back in reserve, unable to strike back at the enemy that it was unable to see, must have been unsettling and a heavy blow to morale. Lieutenant von Brandis of the KGL was acting as aide de camp to Colonel Ompteda, who commanded the 2nd KGL Brigade; he reported:

> Colonel von Hake, whose regiment – the Cumberland Hussars – was standing to our rear, galloped up to Colonel von Ompteda and in the greatest agitation asked him for 'an order to withdraw his regiment from the artillery fire which had become unbearable'. Ompteda referred him to Lord Uxbridge, commander over the entire cavalry. By the way, besides the Cumberland Regiment, several English and Netherlands regiments were stationed behind us who, like ourselves, suffered under the cannonade but still stood calmly in the places assigned to them.[1]

By the time of the great French cavalry attacks, the British cavalry that launched constant counterattacks were suffering from heavy casualties and exhaustion. Just after 5pm, the French managed to position a battery of guns forward of La Haye Sainte, which threatened the centre of the allied position. The remains of the British King's Dragoon Guards and Blues were moved up and the Cumberland Hussars were ordered forward to join them. When the commanding officer, Lieutenant Colonel von Hake, was ordered to support a cavalry charge, he effectively ignored the order and even when formally ordered by Wellington to move forward, decided that he and his men had had enough and the entire regiment turned towards the rear, away from the battle. A dragoon of the 2nd KGL Light Dragoons, on seeing the regiment take off, called out, '*Wat hett den dei Gardehüsaren vör? Dei gaht tum Düwell*'[2]

The British cavalry commander, the Marquis of Anglesey, was horrified at the sight and immediately sent his aide de camp, Captain Horace Seymour, to order them back; Seymour later recorded:

> Lord Anglesey, seeing [the regiment of Cumberland Hussars] moving to the rear (about five o'clock), desired me immediately to halt it. On delivering the order to the Colonel, he told me that he had no confidence in his men, that they were volunteers and the horses their own property. All this time the Regiment continued moving to the rear, in spite of my repeating the order to halt, and asking the Second-in-Command [Major O.F. von Meltzing] to save the character of the regiment by taking command and fronting them. I was unsuccessful, and in the exigence of the moment I laid hold of the bridle of the Colonel's horse and remarked what I thought of his conduct; but all to no purpose.
>
> I then returned to Lord Anglesey and reported what had passed. I was again ordered to deliver the message to the commanding officer of the regiment, that if they would not resume their position in the line, he was to form them across the high road out of fire. They did not even obey this order, but went, as was reported, altogether to the rear.
>
> Shortly afterwards, Major Dawson, the assistant quartermaster general, on behalf of Wellington himself, personally urged von Hake to take up a position out of danger behind the hamlet of Mont Saint Jean, but even this request was ignored, and von Hake continued his retreat towards the forest of Soignies. Some of his own officers, like Adjutant von Dachenhausen, Major von Meltzing and Captain von Landsberg all seem to have urged von Hake to halt the regiment and return, but to no avail.
>
> To continue the pressure on him to remain, Lieutenant Colonel Sir Alexander Gordon, one of Wellington's personal aides de camp, reminded von Hake of his duty according to the formal regulations of warfare, while proposing that he could place his men in a safer place at the edge of the forest. Von Hake refused even this and continued his retreat through the forest. It was here that an officer of the staff

> of the Prince of the Orange ordered von Hake, in the name of the Prince, to return to the battlefield, but with no effect.
>
> Finally, the divisional commander, now Major General von Kielmansegge, sent his own orderly to find the Cumberland Hussars, but he failed to locate them until late that night, long after the battle had ended; this meeting like the others yielded no positive result. The main body of the Cumberland Hussars, apart from those who fled through Brussels spreading alarm, had finally taken up a position about eight miles from the battlefield, in front of the gates of the city. On the grounds that he was suffering from the effects of bruising, von Hake gave up the command and handed over to Major von Meltzing.[3]

In his final dispatch, Wellington praised all the German units under his direct command, as well as giving high praise to the Prussians, and did not single out any of them (including the Cumberland Hussars) for any criticism. However, the subsequent employment of the regiment reflected a complete loss of trust in its capabilities. On 19 June, the regiment was attached to the 3rd Division under von Kielmansegge, but on 23 June this order was cancelled and the regiment was posted to a Dutch division observing Le Quesnoy. By this time we can presume that the chain of command had had sufficient time to investigate the actions of the regiment at Waterloo and it was now attached to the commissariat and split up into different detachments for the ignominious duty of escorting forage and artillery details. The Cumberland Hussars had effectively ceased to be a combat unit.

Despite Wellington's lack of direct criticism, the conduct of the Cumberland Hussars had not gone unnoticed. As early as 20 June, General von Alten, the senior Hanoverian officer in the army, wrote to the Duke of Cambridge who was the military governor of Hanover, remarking on the conduct of the Hussars and criticising their commander. As a result of negative rumours already spreading through the army about the regiment's conduct, Major von Meltzing wrote on 27 June to Lieutenant General von der Decken on behalf of the officers to explain the situation and request an official enquiry into the behaviour of von Hake. Since nothing was done, this was repeated on 21 July to Lieutenant General von Alten and he in turn wrote on the 23rd to both Wellington and the Duke of Cambridge, reiterating the need for a formal enquiry. Wellington consented to this on the 29th. By now, the Marquis of Anglesey's account of events had been passed to the Prince Regent and this document was sent to the Duke of Cambridge, as well as another report written by von Alten on 6 August. As a result, the Duke placed von Hake under house arrest pending court martial and on 13 August ordered a formal investigation into his actions and into those of the regiment itself during the battle.

On 14 August a Hanoverian military tribunal summoned von Hake to a court martial to be held in Brussels, but it did not open until October. The charge against von Hake was that he had repeatedly disobeyed verbal orders given to him by senior officers and had disgracefully led his regiment away from the battle and as far as Brussels. In his defence, von Hake mentioned the lack of forage for the horses, the weakening of the regiment as a result of casualties and its general unsteadiness and confusion during the battle. The court rejected these arguments as simply untrue or as an unjust means of shifting responsibility to his fellow officers and men.

As a result of the court martial, von Hake was cashiered and Major von Meltzing was reprimanded for not having done enough to prevent the situation from escalating into an ignominious retreat. The verdict was published on 14 October 1815 and formally announced in January 1816. Interestingly, the regiment as a unit was not formally charged with anything in the trial but was shortly afterwards disbanded. Von Hake later went as a settler to South Africa, where he served in the local forces and was again reprimanded for insubordination! He died there in 1858.

It seems that a number of officers and men of the regiment (including Adjutant Dachenhausen), appalled by the behaviour of their colonel and comrades in leaving the field, refused to retire, and instead attached themselves to the 23rd Light Dragoons (as well as the 2nd KGL Light Dragoons) and served through the rest of the battle. Although this is unconfirmed, as a number of Waterloo medals were awarded to the regiment this appears to be the only plausible explanation.

Appendix D
Allied Suspicion of the Belgians

We have already studied the concerns over the loyalty of the senior Belgian officers who had served Napoleon and they certainly had the potential to influence and mobilise the Belgian junior officers and other ranks that had also fought for the French by raising a standard around which these others might rally. The behaviour of the most senior Belgians, loyal or not, would go a long way towards deciding the performance of the Belgian troops.

However, the truth is that the Belgians provided only a small proportion of the Netherlands army. The number of Belgians serving in the whole of the army was 4,582 out of a total of 30,280 (15 percent), although this figure also includes over 4,500 Nassauers.[1] This rather neatly puts the Belgian contribution into perspective. Indeed, at Waterloo, it is calculated that there were 4,200 Belgians present, making up only six percent of Wellington's army.

The Belgian units which served at Waterloo were:

2nd Netherlands Division
The 27th Jägers Battalion
7th Line Infantry Battalion

3rd Netherlands Division
The 35th Jägers Battalion
The 36th Jägers Battalion
3rd Line Infantry Battalion

1st Netherlands Cavalry Division
2nd Carabiniers Regiment
5th Light Dragoon Regiment
8th Hussar Regiment

Artillery
Von Krahmer's Horse Battery
Stevenart's Foot Battery

It is certainly true that the British were the most sceptical of their Belgian allies, and what they saw of them did not help to alleviate their concerns. However, when complaining of the courage of the Belgian troops, it was often soldiers from another contingent that had committed whatever 'crime' was being described. When it was indeed the Belgians they were speaking of, a cursory examination of the evidence shows that the commentator was speaking in ignorance. Throwaway remarks such as this from Ensign Charles Short of the 2nd (Coldstream) Guards, 'The Belgians ran at the first shot',[2] when speaking of Belgian behaviour at Quatre Bras, is clearly in error and based on hearsay.

Other stories are clearly exaggerated, like this from Lieutenant Macready of the British 30th Regiment: '[At Quatre Bras] the Belgians behaved vilely; if a man was wounded, he generally left the field accompanied by his whole company.[3]

Earl Bathurst, the British Secretary of State for War and the Colonies, showed that the suspicions surrounding the Belgians in British political circles were widely accepted; writing to Wellington on 31 March 1815, 'All accounts concur in doubting the fidelity of the Belgian troops.'[4]

The *Memorandum Relative to the Dutch Army*, dated 2 April 1815, was also quite blunt:

> The Belgian troops are poor: we cannot count on them. The best way ahead is to put them in the second line as much as possible.
>
> I think there are exceptions, but very few. In general, we cannot count on any resources from Belgium; they are raising 20 battalions of militia there. If they are confiding the command to officers leaving the service of France, this formation will only produce trouble. Old officers from the service of Austria and Holland should be placed with them; there are sufficient numbers; and then young men of the country. In the provinces of Luxemburg, Limbourg and the area of Maestricht the people are well disposed, but all of Flanders [in Belgium] is bad.[5]

It is also true that this suspicion of the Belgian troops was rife in the ranks of the army, even before the campaign opened. Lieutenant Woodbury of the 18th Hussars wrote in his journal in Brussels on 8 May 1815, 'The magnificent Belgian regiment of carabiniers, previously of French service under Napoleon, is in barracks here. These élite men have a fine uniform: most of them are six feet tall. It is said that they are particularly devoted to Bonaparte and it is supposed that they will pass to his side at the first opportunity.[6]

There was also some friction between the Belgians and the Dutch and Hanoverian troops, though in the circumstances this is perhaps unsurprising. When the army deployed close to the border there was some, but not significant,

Belgian desertion into France. The French believed that the Belgians would desert in large numbers and Napoleon even ordered the establishment of a depot at Lille to form them into a regiment for French service. However, the numbers there only reached 378 and included Hanoverians and Saxons as well as Belgians.[7]

A transcript of a French interrogation of a Belgian deserter that took place on 10 June, just over a week before Waterloo, is of interest.[8] Francois-Joseph le Rutte, aged nineteen years, was born in the department of the Sambre et Meuse and had volunteered for the 1st (Belgian) Hussars (which became the 8th Hussars[9] in the renumbering of the Netherlands army), and had served for five months. He claims he deserted because, 'the leaders of the unit treated us very harshly and we were threatened that we would have to go to Holland.' Asked about the spirit of the regiment and the whole of the country people to the war that was coming, he replied, 'The Belgian regiments in general, want to pass over to the flags of Napoleon and all the people want to be part of France once more… one thing is certain, it is that the Belgian soldiers and the citizens will not fight against the French.'

Of course, we must be careful of the claims of a deserter who may have been saying what he believed his interrogators wanted to hear, but in the climate described by many, it perhaps shows why many were sceptical of Belgian loyalty. Some may believe that such deep suspicion of an allied contingent was exaggerated. However, the Saxons had famously abandoned the French to join the allies at the height of the battle of Leipzig in 1813 and the Prussians faced a mutiny among their own Saxon troops in early May 1815, only a month before the campaign opened.

It was noted by Dutch and British officers that Belgian civilians were also split in their loyalties and were probably keeping their options open until the campaign had delivered a clear victor. A number of observers noted the bad feelings of some Belgian civilians towards them; such was Commissary Tupper Carey who wrote, 'but the inhabitants were, I thought, indifferent towards us, and the general opinion entertained of them was that they preferred belonging to France than to the union which had been formed for them with Holland.'[10] Dutch regiments marching through Belgium to the border also met some hostility from the Belgian civilians. The extent to which this was widespread is impossible to be sure of and no doubt varied in different parts of the country. The allies were full of praise for the Belgians of Brussels for their care of the allied wounded after Waterloo, but in contrast, many French officers and men wrote of how sympathetic to the French cause many of the Belgian civilians were in the border areas.

There is evidence that not just the British, but also the Prussians and the Dutch doubted the loyalty of the Belgians. General Kleist, commanding the Prussian forces in the Army of the Lower Rhine, wrote to his king on 19 March, 'About the Belgians one can hardly speak. It is a miserable collection of scum.'[11]

At least one Dutch politician was prepared to give them the benefit of the doubt as long as the allies were successful; on 25 April 1815, Hendrik Fagel, Secretary of State, wrote to his brother, 'As to the Belgian troops I believe we shouldn't put much faith in them, but in my opinion, it will depend on events. If the allies are successful and march forward, I believe the Belgians will fight well; but if on the other hand we have the lesser edge, they will join the enemy.'[12]

It appears a little strange that there was so much more distrust of the Belgians than the Dutch, Nassauer and Brunswick troops (and even some of the Hanoverians) who had also fought for France. However, the Belgians were not considered a Germanic race and if they were not French either, they were contiguous to France, many of them spoke that language, and it is certainly true that they were not only regarded as good and dependable troops by the French, but did also appear rather more enthusiastic in support of Napoleon than the other nationalities. Indeed, many Belgian soldiers had remained in the French army after Napoleon's abdication because of the uncertainty of the future of Belgium and it could be expected that some Belgians would desert from the Netherlands' army given the loss of their independence to Holland and because of insufficient belief in the cause for which they were to fight. This latter point is well made by a later Belgian general who wrote in defence of his nation:

> It is just to ask if the Belgians, at this time, fought for a cause that would excite their courage against a hated enemy. For the Belgians in 1815, for what cause were they going to shed their blood? Was it for the independence of their homeland? No, because their hopes on this subject had been disappointed; England itself had robbed them of this independence, to cast a spell of their fine provinces to a state that they had learnt to hate and which, for two centuries they had received only insults or bad outcomes.[13]

It is only fair to point out that he went on the say that the Belgians had no more love for the French.

Through the wars of the empire, there were several French regiments that recruited almost exclusively from Belgium, notably the 27th Chasseurs-à-Cheval (known as the *Les Chevau-legers Belges du Duc d'Arenberg)* and the 112th Line; when these were broken up after Napoleon's first abdication, those who took French citizenship found themselves fighting against fellow Belgians who had not. Many men of the 27th Chasseurs-à-Cheval were sent to the 4th Chasseurs-à-Cheval who were part of Domon's cavalry division and fought at Waterloo.

King Willem made a special point of mixing Dutch and Belgian units in each brigade, meaning that, because of the different sizes of the respective forces, the Dutch units outnumbered the Belgian by two or three to one. Willem explained that the idea behind this mixing of units was to forge the idea of a national army, but one suspects it also had the added advantage of splitting up the Belgian units to make any sort of conspiracy between them more difficult.

Having gained the suspicion of many of their new allies that they were undependable, these allies were quick to blame the Belgians for many of the shortcomings of other troops. The Cumberland Hussars, whose conduct has already been studied, were named as a Belgian unit in some histories and it seems that whenever something observed by British commentators was going wrong, the finger of blame was automatically pointed at the Belgians.

Towards the end of April 1815, Wellington conducted a number of inspections of the Netherlands units with King Willem. After one such inspection he wrote to Earl Bathurst, the British Secretary of State for War and Colonies:

> The Belgians [are] young, and some very small. The cavalry remarkably well mounted, but don't ride very well. The whole well clothed and equipped for service; and as far as I could judge from what I saw of their movements, well disciplined.
>
> They are completely officered by officers who have been in the French service. It was an extraordinary circumstance that the only corps which cried *Vive le Roi*! were the Belgians.[14]

But Wellington could not help finishing without adding, 'which appears in these good days to be the common cry of treason…'.[15]

Perhaps inevitably, both the Duke of Wellington and the Prince of Orange spoke glowingly of the performance of the Netherlands troops in their letters to King Willem that followed Waterloo, though unsurprisingly neither mentions the Belgians by name.[16] However, using their words as evidence of courageous actions or outstanding performance is rather naïve at best and poor objective analysis at worst. Wellington refused to criticise any of the allied contingents, his officers, his units, or his men after what was clearly a momentous victory. Indeed, he was prepared to overlook potentially embarrassing events that had occurred as in the warm afterglow of victory it served no purpose to criticise, investigate or castigate.[17] Equally, it was unlikely that he would criticise the performance of any of his men in the official correspondence that followed a great victory. The same is almost certainly true of any senior officer writing a report up their chain of command or to their sovereign for reasons that do not need to be examined here. It is pointless, therefore, to quote from such letters as accurate and objective evidence of high performance.

The reader will have already had an opportunity to make their own assessment of the performance of the Netherlands troops in Chapter 5, but there is no doubt that the Belgians performed admirably during the campaign, despite the suspicion of their allies, and had good reason to be dissatisfied about the treatment of their country by the Congress of Vienna. Their casualties bear ample witness to their efforts; of the 4,200 Belgians that fought with Wellington's army, no fewer than thirty-seven officers and 1,146 men became casualties, a rate of almost 27 percent.[18] This does not suggest a reluctance to fight, and as a later Belgian general wrote: 'The Belgians remained faithful to military honour and to their colours. This was because almost all the officers were élite men; a great number carried the cross of the braves [the *Légion d'Honneur*] on their chest, earned on the battlefields of the Republic and Empire… We defy anyone to state and to prove that any of these [Belgian] units that we name lacked honour, deserted the colours or fled the battlefield…we say that these units have conscientiously carried out their duty and that any other assertion is false, slanderous and a lie.'[19]

Appendix E

The Allied Contribution to the Repulse of the Imperial Guard

The repulse of the Imperial Guard at Waterloo has long been one of the most controversial and contentious episodes of the battle. Since the British 1st Regiment of Foot Guards were officially renamed the Grenadier Guards by a general order just a little over a month after the battle, 'for having defeated the Grenadiers of the French Imperial Guard...', the debate over who should have the credit for repulsing the attack has continued to rage over the last two centuries and it is fair to say that the exact composition and phasing of the attack is still fiercely debated today. For the first 100 years after the battle, the argument revolved around which British unit was responsible for its defeat, and having finally established that a number of units were involved, rather than just one battalion or one brigade, the debate shifted to exactly what formation the attack was made in, by which battalions, where it fell and how many waves it was delivered in. In this long debate, the only non-British formation that was given any credit for its involvement was Colonel Detmer's brigade of General Chassé's 3rd Netherlands Division. It was as if no other nation claims to have been involved; either because the British saw nothing outside their own inter-regimental rivalry, or because the accounts of other nations have been deliberately ignored or not considered as worthy of credit.

Examination of the accounts of the Hanoverians, Nassauers and Brunswickers, as well as the Netherlands, reveal that each of these contingents claim to have had some involvement in this key phase of the battle. It is time for their claims to be objectively examined. One of the biggest problems when looking at this event is the timeline. No account attempts to time each act of the battle accurately; nor could we expect anyone to who was directing the battle or intimately involved in the fight to do this. Few combatants give any timings for their activities and those that do always precede them with 'about'. We therefore have to accept that some timings might be considerably inaccurate, and it can be difficult to confidently gauge when any particular event took place, except in those few accounts where the eyewitness claims to have looked at their watch.

Brunswick

We shall start by looking at the official report of the Brunswick contingent, which was written by an officer who was an ex-commander of the Brunswick Oels, but who was not present at the battle: Lieutenant Colonel von Herzberg. His report was based on the accounts of the key officers who were present.

As the climax of the battle approached Wellington ordered that all available allied troops should move to reinforce the centre of his line which, from the movements of the Guard across the valley, appeared to be the object of their attack. These included much of the Brunswick contingent; 'the 2nd and 3rd Light and the 1st, 2nd and 3rd Line Battalions at once marched off by the left.'[1] These five battalions moved towards the Brussels road where a large gap had appeared in the allied line, the cause of which we will examine later, stretching from the Brussels road itself to the left of General Sir Colin Halkett's brigade. As confirmation, a British officer described the units protecting this part of the line, starting with those on the left, next to the main Brussels road: 'It was occupied, beginning from the left, first, by a brigade of Brunswickers; next by Sir Colin Halkett's brigade of the 30th, 33rd, 69th and 73rd regiments; then Major General Maitland's brigade of the 1st Guards, and lastly, stood Major General Adam's brigade…'.[2] It is noticeable that the other brigades of the 3rd Division, which originally filled this gap (Ompteda's and Kielmansegge's), and the Nassauers, are not mentioned as being in the front line.

Having redeployed to the allied centre, von Herzberg's report describes the Brunswick contribution to meeting the final French attack of the battle:

> The corps, after arriving at the decisive point, had hardly begun to deploy and form at the proper distances when the enemy skirmishers had already climbed up the steep slope and were only a few paces away from the troops. Their unexpected nearness, the all-enveloping dense clouds of powder smoke, the men's exhaustion, the partial disorder of the still incomplete deployment and, lastly, the powerful thrust of the attack caused several battalions to hesitate at first and fall back a little. However, the 3rd Line Battalion under Major von Normann quickly formed up again, took a stand against the enemy and received him with such well-directed fire that he ceased his advance. By virtue of the officers' strong efforts, the other battalions had fallen in again, closed up, and, together with the Netherlands Aubremé Brigade [this should read Detmer's brigade] and the Nassau brigade [the 1st Nassau Regiment], advanced upon the enemy. This, as well as the murderous fire of the English artillery, a few splendid charges by the English cavalry under Lord Uxbridge, and the powerful forward pressing of the Prussians forced the enemy to retreat. This turned into a total rout, as the army now moved forward at all points.[3]

It is interesting that the report does not mention the Imperial Guard by name, although we can be sure, given the events he describes before and after this incident, that this is the attack of which he speaks. The key is whether the troops he describes as attacking, preceded by skirmishers, were the Guard or some other formation. At least one French account categorically states that the attack of the Guard was *not* preceded by skirmishers. This could lead us to believe that the Brunswickers faced troops of d'Erlon's corps, launched from la Haye Sainte in support of the Guard as ordered by Napoleon. In the above paragraph, von Herzberg admits that the Brunswick battalions were forced to fall back; the Nassauers also admit that their attempt to counterattack the French Guard ended in failure and that they were also pushed back, although without joining the final advance as von Herzberg suggests the Brunswickers did. The claim that it was Brunswick fire that stopped the Guard and that they subsequently took part in the final advance is uncorroborated and flies in the face of the many other allied accounts of this specific phase of the battle. That is not the same as saying it is not true.

The British 18th Hussars were part of General Sir Hussey Vivian's 6th Cavalry Brigade and had been deployed to the centre earlier in the day; they stood behind the allied infantry line sheltered by the high ground. Their commanding officer, Lieutenant Colonel Murray, wrote, 'The Brunswickers were in the centre of the British position, and on the Duke of Wellington rallying them on their wavering, and reforming them, the regiment came up in brigade and formed line with the 10th [Hussars].'[4]

Murray's account seems to be corroborated by Ensign Macready of the British 30th Foot, who wrote:

> While things were looking badly some Brunswickers had marched up to our left. They gave way once bodily just as they reached the crashing line of fire, but were rallied, and afterwards stood well, throwing out light troops to the left of our skirmishers. A sort of lull now took place, close skirmishing with heavy columns in grey great coats formed to the left of our front [line infantry of d'Erlon], being all our work.[5]

Macready also penned another account to Captain Siborne in which he expanded on the role and position of the Brunswickers:

> A heavy column of Brunswickers came up to our left (30th and 73rd Regiments) in the evening of June 18th. A remark upon them in my journal states that, "they fell back at first bodily, but were rallied and afterwards stood their ground." If I am not deceived, Captain Hughes… received a wound while assisting to rally them. But I do

> not think that these Brunswickers were *engaged* [his emphasis] with the Guard. I saw no troops of the Guard to the French right of that column which advanced on us (30th and 73rd), and which, though it came over the hill in beautiful order, was an inconceivable short time before us, turning and flying to a man at the single volley we fired, and the hurrah that followed it.[6]

These accounts confirm that the Brunswickers were deployed to the left of Halkett's brigade, filling a gap in the line which may have stretched as far as the main Brussels road, and were pushed back during the attack of the Guard. The evidence seems to suggest that it was troops of d'Erlon's corps that faced them rather than the Guard itself and this is supported by Macready's reference to 'grey great coats', which were worn by line troops; the Guard wearing blue. However, it is quite possible that the Brunswickers were engaged by the right flank of an Imperial Guard square and that they may have returned that fire, though it is most likely that they were primarily engaged by the French line troops that had advanced from la Haye Sainte in support of the Imperial Guard's attack.

Nassau

If it is difficult to accurately identify the contribution of the Brunswickers to the defeat of the Imperial Guard, then the actions of the Nassauers are obscured by even more confusion. The 1st Nassau Regiment had started the battle in the second line, but as the battle progressed and the units of both Halkett's and Kielmansegge's brigades suffered heavy casualties, at least one battalion of the 1st Nassau Regiment was drawn into the front line. The graphic Nassau accounts of the disastrous attack of the 1st Battalion on the French guns which had been drawn forward were examined in Chapter 4, and Captain Weiz describes what happened next:

> the remainder of the four companies [of the 1st Battalion] had resumed their position in the line, but, severely weakened, could no longer serve as an independent unit. They were replaced from the reserve and General von Kruse combined the remainder with the 2nd Battalion before the four battalions of the Imperial Guard advanced to the attack…[7]

Weiz does not tell us exactly who replaced the battalion in the front line, merely stating that it was a unit 'from the reserve.' If this had been a Nassau battalion of his own regiment, he would surely have named it, so it is reasonable to conclude that it was actually one of the Brunswick battalions that we have just studied. This takes the Nassauers out of the front line in meeting the attack of the Imperial Guard.

For the role taken by the 1st Nassau Regiment, let's first hear from General von Kruse:

> the French cavalry retreated and the élite infantry, Napoleon's Guard, moved up instead. It took possession of the plateau, from which our infantry withdrew, but only for 100 paces. A heavy small arms fire now broke out. The Crown Prince [of Orange] who had commanded on the plateau throughout the battle and had displayed much courage and judgment, now attempted to end it with a bayonet charge and bestowed this honour upon the Nassauers. I then brought up the 2nd Battalion and advanced with it in column, it was joined by the remainder of the 1st Battalion. This attack was undertaken with much courage. I already observed a flank of the French Guard's square beginning to waver. Caused perhaps by the fall of the wounded Crown Prince, our young men panicked at the moment of their most splendid victory; the battalion fell into disorder and retreated. The remaining battalions of the first line soon followed, and the plateau was then held by only small bodies of brave men. I joined them with the Landwehr [3rd] Battalion and the remainder of the 2nd Battalion, in a position that the enemy fire could have little effect on them.[8]

Von Kruse does not help us when he describes 'our' infantry withdrawing; was this Nassau infantry or other allied infantry? The fact that the Prince of Orange joined the Nassau regiment suggests he went back to join it in order to lead it in a counterattack, rather than stop it falling back. Perhaps inevitably, von Kruse rather glorifies the failure and blames it on the fall of the Prince of Orange, ignoring the efforts of others that we shall come to examine later. The end result was the same: the Nassauers were forced back out of contact with the French.

For a lower level view of this action, we turn to Second Lieutenant Heinrich von Gagern of the 2nd Battalion. He gives a slightly different account in a letter to his mother dated 26 July 1815:

> This immense artillery fire lasted from twelve until after seven o'clock, interrupted only by some cavalry charges, which, however, were repulsed by the brave English cavalry. It was then that our battalion was ordered to make a bayonet attack against a battalion of the French Guard… The major drawback was that our artillery was completely out of ammunition and that we were not supported by a single gun. We attacked two times and were repelled each time.

> The brave Crown Prince of Orange rode by the side of our square during the first time and encouraged our soldiers, but was also wounded next to our square… We had to pause quite a while between each attack, partly in order to re-group the soldiers, partly to allow them some rest.[9]

While Gagern tries to find different reasons for the failure of their counter-attack, the key difference is that he suggests that two attempts were made. Once again, we see the contradictions between first-hand accounts; von Kruse led the attack and so it would seem he is a dependable witness; however, Gagern also took part in the attack and although young and in his first battle (he was aged just sixteen and had only volunteered on Napoleon's return from exile), it is hard to believe he would mention two attacks if there had only been one.

The war diary of the regiment, while generally following von Kruse's account in mentioning only one assault, is perhaps more honest in acknowledging the reason for the failure, 'Most of the enemy mass wavered upon being attacked, in spite of its earlier effective and murderous fire, but failure to press it further kept the attack from turning into a success.'[10] This makes clear that the regiment had shied away from coming into close contact and did not have the necessary fire-power, confidence or determination to cross bayonets with the Imperial Guard if it was indeed them that they were facing.

Von Kruse's account specifies that 'our' infantry had fallen back a hundred paces in the face of the Guard attack, but does not clarify who this infantry was, though we must conclude that it included the 1st Nassau Regiment. A sketch made by Lieutenant Gawler in his article in the July 1833 edition of the *United Service Journal* entitled the 'The Crisis and Close of the Action at Waterloo', does not show the Nassau regiment at all, suggesting it was behind Vivian's 6th Light Cavalry Brigade, which had by this time moved from the army's left flank and formed up behind the centre right of the allied line. However, neither of the Nassau accounts mentions this cavalry through which it would have had to have passed to deliver its counterattack. This suggests that the cavalry were behind the Nassauers and this seems to be confirmed by Vivian's own account in which he says:

> A battalion of foreign troops, with white covers to their shakos, fell back *en masse* against the horses' heads of the 10th [Hussars], and undoubtedly, had this regiment not been formed where it was, would have retreated.[11]

However, we know from General von Kruse that he had ordered these white shako covers to be removed at three o'clock because he had become concerned that they were making his men an easier target. Vivian might therefore have confused the time that he saw these distinctive features and may well have actually seen the Brunswickers being driven back as in describing his position he wrote it was, 'on a line with and immediately behind that you have assigned [in the sketch map] to the Brunswickers.'[12]

To confuse matters further, neither of the Nassau accounts mentions the presence of five battalions of Brunswickers, which is rather strange given that a number of British accounts name them specifically and Brunswick accounts confirm that they had been redeployed to this part of the line. Neither do they mention a large brigade of British cavalry.

The confusion here is clear. It seems impossible to reconcile exactly where the 1st Nassau Regiment was at this time, yet it is vital that we know if we are to be able to substantiate their claims to have faced the Imperial Guard.

The Nassau accounts also do not give us an exact point on which they advanced, other than it was against the Guard. French accounts describe the right-hand battalion of their attack advancing with their right against the main Brussels road and we have already heard from the British officer Macready of the 30th Regiment that there were no Imperial Guard troops to their left; that is, to the front of the Brunswickers or Nassauers. As they approached the orchard of la Haye Sainte the Guard would have been forced to veer to their left to avoid it and may even have been forced further to their left to avoid the French line troops who were advancing from the area of the farm. Like the Brunswickers, it is impossible to know if the troops the Nassauers faced were the Imperial Guard or troops of d'Erlon's corps. Their case would have been helped if they had offered a little more evidence that it was the Guard they engaged. Many British accounts describe the dress of the Guard and especially mention their distinctive bearskin hats; the Nassau accounts offer us no such clues. On the evidence we have, it is impossible to be sure if it was the Guard, but it is possible, if they came up on the immediate left flank of Halkett's brigade, that they would have been able to fire on one of the Imperial Guard battalions as well as troops of d'Erlon's corps.

Hanover

In all the general histories of Waterloo there is no mention of Hanoverian troops having played any role in the repulse of the Imperial Guard's attack. However, a number of Hanoverian accounts claim that they, at least, believe that they were involved and the fact that their open and honest accounts accept that they were beaten back only strengthens their case. Others may argue that their accounts were drawn up in collaboration and that there is insufficient evidence to conclude that it was indeed the Imperial Guard they faced rather than some other supporting unit of the French army.

Let us start by looking at the account of General von Alten, commander of the 3rd British Division, part of which was the 1st Hanoverian Brigade composed of regular troops and commanded by General von Kielmansegge. In his report to the Duke of Cambridge, dated 20 June 1815, just two days after the battle when everything should have been clear in his mind, he did not mention the attack of the Guard, though by this time he had been wounded and handed over command to von Kielmansegge. His account covering what happened after his wound must therefore be based on what he was told, rather than on what he saw for himself, so it is rather lacking in detail and cannot be relied on; he wrote:

> The squares [of Kilemansegge's brigade] advanced against the enemy's cavalry, which had captured part of our position, and forced it to leave the heights in consequence of the well-maintained fire it delivered. But eventually some of the squares were forced to give way to the enemy, as they had been reduced to almost nothing; yet they withdrew in an orderly manner and advanced again when ordered to do so.[13]

Unsurprisingly, this does not give us the clarity we need. However, in his report to Wellington dated 19 June, von Alten gives us some more detail:

> The squares by this time had been so much reduced in number by the continued fire of cannon, musketry and ultimately grape shot of the enemy, that they had hardly enough men to remain in squares, and therefore were withdrawn from the position by Count Kielmansegge; and the remains of the Legion and Hanoverian brigades, and part of the British brigade, reformed on the high road *in rear of the village of Mont St. Jean* [my emphasis].[14]

This is a much clearer, and perhaps more damning report, exposing that Kielmansegge actually ordered the withdrawal of the 3rd Division back as far as the village of Mont Saint-Jean, a full 1,000 metres to the rear. However, it is worth remembering that his report must have be based on verbal reports from his officers and staff.

Let us now hear from the official report of the 1st Hanoverian Brigade that Kielmansegge commanded; after describing the successful repulse of the French cavalry attacks, it describes his brigade suffering heavily from the French guns which had been moved forward and then continues:

> At this very moment the enemy made his last and strongest attack; the fire from a strong column forced the battalions to retire once again, which this time was less orderly than the previous withdrawal because of the heavy loss of officers and men. The remaining officers found it impossible to establish order, as the number of soldiers of all

> arms who were in full retreat at this moment was very great, which added to the difficulty of the situation, and prevented them from realising their aim.
>
> At 8 o'clock in the evening the enemy assaulted the battalions on the right wing in such a lively way that the General commanding the 3rd Division, the Lieutenant-Colonel in command of the square, the Brigade-Major and numerous officers and men were killed and wounded, so that the officer upon whom the command of the square devolved was forced to retire, especially as these battalions, as with those of the right wing, had expended almost all their ammunition. The remaining battalions of the 3rd Division were reassembled in close proximity to these, and thereafter they returned to their former positions, which the enemy no longer contested. The division received the order not to pursue the enemy any further and spent the night on the battlefield.[15]

This account is not absolutely clear, and does not mention the Imperial Guard, but suggests that the brigade was forced back having run out of ammunition and only advanced again once the French had been repulsed. The report does not categorically state whether he was responsible for the brigade withdrawing (though Ompteda's KGL brigade withdrew at the same time). However, a number of eyewitnesses say they were ordered to withdraw and as Kielmansegge was then commanding the division, it seems a fair assumption, and the situation was investigated after the battle as we saw in Chapter 5, von Kielmansegge having been temporarily put under arrest by Wellington's order.

Accounts from eyewitnesses within the 1st Hanoverian Brigade are fairly consistent and specifically mention a confrontation with the Imperial Guard. Several come from the same battalion and all were written some years after the battle, so there was almost certainly, and understandably, some collaboration. Lieutenant von Tschirschnitz was in the Bremen Field Battalion and he wrote in 1824:

> However, our square was finally forced to give way to an attack by enemy infantry formed in square which had cannon in its middle, and which was supported by a heavy musket fire. Our loss of men at this time was very great… The officer's calm and exemplary behaviour enabled the retrograde movement of the square to be stopped in front of the English cavalry, and they started to put the battalion in order, which had been terribly mixed up by the incessant fire. Here, for the last time, we were visited by the Crown Prince of the Netherlands; he praised the diligence of several officers and promised to remember them. Unfortunately, the square advanced some

150 to 200 paces again without being formed correctly, to the position it had lost previously, as ordered by Captain von Bothmer. (The enterprise was all the riskier, because except for the cavalry which was behind us, there was no infantry on our right or left, which could have been extended to unite with us and above all, there was no artillery to support us). We had hardly crossed the short distance when we had to stop to repel an attack by the enemy's cavalry, which attacked us impetuously for the fifth time. It was driven back again and now we had no doubts anymore of our inability to retain our former position until nightfall; at this moment, a square comprised of the French *Garde Impériale*, which could be observed only now through the heavy smoke, advanced under a steady cannonade to within 50 paces of us. Our ranks were so thin that we could not even call our formation a triangle anymore, because everyone just wanted to keep his neighbour close to him and everything was concentrated on the middle. Our ammunition had almost been expended during the fourth cavalry attack, and although an officer had been sent away earlier to get more ammunition, he could not fulfil his mission and the battalion, which was in deep trouble, received some rounds from the Verden Battalion, so that every soldier had three or four cartridges. The soldiers continued to demand more ammunition and new muskets because theirs had become so hot and dirty that they misfired frequently or did not function. In these critical circumstances several skirmishers who volunteered were thrown forward against the enemy's square, which advanced like a tempest; Captain von Bothmer ordered that; 'the square should retire, about turn, march!' and this order was followed by a withdrawal. The officers tried to keep the soldiers calm, because they (the soldiers) started to panic having heard 'retire', and despite the total lack of ammunition and utter exhaustion our small group reached a position behind the English cavalry. Here we stopped and attempted to form four companies and to advance once more, only in better order than before. This business had not been completed when Major-General von Kielmansegge came to us and ordered us to march with him to the village of Mont-Saint-Jean, where the rest of his brigade was assembling. It was towards half past seven.

…we marched forwards again. We reached the plateau, but unfortunately, we were too late to confront the enemy, who was fleeing in all directions; the onset of darkness combined with fatigue meant that it was impossible for our soldiers to pursue the enemy effectively; we were ordered to rest and bivouacked this night almost on the same spot which we had held at midday on the 18th….[16]

We read here that the Hanoverian square had already been driven back before the square of the Guard arrived on the ridge, but it was only a lack of ammunition that forced them into a second withdrawal. Unlike the Nassau accounts, von Tschirschnitz mentions the British cavalry.

Captain von Scriba was also in the Bremen Field Battalion and his account ties in neatly with that of von Tschirschnitz which was also written in 1824:

> Not far from us, I saw a strong column of enemy infantry moving at the *pas de charge* and with beating drums towards the English brigade of Major General Sir Colin Halkett. General Halkett advanced against them and very calmly met them with levelled bayonets and brought them into such disorder that they made off singly in full flight. During this time period (half past seven o'clock), as a decision was nearing, a strong square of French Guards with several guns also advanced towards us, and immediately started firing at a heavy rate. Our small troop could not withstand this strong assault for very long. At first, our men, full of fury, returned the fire but, unfortunately, were running short of ammunition… The gallant battalions (Bremen and Verden) yielded, but slowly and calmly. The officers' efforts and encouraging words brought the men to halt some 300 paces, at most, behind the original position, and still before the cavalry columns in the rear. We were just in the process of reforming and had succeeded to some extent when His Royal Highness, the Crown Prince of the Netherlands came up to us, praised the battalions' conduct and promised to remember us, but at the same time insisted on a quick advance. He could not even allow the completion of our reforming because, as he said, the enemy was already in disorder and had been beaten. Our brave troops, unformed although compact, advanced again, with the Prince at its head, shouting 'Long Live the Prince of Orange!' At our former position we were received by case shot from not more than 200 paces away. The men bravely stood fast as before, but all resistance ceased due to a lack of ammunition. For a time, the men helped themselves to that of the dead that were lying about. The remnants of both battalions retreated slowly. In response to some officers' remonstrances they pointed out the lack of ammunition, even urgently asking them for fresh ammunition, and that they would willingly fight to the last. Both the officers and the men of the two battalions continued to be inspired by the best of will. Most were physically exhausted, but this did not diminish their morale… Our highly revered brigadier, under whose command we had variously been in the campaign of 1813 and 1814, approached us on our retreat and gave the order to assemble at the village of [Mont]

> St Jean, where the remnants of the Duke of York and Grubenhagen Battalions and a company of Feldjäger were to unite with us. The time was eight o'clock.[17]

Both von Tschirschnitz and von Scriba claim their fight was with the Imperial Guard, although both admit that they were driven back each time they advanced. Although their timings are different, both make clear that the order to withdraw to Mont Saint Jean was only given *after* the action against the Guard. Two other accounts from the same battalion offer the same general description of the action, but do not identify the square as belonging to the Imperial Guard. Another officer from the same battalion, Lieutenant von Bülow, writing shortly after the battle, gives a slightly more nuanced account; he does not mention the Imperial Guard, but restricts himself to describing 'a very strong square'; he also fails to clarify exactly when the battalion was ordered to retire:

> A very strong square of enemy infantry moved against us. There was a call for skirmishers, and at this moment when nobody believed anyone could come out alive, there were many volunteers. The square of our two battalions was shot up to a point where no space was left for an officer on horseback. We now received orders from an aide de camp to withdraw, and while we retired to the village [presumably Mont Saint-Jean], the French also took off in wholesale flight.[18]

However, Major Müller of the Bremen Field Battalion, writing in 1824 like von Tschirschnitz and von Scriba, makes a more important observation, reporting that the brigade was ordered to retire *before* it confronted the Imperial Guard:

> Because the fire was more intense, the square was forced backwards and withdrew to the line of cavalry once more; the officers, who remained calm and collected at this critical moment could do nothing to prevent this eventually. Here again the men were made to stop and form, and despite the fact that the two battalions had lost more than half of their men and were almost out of ammunition, although more had been requested, and the soldiers had taken cartridges from their injured comrades, the two battalions were formed into a battalion of four companies and moved forwards once again. In the meantime, the brigade had been ordered to assemble at Mont St. Jean, and the two battalions marched there too. Half an hour later the brigade advanced. The enemy had retired...[19]

We are now faced by trying to reconcile two very different scenarios; one in which at least the Bremen and Verden Field Battalions fought against the Guard, were driven back and only then were ordered back to Mont Saint Jean; but in the second, this order was given before the attack of the Guard, the brigade was rallying at Mont Saint-Jean when the Guard attacked and by the time they advanced once more, half an hour later, the French had already started their retreat.

To help us try and establish the truth, it is helpful to hear from the 2nd KGL Brigade who had been in line with the 1st Hanoverian Brigade during the battle. The brigade had suffered severely; apart from the 2nd Light Battalion which had defended la Haye Sainte and of which comparatively few had escaped the farm when it fell to the French, both the 5th and 8th Line Battalions had been ridden down and dispersed to different degrees by French cavalry, leaving only the 1st Light Battalion that had maintained their cohesion throughout the battle. The adjutant of the 1st Light Battalion was the junior, but very experienced, Ensign William Buhse,[20] In his letter dated Hanover, 24 February 1835, he wrote:

> Immediately after the 5th Line Battalion was attacked in line formation by an enemy column coming from la Haye Sainte, they were overrun in their flank by French cavalry and broken up, *so the whole 3rd Division withdrew somewhat* [my emphasis] and the weak remainder of the 1st Light Battalion successfully reoccupied the house behind the hollow road in the direction of Mont St Jean. The battalion remained in this position until after 7 o'clock, *after the said attack of the French Guards* [my emphasis] on the right wing of the British army. As the enemy suffered a total defeat, the battalion advanced again to the hollow road and took position there.[21]

Buhse states clearly that at the time of the attack of the Imperial Guard the 3rd Division had withdrawn from the front line and were rallying 'somewhat' in the rear and it is perhaps telling that accounts of other British units from Halkett's and Vivian's brigades, whilst mentioning the arrival and presence of the Brunswickers at this critical moment, make only fleeting or no mention of the KGL or Hanoverian brigades in the front line at the moment that the Guard attacked.

In the account from General von Kielmansegge that we have already seen above, he is rather evasive on this point. He does not mention taking command of the division, merely saying that General von Alten was wounded in an attack by the French at eight o'clock and that 'the square' and others were forced to retreat due to a lack of ammunition. He does not mention exactly who ordered the retreat or which units were involved. This may be interpreted as being deliberately opaque given the later examination of his role in this incident.

Lieutenant Colonel William von Linsingen commanded the 5th Line Battalion of the KGL at Waterloo, part of the 2nd KGL Brigade. His battalion was ridden down by cuirassiers in an attack on la Haye Sainte, after which he says he could only muster nineteen fit men. However, he remained in line until 'about half past six o'clock in the evening' when, 'the battalions next to mine and my own were ordered to take position several hundred paces to the rear, where we remained until the time that the enemy began his retreat.'[22]

Although the few accounts from junior officers of the 5th and 8th KGL Line Battalions do not mention this withdrawal, as a battalion commander, Linsingen should be considered a dependable witness and along with the account of Ensign Buhse we should be satisfied that the 1st Hanoverian and 2nd KGL Brigades were indeed ordered to the rear before the attack of the Imperial Guard and therefore took no part in its repulse.

5th Hanoverian Brigade

We must now turn our attention to the 5th Hanoverian Brigade of Colonel von Vincke, as two of their battalions also have a claim to have been involved in the fight against the Imperial Guard. Major von Strube commanded the Hameln Landwehr Battalion and wrote:

> At half past twelve the 5th brigade was ordered to immediately reinforce the centre; the Hameln Battalion was then deployed in line on the left of the high road leading from Brussels to Genappe. At half past one the battalion had to form square four men deep, together with the Gifhorn Battalion, in a position very close to the high road… The battalion remained in this position until almost half past five, when it received the order to occupy a height on the right of the high road and to deploy there, in accordance with a direct order from the Duke of Wellington, who was positioned on this height. On the right of the battalions stood the Nassau contingent and on the left were English regiments belonging to the 5th Division, as well as the 8th Battalion of the Legion. Having occupied the position the battalion fired 30 rounds per man against the enemy's infantry, especially the *Garde Impériale* which was undertaking its final attack, whereupon, the Duke of Wellington waved his hat, which was the signal for the line to advance. The battalion pursued the enemy together with the Gifhorn Battalion until half past ten at night.[23]

The Gifhorn Battalion had not immediately deployed with the Hameln Battalion into this new position, as Colonel von Vincke reports:

> Towards evening everything took a turn for the better. The Hameln Battalion was positioned beside the small house on the right of the high road to Charleroi, under the personal guidance of the Duke of Wellington, and here the battalion fired 30 rounds per man; and at the same time, around six o'clock in the evening, I received the order from Lieutenant Colonel Cambel [sic] of the Quartermaster-General's staff, to march with my remaining battalion, the Gifhorn, across the high road as far as our right wing, where I was to take position a little in front of the 1st Hussars Regiment of the King's German Legion, next to the Brunswick infantry, and to order the men to lie down, because the musket fire was extraordinarily severe. This was more or less the same spot that the Grubenhagen Battalion had held previously. Here the officer commanding the Gifhorn Battalion, Major von Hammerstein, was wounded which caused his death... [he then describes the death of two other senior battalion officers] The men of the battalion were highly affected by these losses, and it was only with the most strenuous efforts and presence of mind by my first adjutant, Captain von Ludowig, as well as Captain von Wick and Adjutant Schwacke, that we were able to form the battalion in the shortest possible time. Shortly thereafter, the Brunswickers announced the arrival of the enemy's cavalry, whereupon we formed square and with the rest of the line, advanced or retired on a number of occasions.[24]

A number of interesting points arise from these accounts. Major Von Strube states that his battalion moved to the right of the main Brussels road at 'almost half past five'; almost two hours before the attack of the Imperial Guard was launched (which left the French lines at about seven o'clock). At this time the presence of the 8th KGL Battalion suggests that the remains of the 2nd KGL Brigade were still in position in the front line, as was the 1st Nassau Regiment, while the Hameln Battalion was positioned by the 'small house' in the second line; the small house was located approximately 150 metres behind the ridgeline on the main Brussels road.

Von Vincke states that the Gifhorn Battalion was ordered across the road 'around six o'clock' and took position next to the Brunswickers. Either he mistakes the Nassauers for Brunswickers,[25] or his timing is out, as the Brunswickers state that it was just as they arrived on the position that the Imperial Guard attacked them.

Although von Vincke mentions a cavalry attack, he does not mention the Imperial Guard; this suggests that the Gifhorn Battalion remained in the second line and only the Hameln Battalion was in the front line during the Guard attack. It is interesting that von Strube does not mention the withdrawal of the 8th KGL Battalion which we know took place, along with the remaining troops of the 1st Hanoverian Brigade and 2nd KGL Brigade, before the attack of the Guard. We must presume that the Hameln Battalion were now in the front line as they fired '30 rounds per man', though von Strube does not mention a move forward. Firing thirty rounds suggests an extended firefight. Positioned as they were, close to the main Brussels road, it is unlikely that they confronted the Imperial Guard, which would have approached the allied line more to their right. We must assume that they were firing on d'Erlon's troops that advanced in support of the Guard from la Haye Sainte.

Von Vincke's description of the Gifhorn Battalion being 'a little in front of the 1st Hussars Regiment of the King's German Legion' is slightly confusing as this regiment, part of Vivian's 5th Cavalry Brigade, were behind the other two regiments of the brigade, as Vivian described in a letter to Lieutenant Gawler of the 52nd Regiment:

> Lord Uxbridge had himself led my brigade from the left… and posted it immediately on the crest of the position, to the right of the road to Genappe [the main Brussels road], where the 10th and 18th Hussars formed into line, and the 1st German Hussars in reserve; the left of the 18th touching nearly to the high road… I should consider as being on a line with and immediately behind that you have assigned [in the sketch map] to the Brunswickers…[26]

It seems strange for von Vincke to name this regiment, as between them and the Hameln Battalion stood the 18th Hussars which do not get mentioned; perhaps this was just a misidentification?

The sketch to which Vivian refers, which is included in Gawler's article in the *United Service Journal*, has troops of the British 5th Division on the righthand side of the main Brussels road; perhaps these were actually the Hameln Battalion, with the Brunswickers to their right stretching to Halkett's brigade. The troops of the 1st Hanoverian Brigade and the 2nd KGL Brigade (or the 1st Nassau Regiment) are not shown, suggesting that at this point they had withdrawn to Mont Saint Jean as ordered by Kielmansegge.

We conclude that although the Hameln Landwehr Battalion were in the front line when the Imperial Guard launched their attack, they were positioned to the left of the Brunswickers and therefore almost certainly faced troops of d'Erlon's corps attacking from la Haye Sainte.

The Netherlands

It is now accepted that the Netherlands have a legitimate and well-substantiated claim to have been involved in the repulse of the Imperial Guard and there are more Dutch and Belgian eyewitnesses to the events than there are from

Brunswick, Nassau or Hanover. Some claim that they took a decisive role in the repulse of at least one square, while other accounts state that they only arrived after the square had been driven back. Therefore, the key question that needs to be addressed here is the extent to which they contributed to the success.

In Chapter 5 we examined the various deployments and manoeuvres of the 3rd Netherlands Division that led up to the repulse of the Imperial Guard, so it is unnecessary to repeat those here. It should suffice to say that by the time the Guard started their attack, the division was deployed in an oblique line along the Brussels to Nivelles road; the two batteries of artillery that were attached to the division (those of Lux (foot artillery) and Krahmer (horse artillery)), had been sent to join the army artillery reserve which was located near the farm of Mont Saint Jean.

Let us first hear from Lieutenant General Chassé who commanded the division; in his report to the Prince of Orange dated Bourget, 4 July 1815, he wrote:

> Towards evening I noticed that the fire of the artillery upon the height in front of us was slackening considerably, although not stopping completely; I immediately went there to enquire the reason and I was told that they were running out of ammunition. At the same time I saw that the French *Garde Impériale* was moving to attack this artillery, and so I did not hesitate one moment; I ordered our artillery upon the same height and its commander, Major van der Smissen, commenced a heavy fire. I then ordered Major General d'Aubremé to remain in two columns one behind another, *en echelon*, and I marched together with the 1st Brigade, under command of Colonel Detmers, in closed column against the enemy and I had the pleasure to witness the *Garde Impériale* retire from the confrontation with our brigade. I followed the fleeing enemy until the darkness of the night prevented us from doing so any longer. I bivouacked with my troops until the morning, when I received the order to go to Nivelles where the 2nd Brigade and artillery awaited my return in the best of order.[27]

This report was written comparatively soon after the action, when things should have been clear in his mind. There are a number of points of interest in this short account. Firstly, he suggests there was little time delay in ordering forward and the opening fire of van der Smissen's battery, yet we shall see that this was not the case. Secondly, it should be pointed out that van der Smissen did not command this battery; he was actually the divisional artillery commander, who worked next to the divisional commander; the battery commander was Captain Krahmer de Binchin. Finally, he makes no suggestion that Detmer's column engaged the Imperial Guard, either with fire or with the bayonet, but that the Guard turned and fled before any contact took place.

Chassé wrote another account to Colonel Nepveu in 1836 which is not significantly different, and which reiterates that, 'Having closed to within a few paces of the enemy I observed that they made a rearward movement, and I pursued them on foot until the onset of darkness prevented us from continuing any further.'[28] Once more we see that he makes no claim that his brigade actually engaged the Imperial Guard.

We next hear from Chassé's chief of staff, Major van Delen, who wrote in November 1815:

> towards the evening General Baron Chassé noticed that the English artillery in front of our position on a height had almost stopped firing, and had certainly diminished its fire, and he went forward with the utmost haste to know the reason for this; as he heard that they lacked ammunition and as he also saw the French *Garde Impériale* manoeuvre to attack the artillery, he did not lose a moment to order our artillery, commanded by Major van der Smissen, to advance upon the height and commence a strong fire. Meanwhile, an English aide de camp came to Colonel Detmers and rode off quickly again, having ordered him to place himself with three battalions in the first line, whereupon the colonel marched with the 35th Jäger Battalion, the 2nd Line Battalion and the 4th National Militia Battalion in columns by division, marching up the slope of the height on which the English army had its position, in such a way that the battalions were partly covered from the musketry with bayonets fixed.
>
> Having finally found a place to deploy on the left of two battalions formed in line [of Halkett's brigade?], who maintained a heavy and steady fire, and between a battalion placed at an angle behind these, the aforementioned battalions marched to the right and entered the line at the moment the battalion placed at an angle, as well as a corps of light infantry on its left flank, began to yield.
>
> Meanwhile, His Excellency had returned with the division and after having made a short but very zealous and appropriate speech, he moved the three remaining battalions of the 1st brigade forward, leaving General Aubremé with the 2nd Brigade in reserve, and now assembled all the battalions of the 1st brigade and advanced in closed column at the head of the 1st Brigade towards the enemy, while the drums beat the attack, and under shouts of 'Long live the King!' the inspired brigade moved forwards against the heavy enemy musket fire and ignored the fact that it was now threatened by a cavalry charge, when suddenly the French *Garde Impériale*, upon which our attack was aimed, left its position and disappeared from our front. The brigade pursued the enemy until late in the evening.[29]

Once more we see that van Delen claims that the Guard withdrew without an engagement, although unlike his general, he intimates that the Guard fired upon their advance. Although he gives more detail than his commander, the key difference between their accounts is that van Delen states that in the absence of Chassé on his forward reconnaissance, an English aide de camp ordered Colonel Detmers to advance three battalions into the front line; we can surmise that this was to replace the Brunswick battalions had been driven back. It was only after these three battalions had deployed into the front line that Chassé brought forward the rest of the brigade and formed it into a single column for an advance.

Colonel Detmers, commander of the 1st Brigade, supports van Delen's account, writing in his report to the quartermaster general (de Constant-Rebecque) which, although undated, suggests it was written not too long after the battle:

> I received an order from an English aide de camp, who immediately rode off, to take a position in the first line with three battalions, whereupon the 35th Jäger Battalion, the 2nd Line and the 4th Militia Battalion marched forward with divisions in column, to a position in rear of the English army, which was positioned on the heights that constituted the position, and along the slope of these heights; the three battalions avoided the musket fire this way which only hit the bayonets.
>
> Having finally found a place to deploy on the left of two battalions in line, who kept up a heavy and well-maintained fire, and a battalion behind the position formed in square, the three under my command changed direction so as to move to the right and marched into the line at the moment the battalion in square and a corps of jägers placed on its left began to yield, and the three remaining battalions of the brigade joined the first three. His Excellency the commanding general then placed himself at the head of the entire brigade, which at this moment came under heavy musket fire and was threatened by an attack from enemy cavalry without wavering, and thereupon pursued the enemy in a lively manner with the entire line, until Major-General de Constant-Rebècque brought us the order to halt. The brigade bivouacked that night on the right of the road of Namur, having the so-called observatory to the right rear.[30]

Detmers confirms that the order came from an English aide de camp, but it should be noted that in places his report is almost word for word the same as that of van Delen, so it is almost certain that one report was based on the other. Although Detmers' report does not categorically state that there was no engagement with the Guard, it certainly does not suggest that there was one either.

Frederik van Omphal[31] was an aide de camp to Lieutenant General Chassé. His account is extracted from his record of military service; it is undated.

> we were now nearly in the centre of the Allied position. General Chassé observed each movement with great interest and provisional measures were taken to act immediately, in case a decisive attack had to be repulsed. As a result, van Omphal was ordered to advance the divisional artillery, which he only found after searching for a long time, because Major van der Smissen, who commanded this arm, on his own initiative had decided to place them further away from the position he had been allocated. Nevertheless, this was accomplished in time so that it could act with the greatest vigilance at the moment a column composed of troops of the *Garde Impériale* advanced to make the decisive attack, and in which the greatest devastation was inflicted.
>
> The time had arrived; the General thought that he could not remain idle, although he had received no orders from Lord Hill. He placed himself at the head of the 2nd Brigade [1st Brigade] of his division, which manoeuvred in such a way that the head of its column was opposite to the one attacking, when a height was reached, which had hidden our troops until this moment. This unexpected engagement stopped their advance and in turn they were attacked and repulsed. This movement soon changed into a rout and the entire column dissolved.[32]

It can be seen that because Krahmer's battery was not where it had been expected to be, its deployment was delayed. We can only speculate how long this delay actually was, but von Omphal describes his search as taking 'a long time'; certainly, its move forward into the front line cannot have been as quick as Chassé's account suggests. Also, van Omphal does not claim that the Netherlands brigade opened fire or made a bayonet charge, merely that they 'attacked' the column, an unusually vague description of close combat with the Imperial Guard.

However, there are eyewitnesses who state categorically that Detmers' brigade did engage an enemy column, but none actually name the Imperial Guard, although it is difficult to imagine what other column they could be referring to. Let us start with Second Lieutenant Hendrik Holle of the 6th Dutch Militia Battalion, part of Detmer's brigade. In a letter to his sister dated 10 July 1815, soon after the battle, Holle wrote:

> Now we were deployed in battle order. General Chassé came before our front (the 1st brigade) and had the muskets shouldered. He said, 'In a few moments you will leave the second line and go over to the first, keep calm, depend upon your command and especially on your brave officers, the battle is not yet decided, but how great it will be for you to have taken part in its outcome.

> The repeated shouts of: 'We would rather die for king and country!' forced him to stop his speech. Within moments we formed closed columns and went into our first line with our 1st Brigade (the only one from our division of the army on that day, and not as the report by the Duke of Wellington incorrectly states of d'Aubremé, but that of Colonel Detmers), the attack was beaten and our army advanced. Our brave colonel was killed with some twenty others, however, this did not cause confusion as the senior captain took the command and I the command of his division. We endured a most horrific canister fire, but luckily, they fired too high, or otherwise we would have been destroyed. In front of us we had an English square which was continuously and bravely charged by the *Lanciers of the Garde Impériale*, but they withstood these charges with equal bravery. When we had closed within 30 paces of the enemy, being at the head of the column, we began to pour a heavy fire into them, which made them turn and run in the greatest confusion, and they also received our canister fire; nothing stopped us. We kept advancing and within half an hour we saw the arrival of the Prussians and the rout of the entire right wing before them.[33]

His reference to the Guard lancers suggests he may have got his order of events somewhat confused, but he is clear on the 'heavy fire' poured into an enemy column. Another junior officer complicates the situation still further; Gerard Rochell was a captain in the flanker company of the 19th Militia Battalion, part of the 1st Brigade. The following is an undated extract from his service record:

> We remained in this position for a further half an hour, when we again formed in front and the whole brigade was then formed in columns. It must have been towards 7 o'clock in the evening. The battle was fought with varying degrees of fortune, and the outcome was still in the balance. Marshal Ney advanced with four battalions of the *Garde Impériale*, and an English aide de camp arrived from Lord Wellington to our brigade commander with the order for three battalions of our brigade, which was immediately executed. A moment later our brave General Chassé came to us, as he saw that Ney was advancing towards our position, and he placed himself at the head of the leading three battalions. He was received with loud cheers and drew his sabre. We advanced at attack pace and soon caught the three leading battalions. At the same time an English division began to waver, as well as a Brunswick brigade; this caused some confusion in our column and the men were pushed against each other. It was impossible to get away with so many troops on one spot, so that our situation became

> precarious. The thunder of the cannon and the small arms fire, as well as the cries of the wounded, as they went to the rear, and the shouts of commands added to the confusion. But the order within the column was soon restored and with renewed courage we advanced further. During this advance our battalion became separated; everywhere one could see small groups of men together; I was lucky to keep my loyal company together and they followed me the whole time… I saw an orchard on the left, from where a well-maintained fire was being delivered by the enemy, and so I hurried to this point with my flankers. The enemy was pushed from it, although we did not stay there long…[34]

Rochell also speaks of an initial order to deploy three battalions forward, stating that the order to advance came from Wellington himself, but also giving details, such as the attack being led by Marshal Ney, that he couldn't have known at the time. His account of the engagement is more confused; he claims to have confronted three of the four Guard battalions, but without giving any detail on if and how they were engaged. Oddly, he describes a lack of cohesion amongst his own column and his battalion losing touch with the rest of the brigade; an unusual occurrence in itself, and then, apparently on his own initiative, he leaves his battalion to attack an orchard, presumably that of la Haye Sainte. But there are two other accounts of the brigade attacking the Guard, both from very experienced men. The first is from Sergeant Jan Willem van de Wetering[35] of the 4th Dutch Militia Battalion:

> The firing began to grow heavier around us. We advanced to the front-line and took part in the fighting. This lasted for quite a while, until the much wished-for "Forward" was heard. Captain de Rechteren van Hemert received orders to advance speedily with his company of flankers and press the enemy hard. We started skirmishing and took many prisoners. We ran into an enemy battery of four pieces. Some of the artillerymen were killed or wounded by us, and we took two guns.[36]

This account is also rather vague, but does state that the battalion was involved in some fighting once it arrived in the front line. However, the next eyewitness is far more explicit in his description of the contribution of his unit. Lieutenant Johannus Koch[37] was another very experienced officer who served in the 19th Dutch Militia Battalion at Waterloo; he wrote:

> an English general rode up to General Chassé and transmitted an order to him. We saw our General draw his sword, and by then we knew what was coming; the General commanded 'Forward', we formed in attack column, advanced to the main road in the pas-de-charge, deployed there and opened a fire by files on the enemy… we advanced on the enemy in quick time, the Lieutenant-Colonel on the right and I on the left of the column, to keep it together, until we saw the enemy looming before us like a mountain; Seeing them, I called out to the Commander "What is to become of us?", to which he laconically replied: "Well, Forward!", and in this direction we went; the artillery, which accompanied the column, handed the enemy a volley of grapeshot, and then we charged in with our bayonets, mounting the height; the artillery, having reloaded quickly, caught up with our column; they gave the enemy another round and now the enemy began to retire, closely pursued by us; our losses were considerable…[38]

Despite these two eyewitnesses describing a fire fight, neither battalion was part of the three battalions that first advanced into the front line before the brigade column was formed. Sergeant Wiegmans described this brigade column thus, 'General Chassé made the First Brigade form each battalion behind the other, in closed columns'.[39] By coming up behind the three battalions in the front line, they would certainly have been towards the rear of the column. This puts their accounts into some doubt; an unlikely position in the column to engage in a firefight. Finally, let us hear from an anonymous chasseur of the 35th Jäger Battalion, the leading battalion in the column, who wrote:

> It was we Belgian chasseurs who in the evening after seven o'clock attacked a square and pursued it to Charleroi [sic]. This square was composed of *vieilles moustaches* of the Guard. We commenced firing square against square, but that irritated us chasseurs, and we called out for an attack with cold steel. This order we were happy enough to obtain from our general. It was then that you should have seen how that fine Guard fled at full speed. Never in my life shall I see again such carnage.[40]

There are few accounts from other contingents that help to confirm what happened. One eyewitness comes from Halkett's 5th British Brigade, the brigade to the right of Detmer's advance. The first gives a dramatic description of the impact of Krahmer's battery (like others, incorrectly credited to van der Smissen):

> But, at this critical instant, Major van der Smissen arrived with his light Dutch brigade of guns, and, taking up a position on our right, between us and the 33rd and 69th Regiments, now warmly engaged, literally cut lanes through the column in our front. There the Old Guard stood firm and undismayed, apparently doubtful how to act; no movement in advance, no movement to the rear. There they stood, with bold and manly front, when their comrades' disasters on their right shook that intrepidity and firmness that had hitherto marked their bearing... With an apathy and coolness unequalled as it was, on our parts unexpected, the French Guards wheeled to the right about and retreated from before us...[41]

The same account later described the fire from this battery as 'destructive and conclusive' but does not mention Detmer's advance. However, in an article from the same officer seven years earlier, he quoted a letter from a fellow regimental officer (unnamed) which does so:

> While things were looking badly some Brunswickers had marched up to our left. They gave way once bodily just as the reached the crashing line of fire, but were rallied, and afterwards stood well, throwing out light troops to the left of our skirmishers. A sort of lull now took place, close skirmishing with heavy columns in grey great coats formed to the left of our front, being all our work. Our regiment and 73rd were in line four deep behind the hedge, and the enemy's columns two or three hundred yards from them, but neither party advanced. All at once the fire of musquetry [sic] thickened so as to tell on our skirmishers, (who were crouched behind dead horses) and to cause many casualties in the line; I believe, among the rest, our brave Major Chambers, as on returning from skirmishing I found him dead, and Howard in command. There was a strange hurly-burly on all sides – firing, and shouting, and movement. And it lasted several minutes. Our grey coated opponents disappeared as if the ground had swallowed them.... We marched obliquely to our right to near the crest of the hill... A heavy column of Dutch infantry (the first we had seen) passed, drumming and shouting like mad, with their chakos [sic] on the top of their bayonets, near enough to our right for us to see and laugh at them, and after this the noise went rapidly away from us. Soon after we piled arms, chatted and laid down to rest.[42]

This officer clearly states that the Guard had been repulsed and his regiment had been engaged with some grey-coated infantry before Chassé's men appeared. We know that French line infantry wore grey great coats and the men described by Macready must have been whichever Frenchy troops had attacked from the area of la Haye Sainte (general opinion is that these were troops of Pégot's brigade of the 4th Infantry Division (Durutte); the only brigade not dispersed during the attack of d'Erlon's corps early in the battle). It was only after they had disappeared does he speak of Chassé's advance, apparently long after the Imperial Guard had been repulsed. Either the slower deployment of Krahmer's battery accounts for this time lapse, or he has deliberately separated the two events to avoid having to share the glory of defeating part of the Imperial Guard.

It is impossible to say with certainty where the truth lies in this particular phase of the action. The British account we have just studied seems to fly in the face of what appears to be overwhelming Netherlands evidence and should be discredited. However, what is noticeable in the Netherlands accounts we have studied is that all the more senior officers – the divisional commander, the brigade commander and one of the unit commanding officers – all of whom would stand to benefit most from being able to claim to have actually engaged and defeated the Guard do not do so. In stark contrast, it is actually the junior officers and non-commissioned officers who appear unequivocal in claiming that they engaged and defeated the Guard.

This author is prepared to allow readers to decide for themselves, but it is perhaps telling that Erwin Muilwijk, who has long studied the Netherlands contribution to this part of the action, concludes in his latest book:

> Although many later memoirs, some printed publications within a few years after the battle, and even official reports from commanding Netherlands officers written within a few weeks almost all state that Chassé charged against the Garde Impériale with Detmers' brigade, we need to acknowledge that in this sector of the battlefield the French Guards had already been repelled by Halkett's men. In fact, the entire assault by the *garde* had been repelled by British troops, who also took the lead in the following pursuit.[43]

Conclusion

While the actions of the various British brigades in this phase of the battle can generally be reconciled, especially when considering the French perspective, this is not so true of the allied contingents. There is clearly much confusion and contradiction in their accounts and without consistent and accurate timings it is unlikely that this tangle will be sorted out to the satisfaction of all those that claim a stake in the repulse of the Imperial Guard.

The possible interpretations of this incident based on these eyewitness accounts are many and almost all conclusions that can be drawn are rather unsatisfactory as it seems impossible to reconcile all the accounts in order to get to the truth. Each writer certainly had his own interpretation and probably his own reasons to describe events in the way that he did.

It's a shame that none of the eyewitnesses from the allied contingents give any evidence that it was actually troops of the Imperial Guard that they engaged. British accounts often mention their 'high hairy hats' and their 'red epaulettes and cross belts put on over their blue great coats', or that they spoke to the wounded. The lack of this sort of evidence leaves us having to do our own detective work, considering timings, positions on the battlefield, and weighing the dependability of the various accounts; none of this is conclusive.

The evidence we have studied *seems* to point to the following.

Brunswick

British accounts seem to confirm that the Brunswickers were deployed to the immediate left of General Sir Colin Hackett's 5th British Infantry Brigade, stretching almost as far as the main Brussels road. Five Brunswick battalions were involved and had marched from further to the allied right in column to their new position. They had only just arrived in position when the attack arrived and had had insufficient time to deploy (into line). As it was probable that there was insufficient space for them to deploy all five battalions into a single line, they were almost certainly deployed in two lines. Given their location facing la Haye Sainte and the British accounts of the action, it is probable that they were pushed back by troops of d'Erlon's corps attacking from that farm. Possibly supported by the fire from an Imperial Guard square, these initially drove the Brunswickers back, but they stopped by the British cavalry behind them, rallied, and then held their position slightly further back from the front line.

Nassau

The role of the 1st Nassau Regiment is perhaps the most problematic to reconcile. The evidence seems to suggest that they initially filled the gap left by the withdrawal of the 2nd KGL Brigade and 1st Hanoverian Brigade, but were driven back by the fire of French line infantry advancing, probably as a thick swarm of skirmishers, from la Haye Sainte. Their position was filled by the arrival of the Brunswick battalions and their withdrawal, having been stopped by the line of Vivian's cavalry behind them, they were led forward once more, this time by the Prince of Orange, but were finally driven back when the Prince was wounded.

Hanoverian

Despite the Hanoverian accounts of their fight against the Imperial Guard, there is strong evidence that General Kielmansegge, who had acceded to command of the 3rd British Division, ordered at least the 2nd KGL Brigade and the 1st Hanoverian Brigade[44] to retire to Mont Saint Jean, suggesting that both these brigades missed the decisive fight against the Guard. Given their position on the battlefield, it is possible that before this withdrawal they launched a counterattack against the French troops advancing from la Haye Sainte, perhaps coming up behind the Brunswickers, but each must make up their own mind based on their own reading of the evidence. The Bremen and Verden Landwehr battalions of von Vincke's 5th Hanoverian Brigade seem to have been forward during the attack of the Guard, but it appears likely from their accounts that they too were engaged with d'Erlon's line troops advancing from la Haye Sainte rather than the Imperial Guard.

The Netherlands

We can conclude that Chassé's division certainly took some part in the repulse of the Imperial Guard, although it is uncertain whether they delivered a close combat assault or drove off an already defeated and demoralised enemy. However, what is clear is that Krahmer's battery certainly took a significant role in the defeat of the column or square that attacked this sector of the allied front and that Chassé deserves great credit for using his initiative and launching a young and inexperienced brigade against the much-vaunted Imperial Guard.

Notes

Introduction

1. Eenens, A., *Dissertation sur la Participation des Troupes des Pays-Bas à la Campagne de 1815 en Belgique*, (1879), p.2.
2. Wheeler, William, *The Letters of Private Wheeler 1809-1828* (Morton in Marsh: The Windrush Press, 1998), p.169.
3. Edward Macready of the 30th Foot, quoted in *Historical records of the XXX. Regiment* (London: William Clowes and Sons, 1887.)
4. See Eenens, Renard and Bolger in the bibliography.
5. See for example, Hamilton-Williams (*Waterloo, New Perspectives*), Veronica Baker-Smith (*Wellington's Hidden Heroes*), Peter Hofschröer's numerous titles and various Napoleonic Wars websites.
6. Gurwood, *The Dispatches of Field Marshal The Duke of Wellington during his various Campaigns in India, Denmark, Portugal, Spain, the Low Countries, and France from 1799 to 1815*, (London: John Murray, 1838), p.590.
7. It is Siborne and his model and *History*, that we have to thank for many of the British accounts of the battle.
8. Heinrich von Brandt, an officer of the Vistula Legion in Spain, taken from his memoir, *In the Legions of Napoleon*, (London: Greenhill Books, 1999), page 71.
9. Franklin, John, *Waterloo, Netherlands Correspondence*, (Dorchester: 1815 Limited, 2010), p.34.
10. Franklin, John, *Waterloo, Hanoverian Correspondence*, (Dorchester: 1815 Limited, 2010), p.68.
11. For an extremely detailed study see Beamish's two volume *History of the King's German Legion.*

Chapter 1

1. The Oxford dictionary defines 'capability' as 'The ability or qualities needed to do something'.
2. Colin, *Transformations of War*, translated by Pope-Hennessy, (London: Hugh Rees, 1912), p.351.
3. This depot was established at Lille and by the 5th June had recruited 378 men, including Belgians, Saxons and Hanoverians. See F. de Bas and T'Serclaes de Wommersom, *La Campagne de 1815 aux Pays-Bas*, Volume II, (Brussels: Librairie Albert Dewit, 1908), pp.385-85.
4. In order to concentrate wholly on military operations whilst he was on campaign in Germany in 1813, Napoleon entrusted the government of France to his wife, the young Marie-Louise, assisted by a Council of Regency directed by Cambacérès. The Decree calling the new conscripts to the Eagles was therefore signed by her, and it is for this reason that these young soldiers were known as *Marie-Louises.*
5. Colin, *op. cit.*, p.146.
6. Gurwood, *Dispatches*, *op. cit.*, Volume 10, p.77.
7. Letter to Viscount Castlereagh in Gurwood, *op. cit.*, p.281.
8. Gurwood, *op. cit.*, p.302.
9. Muilwijk, Erwin, *The Netherlands Field Army during the Waterloo Campaign*, Volume 1, *1815, From Mobilisation to War*, (Bleiswijk, Sovereign House Books, 2012), p.75.
10. Muilwijk, *op. cit.*, Volume 3, p.55.
11. Quoted in Glover, *The Waterloo Archive*, (UK: Frontline Books, 2010), Volume V, p.122.
12. Glover, *Archive*, Volume II, German Sources, p.182.
13. Jomini, *The Art of War*, (Westport: Greenwood Press, 1977), p.351.

Chapter 2

1. Adkin, *The Waterloo Companion*, (London: Aurum Press, 2001).
2. Although it must be remembered that infantry battalions varied considerably in strength from under 500 to over 1,000. The strength of cavalry squadrons varied in a similar proportion.
3. Captain von Reichenau, a very experienced soldier, wrote to a fellow officer that, 'This good man [Saxe-Weimar] would have done better if he had stayed at home.' Letter to Lieutenant Koch, in Glover, *Archive*, Volume II, p.160.
4. Quoted in Glover, *Archive*, Volume II, p.164.
5. Glover, *Ibid.*, p.183.
6. Quoted in Muilwijk, *op. cit.*, Volume 1, p.30.
7. Letter dated 23rd May 1841 to Captain Ernst van Löben Sels, quoted in Franklin, *Waterloo, Netherlands Correspondence*, (Ulverston: 1815 Limited, 2010), p.59.
8. Gurwood, *Supplementary Despatches and Memoranda of Field Marshal Arthur, Duke of Wellington, (London: John Murray, 1858)*, Volume X. pp.167-68.
9. See letter from Wellington to the Prince of Nassau dated 2 May 1815 in Gurwood, *Dispatches*, Volume 12, p.340
10. Quoted in Glover, *Archive*, Volume II, p.180.
11. Report on the Battle of Waterloo by General von Kruse, in Glover, *Archive*, Volume V, p.130.
12. Glover, *Archive*, Volume II, *op.cit.*, p.180.
13. *Ibid.*, p.185.
14. *Ibid.*
15. Quoted by Muilwijk, *op. cit.*, Volume 1, p.86.
16. Letter from Saxe-Weimar to Löben-Sels dated 29th August 1841, quoted in Franklin, *Netherlands Correspondence*, *op.cit.*, p.96.
17. Quoted in Glover, *Archive*, Volume II, pp.171-72.
18. *Ibid.*
19. Glover, *Archive*, Volume II, p.148.
20. For more information on the French perspective of the battle see this author's *Prelude to Waterloo, Quatre Bras: The French Perspective*, (Barnsley: Pen & Sword, 2014).
21. English muskets for this battalion had been sent to the front, but because of the congestion on the roads and the various movements of the different units, they had not been able to get through and the convoy had returned to Brussels. All the Netherlands troops had English muskets by this time.
22. Quoted in Muilwijk, *op. cit.*, Volume 2, p.71.
23. *Ibid.*
24. Van Löben-Sels, *Précis de la Campagne de 1815, dans les Pays-Bas*, translated from the Dutch, (La Haye: Héritiers Doorman, 1849), p.202.
25. Report of von Kruse quoted in Glover, *Archive*, Volume II, p.174.
26. See Glover, *Archive*, Volume II, pp.150-51.
27. *Ibid.*
28. Quoted in Glover, *Archive*, Volume II, p.174.
29. *Ibid.*, p.166.
30. *Ibid.*, p.180.
31. See Glover, *Archive*, Volume V, p.109.
32. See Glover, *Archive*, Volume II, pp.160-62.
33. For Reichenau's letter see Glover, *Archive*, Volume II, pp.160.
34. See Muilwijk, *op. cit.*, Volume 3, p.176.
35. Quoted in Hofschröer, *1815, The Waterloo Campaign, The German Victory*, (London: Greenhill Books, 1999), p.127.
36. Letter of Prince Bernard of Saxe-Weimar, Commander of the 2nd Brigade of the 2nd Netherlands Division to his father dated 'At a bivouac close to Waterloo, in the forest between Brussels and Genappe', 19 June 1815, quoted in *La Papelotte, Les Carnets de la Campagne*, No.4, (Brussels: Editions de la Belle Alliance, 2000), p.32.
37. In the collection Löben Sels dated 29th August 1841, in Franklin, *Netherlands Correspondence*, *op. cit.*, p.97.
38. Quoted in Franklin, *Waterloo, Hanoverian Correspondence*, (Dorchester: 1815 Limited, 2010), p.166.

39. Van Löben Sels, *op. cit.*, p.305.
40. Quoted in Glover, *Archive*, Volume V, p.123.
41. See his account in Glover, *Archive*, Volume II, pp.156-58.
42. He may actually have meant the Hanoverian light companies which were certainly deployed there, rather than Brunswickers, although he should have been able to tell the difference. Some evidence suggests both Hanoverians and Brunswickers were there.
43. Quoted in Franklin, *Netherlands Correspondence*, *op. cit.*, p.18.
44. Quoted in Glover, *Archives*, Volume V, p. 133.
45. This detail and the detail on the specific deployment comes from John Franklin, private correspondence.
46. Lieutenant Colonel Home, 3rd Foot Guards, in Glover, *Archive*, Volume I, p.142.
47. *The Conversations of the First Duke of Wellington with George William Chad*, edited by the 7th Duke of Wellington, (Cambridge: The Saint Nicolas Press, 1956), p.4.
48. Muilwijk, *op. cit.*, Volume 3, p.115.
49. Quoted in Glover, Archives, Volume II, p.158.
50. Pflug-Harttung, *Belle-Alliance (Verbündetes Heer). Berichte und Angaben über die Beteiligung deutscher Truppen des Armee Wellingtons an dem Gefechte dei Quatrebras und der Schlacht bei Belle-Alliance*, (Berlin: Verlag von R. Eisenschmidt, 1915).
51. Franklin, private correspondence.
52. The regimental report quoted in Glover, *Archive*, Volume II, pp.174-77. The following narrative covering the movements of the regiment is from Kruse's report.
53. *Ibid.*, pp.174-75.
54. In Kruse's report of 1836, he says two flanker companies were sent, but the war diary says only one. See Glover, *Archive*, Volume V, p.132.
55. Quoted in Glover, *Archive*, Volume II, pp.182-84.
56. *Ibid*, p.105.
57. *Ibid*, p.185.
58. Constant-Rebecque's account of the 1815 campaign, quoted in Franklin, *Netherlands Correspondence*, *op. cit.*, p.19.
59. *Report of the Hanoverian Field Battalion Bremen on its participation in the Battle of La Belle Alliance*, in Glover, *Archive*, Volume II, p.107.
60. Quoted in Glover, *Archive*, Volume II, pp. 186-88.
61. Report on the participation of the1st Battalion, 1st Nassau Regiment by von Kruse, dated Malplaquet, 21 June 1815, quoted in Glover, *Archive*, Volume V, pp.136-37.
62. Quoted in Glover, *Archive*, Volume II, p.191.
63. Quoted in Glover, Archive, Volume II, p.176.
64. Letter from Sir Hussey Vivian in the *United Services Journal*, for July 1833, pp,310-23.
65. *Letters from Waterloo*, edited by Gareth Glover, Letter Number 57, p.93.
66. *Idem.*, Letter Number 52, p.84.
67. See Appendix E for a detailed analysis of the claims of all the contingents respecting their contribution to the repulse of the Imperial Guard.
68. Glover, *Archive*, Volume II, p.176.
69. *Ibid.*, p.177.
70. This total does not include the volunteer jäger as no casualty figures are available for this unit.
71. Glover, *Archive*, Volume V, p.138.
72. However, the striking similarity between the numbers of wounded and the numbers of missing for some units raises suspicion over the accuracy of these figures.
73. Report dated Malplaquet, 21st June 1815, quoted in Glover, *Archive*, Volume V, p.137.

Chapter 3

1. Ensign St John, 1st Foot Guards.
2. Siborne gives the total *at Waterloo* as 4,586 infantry, 866 cavalry and 510 artillery for a total of 5,962.
3. See Glover, *Archive*, Volume V, pp.142-43.
4. Gurwood, *Dispatches*, Volume XII, p.298.
5. Letter from Wellington to Sir Charles Stuart, *Ibid.*, p.332.

6. In Glover, *Archive*, Volume IV, p.22.
7. Article by Dr Paul Zimmerman in *Braunschweigisches Magazin*, Number 3, 1912.
8. Major Erdmann Von Frankenberg
9. Mercer, *Journal of the Waterloo Campaign*, (New York: Da Capo Press, 1995), p.170.
10. Von Bernewitz was a Saxon by birth but had fought in the Brunswick contingent for the British during the American Revolution (being captured at Saratoga), commanded a Brunswick battalion at Jena, joined the Duke of Brunswick in Austria in 1809 and led the Black Band during its march north after the Austrian defeat. He went with the Brunswick Oels to the Peninsula and commanded them in 1811. Promoted, he commanded a British brigade at Salamanca in 1812 and even temporarily commanded the division. However, he did not impress Wellington who had him removed in 1813. He joined the Duke of Brunswick in London and returned with him to Brunswick to re-build the army. In January 1815 he was promoted lieutenant-general and must have been surprised not to have become quarter-master general; Colonel Olfermann being appointed instead. Von Bernewitz spent the 1815 campaign as commander of the city of Brunswick.
11. Archival research by Andre Kolars.
12. John Franklin on *The Miniatures Page* website, based on archive study.
13. In the 1st Company of the Leib Battalion, 33% had served with the Oels; in the Avantgarde, this was less than 25%.
14. Letter of Private James Gunn of the Black Watch, in Glover, *Archive*, Volume I, p.194.
15. Dawson, Dawson and Summerfield, *Napoleonic Artillery*, (Trowbridge: The Cromwell Press, 2007), p.149.
16. In Glover, *Archive*, Volume VI, p.107.
17. Tomkinson, *The Diary of a Cavalry Officer in the Peninsular and Waterloo Campaigns 1809-1815*, (London: Swan Sonnenshein & Co, 1894), p.295.
18. A study by Andre Kolars of the 1st Company of the Grey Jäger showed only 41 of 185 men as over 24 years.
19. Mercer, *op. cit.* p.154.
20. *Ibid.*, p.154.
21. John Franklin in a post on The Miniatures Page (TMP).
22. Most of the detail on the action of the Brunswick contingent comes from Colonel Olfermann's reports on the two battles to the Brunswick Privy Council dated the evening of the 16th and the 19th June and the campaign report written by Lieutenant General von Herzberg. The first were presented in Volume II of Gareth Glover's *Waterloo Archive* series and the latter in Volume V (See Bibliography).
23. Captain John Kincaid, *Adventures in the Rifle Brigade*, (Staplehurst: Spellmount Limited, 1998), p.316-17.
24. *Ibid.*, p.321.
25. Quoted by John Franklin on *The Miniatures Page* website.
26. Letter from Colonel Olfermann to the Princely Privy Council dated the night of the 16th/17th June 1815. Given in Glover, Gareth, *The Waterloo Archive*, Volume V: German Sources, p.199.
27. *Ibid.*, p.150. Lieutenant General August von Herzberg, '*Detailed Report on the Corps of Troops of His Serene Highness the Duke of Brunswick from the 15th to and including the 18th June of 1815 with two plans*'.
28. *Ibid.*, p.151.
29. From Franklin, quoted on *The Miniatures Page* website.
30. *Ibid.*
31. *Detailed Report,* in Glover, *Archive*, Volume V, *op. cit.*, p.155.
32. *Ibid.*, p.156.
33. *Ibid.*, p.157.
34. Mercer, *op. cit.*, p.170.
35. Quoted in Muilwijk, Volume 3, *op. cit.*, p.187.
36. Glover, *Archive*, *op. cit.*, Volume II, p.200.
37. Private correspondence, Thomas Musahl.
38. Glover, Gareth, *Archive*, *op. cit.*, Volume II, p.158.
39. Ibid.
40. Report by Captain Büsgen, commander of the 1st Battalion 2nd Nassau Regiment. Given in Glover, *Archive*, Volume II, p.158.

41. Von Herzberg's report in Glover, *op. cit.*, Volume V, p.160.
42. *Ibid.*
43. Letter No. 135 by Major Mejer, in *Letters from the Battle of Waterloo*, edited by Glover, (London: Greenhill Books, 2004), p.209.
44. Siborne, *The Waterloo Letters*, (Repr London: Arms and Armour Press, 1983), Letter 6, p. 12.

Chapter 4

1. Lieutenant Hemmelmann, Gifhorn Landwehr Battalion, in Glover, *Archive*, Volume V, p.65.
2. Glover, *Waterloo: The Defeat of Napoleon's Imperial Guard*, (Barnsley: Frontline Books, 2015), p.59.
3. *Ibid*, p.70.
4. *Ibid.*, p.62.
5. Private correspondence; research in the Hanoverian archives (Arbeitskreis Hannoversche Militärgeschichte) by Dr Jens Mastnak and Michael-Andreas Tänzer.
6. Wellington to Earl Bathurst, dated Brussels, 13th April 1815, *Dispatches*, op. cit., Volume XII, pp.305-06.
7. Letter to Hudson-Lowe (chief of staff) in Glover, Gareth, *Waterloo: The Defeat of Napoleon's Imperial Guard*, *op cit.*, p.29.
8. *Ibid.*
9. Glover, *Defeat*, *op. cit.*, p.25-6.
10. Reminiscences of Captain Carl Jacobi. 1865, in Glover, *Archive*, Volume II, p.122. German original: Carl Jacobi, *Erinnerungen aus dem Kriegsjahr 1815 und aus den Occupationsjahren 1816, 1817, 1818*, (Hannover: 1865), pp.6-7.
11. Gurwood, *Despatches*, *op. cit.*, Volume XII, pp.305-06.
12. *Ibid.*, p.314.
13. Glover, *Defeat*, *op. cit.*, p.16.
14. *Ibid.*, p.62.
15. Letter from Lieutenant Colonel Home of the 2nd Battalion 3rd Foot Guards in an undated private letter, in Glover, *Archive*, Volume I, p.145.
16. It is not clear why it served at Waterloo rather than with its own brigade.
17. Jacobi, in Glover, *Archive*, Volume II, *op. cit.*, p.122. German original: Carl Jacobi, *Erinnerungen*, pp.7-8.
18. From *Reminiscences of a Hanoverian Officer in the Verden Landwehr Battalion of the days of the Battle of Waterloo*, in Glover, *Archive*, Volume V, pp.69-70. German original: *Erinnerungen eines hannoverschen Officiers vom Landwehr-Bataillon V[erden] aus den Tagen der Schlacht bei Waterloo*, in: *Hannoversches Magazin*, 1816, pp.95-6. Stück, Spalten 1505-1534.
19. *Report of the 4th Hanoverian Brigade (Best) on its Participation in the Action at Quatre Bras*, in Glover, *Archive*, Volume II, p.136. German original: Julius v. Pflugk-Harttung, *Belle Alliance (Verbündetes Heer) Berichte und Angaben über die Beteiligung deutscher Truppen der Armee Wellingtons an dem Gefechte bei Quatrebras und der Schlacht bei Belle Alliance*, (Berlin: 1915), pp.21-2.
20. In Franklin, *Hanoverian Correspondence*, *op. cit.*, p.109.
21. Reminiscences of Captain Carl Jacobi, in Glover, *Archive*, Volume II, p.127. Carl Jacobi, *Erinnerungen*, p.16.
22. *Ibid.*
23. In Franklin, *op. cit.*, p.138.
24. In Glover, *Archive*, Volume II, pp.7-8. German original: Pflugk-Harttung, *op. cit.*, pp.10-11.
25. Report by Kielmansegge, in Franklin, *ibid.*, p.83. It appears that Kielmansegge has included in this number, 18 men who fell behind during the retreat and were captured by the French.
26. In Glover, *Archive*, Volume II, pp.102-03. German original: Carl v. Scriba, *Das leichte Bataillon der Bremen-Verdenschen Legion in den Jahren 1813 bis 1820*, (Nienburg u. Hameln: 1849), pp.86-87.
27. See Kielmansegge's report in Franklin, *op.cit.*, p.83. German original: Pflugk-Harttung, *op. cit.*, p.17.
28. Gurwood, *Supplementary Dispatches*, Vol X, p.534. Report of von Alten to Wellington, dated Brussels, 19th June.
29. 'Description of the part played by the Royal Hanoverian and King's German Legion troops during the events in the Netherlands in the year 1815, and particularly during the battle of Waterloo.' By Major (captain in 1815) Carl Jacobi, Lüneburg Light Infantry Battalion. In Franklin, *op. cit.*, p.22.

The brigade report on its role at Waterloo states 100 men from each battalion. See Glover, Archive, Volume II, p.94.

30. *Reminiscences of the War of 1815 and of the Occupation of 1816, 1817 and 1818. A Memorial for his beloved family from Carl Jacobi*, translated and published in Glover, *Archive*, Volume II, p.135. German original: Jacobi, *op. cit.*, p.31.
31. In Glover, Archive, Volume II, p.229-30.
32. *Ibid*, p.230. German original: Jacobi, *Erinnerungen*, *op. cit.*, p.34. Jacobi himself rose from common soldier to the rank of captain in 1813 within two months! Vgl. Mastnak/Tänzer, *Diese denckwürdige und mörderische Schlacht. Die Hannoveraner bei Waterloo*, (Celle: 2004), p.12.
33. In Glover, *Archive*, Volume II, p.96.
34. Report dated 3rd December 1824, in Franklin, op. cit., p.128. German original first part: Scriba, *Das leichte Bataillon*, *op. cit.*, p.91.
35. In Glover, Archive, Volume II, p.108. German original: Scriba, *Das leichte Bataillon*, *op. cit.*, p.97.
36. In Franklin, *Hanoverian Correspondence*, *op. cit.*, pp.124-25.
37. Letter No.70, *The Waterloo Letters*, edited by Glover, *op. cit.*, p.149.
38. In Franklin, *Hanoverian Correspondence, op. cit.*, p.85.
39. The 1st Corps was officially commanded by the Prince of Orange, but most accounts state he was wounded later in the battle. See the chapter on the Dutch-Belgian contingent.
40. See Franklin, *op. cit.*, p.85. German original: Pflugk-Harttung, *op. cit.*, pp.78-79.
41. In Glover, *Archive*, Volume II, p.109. German original: Pflugk-Harttung, *op. cit.*, pp.127-28.
42. See Franklin, *op. cit.*, p.26.
43. Gurwood, *Supplementary Despatches, op. cit.,* Volume X, pp.534.
44. *Ibid*, pp.559-60.
45. See Glover, *Archive*, Volume V, p.63.
46. See Glover, *Archive*, Volume II, pp.136-37.
47. In Glover, *Archive*, Volume II, p.71.
48. Letter Number 130 in *The Waterloo Letters*, edited by H.T. Siborne, (London: Cassell & Co., 1891), p.309.
49. Quoted in Glover, *Defeat*, *op. cit.*, p.207.
50. Letter Number 130 in *The Waterloo Letters*, *op. cit.*, p309.
51. It is unclear who gave them this order.
52. In Glover, Archive, Volume II, pp.71-2. German original: Pflugk-Harttung, *op. cit.*, pp.147-48.
53. Quoted in Glover, *Defeat*, *op. cit.*, p.170.
54. Major Heise was actually the divisional artillery commander; the battery of which Best speaks was Captain Rettberg's 2nd Hanoverian Battery.
55. The brigade also contained the 3rd Battalion of the 1st Regiment.
56. In Franklin, *Hanoverian Correspondence*, *op. cit.*, p.164. German original: Pflugk-Harttung, *op. cit.*, pp.83-84.
57. It may also have been the cavalry divisions of Subervie and Domon that Napoleon had sent to observe the Prussians, but the lack of any timings makes this uncertain.
58. Preliminary Report of Colonel Best dated 22nd June 1815, in Glover, *Archive*, Volume II, p.119.
59. Colonel Best to Captain Benne dated Verden, 27 February 1835, Letter No.194 in *Letters from the Battle of Waterloo*, *op. cit.*, p.295.
60. In Glover, *Archive*, Volume V, p.94.
61. In Glover, *Archive*, Volume V, p.90. German original: Carl v. Berckefeldt, *Geschichte des Königlich Hannoverschen Landwehr-Bataillons Münden*, in: Archiv des historischen Vereins für Niedersachsen, Jg. 1848, (Hannover: 1850), pp.185-281 and 230.
62. These represented two of his four captains, which we must presume were company commanders.
63. 63 In Glover, *Archive*, Volume II, pp.120-21. German original: Pflugk-Harttung, *op. cit.*, pp.81-82.
64. In Franklin, *op. cit.*, p.148.
65. In Glover, *Archive*, Volume II, p.111.
66. *Ibid.*, p.112.
67. Report dated 7th January 1825, in Glover, *Archive*, Volume VIII (Ken Trotman Book 2), p.131.
68. For example, some sentences in his report reflect statements made by Major Strube of the Hameln Battalion in his own.

69. Report dated 20 June 1815, in Glover, *Archive*, Volume II, p.112. German original: Pflugk-Harttung, *op. cit.*, p.92.
70. Letter No.191 in *Letters from the Battle of Waterloo*, edited by Glover, *op. cit.*, p.291.
71. Ibid. See Appendix B for a detailed study of this controversial incident.
72. In Franklin, *Hanoverian Correspondence*, *op. cit.*, p.147.
73. *Ibid.*, p.144.
74. In Glover, *Archive*, Volume VIII, (Book 2 in Trotman), *op. cit.*, p.133.
75. In Franklin, *op. cit.*, p.147.
76. *Ibid.*, p.148.
77. The Hanoverian role in the repulse of the Imperial Guard is examined in more detail at Appendix E.
78. Letter No.170 in *Waterloo Letters*, *op. cit.*, p.392
79. Glover, *Archive*, Volume II, p.113. . German original: Pflugk-Harttung, *op. cit.*, p.93.
80. See Glover, Archive, Volume V, pp.173-87, for a fascinating glimpse into this issue, including the surgeon's responses and von Vincke's comments.
81. In Glover, *Archive*, Volume V, p.64.
82. Letter No. 90 in Glover, *Letters from the Battle of Waterloo*, *op. cit.*, p.150.
83. *Ibid.*
84. See Lieutenant d'Huvelé's account in Franklin, *Hanoverian Correspondence*, *op. cit.*, p.153.
85. From Kielmansegge, in Franklin, *Hanoverian Correspondence*, *op. cit.*, p.86-7.
86. Glover, *Waterloo: The Defeat of Napoleon's Imperial Guard*, (Croydon: Frontline Books, 2015), pp.176-77.
87. In Franklin, *Hanoverian Correspondence*, *op. cit.*, pp.169-70.
88. Siborne, *History*, *op. cit.*, p.565.
89. In Franklin, *Hanoverian Correspondence*, *op.cit.*, p.130.

Chapter 5

1. Shaw Kennedy, *Notes on the Battle of Waterloo*, reprint, (Staplehurst: Spellmount, 2003), p.57.
2. Renard, *Réponse aux Allégations Anglaies sur la Conduite des Troupes Belges en 1815, par un Officier Général, 1855*, p.19.
3. All units are Dutch unless specified as Belgian.
4. From Muilwijk, Erwin, *The Netherlands Field Army during the Waterloo Campaign*, Volume 1, *1815, From Mobilisation to War*, (Bleiswijk, Sovereign House Books, 2012), pp180-81.
5. Glover, Gareth, *Defeat*, *op. cit.*, p.30.
6. Journal of Major Macready, reproduced in *Historical Records of the XXX Regiment*, *op. cit.*, pp.122-23.
7. Glover, Gareth, *Defeat*, *op. cit.*, p.30.
8. Letter from Prince of Orange to Wellington dated 23rd March 1815, *Dispatches*, Vol. X, p.702.
9. *Memorandum Relative to the Dutch Army*, dated 2nd April 1815, in *Supplementary Despatches, Correspondence and Memoranda of Field Marshal Arthur Duke of Wellington*, Volume X, (London: John Murray, 1863), pp.15-17. The author of the memoranda is not recorded but the Netherlands historian de Bas states that it was written by the French revolutionary general, Dumouriez, who was then living as an exile in London and seems to have appointed himself as an unsolicited advisor to the British government. See de Bas, *op cit.*, Volume I, pp.207-13.
10. The fourth infantry brigade in the two Netherlands' divisions at Waterloo was that of Prince Bernard of Saxe-Weimar. Solely consisting of Nassau troops, it has been examined in detail in Chapter 2.
11. Evers, a Belgian, had served France from 1792 until captured in Russia in 1812 as a *Générale de brigade*, including three years in Spain and some time as the commandant of the Hanoverian Legion in French service. He joined the Belgian army in 1814, was promoted to lieutenant general and served as the inspector general of cavalry in the southern provinces (Belgium) in 1815.
12. Gurwood, *Supplementary Despatches*, Vol. X, *op. cit.*, p.168.
13. Scheltens, *Souvenirs d'un Grognard Belge*, (Brussels: Charles Dessart, Third Edition, undated), p.197.
14. *Ibid.*, p.193.
15. In Gerwood, *Supplementary Despatches*, *op. cit.*, pp.15-17.
16. See Dellevoet, *The Dutch-Belgian Cavalry at Waterloo*, (privately published, 2008), p.63.
17. A Netherlands military academy was only established in 1823.

18. Letter dated 23rd May 1841 to Captain Ernst van Löben Sels, in Franklin, *Netherlands Correspondence*, *op. cit.*, p.59.
19. de Bas and T'Serclaes de Wommersom, *La Campagne de 1815 aux Pays-Bas*, Three Volumes, (Brussels: Librairie Albert Dewit, 1908).
20. *Ibid*, Volume 2, pp.382-83.
21. None of the Belgian militia battalions had been properly manned and trained before Waterloo and none joined the army before the battle.
22. *Memorandum Relative to the Dutch Army*, in Gurwood, *Supplementary Despatches*, Volume X, *op. cit.*, p.15-17.
23. Gurwood, *Dispatches*, *op. cit.*, Vol XII, pp.291-92.
24. Gurwood, *Supplementary Despatches*, *op. cit.*, Volume X, pp.167-68.
25. Muilwijk, *op. cit.*, Volume 1, p.87.
26. General Renard gives the example of Colonel Duvivier of the 8th (Belgian) Hussars. See Renard, *op. cit.*, p.18.
27. Muilwilk, *op. cit.*, Volume 1, p.84.
28. See Muilwijk, *Ibid*, pp.87-93.
29. de Bas and T'Serclaes de Wommersom, *op. cit.*, Volume 2, pp.384-86.
30. For an outstanding history of the Netherlands cavalry in the 1815 campaign, see André Dellevoet's *The Dutch-Belgian Cavalry at Waterloo*, see bibliography.
31. This seems rather unlikely given his lengthy service with the French army, including command of a French regiment! See Dellevoet, *op. cit.*, pp.56-57.
32. Muilwijk, *op. cit.*, Volume 1, p.85.
33. The information in this section comes from Geert van Uythoven's three part article in *First Empire Magazine*, Numbers 71-73, 2003. These excellent articles give a very detailed account of the Netherlands artillery of the Waterloo campaign.
34. *Memorandum Relative to the Dutch Army*, in *Supplementary Despatches*, Volume X, *op. cit.*, p.15-17.
35. For a detailed account of this battle from a Netherlands perspective I strongly recommend the works by Erwin Muilwijk, Andre Dellevoet and Mike Robinson (see bibliography), as well as translations of the original sources in Franklin and Glover.
36. Account of Colonel van Nyevelt, chief-of-staff of the 2nd Netherlands Division, in de Bas, *op. cit.*, Volume III, pp.299-301. Nyevelt had seen extensive service in the French army.
37. Letter dated 19th August 1841 to van Löben Sels, in Franklin, *Netherlands Correspondence*, op. cit., p.73.
38. The two divisional batteries of Bachelu and Foy, the horse battery of Piré and two guard horse batteries with the Guard light cavalry brigade of Lefebvre-Desnoüettes. The corps 12pdr battery may also have been in action.
39. Meaning 'in small groups.'
40. Lieutenant Josias Barre, 5th Dutch Militia Battalion. Letter dated 22nd September 1841, to Capt Ernst Löben Sels, in Franklin, *Netherlands Correspondence*, op. cit., p.76.
41. Glover, *Archive*, op. cit., Volume II, p.163.
42. In Glover, *Archive*, op. cit., Volume VIII, P.154.
43. Report by Lieutenant Colonel de Jongh from *The Napoleon Series*, www.napoleon-series.org, translated by Hans Boersma. First published in *De Nieuwe Militaire Spectator,* Nr. 1, 1866 as 'Veldtocht van den Jare 1815. Historisch verhaal.
44. Scheltens, *op. cit.*, p.199.
45. Dellevoet, op. cit., p.121.
46. *Report on the Operations of the Second Division by Colonel van Zuylen van Nyevelt*, dated Paris, 11th July 1815, in de Bas, *op. cit.*, Volume III, p.323.
47. *Ibid*, p.319.
48. Van Löben-Sels, *op. cit.*, p.202.
49. Van Löben-Sels, *op. cit.*, p.207.
50. Letter to van Löben-Sels dated 26th December 1841, in Franklin, *Netherlands Correspondence*, *op. cit.*, p.70.
51. De Bas, *op. cit.*, Volume III, p.435.

52. Letter dated 17th April 1836 to Colonel Nepveu, former chief of staff of the 2nd Netherlands Division, in Franklin, *Netherlands Correspondence, op. cit.*, p.68.
53. Letter dated 27th April 1836 to Nepveu, *Ibid.*, p.72.
54. *Statement as to the Conduct of the Third Division of the Royal Netherlands Army on the Days of the 15th, 16th, 17th and 18th, up to the Morning of the 19th June 1815*, by Lieutenant Colonel van Delen, chief of the staff, dated Montmorency, 11th November 1815, in, de Bas, *op. cit.*, Volume III, p.367.
55. *Ibid.*
56. From *Geschiedenis van het 4e reiment dragoners* in Dellevoet, *op. cit.*, p.131.
57. De Bas, *op. cit.*, Volume II, p.395.
58. Nyevelt's report on the battle in de Bas, *op. cit.*, Volume III, p.333.
59. Muilwijk, *Standing Firm at Waterloo, op. cit.*
60. Gruneboscch to Löben Sels, dated 17th April 1836, in Franklin, *Netherlands Correspondence, op. cit.*, p.68.
61. *Report on the Operations of the Second Division by Colonel van Zuylen van Nyevelt*, dated St. Leu Taverney, 25th October 1815, in de Bas, *op. cit.*, Volume III, pp.339-341.
62. *Account of the Waterloo Campaign*, undated, by Constant-Rebècque, in Franklin, *Netherlands Correspondence, op. cit.*, pp.18-19.
63. De Jongh, *op. cit.*
64. Letter No.168 in Siborne's *The Waterloo Letters, op. cit.*, p.382.
65. Letter No. 186 in *Letters from the Battle of Waterloo, op. cit.*, p.283.
66. Letter to van Löben Sels dated 17th April 1836, in Franklin, *Netherlands Correspondence, op. cit.*, p.68.
67. Letter to van Löben Sels dated 26th December 1841, *Ibid.*, p.69.
68. Letter to van Löben Sels dated 31st May 1841, *Ibid*, p.66.
69. Letter to van Löben Sels dated 26th December 1841, in Franklin, *Ibid.*, p.69.
70. Report by Lieutenant Colonel de Jongh from *The Napoleon Series*, www.napoleon-series.org, translated by Hans Boersma. First published in *De Nieuwe Militaire Spectator*, Nr. 1, 1866 as '*Veldtocht van den Jare 1815. Historisch verhaal.*'
71. See account of 2Lt Pronk in Muilwijk, *Standing Firm at Waterloo, op. cit.*, p.144.
72. De Bas, *op. cit.*, Volume III, p.285.
73. Letter to van Löben Sels dated 29th August 1841, in Franklin, *Netherlands Correspondence, op. cit.*, p.97.
74. De Bas, *op. cit.*, Volume II. P.396-97.
75. *Account of events that occurred to the 3rd Division of the Royal Netherlands Army during the days of the 15th, 16th, 17th and 18th June 1815 and until the morning of the 19th*, written by Lieutenant Colonel van Delen, chief of staff, dated Montmorency, 11th November 1815. In De Bas, *op. cit.*, Volume III, pp.365-71.
76. Letter from Lieutenant General Chassé to the Prince of Orange dated Bourget, 4th July 1815. In de Bas, *op. cit.*, Volume III, pp.354-55.
77. Van Delen's report in de Bas, *Ibid.* p.367.
78. We can presume that this was composed of the Hanoverian Bremen and Verden Battalions, as they describe their square being reduced to a triangle (see Chapter 4).
79. *Report on the positions and marches of the 1st Brigade of the 3rd Division during the days of the 16th, 17th and 18th June 1815*, undated, from the *Archives du Département de la Guerre* at The Haig, 1815, no.498 B, signed by Colonel Detmers, in de Bas, *op. cit.*, Volume III, pp.375-79.
80. Undated extract from his military record in Netherlands Institute for Military History, in Franklin, *Netherlands Correspondence, op. cit.*, p.163.
81. I highly recommend Andre Dellevoet's book, *The Dutch-Belgian Cavalry at Waterloo*, which looks in great detail at this subject; see Bibliography.
82. Letter No.9, dated Stoke Chichester, 21st November 1842, published in Siborne, *The Waterloo Letters*, op. cit., p.18.
83. Taken from *The Paget Papers, diplomatic and other correspondence of the Right Hon. Sir Arthur Paget, G.C.B., 1794-1829, 1896*, and quoted in Uxbridge, *One-Leg, The Life and Letters of Henry William Paget, First Marquess of Anglesey, K.G., 1768-1854*, (London: The Reprint Society, 1961), pp.144-45.
84. Dellevoet, *op. cit.*, p.189.
85. Trip's report published in de Bas, *op. cit.*, Volume III, p.407

86. For a detailed examination of the Netherlands artillery during the 1815 campaign see the three-part article by Geert van Uythoven in Issues 71, 72 and 73 in *First Empire Magazine*, 2003.
87. Letter from Second Lieutenant Koopman to Löben Sels dated 11th September 1841, in Franklin, *Netherlands Correspondence, op. cit.*, p.108.
88. Letter from Chassé to the Prince of Orange dated the 4th July 1815, in de Bas, *op. cit.*, Volume III, p.355.
89. Captain van Omphal, aide de camp to General Chassé. Extract from his military service, undated, in the *Nederlands Instituut voor Militaire Historie* at The Hague. In Franklin, *Netherlands Correspondence, op. cit.*, p.132.
90. Macready, *On a Part of Captain Siborne's History of the Waterloo Campaign*, by an Officer of the 5th British Brigade, in the *United Services Journal*, March 1845, p.396.
91. Lux was the least experienced of the Netherlands battery commanders and had not served since 1809.
92. Löben Sels, *op. cit.*, p.305–06.
93. *Ibid*, p.304.
94. De Bas, *op. cit.*, Volume II, p.395.
95. For example, see Ensign Mountsteven's letter No. 178 in *Letters from the Battle of Waterloo*, edited by Glover, *op. cit.*, p.270.

Chapter 6

1. Letter from Count van Zyuylen van Nyevelt, chief of staff of the 2nd Netherlands Division, to van der Hoop, dated 7th July 1815, quoted in Dellevoet, *op. cit.*, p.201.
2. These were the 2nd Nassau Regiment, who had served with the French in Spain and the elements of the Brunswick Oels who had served with the British in Spain.

Appendix A

1. Report dated 7th January 1825, in Glover, *Archive*, Volume VIII (Ken Trotman Book 2), p.131.
2. Major von Berckefeldt in Glover, *Archive*, Volume V, p.87.
3. Preliminary Report of Colonel Best dated 22nd June 1815, in Glover, Archive, Volume II, p.119.

Appendix B

1. Vincke's report dated 7th January 1825, in Glover, *Archive*, Volume VIII (Book 2 in Trotman), p.132.
2. Report by Major Count von Westphalen to Colonel Vincke on his conduct, dated 1st July 1815, in Glover, *Archive*, Volume II, p.115.
3. In continental armies, what the British army called an aide de camp or orderly officer, was described as an 'adjutant.'
4. In Glover, *Archive*, Volume II, p.116.
5. *Ibid.*, pp.117–18.
6. *Ibid.*, pp.116–17.
7. Vincke's report dated 7th January 1825, in Glover, *Archive*, Volume VIII (Book 2 in Trotman), p.132.
8. Gurwood, *Dispatches*, *op. cit.*, p.590.

Appendix C

1. From *Reminiscences of German Officers in British Service from the Wars 1805 to 1816*, in Glover, *Archive, op. cit.*, Volume V, p.56.
2. 'What do the Guard Hussars intend? They are going to the devil!' In Glover, *The Waterloo Archive*, Volume VIII, (published as *The Ken Trotman Waterloo Archive Book 2), op sic.*, p.49.
3. In his account of the campaign, Lieutenant Meier of the 2nd KGL Light Dragoons of the same brigade, describes the disappearance much earlier in the afternoon ('approximately 1 o'clock in the afternoon…') and goes on to say that Adjutant Dachenhausen of the Cumberland Hussars joined his regiment for the rest of the day. See Glover, *The Waterloo Archive*, Volume VIII, (published as *The Ken Trotman Waterloo Archive Book 2*, (Godmanchester: Ken Trotman Publishing, 2019), p.49.

Appendix D

1. Figures come from F. de Bas and T'Serclaes de Wommersom, *La Campagne de 1815 aux Pays-Bas*, (Brussels: Librairie Albert Dewit, 1908), Volume 2, Footnote to p.375.
2. Letter to his mother dated 19 June, in Glover, *Archive*, *op. cit.*, Volume IV, p.146.
3. Quoted in, *Historical Records of the XXX. Regiment* (London: William Clowes and Sons, 1887), p.130.
4. *Supplementary Despatches, Correspondence and Memoranda of Field Marshal Arthur Duke of Wellington*, (London: John Murray, 1863), Volume X, p.8.
5. *Ibid.*, pp.15-17.
6. *Journal du Lieutenant Woodbury*, (Paris: Plon, 1896), p.276.
7. F. de Bas and T'Serclaes de Wommersom, *op. cit.,* Volume 2, pp.384-86.
8. *Ibid.*, Volume 3, pp.242-43.
9. General Renard made the following comments on this regiment, 'The 8th Hussars were in the least good condition... It was composed in part of Germans, French as well as Belgians, and amongst these last were found many young soldiers who had only been superficially trained. The regiment had been organised in November 1814, so it had only been in existence for eight months. During this time it had had three colonels, the first was only 20 years old, but they were seconded by excellent officers, which all, with few exceptions, came from serving France, where they had given proof of their bravery on more than one battlefield. This strong cadre compensated for the shortcomings in its organisation…'
10. Quoted in Glover, *Defeat, op. cit.,* p.67.
11. Quoted in Muilwijk, *1815 From Mobilisation to War, op. cit.*, p.42.
12. *Ibid*, p.85.
13. Renard, *op. cit.*, p.19.
14. Gurwood, *Supplementary Despatches, op. cit.*, Vol. X, pp.167-68.
15. *Ibid.*
16. See de Bas and de T'Serclaes de Wommerson, *La Campagne de 1815 aux Pays-Bas*, (Brussels: Librairie Albert Dewit, 1908), Volume 3, p.475 and Burrell, *Official Bulletins of the Battle of Waterloo*, (London: Parker, Furnivall and Parker, 1849), p.28.
17. Letter from Wellington to an unnamed individual dated Paris, 8th August 1815, in Gurwood, *Dispatches, op. cit.*, p.590. '… you cannot write a true history of a battle without including the faults and misbehavior (sic) of part at least of those engaged. Believe me, all those who you see in military uniform are not heroes; and although in the account of a general action, as of that of Waterloo, there are many examples of individual heroism which do not get mentioned, it is better, in the general interest, to pass in silence those parts of history than to tell the whole truth.' See also Annex B.
18. Figures come from de Bas and de T'Serclaes de Wommerson, *op. cit.*, Volume 3, pp.202-04. These figures must be regarded as approximate.
19. Renard, *op. cit.*, p.25.

Appendix E

1. Von Herzberg's report in Glover, *op. cit.*, Volume V, p.160.
2. Gawler, *The Crisis at Waterloo*, United Services Journal, July 1833, p.301.
3. *Ibid.*
4. In Glover, *Archive*, Volume IV, p.66.
5. Macready in 'On a Part of Captain Siborne's History of the Waterloo Campaign, in the United Service Journal (USJ), March 1845, p.401.
6. Letter Number 139 in The Waterloo Letters, edited by H. T. Siborne, reprinted by Arms and Armour Press, London, 1983, p.330.
7. Quoted in Glover, *Archive*, Volume II, pp. 186-88.
8. Report on the participation of thel[st] Battalion, 1st Nassau Regiment by von Kruse, dated Malplaquet, 21 June 1815, quoted in Glover, *Archive*, Volume V, pp.136-37.
9. Quoted in Glover, *Archive*, Volume II, p.191.
10. Report of the 1st Light Regiment Nassau on the events from the 15 June to 18 June, Pflugk-Harttung's letter no.71, quoted in Glover, *Archive*, Volume II, p.176.
11. Vivian, *Reply to the Crisis at Waterloo* in the United Service Journal, July 1833, p.313.
12. *Ibid.*

13. In Franklin, *op. cit.*, p.67.
14. Gurwood, *Supplementary Despatches, op. cit.*, Volume X, pp.534.
15. Undated after-action report in Franklin, *Hanoverian Correspondence*, *op. cit.*, pp.85-86.
16. In Franklin, *op. cit.*, pp.124-26.
17. In Glover, *Archive*, Volume II, p.109.
18. In Glover, *Archive*, Volume V, p.63.
19. In Franklin, *op. cit.*, p.106.
20. Buhse was an experienced KGL NCO, having served in the Baltic from 1806-07, the Peninsula from 1808 -14, at Walcheren in 1809 and was commissioned in May 1815.
21. In *Letters from Waterloo, unpublished Correspondence by Allied Officers from the Siborne Papers*, edited by Gareth Glover, (London: Greenhill Books, 2004), pp.240-41.
22. In Glover, *Archive*, Volume VIII (Book 2 in The Ken Trotman Waterloo Archive), p.121.
23. Report dated Nov 1824, in Franklin, *op. cit.*, p.147.
24. Report dated Jan 1825, in Franklin, *Hanoverian Correspondence*, *Ibid.*, p.144.
25. Although the Nassauers were dressed in green, this was a dark green, and in the smoke and confusion of battle could easily be taken for Brunswick black.
26. *Reply to the Crisis of Waterloo*, in the *United Services Magazine*, July 1833, p.312.
27. In de Bas, *op. cit.*, p.355.
28. In Franklin, *Netherlands Correspondence, op. cit.,* p.116.
29. In de Bas *op. cit.*, pp. 367-69
30. In Franklin, *Netherlands Correspondence*, *op. cit.*, p.135.
31. Von Omphal was a very experienced officer having joined the Dutch army in 1807, served in the Dutch Guard before coming into the service of the French and ending his career in 1814 as an officer in the Dutch Lancers of the Imperial Guard. He had served in the campaigns of Spain, Russia, Germany and France and was a recipient of the Légion d'Honneur. He re-joined the Dutch army in December 1814 and no doubt fought against some of his old comrades-in-arms at Waterloo.
32. In Franklin, *Netherlands Correspondence*, *op. cit.*, pp.131-32.
33. *Ibid.*, p.138.
34. *Ibid.*, p.148.
35. Van de Wetering had first joined the army of the Batavian Republic in 1803, had transferred to a French regiment and had fought in the French campaigns of 1806-07, 1809 in the defence of Walcheren and in Russia where he was taken prisoner. He joined the Russo-German Legion and fought with them through 1813-14 before joining the Dutch army, serving as a sergeant in the 4th Dutch Militia Battalion during 1815.
36. From Bas de Groot, *Chassé's Division at Waterloo* on the Napoleon Series website. The information on van Wettering and Koch also comes from this article.
37. Koch had joined the army of the Batavian Republic in 1803 and campaigned with the French in Germany and the Tyrol. He then fought in a number of key engagements Spain in 1808-10 before being incorporated into the French army and being commissioned in 1813. Returning to the Netherlands in 1814 he joined the 19th Dutch Militia Battalion as a lieutenant.
38. Bas de Groot, *op. cit.*
39. Wiegmans' account comes from Erwin Muilwijk in *The 3rd Netherlands Division at the Battle of Waterloo*, in *First Empire Magazine* No.86., Jan/Feb 2006.
40. Quoted by Muilwijk in *The 3rd Netherlands Division at the Battle of Waterloo*, in *First Empire Magazine* No.86., Jan/Feb 2006.
41. *The Crisis of Waterloo, by a Soldier of the Fifth Brigade*, USJ, May 1852, p.52. This was written by Ensign Macready of the British 30th Regiment, part of Sir Colin Halkett's 5th Brigade.
42. Macready, USJ, March 1845, *On a Part of Captain Siborne's History of the Waterloo Campaign, by an Officer of the 5th British Brigade*, p.401.
43. Muilwijk, Erwin, *The Netherlands Field Army during the Waterloo Campaign*, Volume 3, *Standing Firm at Waterloo*, (Bleiswijk, Sovereign House Books, 2014), p.199.
44. It does not appear that the British 5th Infantry Brigade commanded by Sir Colin Halkett received such an order; if he did, it seems that he chose to ignore it as only the 1st Hanoverian and 2nd KGL Brigades complied with it.

Select Bibliography

The following books are those that I have drawn information from for the writing of this book or have a specific relevance to the subject matter. The list does not include the many, many books on the campaign that I have read over the years that have served as background.

Adkin, *The Waterloo Companion*, (London: Aurum Press, 2001).

Anon, *Britain Triumphant on the Plains of Waterloo, being a correct and circumstantial narrative of that Memorable Battle with Biographical and Characteristic Anecdotes of the Principal Commanders*, (Burslem: John Tregortha, 1817).

Anon, *The Conversations of the First Duke of Wellington with George William Chad*, edited by the 7th Duke of Wellington, (Cambridge: The Saint Nicolas Press, 1956).

Baker-Smith, *Wellington's Hidden Heroes, the Dutch and Belgians at Waterloo,* (Oxford: Casement Publishers, 2015).

Beamish, *History of the King's German Legion*, reprinted by Naval & Military Press, two volumes, 1997.

von Brandt, *In the Legions of Napoleon*, (Repr London: Greenhill Books, 1999).

Colin, *Transformations of War,* translated by Pope-Hennessy, (London: Hugh Rees, 1912).

Coppens and Courcelle, *Les Carnets de la Campagne*, No.4, (Brussels: Editions de la Belle Alliance, 2000).

Dawson, Dawson and Summerfield, *Napoleonic Artillery*, (Trowbridge: The Cromwell Press, 2007).

de Bas and T'Serclaes de Wommersom, *La Campagne de 1815 aux Pays-Bas*, Three Volumes, (Brussels: Librairie Albert Dewit, 1908).

Dellevoet, *The Dutch-Belgian Cavalry at Waterloo*, (privately published, 2008).

Eenens, *Dissertation sur la Participation des Troupes des Pays-Bas à la Campagne de 1815 en Belgique*, (1879).

Field, *Prelude to Waterloo, Quatre Bras: The French Perspective*, (Barnsley: Pen & Sword, 2014).

Field, Waterloo, the French Perspective, (Barnsley: Pen & Sword, 2012).

Franklin, *Waterloo, Netherlands Correspondence*, (Dorchester: 1815 Limited, 2010).

Franklin, John, *Waterloo, Hanoverian Correspondence*, (Dorchester: 1815 Limited, 2010).

Glover, *The Waterloo Archive*, (UK: Frontline Books, 2010).

Glover, *The Waterloo Archive, The Ken Trotman Waterloo Archive Book 2,* (Godmanchester: Ken Trotman Publishing, 2019).

Glover, *Waterloo: The Defeat of Napoleon's Imperial Guard*, (Barnsley: Frontline Books, 2015).

Gurwood, *The Dispatches of Field Marshal The Duke of Wellington during his various Campaigns in India, Denmark, Portugal, Spain, the Low Countries, and France from 1799 to 1815*, (London: John Murray, 1838).

Gurwood, *Supplementary Despatches and Memoranda of Field Marshal Arthur, Duke of Wellington*, (London: John Murray, 1858).

Hamilton-Williams, *Waterloo, New Perspectives,* (London: Arms and Armour Press, 1993).

Historical records of the XXX. Regiment (London: William Clowes and Sons, 1887).

Hofschröer, *1815 The Waterloo Campaign, The German Victory* (London: Greenhill Books, 1999).

Jomini, *The Art of War*, reprint, (Westport: Greenwood Press, 1977).

Kincaid, *Adventures in the Rifle Brigade*, reprint, (Staplehurst: Spellmount Limited, 1998).

Letters from the Battle of Waterloo, edited by Glover, (London: Greenhill Books, 2004).

Kortzfleisch, *Geschichte des Braunschweigischen Infanterie – Regiments, (Braunsweig: Limbach, 1896-1903, 3 Volumes).*

Mastnak/Tänzer, *Diese denckwürdige und mörderische Schlacht. Die Hannoveraner bei Waterloo*, (Celle: 2004).

Matthias, *Der Feldzug von Waterloo und die Braunschweiger unter Herzog Friedrich Wilhelm: ein Beitrag zur fünfzigjährigen Gedächtnisfeier fes Jahres 1815,* (Braunschweig: Friedrich Wagner, 1865).

McGuigan and Burnham, *Wellington's Brigade Commanders*, (Barnsley: Pen & Sword, 2017).

Mercer, *Journal of the Waterloo Campaign*, (Repr New York: Da Capo Press, 1995).

Muilwijk, *The Netherlands Field Army during the Waterloo Campaign*, Volume 1, *1815, From Mobilisation to War*, (Bleiswijk, Sovereign House Books, 2012).

Muilwijk, *The Netherlands Field Army during the Waterloo Campaign*, Volume 2, *Quatre Bras, Perponcher's Gamble*, (Bleiswijk, Sovereign House Books, 2013).

Muilwijk, *The Netherlands Field Army during the Waterloo Campaign*, Volume 3, *Standing Firm at Waterloo, 1815, From Mobilisation to War*, (Bleiswijk, Sovereign House Books, 2014).

Nafziger, *Napoleon's German Enemies, The Armies of Hanover, Brunswick, Hesse-Cassel and the Hanseatic Cities (1792-1815)*, (Privately published, 1990).

Pflug-Harttung, *Belle-Alliance (Verbündetes Heer). Berichte und Angaben über die Beteiligung deutscher Truppen des Armee Wellingtons an dem Gefechte dei Quatrebras und der Schlacht bei Belle-Alliance*, (Berlin: Verlag von R. Eisenschmidt, 1915).

Renard, *Réponse aux Allégations Anglaies sur la Conduite des Troupes Belges en 1815, par un Officier Général,* 1855.

Robinson, *The Battle of Quatre Bras, 1815*, (Stroud: The History Press, 2009).

Scheltens, *Souvenirs d'un Grognard Belge*, (Brussels: Charles Dessart, Third Edition, undated).

Scriba, *Das leichte Bataillon der Bremen-Verdenschen Legion in den Jahren 1813 bis 1820*, (Nienburg u. Hameln: 1849).

Shaw Kennedy, *Notes on the Battle of Waterloo*, reprint, (Staplehurst: Spellmount, 2003).

Siborne, *History of the Battle of Waterloo*, (London: T & W Boon, 1844).

Siborne, *The Waterloo Letters*, (Repr London: Arms and Armour Press, 1983).

Tomkinson, *The Diary of a Cavalry Officer in the Peninsular and Waterloo Campaigns 1809-1815*, (London: Swan Sonnenshein & Co, 1894).

Uxbridge, *One-Leg, The Life and Letters of Henry William Paget, First Marquess of Anglesey, K.G., 1768-1854*, (London: The Reprint Society, 1961).
Weinhold, *Erinnerungen an Waterloo, Weg und Schicksal des Landwehrbataillons Gifhorn*, (Steinweg: Adolf Enke GmbH & Co., 1985).
Wheeler, William, *The Letters of Private Wheeler 1809-1828* (Morton in Marsh: The Windrush Press, 1998).
Van Löben-Sels, *Précis de la Campagne de 1815, dans les Pays-Bas*, translated from the Dutch, (La Haye: Héritiers Doorman, 1849).

Periodicals

Braunschweigisches Magazin, Edition 3, 1912.
First Empire Magazine, editions 71, 72, 73 (2003), 83 (2005) and 86 (2006).
The Age of Napoleon Magazine, editions 32 and 35 (2000).
Hannoversches Magazin, 1816.
Waterloo 1815, Les Carnets de la Campagne, Éditions de la Belle Alliance, Brussels: Tondeur Diffusion).

Index